CBT + D...

7 BOOKS IN 1

Cognitive Behavioral Therapy, Dialectical Behavior Therapy, Acceptance and Commitment Therapy.

Includes:

PTSD, Vagus Nerve, Polyvagal Theory, EMDR and Somatic Psychotherapy

Emily Torres

Legal & Disclaimer

This disclaimer applies to any loss, damages or injury caused by the use and application, whether directly or indirectly, of any advice or information presented, whether for breach of contract, tort, negligence, personal injury, criminal intent, or under any other cause of action.

You agree to accept all risks of using the information presented inside this book.

You agree that by continuing to read this book, where appropriate and/or necessary, you shall consult a professional (including but not limited to your doctor, attorney, or financial advisor or such other advisor as needed) before using any of the suggested remedies, techniques, or information in this book.

COGNITIVE BEHAVIORAL THERAPY

COGNTIVE BEHAVIORAL THERAPY

Introduction

Do you or your loved one struggle with depression, anxiety, addictions, eating disorders, or phobias of any kind? Do you want to deal with these problems? Have you ever heard of Cognitive Behavioral Therapy (CBT)? Do you know that this technique can help you deal with these problems? The truth is that CBT is a short-term technique that is focused on helping people deal with specific problems. As you go through treatment using this technique, you will be able to learn ways in which you can identify destructive thought patterns. You will also learn how you can change these patterns so that they do not negatively influence your emotions and behavior.

The development of CBT has, in effect, revolutionized the treatment of depression by mainly focusing on how people think of themselves and how they respond to events from their surroundings. For example, if you think about road accidents long enough, you may end up avoiding road travel altogether.

This does not have to be. The main aim of CBT is to help you understand that you cannot control every aspect of your surroundings. However, you have the power to control how you interpret and handle the events in your environment. You have to realize that allowing those thoughts to control your decisions, emotions, and behavior can make the situation worse for you and the people around you. You may be thinking, 'But these thoughts are spontaneous. I don't have anything to do with changing them.' Well, the truth is, they may be spontaneous, but you do not have to allow them to get the best of you. You do not have to accept them as genuine.

CBT will help you examine every thought that comes to mind to identify the evidence from reality that will either disqualify or support these thoughts. In so doing, you will take a more realistic and objective look at the thoughts, and hence, your contribution to what you feel. In other words, when you are aware of the negative, more unrealistic ideas that dampen your emotions and behavior, you will start engaging in healthier patterns of thought and behavior. So, what are you waiting for? Come with me, and let's delve deeper into the subject of cognitive-behavioral therapy.

Chapter 1. Cognitive Behavioral Therapy

Cognitive-behavioral therapy is a technique used by people to change and transform their life. Most of our decisions and achievements are based on our thoughts. Our thoughts influence our behaviors. As such, if we understand our thoughts, we can change them and, consequently, our actions. Cognitive-behavioral therapy has helped people deal with stress, depression, anger, among other mental conditions. Cognitive-behavioral therapy is a technique used by people to change and transform their life.

 Most of our decisions and achievements are based on our thoughts. Our thoughts influence our behaviors. As such, if we understand our thoughts, we can change them and, consequently, our actions. Cognitive-behavioral therapy has helped people deal with stress, depression, complicated relationships, grief, panic disorders, generalized anxiety disorders, marital conflicts, dental phobias, post-traumatic stress disorders, eating disorders, insomnia, and various other mental and physical complications.

We will use cognitive behavioral therapy to identify the thoughts that stir disorders such as depression and anxiety, learn how to deal with negative thoughts, and fight off stress, anger, and depression. Using cognitive behavioral therapy, we will first assess our beliefs, how we interpret the events of our lives, how we behave due to our thoughts, and finally, how we feel.

The most significant advantage of cognitive behavioral therapy is that it is goal-oriented and focuses on specific issues. Secondly, it is convenient, and one must participate fully to get the expected results. Thirdly, it focuses on the daily challenges, thoughts, and behaviors. Another advantage is that you will know what you want to achieve and how you can get there.

Note that cognitive-behavioral therapy focuses on thoughts, feelings, beliefs, and attitudes; therefore, you will be required to face some of the things your mind wants to escape. You might have to face your fears, thought gradually.

Things you will be able to identify are:

- *The unhelpful thoughts that might lead to psychological problems,*

- *The unhelpful behaviors that are affecting your life negatively,*

- *Better thoughts, habits, and beliefs that will add value to your life,*

- *The new patterns you apply in your life to relieve mental and physical conditions and even help you act better.*

- *Did you know that most of your problems mostly arise from the meaning you give to events or situations? If you have unhelpful thoughts about yourself, it becomes hard for you to function well under different conditions.*

Cognitive-behavioral therapy will have a positive impact on how you act and feel. It will also equip you with appropriate coping skills and strategies to deal with the challenges.

Levels of Thoughts in CBT

Cognitive-behavioral therapy recognizes three main types of thoughts, namely, automatic thoughts, assumptions, and beliefs. Cognitive-behavioral therapy explains that our core beliefs are the causes of our premises, which, in turn, initiate our intuitive ideas and, consequently, our emotions.

Core beliefs are the general centralities that we use to assess the standards we set for ourselves, other people, and the world. Our central core beliefs are typically formed at the impressionable stage of life. We use these beliefs to determine what to think about others. In some cases, our opinions are harmful, and they affect our lives negatively. Negative feelings include, "I am unlovable" or "people are not to be trusted. If one believes that he/she is weak, anxiety may kick in. On the other hand, a positive belief, such as "I am a winner," can build one's esteem.

Suppose one has profound negative core beliefs about him/herself. In that case, they will be prone to anger, depression, anxiety, stress, among other adverse mental conditions.

Using CBT, one can identify the negative beliefs leading his/her life in a downward spiral and look for alternative ideas to balance them. You will notice that negative feelings have powerful accompanying emotions. It is hard to shift them even with contradictory evidence.

Underlying assumptions are those beliefs that direct our decisions in different situations. Usually, underlying assumptions arise from personal experiences. For instance, if one was lied to by the spouse, there might be the assumption that every person in that gender is a liar. Another example of underlying assumptions is when one assumes that if he/she allows a person to discover their weaknesses, the person will leave him/her.

Automatic thoughts occur on a day-to-day basis, and they help us to make sense of our experiences. Automatic thoughts influence our decisions unconsciously. Have you ever yelled at someone and then could not understand what triggered you? Automatic thoughts are responsible for most of our automatic responses. For instance, a person might do something that angers you. Immediately, you boil over with anger and let that person have a tongue lashing.

Cognitive-behavioral therapy can help you to understand your automatic thoughts. First, after every episode of involuntary reactions, for instance, a moment of an outburst of anger, assess your ideas. What was going through your head at the moment you were angry? Which feelings were making you act like that? You could write your automatic thought down and assess them carefully.

Types of CBT

- **Acceptance and Commitment Therapy (ACT)**

Acceptance and Commitment Therapy combines traditional behavior therapy and Cognitive Behavior Therapy in an action-oriented approach to resolve behavioral and psychological issues. This approach involves individuals learning to accept their feelings and thoughts as opposed to avoiding them. Goals are established so that the individual can begin to make the necessary changes and learn how to modify their behaviors to live more fulfilling lives. This type of Cognitive Behavior Therapy is an effective way for individuals to address their fears, reduce stress, and confront their anxieties.

15

The focus is on the way you speak to yourself and view the world around you due to a traumatic event or occurrence. You begin to fully understand what is holding you back, why it continues to hold you back, and are taught strategies to overcome and persevere.

- **Dialectical Behavior Therapy (BDT)**

This type of Cognitive Behavioral Therapy is often used to help individuals with severe mood or personality disorders. Those struggling with forming healthy relationships or who struggle in social settings can greatly benefit from Dialectical Behavior Therapy. The focus of this therapy is providing support to the individual. You learn to focus on your unique strengths to build up self-esteem.

You discuss the limiting beliefs, thoughts, and assumptions that run through your mind when in different situations. Specific goals are set to help you identify big emotions you struggle to process appropriately. You learn how to change the way you react to these emotions and change your negative thought patterns when confronting these emotions, so you gain control over them. DBT often combines mindfulness practices with effective thought recognition techniques to regulate their feelings and learn new ways to approach distressing or uncomfortable emotions and situations.

- **Mindfulness-Based Cognitive Therapy (MBCT)**

Mindfulness-Based Cognitive Therapy teaches you how to become more aware of your thoughts. By raising your awareness, you can effectively identify negative thoughts and then learn how to reword and change them to be more empowering and helpful. This type of therapy will provide you with several skills and techniques that can be valuable throughout your life.

- **Cognitive Processing Therapy (CPT)**

Cognitive Processing Therapy is often used to help those suffering from severe mental disorders such as post-traumatic stress disorder. Through this therapy, individuals focus on how they process traumatic events and distort the event. The look closely at the coping skills that have been implemented to deal with the thoughts, behaviors, and emotions when the event is remembered.

You learn to identify the inaccurate thoughts that run through your mind and address the unwanted behaviors you exhibit when trying to work through those thoughts when they arise. You learn to evaluate situations to find the truths in them to rewire your thinking and gain control and overcome the events that occurred to you.

The most effective strategies for identifying limiting beliefs, negative thoughts, and uncomfortable emotions are explained. You will also be taught how you can begin to solve and eliminate these components that are holding you back. Working through each of the exercises will provide you with the foundation you need to set specific goals to empower you to reach your full potential.

CBT Principles

Cognitive Behavioral Therapy's main goal is to help you learn how to resolve the mental blocks, behaviors, and emotions that hold you back. During your teenage years, you will be confronted with unavoidable situations where you will struggle with making the best choices. This can result in unpleasant and significant reactions to the choices you make as you either regret the choice or wished you knew how to change the way you react in situations. Cognitive Behavioral Therapy is effective in helping teens overcome limiting behaviors and thoughts because of its core principles.

Active Participation

Participants are expected to take an active role in the sessions. They help define goals, create action plans, and practice techniques that will move them forward. Being active involves being aware that work will need to be done to overcome what holds them back. It also involves being open and willing to try suggested exercises and techniques to help change the way they think, feel, and act. Though some activities may give immediate results and help them recognize where thoughts are faulty or where behavior needs to be changed, some techniques will need to be practiced. Remaining positive and actively addressing what you want to change will lead you to find great success.

Goal-Oriented

When an individual decides to begin Cognitive Behavioral Therapy, there are specific problems that they want to address and resolve. Stating these problems is the first step to managing them. Goals are clear and matched with specific treatment techniques that will allow them to manage and accomplish what they want. Goals should be personal to you, and you need to have a strong desire to achieve them. As mentioned, changing your behaviors and thoughts will take practice, and you might not always get it right on the first try. Having a clearly defined goal will keep you committed to the process.

Focus on the Present Moment

Cognitive Behavioral Therapy is uniquely different from many other therapy forms because it focuses on the present moment. The goal is to help individuals recognize their thoughts and emotions and how they impact their behaviors now. There is not much focus placed on what occurred earlier in childhood unless addressing them will lead the individual toward their goal. By focusing on what happens in the here and now, the individual can feel more empowered and confident in controlling the factors that they face daily instead of dealing with events that occurred in the past.

Provide You with the Necessary Tools

Cognitive Behavioral Therapy aims to teach individuals how they can manage their problems by utilizing their skills. CBT leads one to strengthen these skill sets and look at things from a different perspective to apply new techniques to situations that have been holding them back. These skills and techniques are valuable tools that individuals can tap into for the rest of their lives to overcome even the most devastating experiences.

Relapse Prevention

Individuals are specifically taught and made aware of the key factors that can trigger unwanted experiences like anxiety and depression. By understanding the factors that can contribute to these intense mental blocks, an individual can recognize early signs of the symptoms that can lead to a relapse.

When these signs are identified, the individual can make the necessary adjustments and implement the right tools that will allow them to avoid falling trapped by their emotions or thoughts.

Time-Limited

Cognitive Behavioral Therapy tends to address and successfully help individuals reach their goals in a short amount of time. Some individuals may find themselves able to move past their roadblocks in just a session or two. These shorter treatment plans give individuals more hope and assurance that they will overcome what has been holding them back.

Structured

Cognitive Behavioral Therapy provides individuals with a predictable order of steps to take that are necessary for achieving their specific goal in a short amount of time. If you are seeing a therapist, sessions will often begin by addressing the particular problem, going over a tool or technique to help confront the problem, and assigning a homework assignment the individual is to complete before the next session. When they meet again, the session will begin with a review of how the homework assignment went, what changes can be made, and a new homework assignment is given. Sessions are straightforward and organized, which makes it such an effective way to help individuals better manage their thoughts, emotions, and behaviors.

Addresses Negative Thoughts

Gaining control over one's thoughts is a key focus in Cognitive Behavioral Therapy. Negative thinking can be the root cause of many problems and setbacks individuals are dealing with. Cognitive Behavioral Therapy provides individuals specific ways to identify, reverse, and create new, empowering, and positive thoughts. Addressing the negative thoughts the individual may or may not be aware of is how they will adopt more helpful ways of thinking.

Incorporates Various Techniques

Cognitive Behavioral Therapy utilizes many techniques in the session and homework assignments. Individuals may learn a list of ways they can help improve their life. This can include meditation, breathing exercises, relaxation training, and exposure therapy, among others.

How Can CBT Benefit You?

The goal of Cognitive Behavioral Therapy is to help you understand your thought process and thought patterns. New patterns are developed by evaluating and assessing past experiences, identifying triggers, and setting goals that will allow you to master your thoughts and live a fulfilling life.

As a teen, this may sound like a complex process. But, from a young age, we learn to behave following our thoughts. It has never been more vital for teens to learn how to identify and redirect their negative thinking in this day and age.

There are many things that Cognitive Behavioral Therapy can help you manage and take control of, such as:

- *How to identify your negative thoughts.*

- *How to process big emotions.*

- *How to manage anger.*

- *How to process grief or loss.*

- *How to overcome trauma.*

- *How to have a better sleep.*

- *How to work through complicated relationships.*

The main benefit, however, is recognizing how your thoughts affect your emotions and behavior. It strives to strengthen your ability to identify negative thoughts and re-program your reasoning process so that you can handle stress, anxiety, fear, and other challenges better.

Cognitive Behavioral Therapy is used to effectively help treat:

- *Anxiety*

- *Attention and focus issues*

20

- *Chronic pain*

- *Depression*

- *Eating disorders*

- *Obsessive-compulsive disorders*

- *Sleep problems*

- *Trauma*

It is used to address the many concerns that involve behavior and the thought process.

Cognitive Behavioral Therapy can help you breakdown challenges into small specific goals. Big emotions like anxiety and depression are organized into more manageable categories (thoughts, feelings, behaviors). Techniques are provided to address each of the categories. By breaking down the problems and issues in this manner, you will be able to specifically target the root cause of the problem and create a more appropriate way to deal with and manage them.

How CBT Can Improve Areas of Your Life

Teens have to process several big emotions and situations. Many of these can be quickly faced, and many can lead to poor decisions and low self-esteem. Teens who undergo Cognitive Behavioral Therapy often find a solution to their anxiety surrounding things like test-taking, time management, speaking in class, socializing, and setting goals that will lead to a successful life well after they leave high school. All areas of your life can be impacted by Cognitive Behavioral Therapy.

Relationships

Relationships have a direct impact on the way you think of yourself and the world around you. Feeling connected with others is essential for social development, but having these deep connections can strengthen the image you have of yourself. Relationships are those that you have with your parents, siblings, friends, or significant other. They can also include the relationship you have with coworkers and teachers.

21

When looking at the relationship area of your life, take note of the following key aspects.

- *Which relationships are going well for you?*

- *What parts of these relationships are working out well?*

- *Where are you struggling in your relationships?*

- *How is your communication in these relationships?*

- *Do you spend enough time with the people in these relationships?*

- *What is your connection like with these people?*

Cognitive Behavioral Therapy can help you recognize how you speak to others and boost your self-confidence to build more meaningful relationships. It can walk you through how you feel others view you and how other people's words and actions can affect how you treat yourself and your behavior. You will learn how to build a clear vision of yourself to help you feel more comfortable and confident being yourself around others.

Create a list of all the individuals (friends, family, siblings, and others) you have a relationship with. How would you like to improve these relationships? Ask yourself how your thoughts, feelings, or behaviors may be affecting these relationships (good and bad).

School/Work

Some teens are entering or are already in the work field while also attending school. Other teens are focused on school and extracurricular activities. In either case, this is a significant area of life for teens. Since school will be the place you spend much of your young adult life, this area of life must make you happy. When you suffer from anxiety, depression, or other stresses, you will feel less ecstatic about this area of your life.

Teens should be taught to find meaning in their school work, extracurricular activities, and their jobs during these years. This will allow them to graduate to pursue careers that give their life more meaning and happiness. Some teens are not challenged enough to become enthusiastic about this area;

others feel insecure, anxious, or afraid of their potential to truly excel in this area.

When considering this area of your life, look at:

- *What your thoughts on having a quality education are.*

- *What classes in school do you enjoy most?*

- *Are there classes you should put more effort into?*

- *What other activities are you involved in?*

- *Which of these activities do you enjoy?*

- *How much do you enjoy your current job?*

- *What career are you thinking of pursuing after high school?*

Spirituality

Spirituality is what makes us feel connected with the world around us. Some people find their spirituality by following a religion. Others find it through yoga and meditation. Some find this connection when they are in nature. Spirituality gives us more meaning and purpose and reminds us that we are part of something much bigger than what we see and experience in our daily lives.

When thinking about this area of your life, ask yourself:

- *What is important to you?*

- *What is it that you really care about?*

- *Are your actions purposeful?*

- *Do you feel connected to something meaningful?*

- *What would you like others to say about you?*

Health

Living a healthy lifestyle may not be a significant concern when you are a teen. Not many are concerned about how all the fast food and chips will impair them in the future. But, poor food choices, lack of exercise, and skipping sleep all impact our mental health and physical health. Individuals who commit to a healthy lifestyle can often overcome all kinds of difficulties, both emotionally and physically. "Healthy" is different for everyone but involves moving your body, eating right, getting enough sleep, and managing stress appropriately.

Questions to ask yourself when thinking about your health:

- *How would you consider your overall health?*

- *Are there any health problems you currently have that affect your life?*

- *Do you exercise or move your body during the week?*

- *Do you have any aches or pains when you exercise?*

- *Does your mood affect your motivation to exercise?*

- *How would you consider your diet?*

- *Are your eating habits influenced by your mood or thoughts?*

- *What is your sleep like?*

- *Do you find your thoughts keep you awake?*

- *Are there things that happen in the day that keep you from getting proper sleep?*

- *What aspects of your health would you like to improve?*

Recreation

While there are many responsibilities teenagers must have, they should also have many activities that bring them joy or help them feel recharged. While many teens are involved in various sports or extracurricular activities, many exert themselves in these areas not because it brings them ultimate joy but to please those around them. The things you spend your time doing must be

24

things that you really enjoy. While you may not want to face your parents' or teacher's disapproval, taking up hobbies or spending time doing something you love are things that will impact your overall happiness.

This is an important lesson to learn at a young age. As you get older, you will often find it harder to make time for the things you enjoy; you may go off to college just to pursue a future your parents or community expected you to follow. In the end, you may find yourself pleasing everyone else, but you find that you are not happy or feel like you are not doing what you are meant to do.

When you do not make time for recreational activities you enjoy, you may fall into the habit of doing for others, which results in being unclear about who you are. You will often find yourself sticking to this pattern as you get older. You might ignore the things you genuinely want to pursue to follow what everyone else expects you to. This can result in developing anxiety, depression, and chronic stress.

When thinking about this area of your life, carefully consider and answer the following questions.

- *What are some things you enjoy doing?*

- *Do you feel you have enough time to do the things you enjoy doing?*

- *Have you noticed that your mood or thoughts have kept you from doing activities you used to enjoy?*

Goal Setting

Being able to set and take action to achieve goals is something many teens are never taught to do. You may know how to start and finish projects or homework on time, but you may not know how you can set your own goals or take action to improve the areas of your life you want to improve.

When it comes to goal setting, you want to think about what you have wanted to achieve. When have you decided you would accomplish something and then took action to work toward achieving those things?

Are there times where you may want to achieve a goal but never actually got started? As a teen, this can improve a grade in one of your classes, working to make the varsity team, or finding a job after school. Many teens need an authority figure to motivate or remind them of what they should be doing. If they do not get this external motivation, they are unaware that they can motivate themselves internally.

Setting goals and taking action on those goals is a skill that will lead you to more success in life. Being able to self-motivate and take the initiative on your own will transform you into an adult who is not afraid to face challenges, try new things, or have big dreams. One of the things most teens never understand is that there are so many possibilities in the world. Still, they get stuck thinking about where they grew up, how they were raised, or the small town that encompasses them is all there is.

Do not be afraid to set goals for yourself. You can begin by setting small goals. You can start by looking at your life areas and identifying where you want to see improvements. Once you have pinpointed the area you want to work on, you can understand what actions you can take to see the changes and reach the goals you set.

Chapter 2. Why is CBT so Effective as a Treatment?

Now that we have talked about rewiring your brain with CBT let's delve a little into why it is such an effective treatment for many people. No pill can be taken or shot to help cure your anxiety, depression, phobia, or any other mental health ailment that you feel is holding you back. There are plenty of medications and treatments that alleviate the symptoms, but there's no "cure" for these ailments.

Cognitive Behavioral Therapy will, however, help you alleviate a lot of these symptoms. It will improve your life and be a powerful tool in overcoming the thoughts that are plaguing you. So, why is it such an effective treatment? The answer is that there is supportive research in its favor.

1.   This study showed that even in a 75-month follow-up, patients showed promising signs of improvement after using CBT.

2.   This study showed that CBT treatment was just as effective as the management of antidepressant medications.

3.   This study used light therapy combined with CBT to prove efficiency.

A common myth about CBT is that there is little empirical evidence to support its efficacy. This belief is simply not true. The more that it is used, the easier it will be to see the long-term effects of this process on patients of a diverse group. There are also many different CBT methods and different approaches that a varying group of people may decide to take. Because of this vast range of treatments, it is much harder to say that it doesn't work altogether. One method might not work for you, but there are other approaches you can take to help you find the most efficient method.

Scientific evidence to support CBT

Data indicates that CBT may be used to treat some ailments. High-functioning people with bipolar disorder and schizophrenia can benefit. It can help with attention deficit hyperactivity disorder, marital issues, eating disorders, social anxiety, panic attacks, major depression, and more! Many people suffer from one or more of these ailments. Still, they shy away from bringing a psychiatrist or psychotherapist into their lives.

These afflictions are extremely personal and have a stigma attached to them, making people hesitate to discuss them. Many instead choose to suffer in silence.

The goals and hope for you are that the techniques listed in this book will be sufficient to give you the confidence and control to push ahead and no longer suffer in silence.

Advantages

One advantage is that CBT can be as effective as medication in some cases. There is no guarantee that this will be the case for everybody. Some people just like you have used CBT techniques to help them establish better control and confidence without worrying about spending weeks or months (or years) finding a medication with similar results (and who knows how many side effects).

Cognitive Behavioral Therapy covers a wide range of ailments. Will it be useful for you in particular? That's yet to be seen, but if you apply the techniques, you will most likely see a difference almost immediately. Most of these techniques can be learned in minutes and applied in many parts of your life, but be patient when learning them. You will need to use them daily to see results and discover which techniques are the most effective.

Cognitive Behavioral Therapy allows you to "rewire" thought patterns. Everyone has trigger events that can make them ill at ease. Tempers may flare, anxiety can occur, and sometimes panic attacks strikeout of the blue. Recognizing what these triggers are, when and where they occur, and in some cases, documenting them in a journal to study them can help you understand them and prepare. Once you have prepared and begun to practice the techniques, the process starts to become automatic. Depending on the severity of the trigger, it can take some time. Still, you will see an increase in the efficacy with patience until you've created a new automatic response.

Cognitive Behavioral Therapy skills apply to many things in life. Once you have begun studying the why's and where your thinking is affected, you will start to find numerous applications for this information. Cognitive Behavioral Therapy is not just about dealing with anxiety or depression; it can be used as a mental discipline to help you in other life areas. One of the reasons that it is so popular is because it works!

Moreover, CBT is time-efficient. Most of the techniques may be practiced immediately and just about anywhere that you go. As such, you may see results in a much shorter amount of time than you could expect with many other types of psychological treatments.

Empowering

Mental illness can take over your life. When you don't know if you can trust your thoughts or what other people are thinking about you, it can be very lonely. Sometimes you end up isolating yourself because the pain of being alone is much easier to manage than the constant stream of thoughts you have about other people. If you suffer from social anxiety, you know that it will be more challenging to go out and do the usual things that everyone else around you is participating in.

When you suffer from any anxiety or depression, you also know how challenging it can be to do simple tasks. These tasks can be exhausting, and on some days, impossible. When you can take back your life and not let mental illness have a front seat anymore, it can be incredibly empowering. You will start to realize that you are in control and that no one can determine how you feel about certain things.

Sense of Independence

You won't have to be dependent on a therapist or medication long term. These things can certainly help initially, but after a decade or so on the same treatment, it isn't as effective as it might have been in the beginning. For your progress to last longer and help take you further in life, it is essential to find a method that will stick in the long run.

Not only is mental illness sometimes isolating, but it can also cause us to be dependent on others. We might look to people online to give us validation, or perhaps we need others' attention to feel better about ourselves. We might need constant reassurance from our friends, family, and even lovers that they still appreciate us and want us around. When we don't get this validation, it can be debilitating.

RISKS

You must commit yourself one hundred percent to the process. Cognitive Behavioral Therapy is fantastic, but it is going to require a commitment on your part. If you aren't using the techniques or are letting yourself get frustrated quickly, CBT will not be of much use. To that effect, just apply patience and try the methods until you find the right ones.

You must evaluate if CBT is suitable for you—you are doing that right now in reading this book. Keep in mind, CBT cannot replace all forms of treatment. If you are currently taking medication, we do NOT recommend stopping it without consulting your physician.

Some treatments require confronting fears. Cognitive Behavioral Therapy has some techniques designed to reduce or remove particular fears through a gradual interface with the subject of said phobia. You may experience heightened anxiety levels, but as CBT is a gradual process, you can rest assured that this effect will be minimal.

Chapter 3. Activate Behavior

Behavioral Activation (BA)

Depressed people often feel weighed down and apathetic. Even small, everyday tasks such as doing the laundry become daunting. Depression drains you of energy, leaving you asking, "What's the point in doing anything?"

As time goes on, you cut more activities from your daily life, which leaves you feeling even more depressed and worthless. Your motivation continues to dive. You start telling yourself things like, "I can't cope with anything," "I'll never get better," and "I don't enjoy anything anymore."

To break out of depression, you need to stop this cycle. The only way to regain control over your life is to deliberately engage in positive activity again, even when you don't want to. This strategy is known as behavioral activation or BA. The first step is to think of the activities you used to enjoy, as outlined in the other exercise.

Exercise: Planning Positive Activities

Make a list of low-key activities you enjoyed before you developed depression. These activities could be as simple as watching a movie at home. Give yourself time to make your list because depression can make it harder to remember things.

Now plan when you can do three of these activities over the coming week. To begin with, 20 minutes is enough. Make a note of each session in your diary. It's just as important as any other commitment, so don't feel guilty about making time for yourself.

Don't expect to feel excited at this stage. Making this list probably felt like a chore. That's normal! The real progress comes when you follow through and keep a record.

Exercise: Pre- and Post-Activity Mood Record

Before you start a planned activity, make a note of your mood. Give yourself a score of 1-10, where a rating of "1" means "very little energy or motivation" and "10" means "very excited and enthusiastic."

31

When you've finished, write down your score. Any increase, even if it's just one or two points, is a step in the right direction. Sometimes your score might not change at all. If you feel as though nothing is making you feel better, it may even go down. That's OK. It just means you need to change your planned activity, or perhaps try another time again.

Choose activities that move you closer to the person you want to be.

BA is more effective if you choose activities that are in line with your goals and values. For instance, if you want to be more sociable, setting yourself the purpose of chatting with an old friend for 10 minutes on the phone would be an excellent BA goal.

Finally, make sure you are choosing the activities you want to do, not what you think you should be doing. For instance, don't set yourself the goal of cleaning the bathroom or doing the grocery shopping. Sure, these are essential activities, but the point of BA is to help you re-engage with the things you enjoy. You don't have to look forward to it, just do it anyway.

When you try BA, the little voice in your head might tell you unhelpful things like:

- *"This won't work. You never enjoy anything."*

- *"It can't be this simple. It won't make you feel better."*

- *"It might work for other people, but not for you."*

The secret? Try it anyway. What's the worst that could happen? Even if you try an activity for 10 minutes and feel no different, you haven't lost out on anything. You can then try the other day again or work another event. If you feel motivated on some days but not others, you can rest assured that this is entirely normal.

Progress isn't always linear when it comes to recovering from depression. Some days, you'll feel hopeful. Others, you'll feel defeated before you even start. The trick is just to keep going. When you complete your BA exercises, give yourself plenty of praise. You have every right to be proud!

Once you have some evidence that BA works for you, you can challenge these negative thoughts using the cognitive restructuring exercise outlined.

Remember: you need to identify unhelpful thinking, look carefully at the evidence for and against it, and then come up with a healthier alternative thought.

When to Get Support

If you've tried BA exercises several times and they don't seem to be working for you, it may be a sign that you need further support from a therapist or doctor. Please don't think that you've failed. Sometimes, depression doesn't respond to self-help. If you feel very low or have no energy for even brief 10-minute activities, finding a medical professional can help you take the first steps to recovery.

Depression, Problem-Solving & Empowering Yourself

A little-known but widespread problem in depression is having trouble making decisions. The good news is that you can sharpen your problem-solving skills. Problem-solving isn't always straightforward, and it can feel overwhelming when your mood is low. At the same time, devising solutions and putting them into practice is very empowering.

When you realize that you don't need someone else to rescue you, your self-esteem will grow. This will help you feel good about yourself, which in turn will help lift your mood.

Seven Steps to Problem Solving

Work out What the Problem is

In some cases, it's obvious. For example, if you know that you need to choose a new school for your child, solving the problem is a matter of evaluating local schools and picking the best option. On the other hand, some issues aren't so easy to pin down. You might know you are unhappy in a specific situation, but the details are a bit fuzzy.

For instance, if you know that you dislike going into work, you'll need to think carefully about the underlying source of the issue. What is it about the environment or the work itself that is making you sad or depressed?

Upon reflection, you may discover that the problem is, "I need to find a new job," or "I need to be more organized so that I can meet all my deadlines, and have a less stressful time at work."

When you've narrowed down the problem, write it in your notebook. Well done! You're off to a good start.

Brainstorm a List of Potential Solutions

Let your imagination run wild. Put aside half an hour to make a list of every solution you can think of. Don't worry if they seem strange or unlikely. You don't have to show this list to anyone.

Get some outside input. Ask a couple of people you trust to help brainstorm with you. They will probably come up with some ideas you haven't thought of. When you are stuck in a depressed mood, your problem-solving abilities take a hit. It's easy to become locked into a single perspective.

If you have a severe problem or can't rely on anyone close to you to help out, get some advice from a specialist. Depending on your problem, this person could be a counselor, a helpline volunteer, or a religious leader at your place of worship.

For each solution, ask yourself:

- *How much time will it take me?*

- *How much money will it cost me?*

- *Will I need any outside help? Will it be easy for me to get this kind of help?*

- *Will I need any special equipment, training, or resources?*

- *Are there any critical long-term consequences I should think about?*

Choose the Best Solution

If you're lucky, you'll have found a perfect solution. Unfortunately, in most cases, we have to compromise when solving problems. Writing out the pros and cons, as in the step, and talking to others is so important. Knowing that you have given the matter serious thought will make it easier to believe in your judgment.

Remind yourself that no one makes the right choices all the time. However, we can all try our best to work with the information and resources available at the time. Don't fall into the trap of postponing a decision just because you're afraid of getting it wrong.

Make a Plan

Having found your solution, you now need to make a roadmap for the way ahead. Your goal is to draw up a step-by-step plan that leaves you feeling empowered rather than overwhelmed. Make each step as specific as possible.

For example, suppose your goal is to sell your house and move to a new town. One of your first steps is to find out how much your property is worth. It would be more helpful to write, "Schedule a valuation within the following seven days," rather than "Find out how much I could get for my house."

Execute your Plan

Start with the first step and go from there. Take it slow and steady—even people who aren't depressed need to be patient and encouraging with themselves when solving problems. You might need to break your steps down further. No action is too small as long as it moves you also toward your goal.

Other strategies that might help:

- *Planning a small reward for every step you take*

- *Asking a friend or relative to give you some support*

- *Working on a stage for just 10 minutes at a time*

- *Keeping a log of your progress so you can see how far you've come*

Evaluate the Results

You've reached the final stage on your problem-solving journey. You've implemented the solution. Did it work? If not, what could you do the other time differently? Perhaps something unexpected happened, or you didn't get hold of the information you needed. We can all try our best, but there are lots of things that are beyond our control.

Even if things didn't quite work out as you hoped, give yourself lots of praise. You tried something new, and that's something to celebrate. Remind yourself that problem-solving is a skill. Like all skills, it becomes more comfortable with practice.

Summary

- *Behavioral Activation (BA) and problem-solving are two practical tools lots of people find helpful in overcoming their depression.*

- *BA involves identifying activities you used to enjoy and scheduling time in which to do them.*

- *It's normal to feel resistance when you try BA, but you need*

Chapter 4. CBT techniques for dealing with anxiety

Strong emotions arise before thoughts related to them are fully formed, not afterward, as it likely appears when you look back on a particularly emotional incident. As such, you will often find that it is easier—and more effective—to change how you feel about a situation than what you think about a situation. As such, if you want to use CBT to help your anxiety, then the following exercises are a great way to work on calming your feelings directly:

Focus on How your Feelings Change

When working with CBT, it can be easy to get so focused on how your feelings are currently aligned but fluid, which means they are always open to change. It is essential to take the new anxiety in your stride and see how severe it ends up being before you get too stressed out about it, possibly causing yourself far more mental strife than you would have had.

You may also find it helpful to verbally acknowledge how you feel in the moment and how you expect those feelings to change once the anxiety has passed. For example, you might say, "Currently, I feel a little anxious, which is natural given the situation. When the feeling passes, I anticipate feeling clear-headed and calm once more."

Additionally, you may find it helpful to keep a close eye out for the first signs that the feeling is passing. The anticipated change is about to begin. Not only will focusing on the anxiety being over actually make the end come on sooner, but it will also stop you from reacting poorly to the anxiety at the moment. Feelings always shift, and keeping this fact in mind may be enough to push things in the right direction.

Act Normally

While Generalized Anxiety Disorder is considered a mental illness, anxiety itself is a useful survival tool when doled out in moderation. It is only when things get out of hand that it goes from being helpful to harmful, sort of like an over-eager guard dog. The truth is that your anxiety response only kicks in because your body reacts to the current situation as if there was a threat.

Regardless of whether the threat is real or not, a perceived threat is enough to set off the response.

As such, one way to train your anxiety to be selective effectively is to give it the type of feedback it understands so that it knows it is not currently needed. Anxiety takes its cues from what you do along with a primary emotional kind of pattern matching, which means that if you act as if everything is currently normal, then the anxiety will back off and calm down. As such, you will want to do things such as maintain an open body posture, breathe regularly, salivate, smile, and maintain a calm and measured tone of voice.

Suppose you can successfully adopt just one of these behaviors when you are feeling stressed. In that case, you can successfully alter your feedback enough that your fear response, directly from the sympathetic nervous system, receives a message that says everything is fine. In fact, one of the most common ways of mitigating an oncoming feeling of anxiety is to chew gum. If you don't have any gum handy, simply miming the act of doing so is going to be enough to make you salivate, convincing your body that nothing interesting is going on.

The reason that this is so effective is that you would never have the luxury of eating a delicious meal during times of serious crisis, which makes your body naturally assume that nothing is a legitimate threat. This, in turn, changes the feedback loop the body was expecting and causes the anxiety to retreat into the background. Just knowing that you have this quick trick in your back pocket can give you a boost of confidence that takes you past the point where your anxiety would trigger in the first place. Remember, anxiety functions are based on the expectation of something catastrophic happening in the near future. All you need to do is prove that this is not the case, and you will be fine.

Discover Underlying Assumptions

Suppose you feel anxious about a specific situation. In that case, this is because you are afraid of some potential consequences that may come about due to whatever it is that is taking place. However, suppose you trace those fears back to their roots. In that case, you will often find that they aren't nearly as bad as you may have assumed they would be when they were just a nebulous feeling of anxiety.

For example, if you are anxious about attending a party, then looking inside to determine the consequence you are afraid of might reveal an internalized fear of meeting new people. Tracing that fear back, you might discover that it is based on the consequence of other people not liking you, which you are determined to avoid due to issues in your past.

However, if you trace the outcome of people not liking you, then you may find that it makes you upset because it reinforces existing feelings regarding your general likeability. Once you get to the ultimate reason that is causing you anxiety, you can look at the problem critically and determine what you can do to solve the issue that you are avoiding. In this instance, reminding yourself of people who do like you is an excellent way to prevent the problems you are afraid of.

This exercise is also especially effective for those dealing with relationship issues, as they can clearly describe all of the fears they have associated with the relationship falling apart. In the process, they will understand that things will continue as usual after the relationship falls apart and that they will move on if the relationship is not intact.

Progressive Muscle Relaxation

Another helpful technique in combating anxiety is known as progressive muscle relaxation. This exercise involves tensing and then relaxing parts of your body in order. This is because the body can't be both tense and relaxed at the same time. Thus, if you feel an anxiety attack coming on, a round of concentrated tense and release exercises can cut it off at the source. Progressive muscle relaxation exercises may be done routinely or before an anxiety-provoking event. Progressive muscle relaxation techniques may also be used to help people who are experiencing insomnia.

To get started, find a calm, quiet place that you can dedicate to the process for approximately 15 minutes. Start by taking five slow, deep breaths to get yourself into the right mindset. Next, you are going to want to apply muscle tension to a specific part of your body. This step is going to be the same regardless of the muscle group you are currently focusing on. Focus on the muscle group before taking another slow, deep breath and then squeezing the muscles as hard as you possibly can for approximately five seconds.

The goal here is to feel the tension in your muscles as fully as possible, to the point that you feel a mild discomfort before you have finished.

Once you have finished tensing, rapidly relax the muscles you were focusing on. After five seconds of tensing, let all of the tightness flow out of your muscles, exhaling as you do so. The goal here is to feel the muscles become limp and loose as the tension flows out. It is crucial that you deliberately focus on the difference between the two states; this is the most critical part of the exercise. Remain in this state of relaxation for approximately 15 seconds before moving on to the next group of muscles.

Chapter 5. How to improve the likelihood that you will respond positively in the future

Indeed, there are so many effective therapies that you can use to address your depression and anxiety. However, the good thing is that there are some strategies that you can choose to practice improving your chances of responding to situations positively.

Some of these strategies include:

Practicing positive self-assurance

You have to realize that anxiety can cause you to pay attention to all the negative things happening in your life. In other words, rather than looking on to ways you can use your potential to do good works, you simply dwell on how you did not handle things the right way. The problem with this kind of perspective is that it can quickly spiral into a damaging thought process that can make your anxiety and depression worse than it already is.

To avoid these negative thoughts, you must turn your attention to the positive aspects of your life. This means that when you start to worry about things that are not going well, shift your focus to the things going well instead. At work, you may be feeling bad about a recent interaction with your boss or colleagues. However, instead of dwelling on what did not work out, try and think of those interactions that go well and what you can learn from them to improve future interactions.

Keeping an anxiety journal

When you are depressed and anxious, one thing is for sure; it is hard to identify what is causing your symptoms.

To work this out, you should keep a journal of your experience.

Whenever you feel anxious, write down all the things that are making you feel that way. Ensure that you capture your emotions, feelings, and actions.

The truth is, by just writing down your thoughts and fears, you can work through some of the situations that cause you to feel overwhelmed.

Going back to your journal whenever you feel anxious or bringing it to CBT sessions plays a significant role in reflecting on your anxiety's familiar sources.

Challenging negative thoughts

Realize that you can easily overcome negative ones when you pay attention to positive thoughts whenever you experience anxiety attacks. Having a fear of negative outcomes can quickly consume your life. Therefore, whenever you feel that negative thoughts are creeping in, try as much as you can to think of the positive outcomes you can get from your situations, such as a travel adventure.

For instance, if you are afraid of heights and often experience sweating, nausea, and an elevated heart rate, try to think about the positive things that can come from your trip and the things you have planned to do. Think of the beauty of the place you are visiting and the beautiful people you look forward to meeting. This way, you can quickly shift your thoughts from negative moments.

Setting up a routine

Did you know that following a routine can help you get through your daily activities with much ease? It is the one thing that will help minimize the occurrence of unanticipated triggers for your anxiety. Setting up a routine ensures that everything you set out to do is achieved by the end of the day. This, in effect, leaves no stone unturned, hence reducing anxiety.

Your routine must include healthy meals and physical exercise so that your mental and physical health is nourished. When you establish a routine for your activities, your mind will shift to the schedule and the small wins of the day to not worry about the day's uncertainties.

Practicing relaxation techniques

Relaxation can differ from one individual to another. This is mainly because each one of us finds our inner peace in different activities. The good thing is that there is a wide range of techniques that you can use to calm down your anxiety. Some of these techniques include deep breathing, yoga, and meditations.

With deep breathing, you can easily relieve the tension and restlessness that weigh you down from the inside. Just close your eyes and focus your attention on your breathing. Take a deep breath from down your diaphragm and feel the anxiety go away.

The other trick is using meditation and yoga to ward off anxiety. These techniques have a soothing and calming effect mainly because, like music, they shift your mind from what is causing your stress to yourself and the good things that life offers. Soon enough, you start feeling relaxed.

Getting some exercise

This is one of the most important parts of a healthy lifestyle. This is mainly because it has both physical and mental health benefits. When you integrate exercise into your daily routine, you are motivated and inspired to get it! You will be determined to achieve healthy goals each day no matter what stands in your way. It is the thing that will shift your focus from anxiety and channel that energy to more positive outcomes.

Practicing acceptance

You have to understand that there will always be things in life that will be out of your control. Often, these things can cause you to be anxious. Overcoming this anxiety, fear, and worries can be daunting, especially with the unknown in mind. However, the thing is, when you choose to focus your thoughts on the unknown, that will not help you make changes.

The best thing is for you to identify situations that trigger your anxiety and determine whether they are under your control. If they are, you must identify the tasks to help you eliminate worries and anxiety and get down to doing them. However, if the answer is 'no,' it is critical that you realize that not everything in life is within our control. Always remind yourself that there are situations that you may not be able to change, and that is okay.

Chapter 6. Identifying Assumptions and Core Beliefs

One of the first steps you engage in when you begin the CBT process is learning how to identify core beliefs and values. When you can do that, you can start the process of identifying problematic thoughts. When you want to identify a core value, you are essentially signing yourself up to delve deep into your mind, diving into your unconscious thoughts and feelings in hopes of gaining insight into your situation. These beliefs and values are largely unnoticed in your day-to-day life unless you actively know how to look for them and decide to do so. Hence, most people struggle to even acknowledge them. When you learn to do so, however, you unlock an essential skill necessary to understand yourself.

When you learn to identify your core beliefs, you begin to understand your own motivators, learning about what makes you behave the way you do. This is crucial to this process, which is about recognizing the cycle between thoughts, feelings, and behaviors. You are essentially learning to identify the thoughts within that cycle to learn how to best cope with them.

What Are the Core Beliefs and Values?

Core beliefs are automatic thoughts that you have that you believe wholeheartedly are true about yourself. They compose how you think of yourself, influencing everything from how you behave to what you think you deserve in relationships.

They determine whether you put up with abuse or assume that you deserve to be abandoned or rejected. They determine how likely you are to anything, and they occur without you being aware of them.

Your core beliefs exist deep in your unconscious, swaying your behavior without requiring you to use up any significant cognitive resources considering things. They decide many of your emotional, instinctive behaviors, and you always default to them. You will always take your core beliefs as factual unless given a good enough reason to reject them. Even then, leaving them can be a long, arduous struggle on its own. In correcting your core beliefs, you are essentially declaring that you do not know how to judge yourself and that you do not have a good understanding of who you are as a person.

How Do Core Beliefs Impact Behavior?

Core beliefs have a significant impact on behavior. They are determining factors for much of your own behavioral patterns. When you act upon your core beliefs, you are essentially behaving in ways that you accept to be true inherently. For example, suppose you have a core belief that says that your family and friends all reject you in the end because you are unworthy of love or affection. In that case, you will always approach relationships feeling guarded and tense. You will constantly assume the worst in those around you, which can have a hugely negative impact on your relationships, pushing people away. Of course, as soon as someone chooses to leave the relationship after being treated accordingly, you automatically assume it is to justify your core belief.

This can go further, with you contorting what has happened around you into delusional interpretations of what has happened. Suppose your friend legitimately is held up at work, for example, and has to cancel your girls' night out. In that case, you may immediately convince yourself that it is, in fact, proof that your friend does not like you. You assume that your friend is intentionally trying to lie to you. Instead of behaving in an understanding manner, you get standoffish and offended before getting upset simply because you assume it was intentionally done to bother you.

Identifying Core Beliefs With CBT

Identifying core beliefs is a relatively simple concept to understand, though the process can cause distress. It is common for people to feel upset or distressed as they parse through their thoughts and feelings simply because they are uncovering some of these distortions that imply that they believe they are not good enough. They are essentially admitting that even they, themselves, think they are unworthy of care and attention. In doing so, they have to admit that the one person that should like them, themselves, has low opinions.

When you want to identify a core belief, you approach the situation first by identifying the thought behind emotion and then attempt to analyze it until you arrive at a statement about yourself. For example, you may feel anxious about your social interactions, believing that they are largely unhappy because no one legitimately likes you.

45

You may point to a recent time in which you felt intense sadness and anxiety. That intense feeling is there to tell you that something was wrong there, and you need to pay attention to it to get to the root of the situation. Identify that situation and ask yourself what happened at that moment. You may notice that it coincided with your friend having to skip out on girls' night because she was too busy at work and was forced into mandatory overtime. You felt sad, followed by anxious, followed by angry.

Now that you have that feeling identified, you should take a moment to understand what those feelings implied about you. You may spend some time reflecting on the situation before finally settling on feeling upset meant that you felt insecure. That is a good observation, but it is not the end of the thought chain. You must then consider what that means to you. You may ask why you feel so insecure and think why. The answer may be something along the lines of feeling that you are unimportant or unwanted in your friends' groups. Again, consider why that matters—you may decide that you feel like people only like you out of pity. One last time, identify why that is relevant to you and what that says about you. You reach the core belief: You feel unworthy and undeserving of love.

With that core belief identified, you are ready to move on to other CBT process steps. There are, of course, several ways that you could go through this process to identify any core beliefs you hold. For example, you could use journaling to go through that process or decide that you would instead do self-reflection, simply letting your thoughts run loose and dictate where they go on their own.

Journaling

Some people prefer to resort to journaling to understand their thought processes. This is actually quite smart—it enables you to have a relatively easy-to-follow written record of your tracking thoughts. In developing them, you will be able to understand how you think. This can be essential, especially if you know behavioral or thought patterns that you may hold. When you want to engage in journaling, one of the most important points is ensuring that you have a quiet time to stop and consider what is happening without stress or interruption. You want to focus entirely on your train of thought as you go through this process. Try setting aside the same time every day for a chance to reflect. Once you sit down to journal, stop and consider any trains of thought you may have at that particular moment. You want to know exactly what is on your mind and acknowledge it. Then, follow that one train of thought, identifying what it means to you, how it is relevant, and searching for the core belief at the heart of it. Over time, you will begin to uncover more and more core beliefs about yourself as you do this. While this does not necessarily have any structure, it helps to keep each journal entry limited to a similar theme so you can analyze it to understand how it relates.

Your thought process likely looks something like this in written form:

Notice how the chain is a repeated attempt to identify the realization's meaning all the way down until you arrive at the core belief or thought behind the process. This is important—you are essentially spiraling down the rabbit hole of your thoughts and implications until you reach the truth that you hold.

Self-Reflection

Self-reflection, again, follows a similar pattern. When you are self-reflecting, however, you are going to follow the trains of thought within yourself.

You are not focusing on writing down what has occurred so much as pursuing your natural trains of thought. You simply allow your thoughts to go without stopping them, waiting to eventually see where they end up.

This is for those who struggle to journal or write about emotions but would like to get to the core beliefs located at the heart of some pretty adverse emotional reactions.

The important part is not so much to get everything written down but rather to ensure you understand yourself. You need to recognize how you truly feel about yourself. When you learn to realize that, you can then begin to cope with it or change it to something effective that you would rather see yourself. Either way, you develop a valuable skill as a result of identifying the core belief.

Remember, no matter how you choose to identify your core beliefs, you will likely feel some pretty intense emotions. This is okay and even expected in many situations. Despite the emotions you feel, you need to recognize that you are worth going through the process. It is worth challenging these beliefs even though doing so can and likely will bring about pain. When you are challenging these beliefs, you are essentially challenging yourself as a person, despite the fact that your perception of you may very well be too negative to actually be healthy or maintained, or even accurate to begin with. It is okay to get upset, and it is even okay to cry—understand that the pain says it is working. All healing processes involve pain, but that is okay—the pain says your body and mind are processing the issues you are facing. In processing them, you can cope in the future better.

Chapter 7. Eliminate Procrastination and Work through Worry, Fear, and Anxiety

The study of the internal mental processes of everything that goes on in your mind and influences it is cognitive psychology. There is perception, thought, attention, memory, problem-solving, learning, and language in every human brain.

Cognitive-behavioral therapy focuses on transforming a patient's behavior by understanding how their brain works and changing their thoughts. In essence, therapists are usually focused on turning a person's mindset from a negative one to a positive one.

Perhaps it would be easier for someone to understand how difficult it is to transform one's behavior by comparing it to anyone that has made a new year's resolution. Most of these resolutions get broken in a few weeks, and some never take off at all. The reason for this is the mindset.

CBT seeks to help a patient make lasting changes to their behavior. It involves investing in time, emotions, and effort. According to psychologists, to create a permanent change in one's behavior, the individual must be willing to transform their minds.

How to Start Changing Your Behavior

Probably you want to stop substance abuse, stop smoking, get rid of your eating disorder, or stop procrastination; no one solution works for all. Through a therapist, a person can try different techniques to achieve their goals.

Cognitive-behavioral therapy professionals use various techniques and focus on their goal at the beginning with the patient. During therapy, a patient can get discouraged and give up on trying to change their behavior. On realizing this, a therapist must come up with ways to keep the patient motivated and focused.

Although change is not easy, psychologists have developed various effective ways to help individuals transform their behavior. Researchers have also developed theories that aim at explaining how change occurs.

If a person wants to transform their behavior, understanding change elements will help them achieve their goals.

The Elements of Change

To succeed in changing one's behavior, one needs to understand the most critical behavior change elements. These are:

• *Willingness to change – ensure you equip yourself with the knowledge and resources to make a successful, lasting change*

• *Obstacles to change – what things act as a barrier to your transformation*

• *Expect Relapse – what triggers can make you go back to your behavior*

Stages of Change

One of the most popular approaches to transformation is the Transtheoretical or stages of change model that researchers introduced to help people quit smoking. Studies have shown that the change model's step is instrumental in understanding how an individual goes through behavioral change.

Just as if cognitive behavioral therapy is gradual, change under this model is gradual too. The model recognizes Relapse as an unavoidable part of a long-term change process. Most people during the initial stages, resistors are unwilling to change. Still, with time, they develop an enthusiastic and proactive approach to behavioral change.

The change model stage illustrates that change is complex and requires a gradual and systematic progression of small beginner steps towards a larger goal.

Stage 1: Pre-contemplation

This is the first stage to change. During this initial stage, individuals do not consider a change and are described as being in denial. They believe there is no problem with their behavior. Ignorance of the problem and denial are what characterize this initial stage.

50

Some individuals in this initial stage feel resigned to their current state and believe they have no control over their behavior. They do not understand the damage of their behavior or are misinformed about the consequences of the behavior. If you find yourself in this stage, begin by evaluating yourself by asking questions like:

- *If you have ever in the past tried to change the behavior,*

- *How would you realize you have a problem and*

- *What needs to happen for you to consider your behavior a problem?*

- *At this stage, a therapist will:*

- *Encourage the individual to re-evaluate their behavior*

- *Explain the risk of continuing with the said behavior*

- *Encourage self-reflection and introspection.*

Stage 2: Contemplation

During this stage, individuals become more aware of the benefits of making a change. At the same time, the cost of the replacement is more evident. The conflict between the interests and the cost of change can cause stagnation. The uncertainty at the contemplation stage can last for months and, in some cases, for years. Not many people make it past this stage.

This stage is characterized by ambivalence and conflicted emotions. An individual may view change as a process of giving up something instead of acquiring emotional, physical, and mental benefits.

If a person is contemplating a behavior change, the person needs to ask themselves the following:

- *Why do they need the change?*

- *What obstacles could be hindering them from changing?*

- *What can things help make the transition more manageable?*

51

A therapist helping a person at this stage may do the following to help:

• *Encourage the individual to consider the pros and cons of behavior change*

• *Help them confirm they are ready to change and encourage them by boosting their confidence in their abilities*

• *Help them identify the obstacles to achieving change.*

Stage 3: Preparation

During the preparation stage, an individual begins to make small transformations to prepare for more significant changes. For instance, if stop-taking alcohol is your goal, you may reduce the quantity you consume. This will help reduce the alcohol content in your body.

An individual may also consider taking therapy more seriously or start reading self-helping reading materials. To improve the chances of making a lasting change, an individual is encouraged to take specific steps.

These may include:

• *Gathering information on how to change one's behavior*

• *Come up with a list of statements that are motivating and draft your goals*

• *Identify an external resource like a support group such as the Alcoholics Anonymous group near you.*

• *Associate yourself with friends or counselors that offer support.*

• *At this stage, a few strategies that would help include:*

• *Preparing an action plan*

• *Developing and writing down your goals*

• *Come up with a list of statements that motivate you.*

Stage 4: Action

In the fourth stage, individuals start taking action directly to accomplish their goals. Many resolutions fail because individuals do not stop giving much thought to the three stages.

If you make a resolution and jump from the initial stage to the fourth stage, changes are you will give up sooner than you thought. If you have decided to make changes, reward yourself for the positive changes you take.

During this stage, ensure you get reinforcement and encouragement for every step because they help maintain positivity towards change. Check your motivations often, your progress, and resources so you refresh your commitment and boost confidence in your abilities.

Stage 5: Maintenance

This stage involves keeping away from past behaviors and their triggers and maintaining new practices. At this stage, individuals are more confident they retain their change, encouraging them to keep going.

To maintain the newly acquired behavior, you must identify ways to avoid temptations. Replace your old habits with new and positive ones. If you successfully can avoid Relapse, reward yourself, but should you Relapse, encourage yourself and keep moving.

To be successful at this stage, an individual needs to:

- *Come up with ideal coping strategies for dealing with temptations*

- *Motivate yourself by rewarding yourself for success*

Stage 6: Relapse

When a person is going through behavioral change, relapses are commonplace. When an individual goes through a decline, they will feel discouraged, frustrated, and disappointed. For success, a person should not allow setbacks to undermine their self-confidence.

If an individual relapses, it is essential to take a moment, analyze what could have been the cause of the Relapse. Once you have identified the triggers, formulate a way to avoid the same triggers in the future.

Evaluate the techniques used, resources, and environment. Come up with a new plan of action that will commit you to your goals and how to overcome temptations in the future.

It is essential to know that relapses do occur at this stage, and you should not dwell on them instead of formulating an action plan for the future.

Change How You Process Information

Learning new habits is difficult for some people and a breeze for others. However, with the right mindset, one can do it. It is all a matter of determination and believing it is possible.

Researchers say that the brain is like plastic. It can allow change because it is static. As you go along with life, your mind is modified. The experiences we go through help the brain to grow or to die. As you focus on change, it is essential to understand that the brain is not hardwired but flexible.

Your brain controls all your body functions, from how your organs function to how you behave and live within your environment. It is essential to maintain the central unit of the human being, which is the brain.

Your brain has two distinct parts, called the hemispheres. The right and left hemispheres of the mind focus on different things. If you find yourself focusing on the big picture, you are using your brain's correct region. To focus on linear and more detailed information, the left hemisphere is in use.

When learning new skills or routines, you will use the right hemisphere. Once the methods become a habit, they are transferred to the left hemisphere. The brain has billions of neurons that are used to transmit information to other parts of the body. Neurons are continuously produced, making it possible for an individual to learn new skills at any age. This is what helps to make change possible.

Chapter 8. CBT & Mindfulness

Over the past decade, mindfulness has become increasingly popular in the world of psychology. Mindfulness-Based Cognitive Therapy (MBCT) combines some of the classic CBT principles along with breathing exercises, meditation, and mindful practices that help you accept reality precisely as it is.

What is Mindfulness?

Mindfulness is simply the act of paying attention. When you are in a mindful state, you are fully present. You aren't obsessing about the past or fretting about the future. You are just in the moment, processing events as they happen. When we are mindful, we're more likely to feel calm and safe.

Why is Mindfulness a Good Thing?

Compare mindfulness with its opposite, mindlessness. If you lead a busy life, as most of us do, you probably go through your days on autopilot.

Have you ever driven to work and realized you have practically no memories of your trip? Or perhaps you've sat down to eat a meal and read the paper and suddenly discovered that all the food on your plate has mysteriously vanished? Living mindlessly means missing out on your life. Mindfulness helps you re-engage with the world, moment by moment.

Understanding the Differences Between Classic CBT & MBCT

You can use CBT and MBCT exercises, mixing and matching as you like. However, you need to be aware that they are based on different approaches to mental health. Some people find it easier to stick to one paradigm, and that's fine!

Here are some key points you need to know:

1. CBT invites you to challenge your thoughts, whereas MBCT encourages you to accept them.

Throughout this book, you've been weighing evidence for and against your thoughts. You've identified your cognitive distortions, asking other people to share their experiences and generally gathering a lot of information. Research shows that these techniques work well in people with mild to moderate mental health problems.

MBCT takes a different approach. Like CBT, it involves noticing destructive thoughts. However, MBCT practitioners teach their clients how to accept them. MBCT techniques help you stay grounded in the present moment and wait for the thoughts to pass instead of fighting them. You don't actively reframe your approach to the world as you would in CBT.

CBT works because it teaches you how to process your thoughts in a new way and arrive at different conclusions. MBCT works because it teaches you how to move through the world mindfully, accepting and letting go of whatever thoughts come to mind. In simple terms, CBT is analytical, and MBCT is more immediate, with a bodily focus—meditation and breathing exercises both involve your senses.

2. MBCT focuses on preventing depression and anxiety. In contrast, CBT is used as a treatment for people who are already experiencing an episode.

MBCT is recommended for people who have experienced multiple episodes of depression. MBCT is also used to help people living with chronic pain or another physical condition.

3. MBCT does not focus on problem-solving or behavioral activation.

Problem-solving is a key skill in CBT because it gives you a framework for taking action. Behavioral activation serves the same purpose; it helps you start taking steps toward changing your environment. MBCT doesn't emphasize these techniques. MBCT is about "being," whereas CBT is about "doing."

4. MBCT is usually delivered in group therapy format.

MBCT is normally given in a structured group format that lasts several weeks. Clients are asked to practice new techniques they have learned between sessions. During their classes, they have the opportunity to practice together and receive guidance from an MBCT-trained therapist.

However, this doesn't mean you can't benefit from some of the techniques used in MBCT. Some research suggests that group and individual therapy are equally effective. Here are three exercises you can try. They are similar to those practiced in MBCT classes.

MBCT Exercise #1: Body Scanning

Sit or lie down somewhere that is comfortable. Some people find this exercise so relaxing that they fall asleep, so if it isn't bedtime, do your body scan in a chair rather than on your bed.

Start by bringing your awareness to your entire body. Notice the weight of your body against the chair or the bed. Inhale, hold the air in your lungs for a few seconds, then exhale. Repeat this several times.

Next, focus on your feet. Notice their weight and temperature. Move your awareness up to your lower legs, then your thighs, buttocks, and trunk. Pay attention to how your back feels against the bed or chair.

Pay attention to your shoulders. If they are hunched or tight, take a deep breath and let them drop. Is your jaw clenched? Let it soften. If your hands are balled into fists, exhale and deliberately relax your fingers. Repeat this exercise at least three times per day, for 20 minutes each time.

MBCT Exercise #2: Mindful Eating

For this exercise, you will need a small piece of food to chew or suck for a few minutes. A raisin or a portion of hard candy is perfect.

Find a place that's quiet where you won't be interrupted for five minutes. Hold the food in one hand. Notice how it feels against your skin. What temperature is it? How would you describe its texture? Put it up to the light. What color is it?

Now, smell the food. How would you describe it? Does it have a strong or subtle smell? Is it appetizing? When you really pay attention to your usual snacks, you might be surprised to find that you don't enjoy them quite as much as you think!

Next, put the food in your mouth. Don't bite into it yet. Roll the food on your tongue. What does it taste like? Is it sharp, sweet, salty, bitter, or a combination? What is the texture like? Is it dry, moist, or somewhere in between?

Finally, swallow the food. Feel it go down your throat and into your stomach. Was it easy to swallow?

This is a great exercise to do at the start of a meal. You will automatically eat more slowly, which will help you digest your food. It's also helpful if you have a problem with overeating or binging; checking in at the start of a meal or snack helps you pay attention to your body's cues. It's not a magic cure, but it can encourage you to stop eating when you start to feel full.

MBCT Exercise #3: Walking Meditation

Most people assume that you need to sit still for hours in the lotus position to meditate. Fortunately for those of us who find it hard to sit in silence for longer than a couple of minutes, this isn't the case! You can try a walking meditation instead.

If possible, choose surroundings that are green and calm. Relax your shoulders and maintain a good posture. As you step forward, notice how it feels when your foot meets the ground. What does the earth or tarmac feel like beneath your feet? As you walk, use all your senses. What can you hear? What can you smell? What can you see? Look up—are there any interesting clouds in the sky? Take a few deep breaths. What does the air feel like in your lungs? If it's raining, you can do this exercise indoors if you have a large room or clear hallway.

What to Do If Your Mind Just Won't Stay Still

Mindfulness and meditation practices are simple, but that doesn't mean they are easy. The biggest obstacle will be your mental chatter. When you slow down and let yourself notice your thoughts, you'll notice just how noisy your brain is. It's normal for your mind to leap from thought to thought, worry about worrying, or idea to idea. The Buddhists have a term for this phenomenon. They call it the "monkey mind" because the mind is rather like a monkey, swinging quickly from branch to branch. No one, however long they have been practicing mindfulness exercises, has a completely still mind. The difference between novice and expert practitioners is that the latter have long ago accepted that their brains will always be hyperactive. However, they aren't bothered. They know that being mindful isn't about removing every thought from your brain. Neither is it about becoming a cold, stoic robot.

Radical Acceptance

Radical acceptance is a technique developed by psychologist Marsha Linehan. In the 1980s, Linehan devised a form of therapy called Dialectical Behavior Therapy, or DBT. Lots of people struggle to confront reality, but this is the first step to change. To help her clients make peace with difficult situations, Linehan suggested they try radical acceptance.

Exercise: Radical Acceptance

You can either wait until you are in a difficult situation to try this technique, or you can practice it by thinking about something that makes you angry or upset. Start by telling yourself that you don't have to approve of a situation to accept it. Take a few deep breaths. Say to yourself, "OK, this is happening. I don't have to do anything about it. I don't have to fight it. I just have to let it be, and it will pass."

This exercise is harder than it sounds! Your mind will still spin, and you'll still feel the urge to blame someone or something for your misfortune. When this happens, bring your attention back to your breathing.

When you feel a little calmer, ask yourself these questions:

1. What led up to this event?

2. Did you play a part in causing this problem?

3. What part did other people play?

4. Did luck come into it?

5. You have a choice—you can choose to accept the situation or rail against it. Which approach do you think will be more constructive?

We like to think that, with enough effort, we can control everything in our lives. It's a comforting illusion. However, it just isn't true. Life is unfair sometimes, and it's often unpredictable. Learning to accept life as it is may be scary, but it is enormously liberating.

Chapter 9: How CBT Can Help You Beat Addiction

One in three people is addicted to at least one substance or behavior. You can become addicted to anything that gives you pleasure or a feeling of reward. Drugs, alcohol, nicotine, and gambling are the most common. Other addictions include shopping, using the internet, and work.

Signs You Have an Addiction

You might be addicted to a substance or behavior if:

• *It's having a negative effect on your day-to-day life.*

• *You've tried to stop or cut down but haven't succeeded.*

• *You get withdrawal symptoms when you try to stop.*

• *You are willing to engage in risky behaviors to get more of the substance or engage in the behavior.*

• *You've lost interest in your old hobbies.*

• *You are ashamed of your behavior.*

• *You've stopped caring about your appearance.*

How Do Addictions Develop?

Addiction begins when you experience a rush of pleasure or a "high" after using a substance or engaging in a behavior. Our brains are very good at working out what makes us feel good, and so we start to crave it again in the future. The more often you use a substance or behavior, the stronger the habit becomes.

When you are addicted to something, you suffer withdrawal symptoms when you attempt to stop. For example, suppose you are addicted to online gaming and try to stay away from the internet 24 hours. In that case, you might feel agitated and preoccupied with gaming. It might be hard to focus on anything else. If you are addicted to alcohol, you might suffer tremors and headaches when trying to stop drinking.

60

The quickest and easiest way to stop these symptoms is to give in to your cravings. This makes you feel better for a while but keeps the cycle of addiction going.

Several risk factors can make you more vulnerable to addiction. Psychologists think there is a genetic component to addictive behaviors. An addiction can also be a coping mechanism. If someone has suffered a bereavement, lost their job, or has an untreated mental illness, addiction can provide a distraction. Spending time with others who have addictions also puts you at risk because seeing others abuse substances or engage in addictive behaviors makes it seem normal.

Caution!

CBT isn't always enough to cure an addiction. If you are addicted to a substance, you might need other forms of help, such as supervised detox or medication that helps you cope with withdrawal's physical effects. If your addiction has damaged your relationships, you and your loved ones may need therapy to rebuild trust.

How Do CBT Therapists Treat Addiction?

CBT for addiction is usually given as a structured program. Treatment is generally broken down into these stages:

Stage 1: Assessment

Stage 2: Behavioral Change

Stage 3: Cognitive Change

Stage 4: Relapse Prevention

Every recovery program is different, but most feature these components.

Stage 1: Assessment

In addiction therapy, assessment is made up of "The 5 Ws."

Ask yourself the following:

When?

61

At what times of the day or night do you engage in addictive behavior? Do you find it harder to control your addiction on weekdays or weekends?

Where?

Where do you buy substances, or where do you engage in addictive behavior? For example, do you drink more when you visit a friend's house or compulsively use the internet when you are alone in your bedroom?

Why?

What compels you to use a substance or engage in addictive behavior? Are there any internal or external cues that seem to come up again and again? For example, do you start to crave alcohol whenever you feel anxious?

With/from whom?

Who, if anyone, usually is around when you act on your cravings? Do you have any friends, acquaintances, or relatives with the same addiction? When you're together, does your addiction feel normal?

What happens?

What feelings do you get when you act on your cravings? Do you get a sense of pleasure, relaxation, or something else? Do you feel distressed by your behavior and, if so, why?

These questions are designed to give you an insight into your personal patterns of addictive behavior.

Exercise: Behavior Record

Draw up a table with the following headings: Situation, Thought, Feelings, Behavior, and Consequence. The next time you act on a craving, make notes under each title. Complete as many records as you can over the coming week.

In time, you'll start to notice that your behaviors follow one or more patterns. For instance, you might see that you tend to go online to play games immediately after coming home from a stressful day at the office. Then suddenly, it's past midnight, and you've been so involved in your game that you haven't eaten dinner. Your partner is mad because you haven't paid them any attention, and you know you'll be tired at work the following day.

In this case, the situation would be, "Coming home from the office." Your thought might be, "I need to unwind." Your feelings could be described as, "I'm really stressed and just want a distraction." Your behavior would be, "Spent all night on the computer." Finally, the consequences would be, "Felt tired, missed dinner, argued with my partner."

Stage 2: Behavior Change

Answering the 5 Ws and keeping behavior records will help you discover your triggers. These are situations, people, and feelings that you associate with addictive behaviors. The more often you engage in behavior following exposure to a situation, the more powerful that trigger will become.

Triggers can be internal or external. Internal triggers include mood states, such as stress, anxiety, excitement, or fatigue. External stimuli include vacations, payday, and spending time with people who also engage in addictive behaviors.

In summary, triggers and cravings work like this: You encounter a stimulus (e.g., a bar), which causes a thought (e.g., "I could get a drink"), which leads to a craving (e.g., for alcohol), which leads to addictive behavior (e.g., drinking).

If a situation involves triggers, a therapist will class it as a high-risk situation. A crucial part of CBT for addiction is to consciously decide to decrease the amount of time you spend in these situations. Instead, you need to increase the time you spend in low-risk situations, i.e., those that don't trigger you.

When you've identified your triggers, the next step is arranging your schedule, so you avoid them.

Here are a few tips:

1. Work out how much time your addiction currently takes up and choose activities that will fill the spare time completely. The less time you have to dwell on your addiction, the better.

2. Choose activities that are totally incompatible with your trigger situations. For instance, do not join a hobby group that meets near a mall if you are trying to overcome a shopping addiction.

3. Try to find hobbies and interests that genuinely excite you. Addictive behaviors give your brain a big jolt of pleasure. You might have to try a few new activities before you find one that fills the void.

4. Reward yourself every time you pick a healthy activity over spending time in a high-risk situation.

5. Spend time with people who aren't struggling with an addiction. You need to spend time with individuals who lead balanced lives and don't depend on compulsive behaviors to have a good time.

Exercise: Avoiding Triggering Situations

How can you plan to avoid triggering situations? What could you do instead? Set yourself a challenge: Over the coming week, replace at least two triggering situations with low-risk activities instead.

Stage 3: Cognitive Change

The way you think about your addiction can make just as much of a difference as to how you manage your triggers. Unhelpful beliefs about addiction and craving will hold you back. Look at the core beliefs below:

Belief: "If I have a craving, that means I'm going to give in."

Reality: It's hard to believe when you're in the grip of a craving, but you don't have to act on your urges. Cravings can indeed feel very compelling, but if you can teach yourself that giving in isn't inevitable, you'll discover that you can resist them.

Belief: "I can't cope with my cravings."

Reality: Overcoming addiction is tough. But people can and do recover. They aren't injured or killed by their cravings. They get through them and keep making strides toward recovery. You can do the same.

Belief: "If I have a relapse and give in to a craving, that means all the days I've spent free from addictive behavior don't count."

Reality: A lapse doesn't undo all your good work. This is a classic example of "all or nothing" thinking. A healthier way to look at the situation is to congratulate yourself on your recent progress. Remind yourself why you want to quit your addiction, and then proceed as best you can.

Belief: "If I have a lapse, it means I'll never be able to quit. I'm doomed to stay an addict forever."

Reality: You have a choice after a lapse. You can indulge in "doom and gloom" thinking, which will only make you feel worse. Or you can look at the situation, try to learn from it, and vow to do better next time.

Belief: "I can have just one drink/visit one store/spend just one hour at the casino."

Reality: Your brain and actions influence one another. Every time you act on a craving, you reinforce addictive behavior, which will lead to further cravings in the future.

Take a moment to review the evidence for and against this thought. Is it really true that you can have "just one"? When you tried to moderate your behavior in the past, what happened? Be honest with yourself.

Practical Tips for Handling Cravings

1. Surf the urge

When you feel the beginnings of a craving, don't try to push it away. Pause, take a deep breath and tune into your body. Do you feel tense? Jittery? Cravings don't last forever; they peak and then subside. Tell yourself that you can observe the craving and wait it out.

2. Acknowledge and talk about the craving

Telling someone how you feel can make a craving feel less scary. Phone or text a friend and describe how you feel.

3. Thought stopping

Picture a big red STOP sign whenever you notice unhelpful thoughts creeping in. For example, if you catch yourself thinking, "I need a cigarette to unwind; it's been a long day," imagine the STOP sign popping up and blocking the thought.

4. Distraction

Choose a distraction and immerse yourself in it for half an hour. Pick something that will hold your attention. If it involves practical work or exercise, so much the better. Good distractions include playing music, reading or writing in a journal, going for a brisk walk, and deep-cleaning the bathroom.

5. Positive self-talk and affirmations

Remember, challenging your thoughts and replacing them with more helpful cognitions is a big part of CBT. When a craving hits, remind yourself that:

You are trying your best

You've already made progress by identifying your cravings;

You'll feel very proud of yourself when the desire passes, and you haven't acted on your urges.

Stage 4: Relapse Prevention

It's normal to have lapses when recovering from an addiction. A lapse is a brief slip-up. For example, if you have a gambling addiction, buying a scratch card or playing online poker one evening would be a lapse.

Lapses can be discouraging, but they don't necessarily mean you are spiraling back into full addiction. As long as you frame your lapse as a slight setback instead of a complete disaster, you can quickly get back on track.

Use positive self-talk. Instead of telling yourself that you are a failure, remind yourself that the road to abstinence is often bumpy. Instead of telling yourself that you'll always be an addict, remind yourself that most people can, and do, recover.

Learning How To Say "No"

Social situations and people can be a big trigger. To conquer your addiction, you need to work out how you will handle high-risk social interactions and maintain your abstinence.

Practice what you will say the next time someone offers you a substance or encourages you to act on a craving. Write down your responses and rehearse them in front of a mirror. Good responses are short, memorable, and assertive.

For example:

"No, thank you, I don't drink."

"I don't smoke."

"No, thank you, I've quit."

"No, thank you, I don't do that anymore."

Make eye contact, and use a firm, even tone of voice. Some people don't take the hint the first time, so you might have to repeat yourself.

"Friends" Who Make You Feel Bad Aren't Your Friends

A friend is someone who wants the best for you. Anyone who tries to stand in the way of your sobriety or tempts you to engage in addictive behaviors is not your friend. People who respect you will respect your boundaries. If they have an addiction of their own, it's their choice to continue, but they have no right to belittle you.

However, being assertive won't change other people. Some addicts find that to change their lives for the better, they need to form healthier friendships.

Chapter 10. How to boost your self-esteem naturally to look at your life from a positive perspective?

Did you know that your self-esteem gives you confidence, hence is a cornerstone to proper mental health? If you do not believe in yourself, there is no way other people will believe in you. The good news is that there are several strategies that you can use to boost your self-esteem. Some of these mental hacks include:

Pushing through self-limiting beliefs

Our thoughts sometimes are like those of a child; we think that we can conquer the world. However, when we get in touch with our adult life, we realize that our dreams, enthusiasm, and beliefs become crushed. This is when the people around us tend to superimpose their beliefs on us. They control what we can and cannot do with our lives, and that can be frustrating!

Rather than getting trapped in what other people want for your life, you must determine your own limits. The best way you can achieve this is by putting yourself out there into different situations. In other words, do not live trapped in another person's image of life for you. Instead, push through the uncomfortable. This will not only help you regain your self-esteem but will help you gain confidence and a different perspective on yourself. The truth is, you will be amazed at what you can accomplish!

Never mix up memory with facts.

It is essential to understand that our memory does not store up information in the same way it is presented to us. Our human nature causes us to extract the gist of a whole encounter or incident and then store the information in ways that make sense. This explains the reason why people who witness the same event often have quite distinct variations of the same.

In the same way, the brain tends to have a built-in confirmation bias. In other words, the brain chooses to store only information that is consistent with what we believe, the values we hold, and what reflects our self-image. This kind of selective memory helps the brain keep us from overloading ourselves with excess information.

It is, therefore, critical that you realize that your memory does not at all times offer you accurate information. For instance, if you are struggling with low self-esteem, the brain tells you that you do not have confidence and hence chooses to store that information. That will be all that you recall about an event.

The trick here is for you to revisit the facts that are loaded in your memory so that you can discover all the self-limiting beliefs stored there. Then try as much as you can to gain a more accurate mindset of the event. Talk to other people with a different perspective so that you can edify your perception and change your perspective.

Talk to yourself

You may think of this as being crazy, but trust me, this works magic! When you are struggling with low self-esteem, talking to yourself and changing your perspective can help. It can make you see yourself as smarter, hence boosting your memory and helping you pay closer attention to increasing your intellectual performance.

For instance, when you talk to yourself, you instruct your mind to be mentally tough and speak positive things. This can override your fears, hence altering your limbic system, the brain's primal part that plays a critical role in helping us deal with anxiety.

The most important thing here is for you to be positive in how you talk to yourself. This is because it has a way of influencing your neurobiological response. When you tell yourself how to do something, you simply have turned your response into a positive one.

Think positive so that you can overcome your negative biases.

Since we were little children, we learned how to get something or be something. We possess the negative bias that has successfully kept us from danger for so many years. However, we fail to realize that not everything that comes our way is a threat that calls for survival responses. This negative bias gradually strips us of our self-confidence, mainly because we are hardwired to believe that we have done something wrong.

Professionals are trained to do good things for the company and the client. However, this can be difficult sometimes because the positive information presented to us easily falls away. In contrast, the negative information tends to stick like Velcro.

If you want to recharge your self-esteem, you must develop at least five positive thoughts every time you have a negative thought. Allow each positive thinking to sink into your spirit before progressing to the next positive thought.

Additionally, learn to acknowledge both the good and the bad emotions you feel rather than suppress the negative ones. Labeling emotions for what they genuinely are allows you to move on. Rather than getting into an inner dialogue about the destructive emotions, choose to dwell on the positive ones to win back your power.

Raise your curiosity

Being curious is one of the essential traits that we human beings have. It is what makes us successful and confident in what we do. It is considered to be the foundation of life-long growth and progression. Therefore, if we maintain our curiosity, we become teachable, which causes our hearts and minds to grow bigger each day.

Yes, we may retain our beginner's orientation. Still, we can look forward to new things and experiences that uncover further information for us. To win back your self-confidence, purposefully ask questions and be curious about them. This will make your mind active, encourage you to be more observant, create new ideas, open new possibilities.

Overcome self-doubt.

If you do not have self-esteem and confidence, there is a good chance that you will feel as though you are at the mercy of other people. By assuming that you are a victim, you give away your resilience to roadblocks and the unavoidable things life brings.

When you have your self-esteem, you will go where you are needed and not comfortable. In other words, you will break out of your comfort zone. You may face challenging situations along the way you have no idea how to solve, but you will not allow fear and panic to get the best of you. This is because you believe that you will come out victorious on the other side no matter what.

Understand that no one but yourself is stopping you from accomplishing your dreams. Therefore, rather than blaming people for your undoing, take the time to identify areas of your life where you have doubt and then work towards getting rid of those barriers.

Stay and face your fears.

Did you know that every time you feel you are in control, you also are not afraid? The truth is, when we are comfortable with something, we are not scared of anything. However, when we feel that our control is taken from us, we fail to think clearly. This is mainly because the emotional brain has shifted into the driver's seat and is suddenly is the one leading the way. This explains the reason why fear is random yet so irrational.

To feel safe and in control, we must learn how to move closer to the threat. In other words, face the thing that is causing us fear. It is no good avoiding or ignoring our worries. Allow yourself to think about your fears. Spend time with your fears and make them even worse by sticking closer to them.

What is the worst that could happen? While close to your fears, focus on your breathing and allow your body to relax as much as you can. You did not die, right? Practicing facing your fears ensures that you are one step closer to overcoming those fears each time.

If you fail to believe in yourself, the truth is, other people will not reciprocate a belief in you either.

Chapter 11. Other types of cognitive behavioral therapy

The Multimodal Model (MMT)

In multimodal coaching, the emphasis is placed on the distinct dimensions of the human personality:

- *Behavior - These are the traits that an individual may present*
- *Affect - Positive or negative influence on our emotions*
- *Sensation - Automatic sensations in our bodies such as sweating, heart racing, tension, etc.*
- *Imagery - Mental pictures*
- *Cognition - Our thought processes*
- *Interpersonal relationships*
- *Drugs – Biological intervention*

These aspects can be easily remembered by using the acronym BASIC ID. While all people experience these exact dimensions in one form or another, it also has room to address each individual's uniqueness. You can think of it in the same way music is composed. Music is always composed of the same notes of the scale, yet no two musical pieces are exactly alike. The same is for the billions of people who have these seven dimensions in their personality: you may find some that are similar, but none of them is precisely the same as another.

The goal of the MMD is to help the individual make the changes necessary to move them from their current personality to become a more progressive and better individual. It is not likely that any of us will ever reach our full potential. However, applying the MMD model can pinpoint the areas in our personality that may need adjusting and help us make the necessary changes.

In this type of therapy, the patient is asked a series of questions relating to these modalities to determine exactly what kind of help they need.

Eye Movement Desensitization and Reprocessing Therapy (EMDR)

This is a form of therapy specifically developed to help people who are suffering from traumatic events. Traumatic memories or images may pop up in their minds without warning, triggering all sorts of negative emotions and actions. EMDR makes it easy to access the part of the brain that processes these images or memories and helps them resolve the issues triggering them.

Through EMDR, in much the same way as the body can heal from physical trauma, people learn that the mind can heal itself from psychological trauma. By learning how the body recovers from physical trauma, such as a cut or a break, you can begin to understand how the mind automatically works to repair itself. If the location of a previous injury is repeatedly injured, the pain will recur. However, once the object that caused the damage is removed and the threat has passed, the body will immediately heal.

With EMDR therapy, we see that psychological trauma can be healed in the same way. The brain actually wants to be mentally healthy. Still, if the system continues to be blocked by repeated recurrences of the traumatic event, it can leave a lasting scar which can cause a great deal of suffering. However, once the imbalance is removed, the mind can begin to heal itself.

During therapy sessions, the patient must address emotionally disturbing material and some form of external stimulus simultaneously.

Once therapy has been completed, the patient can find relief from their own negative beliefs and can move on to more positive things in their life. This healing is done through a detailed series of protocols and procedures designed to activate the brain's natural healing process.

How Does it Work?

There are eight phases of EMDR treatment. Eye movement and other types of exercises that promote bilateral stimulation encompass a significant part of the session. The clinician will first pinpoint the memory triggering the negative behavior by asking the patient to recall various aspects of the traumatic event. At the same time, the clinician will have the patient track his hand movements as it crosses the patient's field of vision.

This will cause the client's mind to process the memory and the feelings associated with it, thus triggering a shift in their emotions. For example, a rape victim may associate a feeling of disgust or horror in recalling the event, but after the change takes place, could demonstrate positive feelings of survival and strength.

All of this is done without the need for a lot of talking.

Therefore, this type of therapy results does not stem from the conclusion that the clinician has gleaned from the talk but instead from the patient's own internal intellectual and emotional processes. The result is that a patient will leave the session feeling empowered by the same traumatic event that originally had broken them.

In this type of therapy, the damage created by the traumatic event didn't just heal the patient; it literally transformed them. The patient's thoughts, feelings, and behavior are part of a delicate balance of emotional and mental health.

Rational Emotive Behavior Therapy Method (REBT)

The theory behind this type of therapy is that humans do not act rationally in many situations. Logic is not always a part of our make-up. Computers and machines all perform their functions rationally. They take in data, analyze its logic, and provide an acceptable output. On the other hand, humans receive millions of tiny little inputs every day, process them very differently from machines, and instantly produce a wide variety of outputs. Some of them may fit in a lot of things, but many others do not.

REBT was designed to train us to think more rationally to change our dysfunctional behaviors. Its goal is to break down our natural instincts to think irrationally, stop us from making unreasonable assumptions, and make realistic assumptions instead. This can change our inappropriate and destructive behaviors to much more positive ones. Since most of our negative thoughts and assumptions come from our beliefs' irrational side, we react to them in inappropriate ways. It was thanks to these theories on negative thoughts that REBT therapy was developed.

Dialectical Behavioral Theory (DBT)

Sometimes referred to as 'talk therapy,' DBT stresses the psycho-social components of treatment. The basic theory behind DBT is that people will react to situations in a much more extreme manner than others do. These are usually the result of emotional reactions to events in their romantic, family, or social relationships.

The general idea is that some people whose arousal levels can increase much more quickly than that of most people. Their emotional reactions are often at a higher level. It takes much longer for them to return to normal after an episode.

These people commonly experience extreme emotional swings; they only see the world in black and white, tend to find themselves in an endless line of crises. They spend most of their life jumping from one issue to another. In most cases, they have no means of coping with these sudden emotional outbursts and, therefore, can get no relief.

Structured Individual Psychotherapy Sessions

In a weekly one-on-one session with the therapist, the emphasis is on addressing problem-solving behavior and issues that may have occurred in the previous week. With these types of patients, there could be issues that spring from suicidal tendencies or tendencies that injure themselves. These will take priority. After that, they will address specific behaviors that could interrupt the therapy sessions.

The therapist focuses on teaching and reinforcing adaptive behavior, emphasizing teaching them how to better manage their emotional trauma when it occurs rather than removing the negative experience entirely. The ultimate goal is to get patients to improve their social skills to have better relationships and interact more successfully with others.

Chapter 12. Setting Goals

How To Set Goals

Goals are fundamental to an individual. They keep you motivated and focused. Going about life without goals is shooting aimlessly. You will not achieve anything meaningful; you will be discouraged and frustrated. To set goals, you must write them down with the expected date to achieve them. They act as a constant reminder and help to keep you in check.

Goals are essential because they give you a target or a purpose. Goals are also important because they enable you to measure your progress. When you set a big goal, you set up other smaller goals to help you achieve the big goal. This allows you to measure your progress and help you celebrate small successes. For instance, if you want to save $1 million to start a business, you set other smaller goals. How much you must save each month to achieve your target of $1 million in 2 years or more. When you set goals, you avoid distractions and stay locked into your course to achieve them.

Another importance of goals is that it helps you overcome procrastination. Setting goals makes you accountable. They allow you to avoid waiting indefinitely to achieve something. They act as constant reminders of what you need to achieve and by when. This enables you to use your time well and avoid postponing doing things. Goals are also motivational. They set a base for your drive and give you a solid endpoint.

You cannot go about life without direction. If you have no purpose in life, then you have no reason for living. Every successful person sets out with a goal in mind that they want to achieve. For instance, if you also desire to be a millionaire, you must also have a goal.

What is your Vision?

Having a vision is one of the most important things if you want to be successful. It is your most important dream or mental picture. It doesn't have to be one; it can be a set of dreams and long-term goals. It defines your desired state in the future; it communicates what you desire to achieve over time. On a personal level, a vision can be termed as your WHY. In contrast, at an organizational level, it should define its purpose for existence.

76

Purpose of a vision

A vision is what describes what you are doing because people want to know. However, every person or organization should have a vision. There are two main reasons why you should have a vision, these are:

> *•First, a vision acts to inspire and give you energy. It helps guide you and gives purpose to all your efforts. When you come to terms with your WHY, you get connected with your core values. It opens up your strongest motivations making a connection between your daily work and strongest values hence making you unstoppable.*
> *•A vision helps give you direction in a world full of choices. It allows you to focus on what needs to be done and what not to do for your future achievements. When you become clear about your vision and goals, it becomes easier to say yes or no with valid reasons and no fear of rejection.*

How to identify and develop your vision

When you are looking to identify your vision, it is best to do this in a quiet place where you find inspiration and no distractions. When building your vision, your main question is usually WHY. What are your dreams, how do you visualize your future? Once you identify your WHY, then it becomes easy to identify your WHAT and HOW. Focus on your biggest and long-term mental picture now.

When coming up with your vision, consider the following:

> *•Unique – ensure that your vision is unique and fits into your values and passion. This means imagining yourself maybe three years from now in the role. How do you see yourself, and do you like your role?*
> *•Simple – a vision must be simple, clear, and easy to understand. You are likely going to need other people to help you actualize it, like employees; they need to understand your vision to work towards its actualization.*
> *•Focused – a good vision is not broad. It is narrow and precise.*
> *•Bold – a vision needs to be brave and big. It must test your abilities and skills*

77

•Beneficial –a good vision has a purpose, and it is intended to benefit you as well as others.
•Aligned – your vision should be aligned to your objectives and ways of achieving them. For purposes of authenticity, ensure that there are no contradictions with your objectives.
•Inspiring – write down your vision in a manner that is inspiring. Your vision must be inspiring not only to you but to your team as well.
•Engaging – a vision should be engaging; it must arouse your curiosity and that of your team.

Overall, to be successful, you must have a vision and work towards that vision as it acts as a road map to your destination.

Making and Achieving Goals

If you want to accomplish anything in life, setting goals is one of the most important things. People that do not set goals tend to have no direction and believe that life just happens to them and that luck is what determines what they have or do not have in life. Setting goals is the difference between having control over your life and letting life have control over you. When you take charge of your life, it means you enjoy it at the same time being aware of where it is headed, and you put work towards it until you arrive at your destination.

How to set and achieve your goals

1.Let your goals align with your purpose

Sometimes you may find that you have set goals, and you are not motivated to achieve them, yet the goals look very good and relevant. The problem is not a lack of motivation but that your goals lack alignment. There are two ways to set goals. The traditional and superficial way is to set goals based on what you think you should do or accomplish. These goals can be achievable, and they do work, but they are the kind of goals that you will likely drop because they are not in harmony with your higher self or purpose. If you get to achieve them, you may not have the feeling or experience you expected because the goal was not aligned to your purpose.

78

When setting goals, focus on your deepest desires, passions or dreams, and your calling. Do not allow anything to dissuade you by telling you that it is unachievable—the purpose of setting goals that are aligned with your purpose and soul.

2.Let your goals be visible

Knowing what you want or how you want it is not enough. It is important to write down your plan for what you want to achieve and how you plan to achieve it. You should also make a point of looking at your goal often so that you never get distracted from them. When you write them down, keep them somewhere to easily see them daily and stay focused.

3.Get a partner for accountability

Goals are supposed to be achieved, especially when connected to your purpose in life. When you set goals, share them with someone to help you stay on course and avoid distractions.

4.Identify a goal that is worth your life

This simply means ensuring that the goals you set are so important. If you find challenges or obstacles, you must still stay motivated and find the strength to keep moving on. When a goal is not important, it is easy to give up on it when facing challenges.

5.Prepare for obstacles

You already know that your journey is not smooth and that you will face opposition and obstacles. You must be mentally prepared for any roadblocks you may come across. Suppose you do not anticipate these roadblocks beforehand and prepare for them when they happen. In that case, they can discourage you, and you give up. As you set your goals, think of all the possible roadblocks and prepare for them.

Stop Procrastination

Procrastination is when a person tries all they can to avoid doing unpleasant tasks. Many people like procrastinating. You have a task that you must accomplish, but you do not want to because it is not pleasant to do it. There are various reasons why people procrastinate. These may include:

•They find the task to be unpleasant, and they prefer to be doing something else instead. For instance, not many people want to change their behavior. They would rather stay with what is familiar rather than come up with ways to eliminate or change the habit.

•Sometimes, a person does not know how to carry out the task and prefers to avoid it altogether. For instance, a person may know that something is not right with how they react to situations and behave. However, they avoid making changes in their behavior because they don't know how to do it or ask for help.

•Most perfectionists have a habit of procrastinating. They do this either because they feel they have nothing to change concerning behavioral change or feel they do not have the time to change perfectly.

Changing behavior is not a pleasant task. However, it must be done, and avoiding procrastination is a sure way to achieving your goal. Once you have identified behaviors and thoughts you want to change, you must avoid procrastination. There are various strategies to help you avoid procrastination. These include:

•A reward system – encourage yourself to do it first, then have a way to reward yourself once you have done it. Try and face the unpleasant task of dealing with your negative thoughts or analyzing your negative behaviors in the morning when you are fresh.

•Do it often – if you find yourself struggling to analyze things in your past that may be contributing to your current behavior, you can break them into small tasks. Practice evaluating yourself every day for a few minutes to establish the unpleasant things. When you do it more often, you start getting used and realize it is not so bad after all.

•Note it down – have a diary or a daily to-do list. When you have things written down, it is hard to ignore them. For instance, if you have indicated meditating for 20 minutes each morning on your to-do list, you will find it difficult to skip to the following task without completing the first one.

•Have an accountability partner – some people struggle with motivating themselves. For instance, if you have decided to get rid of physical clutter that could be causing you anxiety and stress, you may find it hard to part with

80

some items. Get someone you will be accountable to and help you through the journey of getting rid of the clutter.

•Ask yourself the benefits of putting it off against doing it – asking this kind of question will help persuade you to do the unpleasant thing of transforming your thinking pattern.

•Imagine how good it will feel to accomplish your goals – the feeling of accomplishment is great. You want to transform your life for the better, but you keep putting it off. You know how you are living now is not what you desire. Imagine the feeling of being able to accomplish the change and let it motivate you.

•Stop arguing with your mind. Just get up and do it. Once you have started, it gets easier than when you have not started.

•Imagine the pain of not accomplishing it – fear can also motivate you. Imagine losing your friends or your job due to your behavior. Think of what you stand to lose and stop procrastinating today.

Breaking Bad Habits

We all have habits that we need to get rid of. Unfortunately, habits are not easy to break. Whether it is procrastinating or changing from bad behavior, it requires discipline. Below are various strategies that one can use to successfully break from a bad habit.

•For every time you repeat the bad habit, find yourself. Money is a good motivator, and no one wants to part with it. You can decide the money you raise every time you repeat the bad habit will go towards a charity.

•Identify what triggers the bad habit. Knowing this is the first step towards working at breaking it.

•Make slow changes. Most people fail when they try making drastic changes at once. Take time to form new habits as you systematically break the old habits

•Think of the old habit and the new habit you want to replace with. See the best way to break it and how to start practicing the new habit.

81

•Constantly remind yourself of the benefits of breaking the bad habits and gaining good habits

•Change your surroundings. If your environment is the cause of your bad habits, consider changing it to avoid the triggers.

•Train yourself out of bad habits. You can do this by recording each time you behave wrongly and remind yourself to stop. This will make you stay conscious of your behavior.

•If you relapse on your bad habit, don't be too hard on yourself; instead, read why and see how you can do better.

•Think differently regarding your bad habits. Note down facts that are against your bad habits and work towards changing them.

Where to start

So you are at the deciding point if you want to be a change or not. If your answer is No, then there is no point going further, but if it is yes, then there is a journey after. When you decide that it is a Yes, you must change your mind set to start thinking like a changed person and acting like one.

Make an intentional decision to activate the better person within you and analyze all the ideas or critically think of other ideas. Once you identify what you want to do, it is time to develop your vision and set out goals that are in line with your vision and purpose. Follow all the tips in this so far and prepare for the journey ahead.

People without a vision and goals in life have no direction. They go through life aimlessly and often get frustrated. When things do not seem to work, they develop anxiety and depression. They view the world as being unfair, develop anger issues, and often have negative thought patterns.

Breaking bad habits and forming achievable goals is treating anxiety and depression through Cognitive Behavioral therapy.

Changing Your Perspective

Many thoughts that come across our minds are based on opinions instead of facts. There is a story about an elephant. Five blind people were sent to observe an elephant. One person touched the ears and reported back and said that the elephant was like a fan. Another one touched the legs and reported that it was like a building pole. The third one touched the side of the elephant and concluded that it was like a wall. The other touched the trunk and said it was like a snake, while the fifth touched the tusk and reported that it was hard and firm. You can see how people differ about the same thing.

Looking at different perspectives

There are many different perspectives on one thing.

That is why in a court of justice, the judge or jury calls many witnesses, lawyers/advocates, and prosecutors to give evidence. Each one of them gives evidence based on what they saw, heard, and felt about the event or situation.

We may look at something and make our judgments about it without looking from different perspectives. At first, it may seem one way. Still, let's take time to explore other possibilities. We may end up with different facts and opinions about the whole thing.

We attach different meanings to situations, events, interactions, conversations, and all that is happening to us, around us, to others, and the world. Instead of seeing things the way they are, we make our interpretations about them.

Do you need to be realistic about what you are going through? Do you need to drink alcohol? Do you have to smoke? Why are you overeating? What purpose will it serve? How will this affect you? What are the consequences?

You should be rational and ask yourself what would someone else (you respect) do if faced with the same situation?

Learn to view things differently

You should view things from wider perspectives, what is known as "seeing the bigger picture." Stand back and see the "bigger picture." You may be entangled in negative emotions, which make you irrational.

83

Try to balance your moods with your rational thoughts. Apply your reasonable mind (based on facts) to what you are going through. This way, you will be able to respond to what is going on most helpfully and effectively.

Someone might attack you with words. What will you do? The first reaction is to do the same to him. But does it help? We say that two wrongs don't make a right. You feel your moods overwhelm you by doing the wrong thing.

Swallow your pride and think about it first. You may feel like you are choking with anger but doing the right thing will ultimately lift your spirits. You will feel happier for making the right decision.

We all have different belief systems, and how you might see a situation may be different from the way I see it. Think about how other people might see the situation differently. Since you may be overwhelmed by emotions, it is good for you to consider other people's perspectives (those who are not affected by these emotions).

Things to consider

Ask yourself:

- *Am I dealing with facts or opinions?*

- *How am I reacting to this situation?*

- *How am I interpreting the situation? What meaning am I giving it?*

- *How can I look at it differently?*

- *How would others who are not emotionally affected see it? What meaning would they give? How would they react?*

- *What is the best thing to do?*

- *Are the thoughts I have helpful or unhelpful?*

- *What is the bigger picture?*

- *What is the best way of looking at it?*

- *If I was an outsider, how would I look at it?*

84

When you look at the situation from another perspective, your moods will improve, leading to healthier behavior. Your interactions and relationships will improve. Your self-esteem will improve, and you will be more confident and realistically see things.

You will look at people and situations differently. You will be able to communicate more effectively and treat others with empathy. You will feel better about yourself and be happier.

The best thing about CBT is adjusting your mind and behavior so that your moods and emotions can change for the better. To influence the way we react, we need to change our minds to positive, rational, and realistic thoughts.

Chapter 13. Common mistakes and myths about CBT

While most therapists understand cognitive-behavioral therapy, it is easy for the layperson to develop method misunderstandings due to commonly supposed myths. There are also some common mistakes that people may make during the counseling process and misconceptions of CBT flying around. Luckily, CBT is a simple and straightforward treatment to execute with the proper tools when you're trained. Simple mistakes can still be made, however.

Common myths

These myths easily spread, as people with only a small understanding of cognitive-behavioral therapy may misunderstand what they've learned. However, since this person thinks they understand the matter, they start spreading their misunderstanding, creating these common myths. Let's take a look at the commonest myths and the real facts behind them.

CBT is a rigid, one-size-fits-all approach

One of the best things about CBT is that it's a flexible approach applied to several conditions with many methods. While a person with depression will use one set of techniques, a person with post-traumatic stress disorder will employ another set of techniques. While these two individuals will use two different approaches, they will also use a few of the same methods to restructure their cognition, such as journalizing. The fact is, CBT is by no means linear or one-size-fits-all. It is a highly customizable technique that can be modified based on the condition, age, and individual circumstances. This approach acknowledges that each person is exceptional, needing a specific and personalized approach.

This therapist should tailor their treatment plan to their specific needs whenever a person sees a highly trained cognitive-behavioral therapist. A person can also customize their own plan when using this book without a therapist's help. It is, of course, always advisable to seek professional assistance.

CBT only focuses on replacing negativity with positive thinking

Cognitive-behavioral therapy focuses on more positive and less destructive cognitive rehabilitation. This is different from positive thinking, though. A person simply says something positive with typical positive thinking to cover up their negativity. The person may say, for example, "nothing is wrong, I'm happy," even though they've just got bad news and are devastated. This kind of insincere positive thinking is like trying to get rid of your house's deadly mold by simply painting over it.

Cognitive-behavioral therapy helps people learn to see their lives as objectively as possible instead of dressing up their life with insincere positivity. It means you see both the good and the bad, with neither eclipse the other. Having a balanced and realistic cognition allows you to enjoy the good and address and fix any problems.

As well as looking more realistically at the world and yourself, CBT also teaches people to think more flexibly. This means that if a person feels nervous about delivering a speech before a crowd, they can think flexibly about the situation. If the individual said to himself, "I'm not going to mess up, so I shouldn't be worried," it won't help, as it certainly is possible to mess up. The person is taught to think of other perspectives instead. For example, they could think, "I can still do well and succeed even if I make a mistake."

CBT ignores emotions

Nothing could be further from the truth than saying CBT disregards emotions. The truth is that emotions are a very important part of the process of therapy. They are only handled with a different approach from other therapy types. In CBT, they are concerned hand-in-hand with a person's intellect instead of coping with thoughts on their own. This is because it is cognition that affects the thoughts, behaviors, and emotions of a person. Therefore, you must first understand the reasoning underlying them to deal with difficult and problematic feelings.

CBT ignores the past and childhood

There is some reality in this hypothesis, but only partially. The truth is that CBT usually focuses on the issues that currently affect a person, the here and now. However, if possible, a psychiatrist will look back on their patient's past and how that history can affect their memory and cause problems with their present life. For example, if a person has post-traumatic stress disorder, the doctor can look back to see what caused the pain. Suppose a person has a disorder of social anxiety. In that case, the therapist can discuss situations in the past that may have triggered fear of social interaction.

A person may be able to look back on their past and see how it has adversely affected their cognition. Still, only a trained therapist can do this reliably. The reality is that we cannot look completely objectively at our own pasts, particularly where trauma is involved. A psychiatrist, however, specializes in understanding this problematic past and memories with the ability to learn how to restructure thought in a balanced and healthy manner.

CBT only treats the symptoms, not the problem

By definition, cognitive-behavioral therapy treats an individual as a whole without reducing them to a setlist of symptoms. This is because it must first alter a person's attitude before it can even treat symptoms. As a person's comprehension increases, they will learn about the world around them, people, and themselves in a more balanced way. This, in turn, creates a change in the minds, emotions, and behaviors of the individual. The result is a therapy that focuses on external fixes inside rather than just covering up the external symptoms while ignoring the internal problems. You can feel confident knowing that CBT is making a real and lasting change for a person as a whole, allowing them to continue experiencing improvements even after the therapy course is over.

There is limited scientific evidence supporting CBT

The reality is that cognitive-behavioral therapy has a high level of scientific evidence to support its effectiveness, particularly when compared with other types of psychological therapy. A meta-analysis conducted by Boston University reviewed more than one hundred reports on the use of CBT for different disorders, addictions, causes of stress, and other potential situations.

This meta-analysis revealed that CBT was more effective in almost all cases than other forms of therapy employed. Not only that, but people with anxiety disorders, general stress, anger control problems, bulimia, and somatoform disorders were found to be particularly effective.

CBT requires the person to be motivated

Getting started in treatment can be daunting, even if you know that will help. It can be impossible to do anything when you are depressed or anxious, even what is right. Does that mean CBT won't work for people with no motivation? No! Because no! In reality, as they begin, most people struggle with these things and therefore are unmotivated. But, given this lack of motivation, these people find success time and time again and find themselves enjoying incredible benefits.

CBT works if they have a schedule with goals, preparation techniques, and a person to be accountable even for an unmotivated person. In getting someone on your side, even if you are not inspired, you have somebody's support helping you adhere to your routine and try to use the strategies you have learned. For most people, this person is a therapist, but you can also remain accountable to a friend or family member. The person you are caring for should understand the therapy's theory, so try to get them to read this book or give them videos to help them understand the procedure. If the person understands what you need to do, they can make sure that you are doing it well and can advise when necessary.

It's long/short-term psychotherapy

People tend to think CBT is either long-term or short-term. The reality is halfway everywhere. CBT has a set number of sessions, unlike some therapy forms, which require a person to go multiple times a week for an unforeseeable amount of time. By the end of these sessions, the patient should find that they have restructured their cognition and are ready to go out into the world on their own. They may still use the techniques they have learned to maintain a healthy understanding. Still, extensive daily therapy will no longer be required. On the other hand, neither is this necessarily a short-term therapy. While there are typically a set number of five to twenty weekly sessions, the number of sessions can continue for as long as the individual needs them.

You need not worry about getting only five sessions if your case needs twenty.

CBT is straightforward

It's true that cognitive-behavioral therapy is a simple and straightforward therapy that anybody, adult or child, can perform. It is important to remember, however, that no therapy is "really easy." All forms of therapy will have their own difficulties. It is not easy to overcome our inner pain, trauma, or habits. It will take patience and hard work to restructure your mind into a more cohesive and safer mindset. You'll need to make sure you're using your learned techniques daily and keep yourself honest.

Using CBT, you'll find at the end of your time that the effort and work you put into restructuring your cognition was worth it. Of course, it may not always be the easiest thing to do, but it's one of the most worthwhile ways to spend your time. You will consider yourself a lot more comfortable, fulfilled, and content with the concerted daily effort.

Common mistakes

Occasionally, mistakes with any form of therapy are normal. The doctor will usually help correct these errors and lead you along the right path. If you use CBT alone and without a therapist's help, though, you will need to keep these common mistakes in mind so you can stop them.

Not understanding the importance of repetition

People who have tried cognitive therapy may be frustrated or feel that the process is not working, that it is a failure. However, studies repeatedly show us that the process is effective if a therapist specializing in CBT employs the approach on their patients. And, why are the perspectives differing? Simply put, if a person uses a psychiatrist who does not understand the process or does it alone without proper knowledge, they will make mistakes, and these mistakes are not encouraging change.

One of the biggest errors leading to failure is failure to understand the importance of repetition. You can tell a person how they should and shouldn't think, but that doesn't guarantee that they'll automatically change. Rather, they have to use techniques and tools to facilitate the transition in their daily lives. We must use these methods every day - and throughout the day. That is because a repetition of helpful techniques and balanced thinking is the key to successful CBT. It takes steady work.

Unlike other forms of therapy, you're not just talking to a therapist and then going for the week along your way. You have to make an effort to change your cognition directly, and you do that by repeatedly using the tools and knowledge you have been given. Just as you can't master archery by shooting off a dozen arrows, you can't master a single time restructuring your cognition by using a couple of techniques. With both of these, you have to constantly do the same thing to improve and finally learn the art. Before preparation, you cannot expect results.

Using positive thinking in place of CBT

We mentioned earlier that some people may believe that all that CBT entails is positive thinking, which couldn't be further from the truth. A person restructures his / her mentality with cognitive behavioral therapy to function in a more balanced way. On the other hand, positive thinking is either insincere or refuses to see the negativity, which is plain as day. The reality is that while we don't want to think negatively, it's important to be able to see challenges and the bad in our life to resolve and solve them. Ignoring negativity is like failing to see a storm heading straight in your direction. The reverse (failing to see something positively) would be a person lying in the fetal position moaning "We must die" and refusing to do anything similar to the storm tank. You should recognize the tornado coming your way with a balanced cognition and do something about it and move for safety into the storm shelter.

Remember, CBT is not a matter of positive or negative thinking but of balanced cognition.

Not making use of relaxation techniques

Therapists will frequently receive reports from their patients, explaining that they feel stressed and anxious. When asked if they use the relaxation techniques they have been given, such as deep breathing and mindfulness, the person may respond "not really" or "a few times." The problem with this is that you can't expect to benefit from something you don't frequently and actively use. Think about it. While we'd all love it if we could start losing weight simply by eating healthy for one day, we've got to practice regularly eating healthily to see results. The same applies to relaxation techniques. Suppose you want to benefit from these techniques, the reduction of stress and the reduction of anxiety. In that case, you will need to put them frequently into the effort.

Such methods prepare the mind and body in a relaxed and efficient way to deal with negative emotions, thereby making positive emotions. Not only are they useful on the days you use them, but they also get better the more often you use them. Think of such techniques as exercises: the longer and more often you practice, the better and the stronger you become. Soon you'll find it simple to simultaneously complete awareness and deep breathing. However, at first, you might find it challenging to focus and sit still for long periods.

Keep putting these techniques into practice at least once or twice a day, and over the next few weeks, you will find your stress and anxiety greatly decreasing. Once your stress reduces, just don't slack off; keep practicing these every day regardless, as they will keep your stress low.

Believing emotions are irrational

Because our thoughts and emotions are based on our intellect, some people begin to believe that they have to be completely irrational in their experiences. That they wouldn't feel anything if they were balanced and rational at all. But the reality is that sentiments can be rational, irrational, or neutral. After all, when someone makes an innocent mistake, you can feel irrationally angry, or you can be rationally angry at the injustice and senseless violence that has taken place.

Human beings are emotional beings, and you just can't write off all your emotions. We are an important part of ourselves that helps us think, interact with a group, and become more concerned about the world. You're not supposed to be a robot without any feeling, you're way more than someone who makes up scripts and zeros. Numbness and a lack of feelings are a characteristic hallmark of severe depression. So, don't try to get rid of these feelings yourself. You can see a more balanced cognition while still enjoying those valuable sensations.

Using CBT to justify a lack of responsibility

A person is encouraged to accept who they are by cognitive behavioral therapy and value all facets of themselves. This is intended to be used as a basis for growing and improving upon yourself. Yet, some people take this as a justification for simply feeling good about themselves and not caring about progress. They tolerate their flaws to such a degree that they don't care if they hurt others with those shortcomings. You often see that in people who pride themselves on speaking bluntly or honestly.

Yeah, speaking honestly is a good thing. Still, when people brag about it, they only use "honesty" to justify doing cruel and unnecessary things.

With CBT, you must see all your attributes, good as well as bad. Be proud of the good qualities, accept the bad ones and then try to grow and minimize the more negative attributes for yourself. This is nothing to discourage-we all have our own negative characteristics, and we are all human. Such qualities can evolve over life. It is simply our responsibility to constantly work on ourselves, developing ourselves to be the best version of ourselves we can be.

Demanding rationality

You will want to start restructuring your cognition as you learn about the importance of rational and balanced cognition and the benefits it offers. However, some people will take this to the extreme of chastising themselves for failing to match an image standard, believing they should always be completely rational.

The truth is this is not rational in itself, as it is an unrealistic expectation that cannot be achieved. Also, we are human beings making mistakes, so we cannot always be a hundred percent moral. That is not what CBT is or talks about. Improving our mindset is essential to enhance our mental health and depression by having a more realistic view of the world and ourselves.

This is also an irrational thought as it is black-or-white thinking that says, "If something isn't good, it must be bad." You're not meant to see everything in black and white with this therapy, but rather see that there are a variety of shades between these two colors.

93

Not making a lifestyle change

Through cognitive behavioral therapy, you are not just trying to avoid acknowledging unreasonable or pessimistic thoughts. Alternatively, you are consciously teaching your brain to respond to stimuli differently. If you don't put in the practice hours, you can't train your brain; just reading this book isn't going to do the trick! Sure, reading this book is the first move, but if you don't bring it into daily practice, it won't help you.

Think about it, you can't just run a marathon by reading a book on running better. Instead, you have to wake up every day and train at the same time for months. The same refers to cognitive-behavioral therapy. You'll have to regular daily practice for a few months if you're really hoping to make a change and succeed. If you want to restructure your intellect, reading a few words on a page, you can't do it. You must actively use every day, all day, the techniques and tools you have learned.

It may take time, but you'll soon find yourself changing if you make a lifestyle change by thoroughly incorporating CBT into your daily routine. You'll notice a big difference after a few weeks, and the gap will be dramatic in a few months.

Conclusion

Indeed, CBT starts with a relatively straightforward way to understand a challenging situation and how we react to it. You have to remember that cognitive-behavioral therapy focuses on the three major components of a psychological problem: thoughts, emotions, and behaviors.

This simply means that when you experience a challenging situation, it is important that you break it down into these components. When you break it down in this manner, you gain clarity about where to intervene and how to do it. In other words, there is a chain of reactions of both behavior and emotional feelings that arise from having a particular negative thought. The best approach is to go back into reexamining the thought. However, suppose a negative behavior pattern seems to be the main problem. In that case, the wiser thing to do is to learn a new response to the situation.

The truth is, there is no quicker way to fix your anxiety. It takes time and commitment for you to fully overcome your fears. When you go through cognitive behavioral therapy, it is important that you face your fears head-on rather than trying to run away from them. This might make you feel worse at first, but it is only after that you can start feeling better. The most important thing is for you to try as much as you can to stick to your therapy and the advice given by your therapist.

Your pace or recovery may be slow, and this can be discouraging at the time, but you have to remember that it will be effective in the long run. Therefore, rather than giving up, keep pressing on, and you will eventually reap the benefits. To support your therapy, you must start making positive choices. This includes everything from your level of activity to your social life and how that affects your condition. The best route is for you to begin by setting goals and making informed decisions. This will boost your relaxation and functionality levels and offer you a positive mental outlook in your daily life.

Take time to learn about your anxiety so that it becomes easier to overcome it. Education is crucial in ensuring that you know what it takes to get to the other recovery side. True, that alone will not cure your condition, but it will help you make sense of your healing therapy.

Cultivate your support network to be isolated and lonely, as loneliness can make your anxiety even worse. When you establish a robust system of support from your therapist, family, and friends, you will significantly lower your vulnerability level. Make a point to see your support group frequently so that you can share with them your worries, concerns, and progress.

Also, remember to adopt a healthy lifestyle by engaging in physical activities and eating healthy foods. This regimen goes a long way in helping to achieve relaxation by relieving tension and anxiety. Therefore, in your daily routine, make it a point to schedule regular exercises. Also, refrain from foods and drinks that may make your anxiety worse, such as those containing caffeine or alcohol.

DIALECTICAL BEHAVIOR THERAPY

Introduction

Take a moment and think of a life without any anger, disappointment, stress, distress, frustration, or any other undesirable emotions. Think about how wonderful your life would be if you could control your emotions. Even if they seem uncontrollable right now, you can learn to regulate them.

There are various emotions we all experience; some of them are desirable, while others are undesirable. Emotions tend to directly or indirectly influence different aspects of our lives. Since our thoughts are often based on our emotions, it can become difficult to stay rational when your emotions are running high. The inability to cope with intense emotions can quickly hamper your ability to lead a happy and stress-free life.

Millions of people across the globe suffer from a variety of emotion regulation disorders like borderline personality disorder (BPD), obsessive-compulsive disorder (OCD), post-traumatic stress disorder (PTSD), anxiety, and depression. If you are tired of allowing your emotions to guide your decisions and want to learn to control them, the DBT method will come in handy. DBT stands for Dialectical Behavior Therapy. Dr. Marsha Linehan developed the concept of DBT, and it is a clinically proven and evidence-based treatment for emotion regulation and managing intense emotions.

This book is ideal for anyone who wants to learn more about DBT. The information included in this book is presented in an easy-to-understand fashion, making it ideal for beginners and experts. This book is your go-to guide about DBT and mindfulness. The up-to-date information, along with different techniques—including mindfulness—to deal with various mental disorders, makes it different from other guides available on the market. Mindfulness is not just integral to DBT; it is vital for your overall wellbeing. Mindfulness teaches you to live your life in the present instead of dwelling on worrisome thoughts about the past or the future. If you cannot live your life in the present, your thought patterns will be riddled with negativity and anxiety.

If you are eager to take charge of your life and handle your emotions without allowing them to overwhelm you, then let us get started immediately.

CHAPTER 1: What is DBT

Dialectical Behavior Therapy (DBT) is a therapeutic method that merges cognitive-behavioral procedures and mindfulness to impart individuals the skills to keep their emotions under control. It helps improve relationships with people around and manage distressful circumstances.

Dialectical Behavior Therapy was first realized in the 1970s in Washington by Marsha Linehan, a psychologist researcher. It was developed for the treatment of women with Borderline Personality Disorder (BPD). It has since proven successful and is extensively used for various psychological disorders, including anxiety disorders, depression, eating disorders, and addiction.

Dr. Marsha Linehan and her colleagues introduced the concept of DBT during the 1980s. They discovered that certain cognitive-behavioral therapy (CBT) aspects were not sufficient when dealing with patients diagnosed with BPD. So, Dr. Linehan, along with her team, came up with various techniques and a new course of treatment to help meet the unique needs of those with BPD. The primary concept of this technique is based on philosophical processes known as "dialectics." Dialectics essentially suggest that all things are made of opposites. Change occurs whenever an opposing force is stronger than its opposite force. In academic terms, it can be described as thesis, antithesis, and synthesis. There are three basic assumptions on which dialectics are based, and they are as follows:

Everything is interconnected.

Change is not only constant, but it is inevitable.

All opposites can be integrated to form a close approximation of the truth.

In DBT, the patient and the therapist actively resolve any contradictions between self-acceptance and change to bring about a positive change in the patient. Dr. Linehan and colleagues also came up with another technique known as "validation." They observed that when the need for change was coupled with validation, a patient's cooperation increased, and any distress associated with coping with change was reduced.

Research Facts about DBT

Research proving the advantages of DBT for various people suffering from different kinds of mental ailments is abounding. Those who have taken up DBT, suffering from a borderline personality disorder (BPD) specifically, have shown notable improvements, including reducing self-harm attempts and depression. Improvements in feelings of hostility, fury, hopelessness, and detachment were also notably decreased.

It has also been found that people who have completed the DBT program designated less participation in premeditated self-harm and suicidal attempts.

Recent studies have shown that Dialectical Behavior Therapy (DBT) is an effective treatment for those dealing with eating disorders or substance addictions. Throughout the treatment, there was a significant decrease in addictive substances and improved overall functioning.

Research still supports DBT as an effective technique for treating individuals grappling with emotional dysregulation and tolerating distress.

CHAPTER 2: Components Used In DBT

There are four components of full DBT: skill training group, singular treatment, DBT telephone instructing, and consultation group.

• DBT abilities preparing group is focused on improving clients' capacities by showing them behavioral skills. The group is run like a class where the group head teaches the skills and assigns schoolwork for clients to utilize the skills in their regular day-to-day existences. Groups meet on week by week basis for around 2.5 hours. It takes 24 weeks to get past the full skill educational program, which is regularly rehashed to make a 1-year program. Briefer timetables that show just a subset of the skills have also been produced for specific populaces and settings.

• DBT singular therapy focuses on improving client's inspiration and helping clients apply the skills to specific challenges and occasions in their lives. In the standard DBT example, singular therapy happens once per week for around an hour and runs simultaneously with skill groups.

• DBT telephone instructing is focused on giving clients in-the-minute training on how to use skills to successfully adapt to stressful situations that emerge in their regular day-to-day existences. Clients can call their specialists between sessions to get training when they need assistance the most.

• DBT therapist meeting group is expected to be therapy for the therapists and help DBT suppliers work with people who frequently have a serious, intricate, difficult-to-treat issue. The counsel group is intended to enable specialists to remain persuaded and skilled to give the ideal treatment. Groups typically meet weekly and are made out of individual therapists and group pioneers who offer obligations regarding every customer's consideration.

Traditionally, the way to deal with DBT is to be as exhaustive as conceivable and to execute different resources to build up a compelling way to assist a customer in therapy.

In DBT, the accompanying aspects are regularly used:

• Individual therapy sessions: The clients will frequently go to singular treatment once every week. Unique therapy sessions address severe issues and treatment approaches. During individual sessions, the specialist and customer cooperate to understand how their thoughts, beliefs, and desires contribute to their problems. Individuals engaged with DBT stay in individual therapy all through the whole treatment process.

• Group therapy sessions: In a wide range of CBT ideal examples, clients either go to single sessions or group sessions. DBT is one of the CBT paradigms where both individual and group therapy sessions are typically used. Group therapy sessions are regularly a mix of psychoeducational dialogs and talks and formal routines regarding strategies. These sessions are frequently extraordinarily organized and will typically meet once per week over a 20-week (or more) timespan. These sessions are intended to give clients specific skills and to rehearse them to address their issues. Clients are relied upon to go to all the group sessions. The course typically rehashes itself after the whole grouping of classes or practice sessions has run its course to allow people to make up any sessions they have missed (although missing meetings is firmly discouraged).

• Making assistance available: In this present reality, clients in therapy may keep running into situations requiring prompt help. In customary DBT, clients are offered access to a telephone mentor they can contact when they need to counsel somebody. This is regularly a DBT therapist or a prepared telephone mentor; it may even be the customer's close to a home specialist, or it could be some other DBT therapist who is accessible. The use of this asset is intended to enable people to work through issues that might be difficult for them; in any case, the abuse of this asset is disheartened.

• Keeping therapists updated: DBT advisors are relied upon to keep progressing preparing and required to go to periodic training updates, group meetings, and discussion groups. They must stay aware of the research literature concerning DBT therapy and different aspects of psychological well-being treatment.

The above depiction incorporates the complete supplement of services accessible in conventional DBT mediations.

Now and again, the personal coaching option may not be available, contingent upon the kind of issues the customer is trying to determine. The feasibility of having such a service accessible will change from treatment supplier to treatment supplier.

Approach

The approach used in DBT allows for the use of three empirically approved segments to assist in the treatment of clients in therapy:

• Orientation toward the individual: All types of treatment have accurately summed up rules that they follow; nonetheless, these standards can't generally be connected similarly to everybody. DBT endeavors to approach the individual by helping them use their qualities to change and build up their shortcomings, intending to whatever issues they face.

• Thinking and behaving: Because DBT is an intellectual, behavioral type of therapy, it uses both the person's perceptions and activities to accept their issues and improve answers for them. This implies understanding how and why individuals accept the way they do and how that influences their activities.

• Using the therapeutic alliance to accomplish change: The helpful coalition refers to the working bond between the therapist and the customer in therapy. This bond represents an understanding for the customer as an individual and the therapist as somebody with a particular aptitude to support the customer. Research has identified the therapeutic alliance as one of the fundamental components contributing to fruitful results in psychotherapy.

DBT believes the therapeutic coalition is the encouraging instrument of progress for the customer.

The customer's emotionally supportive network outside of therapy is critical in helping the customer address their issues. DBT therapists often attempt to get relatives, companions, and working associates engaged with the customer's treatment.

General treatment objectives comprise of:

•   Developing new skills: A core segment of both individual and group therapy sessions is to assist clients with developing unique qualities and skills to effectively collaborate on the planet.

•   Growing motivation: DBT endeavors to keep the customer's motivation high using uplifting measures and engrossing relations and chums.

•   Accepting what can't be changed: Despite all of the potential therapeutic techniques available in DBT and the steady preparation and refreshing of the advisor's abilities, there are consistently actualities about life outside our ability to control. Frequently, clients are troubled about things they can't change. Helping clients acknowledge certain aspects of the world and evolving by them is a significant part of DBT.

•   Understanding where the customer concerns change: Therapists in DBT are prepared to understand and perceive the customer's ability to adapt and motivation to change. Therapists are ready to work at the customer's level while helping them to build up their motivation and limit concerning change.

•   Functionality: Therapists guarantee that the new skills learned in therapy can be connected in reality by the customer.

Techniques

Like all types of Cognitive Behavioral Therapy, DBT has various methodologies and procedures that the therapist can use contingent upon the specific customer, the customer's issues, and the limit of the customer to use them. There are volumes of books discussing particular techniques that can be used in specific situations.

A portion of the broader systems and methodologies used in DBT include:

•   Incorporating the idea of mindfulness: Although the thought of care is frequently displayed as another idea, it is ancient and built up the concept in numerous types of CBT. The notion of responsibility alludes to the capacity to give one's full focus to what's going on at the time in a nonjudgmental way and facing the minute as it happens. It is an ability that requires unquestionably more practice than one may accept. Still, it allows a person to impartially audit and translates the occasions around them. It is frequently significant for individuals with troubling issues to suspend their desires and biases to understand others.

•   Tolerating stress/distress: This technique is identified with the mindfulness approach. Recall that DBT was created to address issues that were frequently clashing. Much of the time, people come to therapy striving to change unpleasant or upsetting conditions (e.g., loss of a friend or family member, a horrendous experience, and so forth.). Now and again, such change is unthinkable. DBT tries to assist clients in acknowledging such inevitabilities in a nonjudgmental and non-evaluative fashion. This allows them to progressively recognize positive approaches and take increasingly positive activities to address issues they can control. For instance, one can't control past occasions, for example, the passing of a friend or family member. Still, one can figure out how to deal with the stress associated with this misfortune. Stress management techniques are essential in numerous types of Cognitive Behavioral Therapy, and DBT is no exception.

Emotional regulation: Many customers who are primarily alluded to DBT practice extraordinarily attacking and high emotional states (e.g., effectively suicidal clients or clients with a borderline personality disorder). DBT has built up various ways to deal with understanding and controlling one's feelings. This frequently includes an organized methodology that helps identify emotions, decrease one's powerlessness, increase mindfulness, identify obstacles to evolving feelings, figure out how to take inverse activities, and apply stress management for stress/distress tolerance.

CHAPTER 3: Dialectical Behavior Therapy

Dialectical behavior therapy (DBT) gives clients new skills to oversee excruciating feelings and decrease strife, seeing someone. DBT specifically focuses on providing therapeutic ability in four key areas. First, mindfulness focuses on improving a person's capacity to acknowledge and be available in the present minute. Second, distance resistance is intended for increasing an individual's resilience of negative feelings, as opposed to attempting to escape from it. Third, emotion regulation covers systems to oversee and change extreme beliefs that are causing issues in an individual's life. Fourth, interpersonal effectiveness comprises strategies that allow an individual to speak with others assertively, keeps up a sense of pride, and reinforces connections.

What's Unique About Dialectical Behavioral Therapy?

The expression "dialectical" originates from the possibility that uniting two contrary energies in therapy - acceptance and change - brings superior outcomes over it is possible that only one.

A one of a kind aspect of DBT is its focus on acceptance of a patient's experience as a path for therapists to reassure them - and balance the work needed to change negative behaviors.

Standard complete DBT has four sections:

- *Individual therapy*

- *Group skills preparing*

- *Phone training, if needed for emergencies between sessions*

- *Consultation bunch for health care suppliers to remain propelled and examine patient consideration*

Patients consent to do schoolwork to rehearse new skills. This incorporates rounding out day-by-day "journal cards" to follow more than 40 emotions, urges, behaviors, and abilities, for example, lying, self-damage, or self-respect.

106

What to Expect

DBT treatment typically comprises separate therapy meetings and DBT skills groups. Specific therapy sessions contain one-on-one contact with a qualified therapist, confirming that all-important needs are being tended to. The personal therapist will assist the patient in remaining inspired, applying the DBT skills within regular life, and addressing impediments that may emerge through the span of treatment.

DBT skills group contestants learn and preparation skills together with others. Members of the group are urged to share their experiences and give common help. Groups are driven by one prepared advisor showing skills and stimulating activities. The group members are then assigned schoolwork; for example, rehearsing care works out. Each group session lasts roughly two hours, and groups typically meet week by week for a half year. Groups can be shorter or more, contingent upon the needs of the group individuals. DBT can be conveyed by specialists from multiple points of view. For example, a few people total the one-on-one therapy sessions without going to the week after week skill group.

How It Works

DBT is a cognitive treatment created by Marsha Linehan, Ph.D., during the 1980s to treat people with a borderline personality disorder. Those identified with BPD frequently experience very exceptional negative emotions that are difficult to oversee. These extraordinary and wild negative emotions are commonly experienced when the individual collaborates with others—friends, romantic partners, family members. People with borderline often experience a lot of contention in their relationships.

As its name recommends, DBT is impacted by the philosophical point of view of persuasions: adjusting alternate extremes. The therapist consistently works with the person to discover approaches to hold two opposite standpoints at once, helping balance and avoiding black and white —the all-or-nothing styles of reasoning. In service of this balance, DBT advances a both-and instead of an either-or outlook. The persuasion at the core of DBT is getting and change.

107

What to Expression for in a Dialectical Behavior Therapist?

DBT accepts that compelling treatment, including group skill training, must give as much consideration to the behavior and experience of suppliers working with clients as it does to clients' practice and experience. Thus, treatment of the suppliers is a significant part of any DBT program, and therapists should rehearse the skills themselves. They need to know the necessary behavior therapy procedures and DBT treatment methodologies. Search for a mental health professional with specific preparation and experience in DBT.

CHAPTER 4: Distress Tolerance

At any point in our lives, we all need to cope with distress and pain. It can be painful, like a bee sting or a broken arm, or if it can be mental, like sorrow or anger. The pain is often unavoidable, and in both cases, unpredictable. You can't really predict when a bee will sting you or when something will make you feel sad. Sometimes, the best thing you can do is use the coping skills you have and hope they work.

Yet, mental and physical discomfort is more intense for some people and occurs more often than for others. A pain spreads more quickly and sounds like a huge tidal wave. Sometimes, such circumstances feel like they will never stop. The people who encounter them don't know how to deal with their pain intensity. People who deal with intense feelings frequently treat their pain in very risky, sometimes harmful ways, because they don't know what else to do. This is easy to grasp. It's hard to be rational when a person is in emotional pain and thinks about a good solution. Nonetheless, all of the coping mechanisms people with intense feelings use tend just to make their challenges worse.

Take a "rest"

Now that you have recognized some of your own self-destructive and dysfunctional behaviors — as well as their cost — the first approach to pain tolerance you need to know is REST. REST is an acronym that reminds you:

Relax

Evaluate

Set an intention

Take action

Changing some behavioral patterns is hard. You need to learn what you want to do when you want to change them and what else you want to do instead. Although important, you still need to remember why you want to do something differently. Often this is the hardest step — remembering that you want to change — especially when you feel overwhelmed by your emotions.

109

If you're overwhelmed by intense feelings, your first instinct is always to behave impulsively and participate in some form of self-destructive or dangerous repeated acts. This is because you may not even remember that you intended to do something different in those times of heightened stress unless you're prepared. So how do you plan on making healthier choices when you feel overwhelmed? The first move to fix any problem or self-destructive behavior — and not to act impulsively — is to follow the strategy of REST: relax, evaluate, set an intention, and take action.

- **Relax.**

Relaxation represents the first step in the process. Stop what you are doing. Freeze. Breathe in. Pause. Let the situation off for a few seconds and get a new viewpoint. Don't just do the typical thing you do. Don't rely on stimuli. Do your best to note you have the chance to behave differently. Build the "space" between your ability to behave impulsively and your actual reaction. Maybe say out loud, "Wait," "Relax," or "REST," just to warn you not to react too quickly and automatically. And take a couple of deep breaths to help you calm down before taking some specific alternative action.

- **Evaluate.**

Remind yourself what is going on in that situation. What are the facts, exactly? Just do a brief analysis. You don't have to work it all out, and you don't have to do a thorough analysis of why you feel the way you are doing. You don't even have to fix the problem if that is too hard. Just do your best to get an overall feel of what's going on. Observe, for example, what happens to you physically, emotionally, and mentally. Observe what other people are doing around you too. Maybe just ask a few simple questions, like these: "How am I feeling?" "What's going on?" Is anybody at risk?"

- **Set an intention.**

The third step is assessing a desire to do something. In this scenario, an aim is an objective, goal, or strategy about what you will be doing. Decide what action you want to take. Tell yourself, "What do I need?"

110

Then maybe choose one of the coping skills or self-relieving skills you'll learn. Perhaps, you have a bigger problem to solve? Whatever you choose to do, it doesn't have to be the definitive or only solution to the problem right now, but it will ideally be a good thing to help you deal with.

- **Take action.**

Take action, at last. Put your plan into motion. Go forward attentively, which means moving gradually and with knowledge of what you are doing. Whatever your last move goal was, now do it as quietly and efficiently as you can. Now, taking action may not be the perfect solution to the problem at hand. If you follow these steps, the proactive response would certainly be safer and more successful than the self-destructive actions you would have taken.

Although this may seem like a lot to do with practice - especially when you feel overcome by emotions - these steps can be done in few seconds and become a new habit for you. Be conscious also that you may need to use REST in the same case more than once. And if REST isn't working for the first time, go ahead and use it again. You may have missed an important aspect, or maybe something has changed quickly.

So now that you're familiar with the REST strategy, the next step to change your self-destructive and dysfunctional habits is to recognize and predict when REST is likely to be required. Normally, you'll realize that there's a chance to do something better when you're experiencing intense negative emotions. When you do, it is usually an indicator that something will happen that will force you to make a choice: either you are going to act impulsively and do what you always do, or you are going to use the coping skills in this book and do something differently. One good indicator you need to use REST is if you're socially, mentally, or physically in pain; this is usually a good indicator that you need to choose to do something. Eventually, if you have the desire to act impulsively, using one of your usual self-destructive behaviors, even if you don't know why, you might also need to use REST. Each of these three criteria means that you have a moment of choice: either you can do what you usually do — impulsively respond and potentially cause harm to yourself or someone else— or you can calm, assess, set your goal, and take action using this healthy coping ability.

111

Here are two examples to understand how to use that. Let's see how the REST approach is being used by James and Kim.

James had the issue with his friend, Joyce, initiating debates often. This would usually cause him to yell at Joyce that she was "worthless" as a girlfriend and belittle her further. Then, when he felt ashamed, James quickly walked out and went to the local pub, where he would drink too much beer and spend too much money. He knew what skills worked for him, but he often had trouble remembering to use them while his rage and sadness consumed him. He knew he needed to use the REST technique, so in many locations around their home, he put brightly colored sticky notes with the word "REST" on them. Fortunately, the next time James and Joyce continued to argue, James caught sight of one of the sticky notes that he had put up and was reminded to use the tactic. He just stopped what he was doing and tried to relax. He stopped screaming at Joyce, took a deep breath, and relieved some of his body's muscle tension. Last. he assessed the situation. He was able to comment on what was going on. He was debating with Joyce because she hadn't cleaned his suit for work, but until the next morning, he wasn't going to work, and he hadn't been able to tell her he wanted it to be washed first. Besides, it still had plenty of time to do it. He also understood that there was no disaster right now; his frustration just made him feel incredibly stressed. He felt like going home to the pub for a few drinks, but he didn't. He set a goal, instead. He needed to stay home, calm down, and not do anything to ruin his friendship with Joyce any further. James had both focused on his self-reassuring abilities and communication skills, and he knew he needed to use them. So, he has finally taken the initiative. He told Joyce that he remembered that he hadn't asked her to wash his uniform, that he felt angry, and that he had to go into the bedroom to calm down. And he went to lay down on the bed, put on some soothing music, and practiced his diaphragmatic breathing before he was relaxed enough to come out to Joyce and apologize.

Likewise, Kim suffered from overwhelming emotions and would frequently alienate people with her extreme anger— even strangers. One day she took a dress back to a clothing store to refund it, as she found that it had been ruined since buying it. Kim was already annoyed to have to drive back to the store all the way.

112

Then she became even more upset with the "idiot" who made the stain and put it on the shelf to sell it anyway. Instead, to make matters worse, the cashier told Kim that she could not refund it because she bought the dress on sale. Suddenly She was furious. In the past, Kim would have begun to scream in front of everyone at the cashier. Still, she had been practicing her coping skills with her therapist, and she was encouraged to use the REST strategy. And instead of shouting, Kim paused, repeating "Stop" in her mind, taking a deep breath and deciding to relax. She then appraised the situation. She felt extremely frustrated and knew it would turn into an argument very soon if she attempted to talk to the cashier. This was not an emergency of "life or death," but Kim had spent a great deal of money, so she needed a refund. She set out an idea next. She realized she needed to calm down before she addressed this topic with the cashier. She described her coping skills as leaving the shop for a brief while using her calming thoughts to calm down. She told the cashier she had to go outside for a second, but she'd be back right there.

So, Kim stood outside the shop, took a few slow breaths, and echoed her calming thoughts: "I'm not in danger right now" and "These are just my fears, but they will eventually go away. "After a few minutes, when she was relaxed enough, she returned to the store and spoke to the cashier again. Kim explained that when she got home, she didn't notice the mark and requested a refund. The cashier, though, also insisted that Kim's money could not be refunded. So, she became angry and confused. She had hoped that using the technique of REST and calming down would solve her problem, but that did not. And she wanted to give it another try. She stopped once more, breathing steadily and relaxed as best she could. Then, she assessed the situation easily. "What is going on here?" She was thinking about herself. She glanced at the name tag of the cashier and found it said "Trainee." Kim had been to this store for years and had no problem returning things, and she asked if this trainee gave her accurate information. Kim then set out to use some of her newly learned, assertive communication skills and finally took action by politely asking the cashier if she could speak to the boss. The manager, of course, corrected the condition and allowed Kim to return the dress. The problem with Kim hadn't been immediately resolved just because she once used the REST strategy. But with her perseverance, the REST technique helped avoid alienating people with her frustration during her second attempt.

Distract yourself by paying attention to someone else

Another perfect way to distract yourself from suffering is to draw someone else's attention. Below are a few examples. Find out the things you're able to do, and add other events you may think of:

Do something for someone else.

Call your friends to ask if they need help doing laundry, grocery shopping, or cleaning up homes. When you can support them with something, ask your parents, grandparents, or siblings. Tell them that you feel bored, and look for something to do. Contact somebody that you know and offer to take them out for lunch. Go outside, and give the first person you see in need money. If you are overcome by suffering, plan ahead for times like this, contact your nearest soup kitchen, homeless shelter, or volunteer group. Planning to take part in events that benefit others. Join a coalition with neighborhood civic activities, the conservation community, or other organizations to support others.

Take your attention off yourself.

Go to a local store, shopping mall, bookshop, or park. Only sit down and watch people or walk between them. Look at what they do. Observe what they wear. Hear their conversations. Count the number of buttons on their shirts. Observe as much information as you can about these other people. Count the number of blue-eyed people versus the number of brown-eyed people. Refocus on the specifics of the people you see as your mind returns to your own suffering.

Think of someone you care about.

Keep the person's photo in your pocket or in your bag. This could be your husband, father, dad, partner, girlfriend, kids or relative, or somebody else you respect, like Mother Teresa, Gandhi, Jesus, the Dalai Lama, etc. It might even be a movie star, an athlete, or someone that you never knew. Instead, when you're feeling sad, take the picture out and envision a soothing, happy chat you'd have with that person if you could speak to them when you felt upset at that moment. What will they tell you that will really make you feel better? Just imagine them saying these words.

Distract your thoughts

The human brain is a marvelous resource for thought generation. It turns up to millions of views every day. Most of the time that makes our lives much simpler. And we are unfortunately unable to completely control what our brain feels. Here's one such example. Imagine a picture in the movie of your favorite character, like Bugs Bunny, Snoopy, Superman, or anyone else. Close your eyes, and see in vivid detail the character in your frame of mind. Remember exactly what that feels like. Think 15 seconds on the character. Got it? Now for the next thirty seconds, do your best not to worry about that character. Try to block your feelings about this matter. But be frank with yourself, and remember how much the character comes up up your minds. The story is tough not to contemplate. Indeed, the more you try not to talk about it, the more control you lend the picture and the more your brain keeps taking it into your thinking. It's almost as if the hardest you try to forget it, the harder the brain tries to recall it. It's difficult for that reason to push yourself to forgive anything that happened to you. It's also why you can't just push yourself off those feelings you don't want to get rid of.

And try with other memories or imaginative images to distract your mind instead of trying to force yourself to miss a memory or a thought. Here are only a few instances.

Find out the stuff you should do, and add other activities that you should care about:

115

• List things from your life that have been friendly, interesting, or thrilling. Try to remember as many details about those happy memories as possible.

• Look at the natural world around you from outside. Aim as near as you can at the grass, leaves, sky, and scenery. Look out for any animals around. Pay attention to the sounds they make. Or if you live in a city that doesn't have a lot of nature around you, either do your best to observe what you can or close your eyes and imagine a scene you've seen before.

• Imagine yourself as a hero or heroine correcting some past or future event in your life. How would you do it? What would people say to you?

• Imagine having someone whose opinion matters to you earn praise.

• Imagine realizing your wildest dream. What would it be? Who else would take part? Afterward, what would you do?

• Bring with you a copy of your first or alternative offering. Then pull it out when you feel distressed, and read it to yourself. Picture the words that calm you down and soothe you. Use imagery (such as a white light coming down from heaven or the universe) to comfort you while reading the words.

Distract yourself by leaving

The only thing, sometimes, you can do is stop.

Know, if you're already feeling tired, you'll find it difficult to think of a constructive solution to your problem. Maybe putting a distance between you and the situation is safest, so you'll have time to calm your nerves, so think about what to do next. If the best thing you can do is just walk away. Best to add fuel to the emotional flames.

Distract yourself with tasks and chores

Oddly enough, people still don't schedule enough time to take care of themselves and their living conditions. Tasks and duties go unfinished, too. So here is the right chance to do it to look after the world and yourself. The

116

next time you're in a situation where your emotions get too serious, you're getting briefly diverted by engaging in one of the following stuff.

Distract yourself by counting

Counting is a basic ability that can also keep your mind occupied and help you concentrate on something other than pain. Here are only a few instances. Imprint the things you can do and add other tasks you might be concerned with:

•   Count your breaths. Sit in a comfortable position, place one hand on your stomach and take a long, steady breath. Consider eating into your mouth instead of into your stomach. Feel each inhalation expand your belly like a balloon. Count your breath. When you eventually start to worry about something that causes you pain, return your attention to counting.

•   Count anything else. If your thoughts bother you too much, just count the sounds you hear. That is going to take your attention outside of you. Or try to count the number of cars driving past the number of feelings you're talking for, or anything else you can place on a list, like the branches of a tree you're looking at.

•   Count or subtract by increments of seven. Start with a hundred, for example, and deduct seven. Now take the comment and deduct an additional seven. Keep on. This exercise will really separate you from your emotions, so extra attention and concentration are needed.

Relax and soothe yourself

Now that you've learned some healthy and efficient ways to relax while you're overwhelmed with intense feelings, you'll continue to find new ways to help soothe yourself. The exercises in this segment will help you calm and are the first step in the REST plan — calming, analyzing, setting a goal, and taking action. This would provide experience in managing urges, conscientiousness skills, and behavioral success abilities.

117

Learning to relax and soothe yourself is really necessary for several reasons. Once you're relaxed, the body feels amazing. It operates more safely too. In a calm state, the heart beats more slowly, and the blood pressure reduces. The body is no longer in a state of constant panic, poised to fight or sprint away from a difficult situation. It should make it possible for the brain to think about new ways to deal with the issues.

Included here are several simple, soothing, and relaxing exercises that use the five senses: scent, sight, hearing, taste, and touch. Those things are supposed to get you a touch of happiness in general. Don't do it if it doesn't help you feel better or make you feel worse. Look for one more thing. And remember, we're different from any single one. For example, some people will feel more relaxed listening to music, and some will think taking a hot bubble bath works for them. Remember what fits well for you when you approach this topic, and if it sounds intriguing, be willing to try something new.

Self-soothing using your sense of smell

The smell is a really powerful sensation that can trigger feelings and also make you feel something. So, the detection of odors that make you feel good, not evil, is really necessary. Below are a few remarks.

Figure out what you should do, and add any things that you may think about:

• Burn incense or scented candles in your bed or in your kitchen. Choose a perfume that will attract you.

• Wear perfumed oils or cologne that make you feel good, relaxed, or sexy.

• Take perfumed magazine cards out and take them in your handbag or wallet with you.

• Go somewhere, like a bakery or restaurant, where the smell pleases you.

• Bake your own scented food, including chocolate chip cookies.

• Lie down in your local park, enjoying the grass and the scent of the outside.

- Buy freshly cut flowers or look for flowers near you.

- Embrace somebody whose scent makes you feel happy.

Self-soothing using your sense of vision

Vision is highly essential to humans. A substantial portion of our brain is dedicated mainly exclusively to our sense of hearing. The stuff you see will also have very strong effects on you, for better or worse. That is why it is important to find images that have a very calming impact on you. And again, it's down to each user's particular taste and preference. Below are a few remarks.

Find out what you should do, and then add other things you might conceive of:

•   Look through newspapers and books and take images you'd like. Make them a collage to put on your fridge, or keep some of them in your handbag or wallet with you to look at when you're away from home.

•   Find a place to look at, like a park or museum that is relaxing for you. Or find a picture of a spot, like the ocean, that's calming to look at.

•   Go to the shop to select soothing images or drawings, such as the Ansel Adams nature photos.

•   Sketch or paint an image of your own that pleases you.

•   Hold a snapshot of someone you love, someone you find attractive, or someone you respect.

Self-soothing using your sense of hearing

Any sound will soothe us. Listening to soft music, for example, can be soothing. About the same, every one of us has his own preferences. You need to figure out what suits you best. Using these explications to find the sounds that help calm. Check all the stuff you should do, and add some activities you might be dreaming about: listen to soothing music. This could be anything that fits you. It may be music, whether with or without singing. Go online to download some soothing music before you buy it, then listen to a wide range of genres to determine which ones will help you relax.

Then add the song to your cell phone so that you can listen to it anyway.

Listen to audiobooks. Most public libraries will encourage you to borrow books on Dvds, or temporarily borrow audiobooks. Borrow some to see how they're going to make you sleep. You don't need to understand the storyline. It can also be profoundly calming to simply listen to another talking softly. Keep some of those videos with you in your car, or add them to your smartphone.

Turn on the television, and just listen. Find a bland or sedating broadcast, not something agitating like the press. Sit in a cozy chair or lay down, then close your eyes and just listen. Be sure to turn the sound down to the point that it isn't too loud. Many years back, there was a national television series starring a painter called Bob Ross. His voice was so soothing and consoling that as they listened, several people started falling asleep. Choose a show that will make you happy.

Hear a relaxing podcast or video sharing, or listen to a fun chat show on the radio. Remember — a relaxing podcast or chat show, not one that leaves you irritated/frustrated. So keep away from the news shows and the political talk shows. Finding something that's fair in speech, like the online TED Talks series on public radio or This American Experience. Often, just hearing someone else talking can be calming. Bookmark the smartphone links or download your favorite podcasts so you can listen to them when you're irritated or annoyed at them.

Open the doors, and listen to the sounds of quiet outside. Or, if you live in a city without calming sounds, go to a spot with relaxing sounds, like a park.

Listen to a compilation of nature-based sounds like birds and other species. It will also be downloaded digitally and then taken to your cell phone to listen.

Listening to a white-noise screen. White sound is a tone that hides certain irritating sonorities. You can purchase a rotating air machine that produces white noise, turn a fan on to stop the noise or add a no-noise feature to your smartphone. Some white-noise machines and applications even capture other sounds, such as bird sounds, waterfalls, and rainforests. Many people find the sounds incredibly calming.

Listen to the sound of a single water fountain. These tiny electronic fountains can be purchased online. Many people in their homes find the trickling water sound very soothing.

Hear a sound of sleep or calming practice. Exercises like this will encourage you to consider different forms of soothing yourself. Some recorded exercises could also show you the self-hypnosis techniques to help you relax. Look at the sound of water flowing or pumping! Maybe your local park has a waterfall, or the nearby mall has a swimming pool. Or maybe just chill in your shower with the tub running for a few minutes.

Self-soothing using your sense of touch

We sometimes forget about our sense of touch, and yet we always touch something, like the clothes we wear or the chair in which we sit. Our skin is our largest organ and is completely covered by the nerves that bring thoughts to our brain. Many physical stimuli, such as petting a fuzzy puppy, can be pleasant. In contrast, other sensations, such as feeling a hot stove, are disturbing or unpleasant for contact danger. Each one of us experiences various sensations once again. You've got to select the ones that better suit you. Below are a few ideas. Find out the stuff you can do, and then add other items you can dream of: Have something cozy or velvety in your pocket or a piece of fabric to carry when you need it.

Take a hot or cold shower, and enjoy the sound of water falling on your skin.

Take a warm bubble bath or drink up a fragrant wax, and enjoy the soothing skin sensations.

Put a message on. Many people who have suffered physical and sexual violence do not want to see someone near them. To grasp this is very clear. But not every form of massage lets you get off your clothes. Most treatments, like conventional Japanese shiatsu therapy, simply allow you to wear loose-fitting clothing. A shoulder and neck massage, given when sitting in a massage chair, can also be done without removing any clothes. If this is your problem, just ask the massage therapist what kind of massage to wear. Your clothes are perfect for you.

Give one massage to yourself. Often, it's very good trying to rub your own sore muscles.

122

Play with a cat. Many will get health benefits from owning a pet. Sometimes pet owners have lower blood pressure, lower cholesterol levels, and lower risk of heart disease, as well as other health benefits. On top of that, you will have a soothing sensory time playing with your pet and stroking the animal's hair or skin. If you don't have a cat, then you should think about getting one. If you can't have one, visit a friend who has a pet or volunteer in your local animal shelter where you can play with the rescued animals. Wear your clothes as comfortable as a T-shirt, a baggy sweatsuit, or faded jeans were worn in your youth.

CHAPTER 5: Mindfulness

You might be having a snack while watching a show on TV or reading through a rather uninspiring article when your mind just wanders off. Perhaps you are thinking of the day's event or tomorrow's hectic schedule. Still, you most certainly are not giving attention to anything you're doing presently.

How often does that happen to you? Probably, more often than you can count. The greatest portions of our lives are spent in our absence. We do one thing while thinking of something else—we never are wholly in the moment.

Now, why does that happen? Well, to phrase it nicely, we are automatons of our emotions and thoughts. They dictate how we think, react, and, unfortunately, how we live. We're automated to react in a certain pattern that has already been inscribed on our brain.

Mindfulness is about tipping the balance; it allows you not only to dethrone but to regulate your emotions and thoughts. You start scraping off those inscriptions and creating your own patterns of reaction to situations and patterns of thinking. Mindfulness bestows you the chance to become present in the world you live in, to pay attention to the details that matter.

Mindfulness is the epicenter of DBT. It is indeed an ancient concept that has existed in religious and spiritual traditions like Buddhism, martial arts, yoga, tai chi, and Taoism. Over the last three decades, Western psychology has adapted to treat psychological and mental health disorders.

This module aims to have the individual control their attention and focus it on the present without dwelling on the past or fretting about the future. Often, people are ensnarled in the anguishing experiences of their past or harrowing prophecies of the future. Mindfulness amplifies one's awareness, which in turn helps him/her exist in the here and now. Eventually, one learns to prohibit the past or future from coloring any experience.

After developing the skills to have the unclouded perspective of the present, the individual can begin to understand his/her emotions and thoughts better and learn how to control them instead of being dictated by them.

The practice of mindfulness has been proven to reduce depression, irritability, and anxiety, enhance mental stamina and memory, decrease chronic stress and hypertension, and mitigate cancer's impact. It helps reduce chronic pain, relieve the dependency on substance abuse and reinforce the immune system to ward off diseases such as flu, colds, and so forth.

Mindfulness allows for a healthier and happier life. It bestows you binoculars to look within and understand yourself profoundly.

Three States of Mind

Mindfulness tackles three primary states of mind.

Reasonable Mind:

This is where the individual takes a reasonable approach to address issues and engages with focused attention and planning behavior.

Examples of the reasonable mind are: preparing for an event, measuring the ingredients before cooking a meal, studying for a test, scouring the net for information.

Emotion Mind:

This is a state of mind when the person is so overwhelmed and highly influenced by emotions that they control his/her thoughts and behavior. His/her thoughts are completely controlled by emotions. For instance, if a person feels anger or fear, it keeps his/her thoughts so volatile that thinking reasonably becomes nearly impossible. It makes the application of planning or logic hard as gathering the individual's attention is quite difficult at this state.

This mind state is disproportionately present in people who find controlling emotions challenging, as those with a borderline personality disorder.

Examples of the emotional mind are: going on an unplanned excursion on an impulse, paying an exorbitant price for an item just because you like it, cuddling a puppy, having a fight with somebody you don't agree with, going out for a ride for the fun of it.

Wise mind:

At this stage, the individual acquires intuition and the sense of what is wrong or right.

It is more like the "aha" moment. A wise mind is the coming together of the reasonable mind and the emotional mind. They are bound together by intuition.

Intuition is a feeling of knowing what is right or wrong. You can experience intuition without an intellectual approach.

Examples of the wise mind are: following your intuition; going for what you sense is the right choice in a dilemma.

Core Mindfulness Skills

Core mindfulness skills could be categorized into two.

I. The "what" skills comprise: observe, describe and participate. They give answers to the question: What do I do to practice core mindfulness skills?

II. The "How" skills. They include non-judgmentally, one mindfully, and effectively. They answer the questions: What do I do to practice core mindfulness skills?

Observe

This is the first "what" skill. Generally, it's about addressing emotions and other behavioral responses—induced by certain events—without trying to eliminate them. In other words, an individual allows him/herself to experience a moment with awareness rather than leaving a situation or trying to stop an emotion.

In mindfulness exercises, the individual is encouraged to observe the emotions, sensations in the body, and thoughts that manifest in situations. Without reacting or being devoured by these feelings, the person is taught to study them. Preserving from all forms of judgment, he/she studies the emotions, thoughts, and sensations and notices them disappear. The technique is purposed to have the individual control his/her attention but not the experience.

To carry out this practice, one needs to develop the Teflon mind— this is a mental state in which one can allow feelings to pass by like clouds in the sky without clinging on to them.

Observe is a significant practice for those with a borderline personality disorder or traumatic history. It lets them discern sensations that occur in the mind and body and teaches them how to control them. It helps mitigate situations where emotions become too domineering.

Describe

Proceeding to the second part of learning mindfulness, one is encouraged to describe the thoughts and emotions that have come into his/her awareness. The individual could depict them as such:" I am feeling hurt," or "A thought of ___ came into mind."

When the person depicts them in words and expresses internal emotions, a feeling becomes a feeling, and thought becomes just a thought. The possibility of becoming engrossed in the emotions or thoughts that arise is reduced. If the situation is an infuriating matter, the individual acknowledges it as one and simply moves on instead of obsessing over it.

The first step to adopting coping strategies is to identify feelings that arise; once you know what they are, you can learn to deal with them.

Participation

Participation is about being fully present in an activity. A person fully immerses him/herself in what he/she is doing, whether it be eating, washing dishes, or mowing the lawn. The individual is encouraged to apply the mindfulness skills to everyday life and focus on the present. The skills would allow one to exist in life with awareness and thus live in the present with more control over his/her life.

This is an essential tool to guard against distress. A person who is devoid of mindful awareness in life is more susceptible to mood disorders and various mental ailments.

Non-judgmental Stance

This is the part of the practice that aims to have the person disassociate his/herself from the judgment of their feeling; in other words, the focus is on the "what," not the perceptive of the condition.

For instance, say a person feels angry. He or she simply defines it as "I feel angry." A judgmental interpretation of this feeling would be "I should not feel angry" or "Do I have any right to feel angry?" Such an evaluation of our emotions and thoughts impedes learning mindful awareness. This is why the individual is taught to view and study thoughts and emotions from a neutral perspective—from a non-judgmental stance.

This could be a challenging skill to acquire for the highly self-critical ones or those with rather low self-esteem.

Mindfulness Exercises and Worksheets

Various forms of exercise are applied in DBT. From meditative mindfulness to everyday mindfulness—there are quite a lot used in individual and group therapies.

Here is a simple technique for a short meditative practice:

- *Sit down comfortably and shut your eyes.*

- *Concentrate on your breathing; you're exhaling and inhaling.*

- *An abrupt thought or emotion may corrupt your focus. That's okay. Acknowledge its presence and simply return to your focus on breathing.*

- *Don't forget that this is not an exercise to relax you but to allow you to observe your state.*

- *Do not stop to judge or digest these fleeting thoughts and emotions. Just carry on.*

Conscious breathing is an essential component of mindfulness. It is the launching pad for the focus of sensations in the body. After acquiring this skill, the individual can use discerning other elements like anxiety, stress, sorrow, etc.

Through mindful meditation, one is taught to abandon all entanglements with the past or qualms of the future and concentrate on the here and now. Mindful meditation teaches the focus of one thing and allows a person to study, discern and control thoughts and emotions.

Observation Exercise

•   Observe your surroundings.

•   Notice what is taking place around you without instantly or reflexively reacting. Awaken your senses. Take heed of the scent of the environment. Listen to the sounds.

•   Allow thoughts and sensations to liberally pass you by.

•   Do not let past experiences or worries of the future interrupt your focus. Concentrate on the present.

•   Address your inner thoughts and feelings as they come. Do not allow them to consume you or lure you into pondering over them; simply observe and let them fade away.

Description Exercise

Say you have an important interview for a job you have been pinning for. You're nervous, and you don't want to ruin your chance; you might even think, "I am going to fail this interview." Describe everything you are feeling.

•   What are your bodily reactions? Are you perspiring? Do you feel Nauseated? Are your jaw muscles tense?

•   What are the thoughts going through your mind? What are your thoughts about the interview?

•   Ask yourself if these thoughts are really connected to the matter at hand.

Learning to describe the situation helps you understand that thoughts and feelings are different from the actual matter.

"Thoughts are just thoughts, feelings are just feelings," Marsha Linehan says. This is not to say that thoughts and feelings are not real; they are. But they are not the situation; they don't explain or prophecy events.

Apply this practice to any activity: walking, cooking, and watching TV, etc. Try writing down descriptions of your thoughts and feelings.

Mindful Eating

Examine the food you are eating (let's say it's a hamburger). Observe your hand, bringing the food towards your mouth. Take a moment to smell the food. Notice the emotions, sensations, and thoughts that are induced by the smell. Feel the texture of the bread. Now take a bite. How is the food positioned in your mouth? Start chewing and observe the experiences the taste is giving you. Swallow it. Notice the muscles that contract as you push the food down your stomach.

Try eating with your non-dominant hand, which would maximize your attention. It will make the experience new and awkward.

Walking Mindfully

Walking is a great opportunity to cultivate mindfulness. Movement can empower and sharpen awareness.

Choose the place for conducting the exercise. Don't obsess over your selection; just pick a spot about 20-30 feet apart and just walk back and forth. (You don't walk towards a certain destination; this will eliminate the distraction of "getting somewhere.")

Stick to the following steps as you walk:

•   Begin by focusing on the sensation of walking on the ground. Feel what your heels sense as they are touching the floor. Observe the stepping motion on the floor. Try taking shorter strides and lifting your knees slightly higher for each step—stepping, stepping, stepping.

•   Now reduce your stepping pace to see the lifting of your feet and its landing on the ground. Feel your toes propel you forward as your feet lift. Lifting, stepping—lifting, stepping.

•   Slow down further— enough to observe the shift of pressure and the shift of weight from one foot to the next. Take stock of muscular movement when the foot rises; notice how it just hangs and how it steps on the ground. Watch the shift go from one foot to the next. Stay focused on the process of lifting, stepping, shifting—lifting, stepping, shifting.

Once mastered, this can be applied on even your busiest days. You can practice it on your way to work, supermarket—anywhere. It anchors you to the moment, making you fully present.

Exercise for One Mindfully

In no way is learning to be fully present, fully aware of your daily tasks, interactions with others, and every moment easy. And with worries about work, family, friends, and money hovering over us, the endeavor becomes all the more challenging.

Here is the DBT skill: One Mindfully, that will help you focus on one task at a time.

•   Relinquish all worries and disturbances.

•   Concentrate on the here and now.

•   Let the stream of distracting and disturbing thoughts and emotions enter and exit your mind. Just breathe.

•   Gather your thoughts on what you're doing now. Say you're washing tableware; direct your attention to the senses. Listen to the sound of water streaming down the sink. Feel the warm sensation of the water.

•   Should any thoughts emerge to corrupt your focus, acknowledge them, and then return to your attentive state.

•   If judgmental thoughts enter, notice yourself judging yourself and block them.

•   Return to focus on your present task. Put aside other worries and thoughts for another time.

CHAPTER 6: Master your Emotions

Emotions are the most outstanding nature of our being. They traverse all aspects of our lives in social and professional terms. Emotions also have a way of uniquely influencing how we think and behave, thus, ultimately shaping how we \relate and socialize with others. Fundamentally, our feelings have crucially been embodied and, at the same time, been subjected to various studies as single concerns. While in this regard, research has mainly been focused on the aspect do with the cognitive and expressive attributes regarding the physiological and neurological tendencies, which form the basis of emotional reactions. However, in the last decade or so, scholars have been able to create a full awareness explaining further that our feelings result from the influence of nature. They are also a result of interactions with other people. The main reason is that these emotions are usually exhibited by individuals and aimed at others. Hence, they have also been regulated to either influence other parties or to comply with social norms. However, despite an increase in awareness, studies are yet to make a concrete conclusion about the effects of socializing and dimension as a critical factor in research on how our emotions affect our lives.

Furthermore, there has been evidence fronted by scholars suggesting that emotions have been tightly intertwined with the fabric of our social lives. To further support this phenomenon, research has clearly shown that how we interact socially profoundly affects our practices and values. It systematically shapes our experiences, regulates, and expresses what we feel in more ways than one.

Several studies have also unearthed how the attributes of our interactions socially, like the trappings of power and other cultural practices, have a significant effect on how we eventually come to recognize and interpret how we feel.

It is only natural that our feelings are significantly viewed in four different groups. They include the individual level, dyadic level, and cultural level of analyses. Even though most of the time, they are not separate from one another, some studies can be done in more ways. This phenomenon helps form the basis of the organization of the principles used for discussing the importance of each level towards our contemporary emotional levels.

The Individualistic Level

During this analysis phase, crucial evidence and queries abound on how the social context can influence our experiences and regulate and express our feelings. Even though it is viewed in contextual levels of individual interpretations, we can see the deep connection and nature exhibited by social emotions. One such excitement at the personal level is gratitude, as it manifests itself during social interactions. Thus, it has been discovered to be beneficial to our mental health, also improving the quality of interpersonal interactions.

The feelings that come with gratitude mean that an individual relates in a positive way to another person. However, the flow of negative emotions such as sadness manifests itself when we experience first-hand other people's misfortunes (schadenfreude), or the root cause of other people's paint actions such as gloating might translate into a negative relationship.

Nostalgia is also another inherent social emotion, involving fond memories of people and past events. This emotion has been found to increase the positive outcomes while, at the same time, decreasing the adverse effects. However, alleviating any significance brought about by nostalgia based on negative emotions of being sad is hinged upon an individual's interactive abilities and connectivity socially. Compared to ordinary occurrences, they both can influence an individual to recover from a negative situation, much depending on their emotional attachment and insecurity. Those with low levels of uncertainty benefit more from nostalgia. On the other hand, those with high levels of danger were not so lucky. Therefore, the benefits of nostalgic events dramatically depend on the confidence levels and the quality of an individual's social relationships.

Aspects of our sexual orientation very much control emotions related to responses about social abilities and cohesiveness brought about by other people. Positive feelings, which were exhibited by males, showing powerful facial expressions. In the two genders. In contrast, it was also discovered that there were high levels of arousal. This was mostly seen in situations where the opposite sex positively and freely expressed emotions. This then indicates that the processes, which exhibit emotive processes, usually unfold in different manners depending on the gender of the interactive partners.

Dyadic Level

In this analysis phase, parameters of dominant research themes usually are about how we typically view, translate, including how we also respond to different emotional stimuli exhibited when we interact with others. This is inclusive of the levels of the effects and how our social settings can also influence it. Another method of determining if the way we express ourselves emotionally has an overall influence is providing information on the other party's outlook of that particular situation. In such circumstances, expressions of regret can be influenced by inferences. The other party was the one responsible for a very tragic occurrence. Where expressions of feelings such as anger show that another party was the one involved in the act. Thus, such results indicate that emotional expressions have a way of helping individuals interpret those ambiguous social situations.

Therefore, the ultimate decisions we make in the social context will be significantly influenced in the most reliable possible manner by our feelings in the method by which we interact with other people.

Apologies can, in more ways than one, dampen any reactive aggression that might arise after wrongdoing.

When it comes to building new relationships, can the concept of improving other people's feelings help them to connect in social networks? Strategies used to regulate interpersonal emotions went ahead to predict growth, which is popular in our work environment, including our non-work issues. Even though different planning, in terms of regulations regarding interpersonal emotional reactions, usually have different results. Those plans involving behavioral patterns like provisions to do with comfort or reassurance have been identified positively and popular, while cognitive strategies, including changing someone's appraisals about a situation, negatively impacted popularity.

Group Level

In this segment, researchers conduct studies on how emotional tendencies in group dynamics often play out on the formation of these groups, their primary practices and objectives, interaction, and how different or similar they are to other groups about individual characters by their members, among other traits. That is why group identification leans more towards development and is more exhibited in groups, which have physically displayed individuals rather than groups with clusters whose individuals have been positioned within various levels. On the one hand, the reality is that text messages can physically, in a way, end up increasing someone's heart rate in a synchronized way. While on the other, heart rate visualization can only end up expanding this synchronization in non-co-located dyads.

What is the Ego?

This is our conscious mind, which is innate; therefore, part of our identity, which is generally considered the "self." Have you ever heard of someone being referred to as having a big 'ego?' It merely means that the individual, in particular, is too full of himself to care about anything. The Id, Ego, and superego are all parts, which combine to make a human personality. The three are all parts involving the psychoanalytic personality theory, put forward by Sigmund Freud. These, according to him, combine to create some of the complex behavior we see in humans. What are some of the examples of the three?

Meeting Basic Needs

This is the most fundamental bit of the personality, representing our innermost animalistic urges more often than not. It could be any urge like the desire for food. In most cases, the id looks for instant gratification concerning our wants and needs. However, they are not met, then the individual, in particular, may end up being angry, tense, or anxious.

How we Use Our Ego to Deal with the Realities of Life?

Our self-centered nature handles reality when it tries to address our various desires presented by our identity in a more socially acceptable way in the eyes of society. It then means that there will be delayed satisfaction, which might assist in doing away with the tension brought about by the id, in case a desire is unmet in an instant. Therefore, this Ego recognizes that others, too, have various needs and wants as well. Being selfish will not be a good idea in the end.

135

Superego: Adding Morals

This is the last bit of our human nature that comes out in the end.

Although both inflated Ego and vulnerable Ego could end up having similar conclusions on a matter, this cannot be said for the superego, as its reasons for that particular conclusion is customarily hinged on moral values, as opposed to Ego's, which is leaning more towards what others think or the effects that come about as a result of other people's actions on a person.

Our Identity, Ego, and Super/inflated Ego

Therefore, it matters to do with our identity in the real sense, being either selfish or having a superego combine to create human characteristics. Whereas our character can have its own wants, it is our egoistic nature, while our inflated Ego is solely responsible for adding bits of morality to the decision, which an individual makes in the end. While on the one hand, each of these elements constitutes human behavior; on the other, they also comprise some of our favorite characters in those books we usually immerse ourselves in.

How the Ego affects your emotions

Understanding the stages of our emotions and how we respond to them can enable us to develop high levels of emotional intelligence. This is because we shall easily relate to and control our reactions to daily occurrences and thoughts.

Moreover, it is a good thing at all times to be aware of your emotions. You can also try breaking them down bit by bit to ascertain exactly what you are feeling. This will greatly help you find ways on how we process these emotions.

Below are some of the general emotional processes that we normally go through:

1.   We normally come into contact with a stimulus. This could be in the form of an event, object, situation, sensation, or thoughts.

2.   How we pay attention to that particular stimulus

136

3.   The third step involves how we interpret the stimulus at hand.

4.   Lastly comes our emotional and psychological reactions to the stimulus.

At times, you can face situations, which can put your emotional intelligence to the test. Such conditions can either force you to react instinctively or deliberately. In normal circumstances, when we encounter situations, which require that we interpret these emotions, one way of going about it is acting naturally. However, if someone steps on your toes, our reaction becomes twofold: intuitively or deliberately. This is because we can choose to get very annoyed by the incident or take a step back and try to understand if the action was deliberated to cause discomfort or just a minor mistake with no malice involved. You should bear in mind that how we respond to situations in our lives tells a lot about our Ego.

Our Ego plays a huge role in how we see things at the interpretation stage. Thus, those with inflated egos tend to view themselves in high regard, who tend to confront anyone in the slightest of provocations. This comes about due to the interpretation that you will be viewed as a weakling if you do not do something drastic about the situation. This kind of reaction is common in almost everyone. Our inflated egos control us making us think that everyone is against us, while in the real sense, it is not valid. We tend to take everything personally, even when the situation does not warrant it that way.

We become the star attraction in our lives; hence, the belief that our values, norms, and expectations are superior to others. That is why, in most cases, we will always try to find ways of forcing our moral code and convictions onto others. The faster we come to terms with our overly inflated Ego, the more control we will have over how we respond to different stimuli in our lives. We will be able to approach any situation in your life with a calm and reasonable mindset, presenting you with the opportunity to make sober decisions in the long run. This can only be a possibility when you go out of your way to give priority to your emotional intelligence while, at the same time, lowering your inflated Ego.

The interpretation stage is the most crucial in this whole process. When making any conscious decision, you do not just wake up one day and decide to do it. It is a gradual step, which requires absolute time for recollection and

CBT + DBT + ACT

gathering of vital information, including factors, which will help you make sober conclusions.

Emotional degradation can become a significant concern in cases where our Ego gets attacked. Such situations thus call on us to erect our defense mechanisms to keep these attacks at bay, keeping us physically safe in the end. That is the main reason it can be interpreted as a life-and-death scenario. The transfer of such defenses is generally hinged on the species' survival, concerning the Ego's protection, which gives emotional rot a stranglehold on our mental being. Besides, psychological decadence brings about feelings of low self-esteem; secondly, be it that you feel let down, shut out, belittled, and diminished, it does not matter whether or not we are consciously aware of such feelings.

Interestingly, some of these defenses that we end up creating to curb our Ego against emotional degradation create more problems for us. Sadly enough, this comes about when we try to block other people from making trampling on our emotions. The temptation here will be finding a way of dismissing the emotional degrader who, in more ways than one, needs to feel more important than you do: "He is just crazy." You might bellow, but without knowing, you might be doing precisely the same thing as that person by making yourself feel more important when you regard him as a nonstarter.

Thus, in one way or the other, such sentiments from you may help erect a defensive wall for your Ego against the barrage of his assault. Nonetheless, when you react to a jerk in the same manner that he is doing to you, the fundamental question that should come to mind is: Where does that leave you? Furthermore, emotional pollution can be described as an ego-defensive mechanism of subtle psychological aggression, which makes other people defend their egos in response; therefore, in a real sense, becoming inexorably self-seeking.

Even though the Ego is mostly the point of attack, the toxic effects of emotional pollution can extend beyond the psychological. This is because the defenses keep us physically safe and are emergency systems powered by corrosive stress chemicals. These can be harmful in the long run in our lives and were never intended to be used daily.

Hence, we can end up paying a very high physiological price, which adds to the excesses for dealing with any nervous infection that might occur daily.

How are emotions formed?

Feelings to do with sadness and anger are usually exhibited by people as they respond to different thoughts and stimuli. At times, we can be overwhelmed by more than one emotion at the same time.

CHAPTER 7: Emotional Regulation

At this point in the game, we reach the second to last major skill you're trying to train through these dialectical behavior therapy techniques. This is emotional regulation.

Note that all of these skills intertwine with one another in a very necessary way. Mindfulness, for example, gives you the ability to treat distress tolerance and emotional regulation with the detachment that they deserve. Distress tolerance gives you an important base for regulating your emotions when times get especially difficult. Emotional regulation builds on mindfulness skills and distress tolerance skills to allow you to regulate your emotions to the greatest extent possible. Interpersonal effectiveness is about working on your ability to make your conversations with others more effective about the things we've already discussed.

So, what is emotional regulation, and what is the reason behind it? Well, to answer the first question, emotional regulation is relatively self-explanatory. It's a set of different procedures and systems that have been developed to help people who have difficulties controlling their emotions in a more consistent, regular, and healthy way.

Ultimately, it's just the idea of metering your negative and harmful emotions so that you can become a better person and deal with various different problems in a more conducive way. It also allows you to build a better sense of detachment and acceptance from your problems so that you can better isolate their root causes and figure out what you could be doing to better help yourself.

This is important to people suffering from a borderline personality disorder, suicidal thoughts, or are emotionally unstable because they tend to have unpredictable and intense emotions. For example, you might feel angry, depressed, anxious, or inexplicably annoyed. While these things are appropriate and understandable emotions in various cases - completely blocking out your emotions is just as unhealthy as having too intense of emotions - you need to learn to feel them at an emotionally healthy level and not allow them to become irregular or irrational.

The first skill you need to learn to regulate your emotions is understand your feelings and why you're feeling them. You can do this by breaking them down with what's called the story of emotion.

The story of emotion is a crucial skill in breaking down your emotions and knowing what exactly it is that you're feeling. Some emotions are particularly difficult to process. You don't always feel just one emotion; often, you'll feel multiple at once in a very disconnected sort of way. What do you do in this kind of situation? Well, you break down multiple signals and think about what they might indicate that you're feeling.

The first thing you need to analyze is what exactly prompted what you're feeling. This can be a massive tell in whatever emotion you're experiencing. If somebody cuts in front of you in traffic, you might have cause to feel angry, for example.

The second thing you need to analyze is how you interpreted the event. What happened in your eyes, how did you take it in? What can you do to distance yourself from the event a little bit and analyze it with somewhat clearer eyes? All of this can have a massive effect on your reaction.

The third thing you need to analyze is what you're feeling in terms of your body. Do you have a pit of fire in your stomach? Does it feel like your stomach is churning? Our brain has all kinds of interesting ways of indicating that we're feeling a certain way about something. It's a very interesting sort of intertwining phenomenon between our brain and our body.

The fourth thing you have to analyze is how you're subconsciously reacting to the event. Are your arms crossed? Do you feel more emotionally closed off than you did before the event? Is your jaw or face tense, or are your eyes wider than usual? All of these sorts of things indicate different emotions.

The fifth thing that you have to analyze is what you feel the urge to do. If you feel the urge to ram into the back of somebody's car when they cut you off, the chance is good that you're feeling anger, for example. You can understand your emotions based on the thing that they make you want to do.

The sixth thing that you have to understand is the action that you took. Did you curse when they cut you off or flip them off?

141

This is yet another indicator that you are angry. These sorts of things tell you what you're feeling.

The last thing you need to analyze is the name of the emotion, taking into account all of the other things on the list. If you're feeling angry, recognize that you're feeling angry based on the fact that you did angry things and had what you perceived as a reason to be angry.

There's a great amount of importance in all of this;. At the same time, it may seem silly to tell yourself what you're feeling. It can be a fantastic tool for putting things into perspective and analyzing what you're feeling under the hood. It can also make you realize that you're feeling irrational about something and that you need to take a step back if at all possible. Recognizing what you're feeling can do a lot in terms of metering what you're feeling.

The ultimate goal is to distance yourself from what is called the "emotion mind." In doing this, you build your ability to recognize and adapt to things with your conscious and mindful thoughts rather than reacting viscerally based on whatever your wit and whimsy may be.

You can do several things in terms of your physical health that will allow you to better regulate your emotions. You can remember these through the acronym PLEASE.

The first thing in the PLEASE set is Physical health. Pay close attention to your physical health; if you are sick or hurt in some sort of way, you need to do what you can to get to a doctor and get it taken care of. When you're sick, you don't have as much energy as you normally would maintain control of your mind.

The second thing in the set is proper Eating habits. Don't eat too much or too little and eat proper food if possible, instead of junk food. Sometimes, finances get in the way of this; don't make the mistake of thinking that cheap food can't be healthy food, though. Things such as canned carrots and spinach, beans, rice, and so forth are all healthy staple foods that can be prepared in numerous ways and pack a ton of nutrients.

The third thing is the avoidance of drugs. Essentially, drop all things that you can which alter your mood. This is often a big deal for people who suffer from a borderline personality disorder because they tend to have high rates of substance abuse. This isn't me trying to be D.A.R.E.; this is a genuine suggestion; drugs may make you feel better in a short time, but they have an overall unpredictable impact on your long-term mood. Some people find therapy in certain things that can be prescribed, and that's alright. The concern is more with things like alcohol, opiates, and stimulants. Things of this nature can cause your moods to be unpredictable and more volatile than usual, especially their addictive potential.

The fourth thing is sleeping habits. Be sure that you're getting the proper amount of sleep. Try to get between seven and nine hours per night. Can throw your body's chemistry out of whack in major ways, which will ruin your mood generally.

The final thing is exercise. Exercise is a cornerstone of both mental and physical health. You'll feel like you look better in terms of physical health if you do a proper amount of exercise. In terms of mental health, exercise causes the release of endorphins and various chemicals in your brain, which causes you to feel better and happier in general.

That brings an end to the PLEASE set. In addition to the PLEASE set, you need to build self-discipline by working on at least one thing every day. Try to end up mastering something. This will make you feel better about yourself and teach you a lot about self-discipline and self-control, in addition to making you generally feel more competent.

A big cornerstone of this block of dialectical behavior therapy is that you can effectively use the concept of opposite action. Opposite action is used to curb your urges and do and feel the "right" thing when you have an emotion that is difficult to justify. Through emotional reflection and detachment, you should realize when it's right or wrong to feel an emotion. If you feel something that you ideally shouldn't be feeling, use the opposite action. Opposite action is the idea that you do whatever is the exact opposite of the urges that you're having in that given moment.

This is used for unhealthy and self-destructive emotions like unjustified anger or annoyance.

143

Instead of doing whatever the emotion makes you feel specifically compelled to do at that moment, do whatever is the polar opposite of that.

This, in effect, causes you to leave the emotion you don't want behind by instead feeling the emotion which is the exact opposite. While this does come across as a bit reductionist, its use is actually rather intuitive, and you'll likely find that it can help you feel a lot better in emotionally volatile situations.

So, what if your emotion is justified? What can you do? This is the skill of problem-solving. Detach yourself from the situation and see what you really can do to solve it. If you can't do anything, then accept the situation at hand and allow yourself to feel the emotion. If you can do something, then take reasonable, actionable, and effective steps forward to ameliorate the situation that is troubling you.

The last key concept of emotional regulation goes hand in hand with the acceptance and mindfulness topics. This is letting go of your emotions. As said earlier, the idea isn't to block out your emotions entirely but rather to feel them in a rational and relatively healthy way.

Think about the emotion that you're feeling; give it genuine thought and accept that whatever it is, it's happening. Acceptance of an emotion does not necessarily mean a reaction to it; it simply means that you acknowledge that the sentiment is occurring. Once you've done so, you can simply let the feeling pass over you.

CHAPTER 8: DBT & Stress

Stress is often accompanied by anxiety and fear. These feelings simply go together so often that often people interchangeably use the words "pain" and "anxiety." However, what you may not know is that although stress and anxiety are closely related, they are not the same thing. There are some important differences that you should be mindful of between both situations.

What Is Stress?

We all experience stress just as we all experience fear. That is inescapable. How exactly is pain, though, and how does it vary from anxiety? A much wider term than "anxiety," stress refers to your body's response when faced with situations that require you to behave, alter or react to your situation. Stress also plays a highly significant role. Essentially, the stress feeling is an indicator that somehow the body's resources are being drained or used up.

This way, you might think about it: Consider your body as a giant machine. Today computers are getting faster and faster every day. Still, in the end, there is only a limited amount of processing power on even the biggest and most sophisticated computer. So, if you run a small program on your computer, it will use up a bit of your computer's processing capacity.

It means that the machine will have far less processing power for other programs, but, with only one specific program operating, the computer's output will possibly not be affected so much. Now, let's say that, on your computer, you start running program after program. At some point, you'll note a drop in the output of your computer. Basically, the more programs you run on your machine, the harder it will be for each program to handle. However, in extreme cases, if many programs are running all at once for a long time, the machine could be drained so much that it would fail.

The organs do the same. We have few resources at our disposal for coping with the circumstances we face. Essentially, at any given time, we only have so much mental or physical capacity. The more scenarios or events we face that use these tools, the more anxious, nervous, or exhausted we will feel and the less successful we will be in coping with them.

145

Therefore, the more we live in these conditions or participate in those behaviors, the more we will begin to deplete our resources.

Consequently, we can find it harder to regulate our emotions or become more emotional, or our feelings may seem more out of balance. Their focus and attention will fail, too. They may have sleeping problems and may even increase our chances of getting physically sick.

However, people do not always know that tension will come from both friendly circumstances and unpleasant ones. When many people think about stress, they just think about stressful or upsetting circumstances, situations that they don't like and would rather not have to encounter, such as losing a job, having money issues, or coping with an injury are really bad. Even the term "stressful" has literally come to mean unpleasant or disagreeable. Pleasant incidents, however, circumstances that produce positive feelings, can also contribute to tension. For e.g., it can all be difficult to plan a wedding, have a baby, and get a promotion. Such circumstances can have advantages, and you may be grateful that they have arisen. Still, they can also be a source of stress.

It's important to be aware of the types of events that place you under tension. The more informed you are of these conditions, the more comfortable you can be to cope with the stress when it comes up.

Stress in Anxiety Disorders

While stress is generally not thought to be a particular symptom of any anxiety disorder, the only exception may be in the case of a widespread anxiety disorder (GAD). A person may undergo several stress-related physical symptoms more days than during the past six months to be diagnosed with GAD, along with other symptoms such as uncontrollable and overwhelming concern. GAD's stress-related symptoms include muscle tension, exhaustion, sleeping difficulty, and trouble concentrating.

While stress is not listed as a particular symptom of other anxiety disorders, stress definitely goes hand in hand with all disorders of anxiety. A person with panic disorder can feel some stress-related physical symptoms, such as muscle tension, during a panic attack or contribute to one. Someone with PTSD may feel high-stress levels as a result of being constantly on guard.

146

Another individual can find social experiences very upsetting in a social anxiety disorder. In fact, signs of anxiety disorder can be very difficult to cope with and can have a tremendous impact on a person's life. As a consequence, they also cause a tremendous amount of stress. Essentially, the presence of signs of anxiety disorder can be incredibly stressful and exhausting in general, taking away some of the ability to deal with other stressful life experiences.

Managing Stress with DBT Skills

The good news is that various DBT strategies will help you reduce your susceptibility to stress and mitigate some of the stress effects.

Identifying Where You Experience Stress in Your Body

First, it is important to recognize where you feel stress and tension in your body before we go into the basic DBT skills. This is because the first indication that you are under stress is often emotional or body experiences; they are the warning signals you need to pay attention to.

Using Self-¬Care to Reduce Your Vulnerability to Stress

As described above, our ability to handle stress well has a great deal to do with the mental and physical resources available to us. By making sure you take good care of yourself, we will maximize our available resources (and our susceptibility to stress). In fact, this is so critical that there is a whole collection of DBT strategies committed to doing just that: taking care of our bodies, so we have more resources available to handle all of the stresses and stressors in our lives.

So how can you make sure you take care of yourself? Okay, you can do many things.

Maintain balanced eating

Another way to ensure you have as many resources as possible to cope with stress is to put nutritious food on your body to develop healthy eating habits. Your body needs nutrition to survive and work. Ensuring that you maintain a healthy diet should ensure that your body has the requisite food. Think about it: if it runs on fumes, your car doesn't work well, does it? Yes, it can start malfunctioning at that point or even stop running. The body does the same. If you don't have a full tank of gas, you can't work well, so be sure to give yourself the fuel you need throughout the day.

Today, there are really two aspects of healthy eating. First, you need to feed at regular intervals throughout the day, spread out meals and snacks to "fuel up" several times a day. Try your best to achieve as steady a blood glucose level as possible. Some studies have shown that blood glucose reductions can reduce coping abilities, make it harder to cope with stress, and prevent negative coping strategies. Holding your fuel tank at a steady level would allow you to drive and deal with stress better.

The second part involves choosing healthy and good things for you. You probably won't have many resources available to manage stress if you only eat junk foods or processed sugars every time you eat. And make sure you get plenty of nuts, berries, whole grains, and proteins; these are the top fuels that really help your body run at full potential. The odd indulgence is nothing wrong, but usually, you want to eat a consistently healthy, balanced diet. Suppose you're uncertain about what to eat or how to maintain a healthy, well-balanced diet. In that case, you may consider talking to your family physician, speaking with a nutritionist.

Maintain balanced sleep

Just as the body needs proper nutrients to function properly, so it needs adequate space, too. Sleep is another fuel source for your body, and your body doesn't work as well without it. When you don't get enough sleep, your physical abilities are greatly reduced, and your ability to manage stress is decreased. Ultimately, the body recovers its strength when you're asleep and works up the mental and physical energy for that day. Therefore, if you don't get the full amount of sleep you need every night, your body won't have time to fully restore your energy, so you'll have fewer resources at your fingertips to start the day. And that means you'll have fewer available resources to manage pain.

Have you found that you're more on the verge when you're not getting enough sleep, and stuff that wouldn't normally bother you seem to bother you a lot? That's presumably because you don't have the same level of resources to manage the stress that you usually would have after a full night's sleep, and you can't handle it as well. That is why it is so important to get a full night's sleep every night. So, one way to make sure you get enough sleep is to follow a regular sleep routine, go to bed every night at about the same time so wake up every morning at around the same time. Daily sleep means more stress-management tools.

Needless to say, this is better than done. People with anxiety problems often have trouble sleeping, having depression regularly, falling asleep issues, or anxious early awakenings. Another way of tackling these things is to use what is considered sleep hygiene. Sleep hygiene provides a set of strategies you can use to make your sleep healthier. The first step is to upgrade your sleep area by getting rid of the clutter in your bedroom and making sure it's an ideal sleeping space. First, see if you can recognize and change some of the reasons that could make getting a good night's sleep difficult. Some of these causes could include taking long afternoon naps (short naps are okay), consuming coffee, watching relaxing TV shows, smoking, using alcohol or drugs too close to bedtime, and eating a big dinner. Do your best to improve your sleep and change your behavior. Second, optimize productivity in your night. Sleep output is the proportion of sleep to bedtime expenditure. So if you're spending eight hours in bed but just sleeping six of those hours, the sleep performance is 75%.

The goal is to get that percentage as close as possible to 100% by preventing anything other than sleep (sexual activity is all right) in your bed. Don't work, read your e-mail, watch TV, or have extensive bed discussions. You want your brain to create a link between the bed and sleep, not between bed and waking.

Get regular exercise

Another way to reduce your pain susceptibility is to take regular workouts. Regular exercise will actually strengthen the body, building up physical resources over time. And this means you'll have more resources to handle pain. So, when we think about regular exercise, we don't mean you've got to work out five days a week at a gym. Don't get us wrong: if you have the time and money to go to the gym, that often is fantastic and can definitely help improve your strength; however, you don't need to see the exercise's physical benefits. All you need to do is do some kind of mild physical activity thirty minutes a day for five days a week to get the health benefits of exercise. And that shouldn't mean running or using exercise equipment. It could mean walking, cooking, vacuuming, walking up the stairs at your home or office, or anything else that's bringing the heart rate up. The only thing that matters is that you take at least thirty minutes to do something moderately active. And, the happier you are, the more imaginative you become. One factor that can lead to tension, as already described, is being busy and have many demands on your time. This is the same problem that can make maintaining a regular exercise schedule challenging.

Yeah, go easy on yourself and concentrate everywhere you can on getting exercise. If you need to go to the supermarket, park as far away as you can so that you can walk a little. Use the stairs instead of the elevator to work in a multi-story building or have appointments in such buildings. Focus on making the cleaning as functional as possible, rigorously pushing the broom, and really pouring yourself into scrubbing the floors or polishing the furniture when you need to clean your house. Furthermore, taking a bike to work is another way to incorporate fitness into your routine.

Take care of any illnesses you have

It is also important to remember that physical illness will drain your body's energy, making it more challenging to cope with the stressors of daily living. Therefore, one way to conserve your resources to survive a hurricane or stressful situation is to take care of any diseases. And, if you suspect you're coming down with something or you know you have an infection, go to the hospital. Take drugs accordingly. Make sure you get some extra sleep. Gain plenty of liquids. Have some chicken soup with noodles. Take a day off work, or temporarily reduce your workout routine. Ultimately, do whatever you can to take care of that illness and regain physical health. You'll be shocked at how much happier you feel when you're physically healthy to manage stress.

Limit alcohol and avoid drugs

People do not always know that too much drinking can take a toll on the body and use many of the body's physical resources. Likewise, alcohol consumption or mood-altering drugs will tax your emotional resources. Therefore, one way you can reduce your susceptibility to depression is to avoid taking drugs and minimize alcohol intake.

Increase your self-¬efficacy by doing things that make you feel capable

Have you ever found that you are better at handling stress than you do when you feel bad or less capable of your abilities? This is presumably because even physically, stress will wear on you mentally. Therefore, mentally feeling stronger and able transforms into an improved ability to handle and manage stress. Therefore, one easy way to reduce your susceptibility to stress is to do one thing every day, making you feel confident and in control of your life. It doesn't matter what it is; it's all-important that you do something that makes you feel happy.

151

Using Self-¬Soothing Strategies to Calm Your Mind and Body

As with the opportunities to mitigate your susceptibility to pain, you can use DBT's self-relieving techniques to avoid the detrimental effects of stress and improve the ability to manage the stress you face. Throughout the day, these techniques will help you recover your wealth and start to replenish the resources, so you can handle it better when tension occurs suddenly. The aim of these skills is to care for and soothe your body by exposing each of your five senses to soothing stimuli. First are some of the feelings that people find most calming and relaxing.

Touch

Take in feelings that soothe your body and feel good about your skin. Take a hot bubble bath. Rest in a sauna or whirlpool. Have a massage. Chat with your favorite pet and concentrate on the pet's fur sound on your skin. Relax in the light, and concentrate on your skin's warmth. Hug a friend or someone you dated. Throw on soft, comfortable textured clothes, like a light jumper, a soft flannel shirt, a soft cotton sweatshirt, or a silk coat. Wrap yourself in a soft, warm blanket. Stand outside fire and concentrate on the love you find.

Taste

Sip a cup of chocolate or hot tea (or some other soft beverage). Drink something cool on a hot day, or have a Popsicle or an ice cream sandwich. Eat your favorite food of convenience, including macaroni and cheese, pasta, grilled sandwich, mashed potatoes, fish and chips, or freshly baked bread. Eat dark chocolate (this activates molecules that are "feel good" as well). Eat a very new piece of fruit.

Smell

Go to a flower shop (to say it even if you're not shopping). Light a scented candle or burn incense. Inhale the scent of Vanilla or Lavender. Go outside and grab a breath of fresh air. Bake fresh bread or cookies, and take in the aroma. Smell new beans from the plantation, or brew some fresh coffee.

Sight

Find out pictures of loved ones or a favorite holiday place. Look at pictures that you find calming or inspiring, like ocean pictures, a sunset, or a majestic range. Go to the ocean to hear the tide reach the waves. Look at the sunset. Look into the sky at the clouds. Watch play with or sleep with your pet or kids. Go to a park to watch the kids play.

Hearing

Listen to the music to relax. Hear birds singing. Hear children playing. Walk through the woods and listen to nature's sounds. Listen to the crickets and sit outside in the dusk. Go to the beach and hear the sound of crashing waves on the shore.

Using Mindfulness Skills to Deal with Distraction and Poor Concentration

Stress can be highly frustrating. Because people are often under a lot of stress, they often feel that they have a hard time focusing on anything else. Is this one way that you get affected by stress? Will you find anything else hard to worry about when you're stressed? Will you find that you're spending a lot of time worrying about the causes of your tension and how this stress affects you? If this is one way that stress impacts you, you may find it's getting in the way of accomplishing certain things in your life, which can contribute to your frustration by making you feel like you're behind or not successful in your activities. Or it may take away your focus from non-stressful positive things in your community and facets of your life.

Luckily, DBT has an ability that can help you focus your attention and control the tension feeling. Specifically, the DBT conscientiousness ability to focus attention on one thing at a time can be used to help you focus your attention on whatever you're doing right now, making sure you turn your attention to the present moment and the task at hand when distracted. As already mentioned, this ability is all about doing one thing at a time: keeping all your energy on just one thing and letting go of distractions.

153

Therefore, you write when you're learning. When you play with your parents, then you can play with your kids. If you're doing something relaxing or self-supporting, just focus your attention on that. Often, when people are stressed out, they believe it will be better to attempt multitasking at once and work on many things. They think this will help them get more done, and they feel less stressed as a result. But, however common that belief may be, it's just not true. Alternatively, putting all of your energy on just one thing at a time and letting go of the obstacles that pop up will help much more than multitasking the tension.

And, the next time you get overwhelmed by everything that makes you anxious, take a deep breath and then bring back your mind to what you were doing at that moment. Center all your energy on just one thing, throw yourself into that task, and center only on that. Remember that if you get overwhelmed by the tension, then return your attention to the task at hand. Do this as many times as you need, focusing your mind over and over again. Note that minds get distracted; the purpose of mindfulness is simply to note when this happens and then to focus your attention again and again if needed.

This ability can also go a long way in helping you better endure tension. As Dr. Marsha Linehan said to one of us lately, "You never really get stressed when you just do one thing at the moment" (personal communication). Have you ever found that what really stresses you out is not what you're doing well at that moment but a sense of doom or a bunch of anxious ideas about what to do in the future? Admittedly, sometimes the present moment can be quite overwhelming. Still, if you just concentrate on what you are doing right now, rather than the pile of stuff you need to get done in the future, you'll feel like you're dragging much less weight around. Stick to that task you're focused on; just concentrate on the process of walking as you walk from one position to another (rather than going to your destination or all the stuff you'll need to do when you get there). The next time you find yourself frustrated by all of the pressures or stressors in your life, try this technique and see if it helps.

Using DBT Skills to Deal with Emotional Reactivity and Stop Unwanted Behavior

Have you ever found that you are more likely to fly off your handle or burst into tears easily when you are stressed out? That does make sense. When the constant stress causes your energy to be exhausted, you have fewer resources left to control your feelings. Therefore, there may be occasions when you feel much more sensitive physically or when your feelings feel out of balance. It is hard not to be emotionally reactive when you are feeling a huge amount of stress. Even though you may not be able to control how emotional you are, you may be able to control your actions. A few DBT strategies would concentrate on how you can control your actions while you feel intense emotions. Some of the qualities we feel can be most useful in this respect are the ability to observe your actions with caution and focus on the effects of your activities before you act. Here's a list of steps you can take any time you feel like you're almost ready to snap at the end of your string.

• Stop whatever you are doing. Sit down somewhere in a relaxed, quiet spot, where you won't get distracted and don't move a muscle.

• Step back and notice your experience. Use the ability to be mindful of your experience to step back in your mind and observe how you feel. Remember what an emotion you perceive in your body and where you feel it. Use your attention's flashlight to search where you are retaining anxiety, what you know about your heart rate and body temperature, and what other feelings you have. If your mind wanders, that's all right; just turn your attention back on your body. Do not push away any of your emotions or try to escape them. For now, just consider them.

• Notice any urges to act. If you're feeling particularly upset, annoyed, or frustrated, perhaps you've got the urge to lash out at someone. If you're feeling desperate, ashamed, or miserable, you might want to run upstairs and curl up in your bed. Everything you feel like doing, which we call your response instinct (what you feel like doing when you feel an emotion), just remember. Note what you feel like doing, watch and note the temptation or desire to act, and let it come and go, rise and fall on the ocean like a tide. Just step back and have a little time paying attention to it. Don't push it away or

155

try to hold it back. Start visualizing yourself navigating this desire as if it were an ocean storm.

•   Think through the consequences of what you want to do. When you're stressed out and otherwise aggressive, one of the best ways to direct yourself onto a more successful path is to think through what would happen if you'd just move on the urge and do what you feel like. When you're stressed out, the immediate positive results of acts like screaming, smoking, substance use, throwing things, and so on may seem pretty tempting. Therefore, you need to train your attention on the negative effects of these behaviors. Another approach to do that is to list all the effects of different behaviors, both positive and negative, in the short term and in the long term.

CHAPTER 9: DBT & Anxiety And Phobias

There are plenty of causes for anxiety. There are also many different treatments available, depending on the degree of the disorder. Consulting a doctor or a therapist is the best route because the therapist or doctor will create a combination of treatments, ranging from medication, meditation, self-care methods, breathing exercises, and so on. They do this by assessing the degree of your anxiety and recommend the necessary treatments. In almost all degrees, meditation is one of the elements of treatment. Meditation is, in no way or form, meant to be a focal treatment for anxiety. It is a complementary treatment with benefits that extend way beyond what science and research have given proof.

Through meditation, you are simply breaking down negative thoughts or triggers, fear, and worry. You focus all that energy on thinking on purpose. You also focus on your sensations mindfully and accept what you can control and what you cannot. Even if you do not suffer from chronic anxiety, you often find yourself worrying too much. This book is for you, especially if you go through stress daily or find yourself needing some self-care.

You will not only know what anxiety is and its triggers, but you also learn how meditation benefits anxiety relief and the kind of meditations one can do for a mere few minutes. Finally, you will also know how to introduce peace and serenity into your life.

Anxiety, if left untreated, can cause serious damage to a person's life. It may start as something relatively small. Over time, it builds up to the point that it becomes chronic and starts to interfere emotionally and mentally in the aspects of day-to-day life.

Understanding Anxiety

I can't breathe!

My heart is pounding!

Why are my legs shaking?

Why am I feeling sick to my stomach?

I need to drink or take my pills to calm my anxious heart. I can't stand this.

Why does it seem like the world is crashing on me?

You may have experienced all these symptoms before. It could be anxiety, and it even could be a panic disorder. When it comes to anxiety, it is a natural human response to stress. It is a feeling of fear or nervousness about what may or may not happen. The American Psychological Association (APA) defines anxiety as "an emotion characterized by feelings of tension, worried thoughts, and physical changes like increased blood pressure." Some people feel anxious about major events like examinations, childbirth, or going for interviews. Likewise, anxiety can also arise from common issues like financial problems, health issues, or work stress. It is also not uncommon to fear getting an injection, taking an airplane, or encountering a wild animal. Although different people are triggered by different causes of anxiety, everyone will experience anxiety sometime in their lives.

In the early days of mankind, incoming danger or the approach of predators triggered alarms in the body that enabled quick response to danger. These alarms come in as increased heartbeat, perspiration, and increased awareness or sensitivity to surroundings. An adrenaline rush is triggered that sends a message to the brain, which, in turn, prompts reactions that are called the 'fight-or-flight response. Individuals, through this, can escape or confront their threats or crisis situations.

However, escaping predators could be the least of our concerns today. Causes of anxieties nowadays revolve around work, health, money, family, and other issues without requiring the 'fight-or-flight' reaction.

Before an extremely new experience or important event or even something difficult to handle, the fear and worry are kin to the original 'fight-or-flight' reaction, which can still be vital to survival today. For example, the fear of being struck down by lightning could mean that a person instinctively ensures that you do not be out in an open field during a thunderstorm.

Stress, fear, and anxiety are common feelings and experiences, but they are different from anxiety disorders. If feelings of severe anxiety exceed six months and impede your daily routine, you could potentially be suffering from an anxiety disorder.

Although there are many anxiety-related disorders, they are classified into three main categories:

1) anxiety disorders

2) obsessive-compulsive and related disorder

3) trauma-related disorders. In an anxiety-related disorder, your worry or distress lingers and continues to intensify over time and disrupts your daily activities and relationships.

One way to determine whether you are suffering from an anxiety disorder is to identify the cause of the anxiety and then evaluate whether the severity of the symptoms is proportional to it. For example, someone with an anxiety disorder will respond as if they are in real danger when, in reality, they are not.

It can be difficult to determine whether your anxiety is linked to a disorder, which is why it is wise to refer to licensed professionals, such as psychologists or psychiatrists, to make the diagnosis.

The common types of disorders concerning anxiety include:

• Universal anxiety disorder: Extreme fear and worry about anything and everything

• Social anxiety disorder: Stress and fear in social settings, which often arises from the fear of other people's negative perception of oneself

• Panic disorder: Repetitive panic attacks and worry about subsequent panic attacks

• Agoraphobia: Fear of having a panic attack and not being able to reach out for help

• Specific phobias: Intense fear of certain people, things, or situations

When is Anxiety Diagnosed?

According to Dr. Tracy Dennis-Tiwary, Ph.D., Professor of Psychology at Hunter College, "We obviously struggle with anxiety, as well as stress, at different times in our lives. The big question is, if you have these experiences, to what degree are they interfering with your ability to lead life?"

If you are wondering if it's time to seek help, here are some things to think about:

• Your chronic worrying is interrupting your life

Struggling to decide or taking too much time making a decision (especially for a small issue), whether at home, at work, in a relationship, or even as a parent, may be a sign that you need help. If you constantly get in the way of you living an otherwise happy and full life, it is worth reaching out for help.

• You no longer want to travel or do the things you love

If worrying and stress keep you away from enjoying the things you love, Dr. Ilene S. Cohen says that this is another sign that something is wrong. Dr. Cohen, a psychotherapist and an instructor at Barry University, says that if you usually love to travel but suddenly feel the need to bail, and this keeps happening often, speak to someone about it.

• You bailed on a work project

If your fear of speaking in public is so great that you bailed out on giving a presentation, it may be time to find a therapist. Bailing on a task important to your role is a sign that something is up.

• You feel isolated

If you feel isolated or you isolate yourself. Such behavior could also indicate a problem.

• Your anxiety has lasted more than a few days or weeks

Dr. Dennis-Tiwary also points out the consistency of the anxiety. If you are going a day or two with anxiety and stress, and it has made life harder, but then you go back to normalcy after that, this is okay. But if you have been anxious and stressed for three to four weeks, then it is time to seek support from your counselor, doctor, or therapist.

Signs & Symptoms of Anxiety

Up until today, medical professionals cannot completely understand what leads to anxiety disorders. The current premise is that traumatic incidents can act as triggers to those who have suffered from them. It is believed that genetics also plays a part in anxiety. Likewise, health issues could cause anxiety but in the form of a physical instead of a mental condition.

With anxiety disorders, a person could suffer from one or more disorders simultaneously. Usually, there could also be other conditions that come together, such as bipolar and depression. This is especially concerning common or universal anxiety disorder, which most frequently is associated with mental or health disorders.

Suppose your fear or worry is not the outcome of a serious health condition. In that case, you may be referred to a mental health specialist, either a psychiatrist or a psychologist, depending on the seriousness of your condition.

161

• A psychiatrist is a certified medical practitioner licensed to diagnose and handle mental health conditions with or without prescribed medications.

•A psychologist is a mental health specialist who can do treatment and diagnosis of any kind of mental health issues but is usually administered through counseling and often without any medication.

It is vital to get treatment from a mental health provider whom you are comfortable with and trust. Ask your doctor to refer you to a few, and take the time to meet them. It is not unusual for it to take a few meetings to find the one that is suitable for you.

A psychological evaluation will help your mental health provider to diagnose an anxiety disorder. This could look like a therapy session of one-on-one with your mental health provider, asking you questions regarding your feelings and behaviors.

What Are the Symptoms of Anxiety?

Different people experience anxiety differently. The feelings can vary from a churning stomach to an intensely racing heart, feeling like things are out of control, and a total disconnect between your body and mind. Some people experience cold sweats, panic attacks, nightmares, and uncontrollable thoughts. Other symptoms of general anxiety include restlessness, insomnia, difficulty in focusing, difficulty in breathing, hyperventilation, twitching muscles, lethargy, strong aversion to certain things, and obsession about certain things, and digestive problems, such as gas or diarrhea. A sudden outbreak of fear that can escalate in a short amount of time can constitute a panic attack.

The symptoms of panic attacks are more severe. They can be confused with medical conditions like heart disease, thyroid problems, and breathing disorders. Panic attack symptoms include heart palpitations, shaking, smothering, nausea, sweating, chest tightness, feeling faint, a sudden feeling of hot or cold, numbness, or acute fear of dying or losing control.

162

DBT for Anxiety

Our emotions are very important. We are given emotions because it makes us alive. It services an important function in our lives. As much as we hate having emotions, especially when something bad has happened, emotions help the mind and brain make sense of what is happening. The core emotions that we have been linked to anxiety. These emotions are such as abandonment and fear, which make perfect sense if you think about it. When we experience a threat or danger to our life, our well-being, or our health, fear is what motivates us to get out of the way. It gives us a near-instant reaction to protect ourselves.

But sometimes, our emotions rise up, and it can be catastrophic. Emotions such as fear that suddenly crop up when we least expect it can be extremely unproductive and unhelpful. Using DBT helps us work through learning the necessary cognitive and emotional skills and applying these skills to our life. Essentially, we go through the acquisition process through the skills we learn; next is generalization through applying these skills.

DBT enables us to tackle distressing and difficult emotions. It also enhances our propensity for emotional regulation, which improves our ability to control our feelings, how we experience them, and finally, how we express them.

Training Mindfulness and Distress Tolerance Skills with DBT

DBT has both individual-based therapy as well as training in groups. Through skills-based training in groups, people learn important skills such as distress tolerance and mindfulness techniques that are huge elements in enabling ourselves to access the present moment.

Some of these techniques can involve walking, counting up to 10, or holding an ice cube, to increase awareness and acceptance. These activities allow us to understand what is going on right now, at the moment.

Some of these skills that are taught through DBT's emotional regulation are observing and describing emotions. There is also a step-by-step toolkit for managing and changing emotions that you want to change.

Some of these tools are:

- Fact-checking in any given situation

- Counter-behaving to the emotional drive

- Resolving problems to alter an event by prompting a specific emotional reaction

The central goal of DBT is changing and influencing emotions. Before beginning this step, it is vital to comprehend and understand the root cause of these emotions and why they come about. This aspect of 'understanding and acknowledging' in DBT is one of the main elements distinguishing DBT from CBT.

This methodology encourages the analysis and explanation of emotional experiences in a mindful and non-judgmental way. Adding this element enables DBT powerful in a range of problems, including anxiety, since the skills you learn will help you separate feelings from reality, allow you to work with emotions effectively, and handle them efficiently.

Using DBT to Develop Emotional Skills and Alleviate Anxiety

Detailed DBT includes various elements like individual therapy with a DBT therapist, training in group skills, skills coaching usually done by telephone, and the inclusion of the therapist in a support and consultation team.

These different elements work together to ensure that the DBT provides skills that you can immediately put into practice. If an anxiety disorder is part of life, then you probably have a good idea of how the feeling of not being in control of your thoughts is, which means feeling in control is an extremely validating and valuable feeling.

Mindfulness in anxiety can you approach and not avoid situations where you are fearful in. It also enables you to accept the present moment you are in, bringing you more joy and meaning, especially in establishing healthy relationships.

164

The things you learn from DBT are useful for anyone, even when you are already doing so well. DBT teaches and gives healthy life skills that are sustainable and remain in use for a lifetime, enabling us to use them in many different facets of our lives.

DBT comprises four main sets of skills: attention, emotion control, tolerance for distress, and interpersonal efficiency, and when necessary, these skill sets can be used in many different ways.

It is not the same as mindfulness meditation

In DBT, the image of mindfulness is not the same kind that you think of when talking about mindfulness, which includes meditation. In DBT, it is more than this. The most vital component is the training of our attentional muscle, which gives us a better focus on what is going on in the present rather than thinking ahead into the future.

This is incredibly important for many people with anxiety disorders who constantly worry about what is coming!

The element of Wise Mind

A DBT therapist introduces mindfulness to help them stay more present. Another important aspect of mindfulness is that element of a wise mind, acting and making decisions from a place in the mind that evaluates and balances what is logical and emotion-based. For anxious people, this means owning up to their fears and being sensitive to the level of emotion they are in and also striving towards moving forward in life.

165

Emotional Regulation Skills

In anxiety, this skill focuses on decreasing your vulnerability to negative emotions and using strategies that can change negative emotions as they bubble and threaten to arise.

It also involves incorporating sleep, including a healthy eating schedule, exercising, and other productive and healthy behaviors to reduce their emotional vulnerability. The DBT concept used here is to change negative emotions and act against them, which are not justified by the situation at hand, even when they feel their feelings are justified.

The concept of acting against anxiety and fear is very much in accordance with how therapists usually treat anxiety—by empowering people to face thoughts, emotions, and circumstances that scare them instead of trying to escape them. To behave against it also involves approaching other people rather than going to bed when you are sad, treating people with empathy, and doing something positive when you're angry. Most people were surprised to find that their feelings actually change for the better when they act against their negative emotions!

Interpersonal Effectiveness

This means that you need to be assertive, whether in asking people to make certain changes in the way they behave or even saying NO to things asked of you that you do not feel comfortable doing. This assertiveness also means assessing how willing you are to stay in a position and maintain your position in the face of demanding reactions from others. This can be an essential capacity for people who are socially anxious or simply stressed because of a complicated interpersonal situation.

The effectiveness of DBT in interpersonal skills has a wide range of benefits for different types of patients, from businesspeople navigating high-pressure situations at their workplace, co-workers dealing with deadlines, numerous meetings, and teens dealing with tough situations.

166

Distress Tolerance in Anxiety

Finally, distress tolerance skills involve doing things to ride out your feelings to not make things worse. It isn't aimed at making people feel better but rather at helping people stop acting abruptly. These are all merely distraction tools. Since not moving away from emotions is extremely important for individuals with anxiety, these skills are usually introduced to patients through DBT. Distress tolerance is highly crucial for people with anxiety who can also act impulsively just because they cannot sit with their own uncertainty in provoking scenarios.

Benefits of DBT for Anxiety

Obviously, with DBT, people can continue practicing skills that enable them to live in the present moment and observe their feelings. It also helps people with anxiety manage the intensiveness of their feelings. They are also able to tolerate their feelings and alter their behaviors to create new emotional experiences.

DBT also teaches the anxiety-ridden person mindfulness skills that can be used as tools to set aside their worries about the past or the future to address all that is happening around them in the present.

Exercise: A Quick Mindfulness Technique for Anxiety

Using mindfulness in anxiety is extremely effective as it has been found to improve moods. The effects from each session of mindfulness last even beyond initial improvements. Interested in adding some mindfulness into your anxiety therapy?

To start, here are some 10 attitudes to create the basis of addressing anxiety successfully:

- Beginner's mind

- It applies to a way of looking from a new perspective

- Volition or intention

- This will be the foundation of all other behaviors. First of all, you will need to bring all your focus to work with your anxieties.

- Considering new approaches regarding the treatment of anxiety.

- Patience: a much-needed mind-frame to grow and nurture, which can instinctively sharpen and widen your perspective and make you persevere even through the toughest of times and the hardest of obstacles.

- Acknowledgment

- This means grasping all the experiences you have and understanding what it represents. It also means accepting the things you went through, both good and bad, and acknowledging that you are safe and secure in the thought that all of these bad things will pass.

- Non-judgment

- This approach involves noticing and evaluating the present situation. This ensures that you can make valuable decisions about yourself and how you feel and start working with a more positive entry point.

- Non-striving

- This approach is about being ready to accept, without trying to change, a circumstance or an event as it is. You first need to be present and acknowledge your present condition to combat your anxiety.

- Self-reliance

- The way of thinking of yourself is characterized by your self-belief and the ability to manage your feelings. Working on your self-confidence, recognizing and appreciate that you will, in time, let go of whatever binds you with fear.

168

- Permitting or allowing

- Similar to the non-straightening mentality, letting or allowing refers to the mindset that causes you to experience anxiety. It is better to focus on dealing with depression more successfully than hiding it away or not dealing with it.

- Self-compassion

- As mentioned earlier, compassion is the core of mindfulness. This leads to being self-compassionate and kind to yourself. This will help alleviate the depression symptoms by being your very own support, the same way you show support to a friend or loved one.

- Equilibrium and equanimity

- These attitudes enable knowledge and wisdom to develop by expanding and diversifying your perspectives. You need to understand that your entire experience, whether positive or negative, is more than your current feelings.

You can try this short exercise in a rather simplified way to apply mindfulness to anxiety:

To do this mindfulness exercise, you need to first take note of how you feel. The next step is to reflect on your experiences, and then you proceed to describe these feelings and experiences.

Pay special on how you feel throughout this entire process.

- Wherever you are, whether you are sitting or standing, just as long as you are in a safe space, either close your eyes if you can or keep them open

- Place your hand on your heart to feel the rhythm of your heart beating

- Breath in and out as comfortable as you can

- Pay attention to the sensations that arise in your body when you are anxious, your heart beating faster, your face feeling hotter, etc.

169

- Bring yourself into the present awareness

- Give yourself fully in the present

- You can give in to anxious and distressing reflections.

By knowing these thoughts, you can realize that they are not valid. Thus, you can be stronger in letting these feelings go instead of focusing on feelings that bring calm, slowing down, and steadying your beating heart.

CHAPTER 10: How To Support Someone Who Is Going Through Therapy

It takes a lot of guts to decide to go into therapy. Many people choose not to do it because they do not want to face the reality of the situation. They don't want to know if they are ill or there is something wrong with them.

But someone you know has taken that active step, and by doing so, they have acknowledged that they want to get better or find out if there is anything wrong with them that needs fixing.

No matter the reason, your role is vital depending on how close you are to this person. It could be your spouse, your best friend, your colleague, your sibling, or even your neighbor. If they have chosen to open up to you and tell you that they are going through therapy, then you can be actively involved to help them through this time.

How can you help?

How do you help someone going through therapy, especially when you do not know anything about therapy or any therapeutic process yourself? What should your level of involvement be? Are you required to show up with them for every session? Do you stay out of it? Do you talk about it?

These may all be a little stressful for you but remember that the person going through therapy is even more stressed about this than you are. One of the first things to do is to remind yourself that sharing the fact that they are going through therapy is a sign that they trust you and that your relationship with them means a lot.

Your first move is to make sure that you will continue to be their friend and confidante whenever you need them due to this trust. If you are their partner or spouse, reassure them that you will continue to love them no matter what and will help as best as you can.

171

Here are eight ways that you can help, being a partner or friend support:

1 - Be available

A big warning sign to you, therapy can lead to places that neither you nor your partner was planning to go to, and the fallout from it could be intense. There will be tears; there will be anger, confusion, and exhaustion afterward. Therapists often administer 'deep work,' a segment of intense psychotherapy that involves diving into a very primal and usually upsetting part of your life. Sometimes, it can be a place we never thought existed. This place could be the reason for your anxiety, worry, and fear. At this point, remember to give your partner the space he or she needs to allow this information to sink in. They need time post-session to process what they have been through. It's like resting after a session of chemotherapy. Cook dinner, give back rubs, do extra chores around the house. Essentially, be present.

2 - Allow them to talk about it with you

Some people are open to talking about their sessions and what they've discovered, whereas some aren't. The important thing to know is that you don't have to act like a therapist when they open up to you or talk to you about their sessions. Be open and let them talk. There will be things that would only come up now and don't be upset if it does. That's what therapy does. It unleashes certain issues that you and your partner or friend have not spoken about before. Patients after treatment need support to deal with these matters.

There may be instances that you might be invited to join in any of the sessions, especially if the patient has brought you up in the conversation. Depending on how close you are to them, the therapist will ask you to join in if they deem it necessary to unpack certain issues and problems. As a friend, partner, sibling, or parent, be prepared for this. You must be willing to be part of this process if you want to help your friend.

You could also become worried or panicked and weighed down because you do not know what to expect.

This is a sign that whatever it is that you are concerned about, it needs to be out in the open and help in the healing process of both parties. Having a conversation in a neutral space with an intermediary (the therapist) helps heal and support.

3 - Respect their rights not to talk too

You might be anticipating that your friend, partner, spouse, sibling, parent, or child might come back and want to talk about their therapy session. While it is perfectly okay to ask how their session went, expect not to have an answer. Communicating with a therapist is a different and unique talking. More often than not, it's hard to translate or relay it again outside the therapeutic space. It could also be that your partner or friend may not be ready to discuss what has happened or they are too exhausted to talk about it. If you get this vibe, it is best to respect their right not to speak about it. You can also establish a ground rule with them on the level of involvement they would like to have from you. As their therapy journey continues, revisit this level of commitment. Your partner, friend, spouse, sibling, parent, or child may find it easier to engage with you for all you know.

The prime route to maneuver around this is to remember privacy. Respect their privacy the way you want your privacy to be respected too. Sometimes, they may not be too eager to share information immediately because they don't feel like it or feel the time is not right. But that does not mean they do not trust you. If they share information with you that is sensitive, ensure that you will maintain confidentiality. Ultimately, talk things out and remember not to be a therapist or contradict the therapist. Whether silently or just by being there, your support means more than anything to a person who is undergoing therapy.

4 - Understand their distress

Having a loved one come out of therapy crying may seem like an alarming situation, especially when you have never had any experience with therapy. The therapist's job isn't a standup comedian to make your partner or friend feel happy all the time. Their job is to determine psychological problems, help them deal with them, and find solutions. Some bad therapists make patients feel bad about them. So, it is critical to find a good and trained therapist. But distress is often a natural response to any therapy session.

Also, if there is no crying, weeping or distress doesn't mean that the therapy sessions aren't working. People respond differently to therapy sessions. It is a different experience for everyone.

5 - Support their decision on getting help

Sitting and confronting things once every week (or how often you are required to attend sessions) can be depressing. It is depressing to talk about issues we do not like or things that are bothering us. However, having a support system outside the therapeutic space is essential. Having caring parents or siblings, or friends can help the healing process for any individual going through therapy. Sometimes, the patient might feel that it is a waste of their time going for therapy sessions. This is where you come in and support them and remind them that benefits will come; it will just take time.

6 - It isn't about you

A person going for therapy is going for it for themselves alone and repair and fix their relationship with the people around them. Sometimes, it has nothing to do with connections and relationships, but just how that person deals with life in general. If you are someone close to the patient and your relationship with them is a spouse or partner, do not demand to know what they talk about in therapy.

7 - Don't expect them to get better fast

It will take some time before you or even your friend or partner sees the results. Unknotting problems of the mind is a drawn-out and fraught process. It involves trust with the therapist, trying out different approaches, going through tests and deep examinations, and many exercises. It is hard for the patient, and sometimes, it is also hard for loved ones to understand what the patient is going through. Just remember that all good things take time. Your love and support will go a long, long way and always encourage them to be committed to their therapy sessions, not for anyone else but themselves.

8 - <u>You might want to get support</u>

If the patient is someone close to you, a family member, a spouse/partner, your parent or sibling, chances are that you may need emotional support to help deal with this as well. You need to get enough emotional nourishment as well, especially if the patient was your support all this time. Speaking to another family member you can trust with confidential information or even a friend is helpful for you to help you get through this together.

Bottom Line

Depending on who the patient is and your relationship with them, being part of their support system is vital in ensuring that they come out of their disorder healthily. Having a good support system helps the patient. It also makes the therapists' job easier knowing that the patient is surrounded by positive influences.

Therapy will be good on some days and bad on some days, and sometimes, all the patient needs is space or a shoulder to cry on or an ear to listen. Being there or just listening to them speak can be extremely helpful in so many ways. If things get too much for you to handle, seek help. Psychological problems are not something that should be kept secret or isolated. Treat it as you would a physical problem such as cancer or surgery.

How to solve Problems?

All people have problems in their daily lives. Sometimes these surpass us, and anxiety, stress, and sadness appear. So, what can you do? We can help you solve your problems by teaching you specific strategies called "Problem-solving techniques."

They consist of five steps:

<u>Step 1: Identify your problems</u>

Before you can solve a problem, you have to know what it is. What problems do you have now? Some of them can become serious, like "I'm going to be fired." In contrast, others are smaller "I'm going to need the help of my brother-in-law to paint the garage," others are in a medium-term "I have to fix some papers and not I know how to do it".

175

Make a list of your problems.

Tips:

•   Evaluate if the problem is yours: most people complicate their lives trying to find a solution to a problem that does not belong to them. This is because we are very given to bear the burdens of others. After all, socially, we require this attitude. In case the problem is not yours, dismiss continuing to worry about it.

•   Concretely define your problem: it will help you find a solution.

•   You do not have to think about the problem, just list it and move on.

•   Do not worry if you think that these problems may or may not be solved at that moment. Remember that you do not have to have the solution, only the problem.

•

•   Take your time; it is not necessary to make a list hastily.

•   Sometimes it is difficult to be clear about precisely what the problems are. Ask for help from someone around you if this is the case.

Do not worry about the number of problems you have written. Remind yourself that this is the first step in solving them. Sometimes people discover by writing their list that this is not as long as they thought.

<u>Step 2: Choose a problem.</u>

Now select a problem from the list you have made. It should have a lot of interest in solving and that there is a possibility of resolving. Later you can tackle the ones that are more difficult for you. What problem would you like to pursue first?

Try to make it as concrete as possible. For example, a chosen problem could be: "my co-worker is a lazy man." This approach is a little generic; it would help if I specified it a little more.

For example, "my partner asks me to answer his phone calls." Try writing the problem you have chosen as clearly as possible in the box below.

MY PROBLEM IS:

Now I answer the following questions: Have you solved similar problems in the past? If so, how did you do it? What resources or skills did you use?

Would you have someone who supports you in that effort to solve it? Ideally, these people will not solve it but only help. Who are they?

Next, think about things that might help you solve the problem:

• Try using a "brainstorm": Propose as many solutions as possible. The greater the number of options that are generated better, because the greatest discomfort that is created by having a problem is due to the idea that it is not going to be resolved, that it has no solution.

• Do not worry about how good the solutions you have looked for are.

• Do not worry if some of them seem silly. Now it is about looking for as many possible solutions as possible. Then he will look at them and value them.

In the example, the list of possible actions could be:

• *Talk to him directly.*

• *Complain to your boss.*

• *Do not take your calls.*

• *Pass mine to him.*

• *Disconnect your phone.*

Possible actions that can help you solve your problem.

Step 3: Choose one of your solutions

Choose three solutions: not necessarily the first is the most viable. It is good to know that there are two alternatives in case the first one fails.

Now start with the one that seems to be the best. There are no fixed rules on how to make this choice. Think about the pros and cons of each and then choose. Remember, if you try one option and it does not work, you can try another.

What solution do you choose?

Do not think about the problem: the problem was a problem while there was no solution.

Now he has it.

Step 4: Create an action plan

There are not many problems that can be completely solved with a single action. Often, it is necessary to carry out many actions to find the solution; for example, if you have to prepare a talk, your first action could be to gather all the documents you will use to make the speech. Only collecting the documents will not solve the problem, but it will bring you closer to a solution than before.

Execute the action: no problem is solved if you sit down to wait for your plan to be implemented on its act.

Your action plan should follow four rules. In other words, your plan should be:

•   Achievable. It is better to achieve a small objective than to fail in a large one. Here is a bad example: I fix all the cabinets in the house. A better example: I fix my bedroom.

•   You are oriented to action. Make a plan with what you will do without thinking about how you will feel while doing it. You have some control over your actions, but less about your emotions. A bad example: Have fun with my friends. A better example: Spend an afternoon with my friends.

•   Specific. Make it very clear what you need to do. A bad example: I spent time with a friend. A better example: I accompanied a friend for a walk.

178

• It is limited in time. This makes the solution affordable and easy to start. Being limited in time, the expected changes will not be radical. For example, it is more realistic to say: "Today I will dedicate an hour to make reports of the work" than to say: "Today I will finish all the work reports."

What is the plan, exactly?

ACTION FOR WHEN

Carry out your plan in the time set in your table above. When you have complied with it or when the deadline has passed, go to step 5.

Step 5: Think about how your plan was

Now, think about how the plan turned out (even if the problem has not yet been solved in its entirety).

What happened? What went well? What went wrong?

Use this experience to plan your next step. You have three main options:

• Continue with your initial plan. For example, I spent twenty more minutes doing reports.

• Review your goal and make another attempt. For example, the reports are very complicated, and I do not have time to finish them soon, so I plan to have half for this week.

• Face it from another perspective: Perhaps your first effort has allowed you to find another way to handle the problem. Take another alternative solution from the ones outlined above.

For example:

Talking with my partner did not work, so I will talk to my boss.

What will be your next step then?

Work with these five steps. Keep a rec

ord. Recall the progress you make.

179

CHAPTER 11: Frequently Asked Questions

How are CBT and DBT different?

DBT has its roots in CBT, but it uses a more dialectical approach than traditional CBT therapies. Although most people can get significant results from CBT, it was found that there was a specific group of patients who were not getting the results that the average person was receiving. Instead, this group got frustrated with the process and quickly dropped out because they did not feel validated. So, a revised CBT process that combines emotional validation with behavioral change was developed. This is known as DBT.

Are CBT and DBT more effective than other therapies?

These therapies have been scientifically proven to be very effective, and most clients make lasting changes quickly.

All therapies have their positive points; however, cognitive-based therapies are often favorites among clinicians because they are action-oriented, thus obtaining quick results. Most people get in a year of talk therapy can be easily obtained in 3-4 sessions of CBT or DBT.

How does the therapy work?

The amount of therapy you need varies based upon your own individual needs. However, most people do well with one individual session per week. DBT also includes one additional skill-building group session per week. Your commitment to the therapy process really is the best determining factor in how the therapy will work. Some people do more than one individual session per week, while others are comfortable with the one session. That is something that you should discuss with your therapist to determine a specific treatment regimen.

How long does it take to see progress?

Progress varies depending on the person, but most people start seeing results very early, typically within 3-4 sessions. Of course, this depends largely on how much effort you put into the program. Doing the homework consistently and attending the group skill-building sessions every week is critical to your success in DBT.

What if I'm skeptical?

Give it a try. You won't know whether it works or not until you try it. Just like almost anything else in life, you won't know how effective it really is until you try it. Commit to doing your first behavioral experiment and see how it goes. If it works, great, keep going. If it doesn't, you can always stop.

Can I discontinue medication?

Although both CBT and DBT are quite effective treatment approaches even without medication, the decision to discontinue your medication should be taken very seriously and supervised by a medical professional. You should discuss that decision with your psychiatrist or another physician.

How does DBT prioritize treatment goals?

- *Target 1: Life-threatening behavior and behavior that interferes with treatment*

- *Target 2: Decrease emotional suffering*

- *Target 3: Daily living management*

- *Target 4: Sense of wholeness and connectedness*

This is the priority of the goals for DBT treatment. Of course, life-threatening goals prioritize, and moving through suicidal ideation or self-harm behavior is addressed first. Also, behavior that interferes with treatment is high-priority. No progress can be made unless there is a commitment to the therapy process. The ultimate goal is to get you to a place of complete wholeness. You are one out of a whole universe, and you are universally connected with every other person in the universe. Whatever your religious or spiritual beliefs are, the ultimate goal of DBT is to help you embrace yourself, your life, and other people so that you can fully experience and enjoy life.

CONCLUSION

Initially, dialectical behavior therapy was developed by Dr. Marsha M. Linehan as a treatment for borderline personality disorder. However, DBT is now being used to treat various mental health conditions and isn't restricted to BPD. DBT can be used to improve your ability to handle any distressing situations in life without losing control of your emotions, your emotional stability, or resorting to destructive behaviors. It is a great technique for rectifying emotional dysregulation.

The core principles of DBT are based on mindfulness, distress tolerance, emotion regulation, and interpersonal effectiveness. These basic principles come in handy while dealing with difficult emotions. Certain situations in life cannot be changed regardless of how hard you try, which can be a source of immense stress and distress. Learning to cope with such situations and get out of them takes mindfulness. Mindfulness is one of the most important aspects of DBT.

Mindfulness is the ability to live life at the moment without allowing any thoughts about the past or the future to hijack your thinking patterns. Unless you are mindful of yourself, your emotions, thoughts, feelings, actions, and life in general, you cannot lead a happy and stress-free life. It is where DBT steps into the picture. To regain control over your emotions and maintain emotional stability, you must commit yourself. Health isn't just restricted to your physical wellness; it includes your mental and emotional wellbeing too. Unless all these three aspects of your health are in balance, you cannot attain mental peace.

In this guide book, you were provided with the information required to develop and improve important skills that help you focus on your current state while reducing stress, worries, and PTSD. You were also provided information about effectively counteracting any impulsive behavior using DBT and tips for dealing with extremely stressful situations in life.

Every technique and tip given in this book is simple to understand and easy to follow. All the advice is curated to help you stay in the present moment, increase your understanding of your emotions, understand your true self, and curb impulsive behaviors. You can do all this even in times of distress.

All the techniques covered in this book will help improve your ability to regulate your emotions while promoting your mental and emotional health.

The key to your emotional and mental wellbeing lies in your hands. The first step toward regaining control of your emotions is DBT. A little consistency and effort are all it takes to master the different techniques of DBT and mindfulness within this book. Once you start following these techniques, you will notice a positive change in your emotional health. So, what are you waiting for? There is no time like the present to get started.

Thank you and all the best!

ACCEPTANCE AND COMMITMENT THERAPY

Introduction

Acceptance and Commitment Therapy (said as a single word, 'ACT') is a proof-based psychological mediation that uses acceptance and mindfulness systems close by conduct change strategies to assist you with living life as per the main thing to you. Considering late leaps forward in understanding how language works, ACT offers a unique viewpoint on the human condition and the test everybody faces in living a life with importance and reason. We tie ACT in with doing the things that truly matter to you and not letting your mind disrupt the general flow. Frequently, without you understanding it, your mind — what goes on in your mind — can push you around and meddle with your everyday life. You're so associated with your thoughts that you rarely see what they do and, significantly, what they stop you from doing. But your mind is the only exceptional tool that is, similar to all tools, acceptable at taking care of specific problems and miserable attending to other people. ACT tells you the best way to use your mind for what it's fair and then put it aside when your thoughts are less useful. To assist you with continuing ahead with the life you need to be living, ACT uses a scope of activities to empower you to turn out to be progressively open, mindful, and active:

Openness includes venturing forward into life and accepting all that accompanies it.

Awareness implies expanding your association with the world around you as opposed to living in your mind. Being active is tied in with doing the things that matter to you. This is an energizing time for the ACT. Consistently, new research articles and books investigate how it is applied in different settings and many human problems.

Truth be told, so many new applications are being built up that lack space right now spread them all. Or maybe, we furnish a general prologue to ACT with the point of helping you understand the focal standards, thoughts, and practices that support the model.

In opposition to prevalent thinking, doing the things that truly matter to you can be very difficult. And the explanation behind that, as per ACT, is human language. While language empowers you to do stunning things, it additionally permits you to ruminate on the past and stress over what's

185

coming. And when you become excessively snared in your thoughts, you quit living the life you need to be living — and rather, your life is directed by your outrage, fears, stresses, and questions.

This understanding isn't especially new, but where ACT differs from different methodologies, it reacts to these occasions. As opposed to handling this cynicism head-on, ACT shows you better approaches to identify with your thoughts, feelings, and emotions, so they have less effect on your everyday life.

Chapter 1: Dissemination of ACT Therapy

Acceptance and Commitment Therapy, or ACT, is a form of therapy that draws from mindfulness practice and cognitive-behavioral psychotherapy. It is also known as contextual psychotherapy because it encourages patients to exhibit values-based positive behaviors even if they experience negative sensations, emotions, or thoughts. In other words, it helps patients increase their psychological flexibility.

As the third wave of Cognitive Behavioral Therapy (CBT), ACT (said as one word) is strongly connected to the power of behavioral change. However, ACT differs from CBT. It can change the relationship you have with your thoughts rather than change them directly. ACT promotes the notion that you don't have to do anything with your thoughts to push change in your behavior.

ACT focuses on mindfulness, diffusion of challenging thoughts, and acceptance of unpleasant emotions. With ACT, your efforts are concentrated on moving you towards a momentous life by helping you learn to separate yourself from your thoughts. Your efforts are based on your committed action towards establishing your values.

ACT mindfulness skills have 3 categories:

•Acceptance: enables patients to make room for sensations, urges, and painful feelings and allowing them to easily come and go

•Defusion: enables patients to let go of and distance from unhelpful thoughts, memories, and beliefs

•Contact with the present moment: enables patients to fully engage, with an attitude of curiosity and openness, with their here-and-now experience

ACT can be delivered in many different ways:

•Ultra-brief ACT – ACT can be highly effective even in one or two twenty to thirty-minute sessions. A good example is a treatment by Kirk Strosahl, co-founder of ACT, in primary care medical settings.

187

•Brief ACT – ACT is done with only four sessions at 1-hour each. A good example is a treatment by Patty Bach, assistant professor of psychology at the Illinois Institute of Technology, used on patients with schizophrenia.

•Medium-term ACT – ACT is completed for a total of eight hours. An example is a protocol for chronic pain by a professor of psychology at Uppsala University in Sweden, JoAnne Dahl.

•Long-term ACT – ACT takes forty sessions at 2-hour each. This is very effective in treating patients with borderline personality disorder (BPD).

One of the only few known users of long-term ACT is Spectrum, the Personality Disorder (clinic) Service in the state of Victoria in Australia.

Note: Therapy Affects the Brain

According to a study published in the American Journal of Psychology in 1998, several decades of research have revealed that all mental processes derive from brain mechanisms.

This means that any change in our psychological processes is reflected by changes in the functions or structures of the brain.

It doesn't surprise that the outcome and effects of these therapies have been studied on the social and psychological levels. Changes in social functioning, personality, psychological abilities, and symptoms were carefully measured. These changes are, in a way, brain mechanisms.

This approach looks for non-physical causes for mental disorders, understanding that experiences such as depression, addictions, obsessive-compulsive disorder, and schizophrenia arise out of multiple complex factors. It considers genetic, epigenetic (not inherited through DNA), psychological, and cultural conditions. As a syndrome strategy, it identifies sets of symptoms as syndromes related to sets of conditions (Hayes and Lillis 2012, 5).

Conceived by Steven Hayes in 1980, it was developed into a full-fledged therapy model by his students and colleagues, especially Kirk Strohal and Kelly Wilson in 1999 (ibid, xv).

These researchers were concerned with finding a more successful way to ease human suffering and help people address problems within relationships and daily living. They were puzzled as to why people often suffer even in conditions of affluence. They see human suffering as common despite the high-level accomplishments that any individual may make. Hayes and his students and colleagues thought it best to examine the root causes more than the symptoms. Considering the context of each case, this approach is inductive and process-oriented for comprehending human misery and failure (ibid, 6).

Very few therapists practiced ACT until the new millennium (ibid, 15). That may be because Cognitive Behavior Therapy (CBT) was in vogue until the end of the 20th century. As CBT declined, ACT carried on and grew.

History

As behavioral therapy based on empiricism rose through the 1960s, there was little research on psychological intervention methods. Empirical results were easily measured, and theoretical foundations tended to be weak, according to Hayes and Lillis (2012, 16), based on humanism and psychoanalysis. Misdiagnosis frequently occurred, they say, citing some of Freud's cases where analytical symbolism revolving around things like defecation and sex went too far.

Perhaps in a backlash to analytical psychology, reliance spread on clearly measurable empirical evidence observed in controlled conditions. Behavioral principles were rigidly set, and the application of technologies rigidly tested. ACT arose out of behavioral therapy but made concessions to psychoanalytical and humanist approaches. It, thus, began as a less conventional approach that demanded direct and overt modifications to the behavior of the treated person (ibid, 18). Acceptance and commitment therapists want to see behavioral changes. Still, they also want to explore the underlying human issues to problem behavior. They view social conditions as deep, rich, and complex (ibid.).

Behaviorism sets great stimulus-response training and behavior choices. It is inadequate because it does not consider language and higher-level cognitive processes –meaning, conceptualization, and symbolism (ibid.). In laboratory experiments, only the external factors that the scientist can manipulate can be

189

altered. Cognition, internal processes of the mind, were harder to decipher. Cognition psychology was likewise insufficient. Models sprouted up, but the evidence for them was lacking. Achieving practical results from cognitive therapy seemed too difficult. However, Cognitive Behavior Therapy began to develop, teaching clients to acknowledge and self-direct themselves to correct "behavioral errors" (ibid, 20) while tending to abandon evidence-based treatments in the beginning. Alternative approaches started to be put forward.

Chapter 2: Strategies for Relief From Anxiety And To Improve Your Quality Of Life

Here, you will be introduced to just a few more techniques that are not as specific as those you have read about thus far. Here, you will learn about strategies that can be used in a wider range to develop the changes in your life that you wish to see. You will learn how to improve your general quality of life as well.

Strategies for Anxiety Relief

When you suffer from anxiety, it can become easy to get so caught up in the negative that you feel as though there is no hope for survival or freedom from the negativity. You get so stuck in that negative mindset that you fear that you will be there forever. However, that could not be further from the truth. You can, in fact, achieve anxiety relief.

Realistic Thinking

This is one more method of controlling your emotions and reasoning—when you engage in realistic thinking, you identify which thoughts are realistic. If you find unrealistic ideas, you are making them reasonable somehow. When you do this, you are essentially ensuring that you can correct thoughts on the go.

The first step to this process is knowing what you are thinking about in the first place. This is where your mindfulness tools come in. When you utilize those skills, you can identify where your mind goes, and that can help you locate all sorts of loose ends and thoughts that are unrealistic. Identify which of those thoughts make you feel bad somehow, and target those. For example, if you feel devastated that your date night you get weekly fell through, you have an unrealistic thought. Pay attention to how that makes you feel and identify the thought behind it. Why do you care about why you were unable to attend your date? Yes, this is similar to identifying negative automatic thoughts. In fact, that is exactly what you are doing here—you want to identify that negative thought so you can simply correct it with one short sentence.

Your answer to being upset about the date night may be that you do not want your partner to feel like you no longer love him because your partner always leaves you. You really want to make sure this one is the one. When you stop and look at that thought, you may recognize that the thought is quite the overreaction for missing a single date night. You remind yourself of that: You tell yourself that if a relationship were destroyed over a single date, then it was not a worthwhile relationship in the first place. By correcting that thought and making it more positive, you essentially fix the problem in your mind. You can calm yourself down a bit because you see the truth.

Seeking out a Therapist

Sometimes, the best thing you can do for persistent anxiety is seeking out a therapist. This is far easier said than done, but even if you feel like you do not need one, it may be worthwhile to consider. Therapists are not evil or a waste of money—they are actually quite useful. They can help you navigate through all sorts of negative thoughts and ensure that you can better handle yourself no matter what the situation at hand. You will get real-time feedback, telling you how you are doing and whether you are making a mistake in executing something you are doing.

Suppose you think that actively seeking out a therapist may be useful to you. In that case, you should make an appointment with your primary care provider to get advice or a referral. Sometimes, insurance will not cover any therapy without a referral, so this is one way to skip that step. As a bonus, your doctor will also ensure that there are no physical causes to the symptoms you are having, particularly surrounding your heart. You only have one of those, after all.

When you have gotten a referral for therapy, you can then begin to consider what kind of therapy would work best for you. Would you want a cognitive behavioral therapist? Traditional talk therapy? Some other kind? There are several different forms of therapy for anxiety, and ultimately, the one you pursue will be your own choice. When you have decided, you should then check out any in your area that accepts your insurance, or if they do not, that is affordable to you.

When you do eventually meet your therapist, keep an open mind and keep in mind that you need to click with the individual. You want to make sure you feel comfortable with the person that you are talking to. However, it is hard to judge that after a single session in many instances. Try to meet with a therapist at least twice before deciding that he or she is not right for you. Finding the right match for you is essential if you want to make sure that your therapeutic process is effective.

Worst Case Scenario Roleplay

Another technique some people find useful in managing anxiety is to engage in what is known as a worst-case scenario roleplay. In this case, you are challenged to imagine the worst possible ending to whatever you are anxious about. For example, suppose you are anxious about getting a divorce. In that case, you may then stop and consider what the worst-case scenario would look like—you plan out exactly what would happen. Perhaps you fear that your soon-to-be-ex will get full custody of the kids and get to keep possession of the house, leaving you with a massive child support bill for children you never see. Your children are quickly alienated from you, so they no longer want to interact with you at all. Maybe this goes a step further, and you lose all contact with your children. All you become is a wallet for all of the activities, medical insurance, and everything else the children need. At the same time, your ex marries someone else who gets to be the parent to your child that you wish you could be.

Stop and play out that situation. Then, you need to consider how realistic that is. How often do parents lose all contact with their children unless they do something bad for them? How often do you hear about people who do drugs retaining custody of their children or people who abuse their kids retaining custody? How likely is your ex to stop, take the kids, and run? Why would your ex want to do something so bad for your children, who would benefit from having both parents present, barring any abuse or neglect?

As you dismantle the situation, you start to realize that the chances of your worst-case scenario actually happening are exceedingly slim, and that gives you some of the comforts you need to move on without further anxiety over the subject.

Play out a Situation to the End

The last of the methods to cope with the anxiety you will learn is playing out a situation until the end. In this case, you will be thinking about considering your fear and allowing yourself to think through what will really happen in that particular situation. For example, perhaps your fear is that you will lose your job when you go to work tomorrow because you were sick for a week and missed a lot of work. Your anxiety keeps you up, and you know you need to sleep, but you just cannot manage to do so.

In this case, what you should do is stop, think about that fear, and then play out how you think the situation will go. If you are afraid that you will be fired when you show up, imagine what you think will realistically happen. Perhaps you imagine that you will arrive, and your boss will come over. Rather than telling you that you need to talk in private, your boss asks you if you are doing better and says that you were missed. He does not say a word about being sick because he is a good boss and understands that people get sick sometimes.

Because you play out the realistic ending, you can contrast it with the worst-case scenario that you may have also developed for that particular situation. You can look at the two and realize that you will be okay. You know that being fired is a possibility, but it is always a possibility. There is always a chance of being fired from any job for any reason. You can then relax a bit and tell yourself that things will be fine, which enables you to finally fall asleep and get the rest that you need.

Strategies for Improving Quality of Life

Now, you will be walked through several steps to improve the quality of life you have. These are other ways that can benefit you that are not necessarily directly designed for anxiety in particular but can help you find more enjoyment and value in your life. As you go through this process and read through these four different activities, imagine how you could apply any of these possibilities to your own life to develop the life you want to lead. You may realize that there are several different ways you could implement more positivity into your life that may have a pleasant side-effect of lessening your anxiety.

Goal Setting

The first skill you are being introduced to is how to set proper goals. Goals are one of those things that everyone sets, but most people set poorly, and then they fail and give up without much more thought. However, that is largely due to not creating well-formed goals. When you know how to set effective goals, you can up the chances that you can succeed.

When you are setting goals, you have three key things that should never be the subject of a goal: your goal cannot be an avoidant goal, a goal rooted firmly in an emotional state, or a goal in which you wish to go back in time. Each of these three subjects for your goal will do nothing but set you up for failure, and they should be avoided at all costs.

When you are setting a goal, however, you want to make sure that it is SMART. When you make a SMART goal, you are reminded of an acronym that is crucial to good goal-setting. You want your goal to be specific, measured, achievable, and relevant. All five components work together to create a goal that you can actually accomplish, enabling it to be more effective in general.

When you begin this process, start by making it specific: You want your goal to define exactly what you want to do. If you want to learn to cut your anxiety symptoms, you can put that down. Notice how cutting the frequency of your anxiety symptoms is not an emotional state but rather seeking to eliminate how often your feelings of anxiety trigger an anxiety attack.

Next, you want to make your goal measurable. This is difficult when you are talking about something that is not easily quantifiable. Still, the easiest way is to transfer whatever you are doing into a percentage. Perhaps you want to cut your anxiety attacks by 50%. You could also want to build up to running an 8-minute mile or lifting 300 lbs., or anything else. The key point here is to make sure there is a numerical way to measure your success.

Third, you want your goal to be achievable. Spend the time to identify whether the goal you have set is something that you can do, and if it is, you want to break it up into smaller steps. If your goal is to learn to control anxiety attacks, you may decide to eliminate the 10% a week. If it is to write a novel, you may assign 1000 words a day.

Fourth, you want to check to see if it is relevant to you. Does this goal have a significant impact on you? Is it something you can actually do? Do you want to do it? If you can answer yes to those questions, move on.

Lastly, you want to set a deadline for your goal, setting a time limit during which you will work toward the goal. This keeps you from going at it indefinitely, never really claiming you have failed because you never had a limit in the first place.

Together, those five steps culminate into a SMART goal, making it easier to achieve. In this instance, you have a goal: you will eliminate 50% of your anxiety attacks within 3 months, eliminating the 10% a week until you reach your goal. That gives you an action plan in which you know exactly what you are doing and guides your behavior to ensure that you actually accomplish your goal.

Positivity Challenge

The positivity challenge is designed to get you thinking in positives more frequently than you already were. This is essentially the quintessential emotional intelligence development challenge. When you engage in this process, you effectively teach yourself to think in positives more frequently than you already were. The hope of doing so is encouraging you to engage in positive thinking more frequently, encouraging the development of engaging in positive thinking more. When you engage in this challenge, you are essentially forcing yourself to engage in positive thinking.

The challenge is that you must replace it with two more positive thoughts every time you have a negative thought. The positive thoughts must be related to whatever you were just thinking negatively about, forcing yourself to find the good in even negative situations or that you hated. By recognizing the positive, you teach your mind to think in positives.

For example, imagine that you tried out a new pizzeria that opened near your home. It was heavily advertised, and you figured you would give it a shot. You ate it and discovered that the big gimmick was that it was made with cauliflower crust, which you learned that you hated. You found yourself thinking that the food sucked and you hated it.

196

In thinking that negative thought, you then had to engage in two positive thoughts about the pizza. The first could be that you are thankful that you were able to eat something healthy and nutritious, recognizing the nutritional value in eating something made almost entirely with vegetables. The second thought could then be that you can get food regularly in the first place. You recognize that several people out there are food insecure and would not actually be able to get food as easily as you could. In engaging in those positive thoughts, you realize that it was not all bad after all and that eating there could have been much worse.

Understanding Body Language

In learning to better read other people's body language, you do two things: you teach yourself how to read others, so you know what they are thinking at any given moment in time. You also ensure that you can develop the skills to get yourself acting in ways that are directly related to the mood that you would like to be in. Remember, fake it until you make it. When you learn to read other people's body language, you can better engage with yours. Further, you also develop the idea of recognizing your own body language and learning what your own body language means. In doing so, you can better understand your own moods when you are struggling to read them.

Chapter 3: Core Processes in Act

ACT addresses every principle inflexibility mechanism simply described, with the overall purpose of developing mental flexibility. It can touch the existing second higher very well as an aware person and regulate or maintain in conduct to meet favored functions on the idea of what the scenario affords.

Each of those fields is conceptualized as a high-quality mental capacity; this is instigated, modeled, and assisted in the route of treatment. All the techniques of ACT are designed to foster those versatility traits. Consequently, this method may be considered as a foundation of the remedy itself.

Such approaches are well worth noting now no longer simplest due to the fact they may be the favorable comparisons to the mechanisms of psychopathology, however additionally due to the fact they may be scaled as much as dyad or organization level. This is why variation mechanisms are so carefully related to the behavioral abilities of ACT: the version shows that those approaches want to be pondered in therapist-purchaser relationships on the remedy stage. He added the versatility techniques in ACT, encompass a blueprint for a green healing courting and a hit treatment.

Acceptance

Acceptance encourages tolerance of personal occasions as an opportunity for experiential avoidance. This way calls for the energetic and conscientious popularity of particular times that our beyond offers upward thrust to without undue tries to alternate their incidence or type, especially while doing so might reason mental harm. Clients dealing with fear, for example, are taught to experience tension as an emotion, absolutely and without intervention, and to allow movement in their soreness with the shape of mental misery.

Acceptance, in ACT, isn't always a lead to itself. Alternatively, tolerance is advertised as a manner of growing value-primarily based practice. Acceptance is fostered with the aid of using sports that sell a wealthy, flexible courting with reports formerly ignored. For example, feelings are converted into items described, complicated reactions are damaged down into

198

experiential elements, and interest is given to the surprisingly diffused components of the occasions avoided. To a few degrees, they experience like stimulation tests; however, they have the feature of growing versatility of choice and reaction in place of genuinely reducing emotional response.

When popularity is scaled to the extent of the healing courting, accepting and modeling demand is critical for therapists. At the same time, their very own tough moments come into remedy. Acceptance also can be carried out to people, families, or different groups with the aid of using kindness toward others; that's why a strong partnership exists among ACT and compassion-centered remedies.

Cognitive Defusion

ACT is one of the cognitive and behavioral healing procedures; however, like different so-known as 1/3 technology CBT strategies. It now no longer includes one among conventional CBT's center principles: enhancing distorted or unrealistic mind is an essential precursor to profound behavioral alternate.

This significant conventional argument for CBT has the simplest obtained little medical assist. From an RFT factor of view, this is no surprise.

The quandary is this: efforts to alternate social networks (i.e., questioning styles) commonly make those networks bigger to make the person's incidence (e.g., the concept or emotion) even greater critical. In technical phrases, however, a contextual context is often a logical framework.

People are commonly excessively centered at the terrible non-public interactions. By flip, they have got decreased their behavioral repertoire.

It might not be maximally powerful to spend even more significant time in those fields. The task of converting cognitive content material ultimately and carefully is tough because the mind is historic, regularly automatic, and typically well-established in clinically applicable regions. It can take a long term to alternate them, or even. At the same time, the attempt is "a hit," they may be nonetheless now no longer absolutely long past, as proven with the aid of using the propensity for older verbal/cognitive networks to reappear below stress.

199

In truth, people are typically very inclined to try to suppress or get rid of unsightly minds and emotions. They might have already tried to do so. However, this regularly has paradoxical outcomes, usually doubtlessly growing the frequency and severity of those encounters, in addition to their capacity to modify conduct. Although cognitive stimulation strategies aren't typically meant to be suppressive, this propensity uses such techniques dangerous. Nevertheless, little or no records show that cognitive battle and development are useful or a first-rate mechanism to alternate conduct. So far, research recommends that those strategies are pretty ineffective or maybe terrible in a few situations.

RFT shows one-of-a-kind methods: that as a way to alternate the jobs of mind of our lives, we no longer want to rotate the content material of the brain. The social and cultural dynamics of literality, the giving of reason, and emotional management typically dictate the jobs of intellectual mastering.

The outcomes of questioning movement in contexts consisting of those are machine-like; mind or emotions appear to reason movements simply as one billiard ball putting a 2nd reason the second one ball to transport in.

In the traditional behavioral scenario, we want to alternate the mindset and alternate the practice. With a theoretical factor of view, though, we will see that the outcomes of notion appear simplest to be mechanical: they seem to reason acts; however, they do now no longer in truth. Alternatively, person thoughts are associated simplest inside a given context to specific movements or feelings. Therefore, they affect the mind that may be modified to use positive organizing meanings (e.g., with the assistance of using defusion or popularity) without first having to alternate their type. Those perspectives don't want to regulate. In truth, research recommends that contextual techniques can also additionally result in a long-lasting alternate of conduct greater quick than techniques that immediately goal the content material of mind and emotions.

From an ACT angle, while clients interact in warfare with their very own non-public reports as though their lives trusted it (as appears to be the case while the mind is taken actually) and create testimonies to justify and give an explanation for their movements, the end result may be an amplification of struggling and a pressure of response, each of which may be difficult to overcome. A foremost motive for this has an effect on is that those very movements set up ubiquitous and static systems of literality, the giving of reason, and the law of feelings.

Defusion, a summary phrase meaning "to opposite fusion," refers back to the system of organizing non-literal meanings where language may be interpreted as an intentional, persevering, interactive phenomenon that's historical in nature and contemporary at the existing second. This manner is looking at the mind with a mindset of dispassionate curiosity, in much less technical phrases.

Language and notion can continuously be determined as language and knowledge on the second. In place of being a slave to it, we will watch what the thoughts say.

A word is visible as a phrase, now no longer what it might appear to say. Having a non-literal meaning loosens the affiliation among language and conduct, giving more versatility in manner. We oughtn't to be encouraged with the aid of using our mind or allow our movements to decide them.

Defusion is possibly certainly considered one among ACT's maximum precise capabilities. Scores of defusion techniques for a wide variety of medical displays had been developed. For example, a terrible notion may be considered dispassionately, echoed loudly till it will become only a tone, meaningless, or appeared as an outwardly visible phenomenon with the aid of using assigning it a name, height, color, intensity, shape, or different bodily attributes. The result of the defusion is commonly a decline in the notion's believability or connection to it, in place of a sudden boom in its duration. Therefore, defusion isn't always a technique of suppressing feelings or maybe changing the effect on the mind. The concept is to have a greater aware view of opinions, which complements behavioral versatility related to selected beliefs.

Defusion techniques are directed at taking pictures of language structures in movement and getting them below qualitative effect to check out in place of visible from wherein possible. Defusion, while scaling to the healing courting, promotes an open, non-judgmental area in remedy wherein all mind is open for review. This manner growing a non-judgmental courting wherein judgments don't entice the purchase or, if they do, the therapist accepts this after each movement.

Being Present

ACT allows steady, non-judgmental verbal exchange with incidents of social and environmental importance as they happen. The goal is the know-how of the existing-second, wherein attention is paid to the right here and now that this is flexible, dynamic, and voluntary. Humans are adaptable, touchy, and conscious of the opportunities and mastering possibilities supplied with the aid of using the contemporary scenario while in contact with the existing second. Compared to dwelling in a beyond or destiny conceptualized, the belief of the existing-second is higher clean and touchy and much less good and fused. Suppose touch with the existing second is inadequate. In that case, the conduct tends to be greater ruled with the aid of using fusion, avoidance, and motive, ensuing in greater of the same manner that happened in the beyond, commonly. It forecloses on new opportunities.

Throughout ACT, being a gift is associated with the advent of experience of self-as-system— a sample of open self-awareness marked with the aid of using steady statement and concise marking of feelings, emotions, and different non-public occasions in a defused and unjudgmental way. An experience of belief is likewise welcomed, so human beings can admire higher very well the wealthy series of reports which are supplied at any given second.

If socially scaled, the focus of the existing second contributes to an environment wherein the continuing system in the healing courting itself is observed and used as a foundation for flexibility work. In addition to the purchaser, the psychiatrist is known as upon to be a gift and to concentrate on something that matters.

Self-as-Context and Flexible Perspective Taking

From an RFT point of view, it argues that language schooling calls for cognitive constructs related to insight (technically known as deictic framing RFT). Those abilities in flip create an experience of self as a significant locus. From an RFT factor of view, the self is greater like an experiential experience or area than an occasion itself. Remember what those questions

202

have in a not unusual place, for example: "All did you eat?" What are you going to want? " Who have you been speaking to?" Why have you been doing this?" Why have you ever accomplished this?" The simplest element they have got in not the unusual place is wherein the solution lies: the" I "who will solution all of the questions.

ACT facilitates human beings to talk this experience of self-as-context to use experiential reports and metaphors— a steady and stable "I" from which occasions are perceived, a fact that consists of however are likewise cut loose those occasions. This system facilitates human beings to disentangle among our ears from the phrase machine. The intention is to assist people in creating a greater secure experience of themselves as witnesses or experiencers, no matter the specific enjoyment they have got on the second.

Additionally, inside awareness or focus, the boundaries of knowledge and attention cannot be contacted. The angle fostered with using human language can result in transcendence, giving regular humans enjoy a non-secular aspect. Communication is a double-edged sword. Indeed, one among its maximum high-quality functions is selling a sense of transcendence.

It can also be useful to set up this transcendent experience of self in reducing attachment to content material. This concept became one of the seeds from which each ACT and RFT grew. Proof exists of its significance to the language capabilities that underlie such phenomena as empathy, compassion, and thought theory. A transcendent experience of self is essential in ACT, in component, because human beings may be conscious in their persevering with a float of interactions without connection to them from this angle. Thus, this naturalistic, metaphysical aspect of human enjoyment fosters defusion and recognition.

The different motive that taking self-as-context and angle is essential to ACT is that they may be the number one supplier of the version's social extension. In RFT, you and I have the three critical angle-taking sets, right here instead of there and now as opposed to then. Such contexts are significant to how human beings expand a clean experience of angle and information that their view isn't like others'.

Both interplay frames are bidirectional and having to study the sector from the viewpoint of I-right here-now mechanically permits human beings the capacity to analyze the industry from you-then. Metaphorically, as an utterly aware member of the organization, you get to reveal up in the back of your eyes simultaneously as you notice that others are privy to theirs. A self-focus in angle-taking connects us to the reports of others and from different instances and locations. The extension of awareness is why self-as-context is significant to religion and transcendence, empathy, love, and self-compassion encounters. Such human abilities are partly nonverbal (for example, they affect replicate neurons). However, they are considerably more suitable with the aid of using verbal interactions now regarded to assist angle-taking.

Defining Valued Directions

The versatility mechanisms stated above are regularly intended to disrupt temporal and evaluative language in dwelling locations wherein those styles of communication are surprisingly ineffective. The approaches of rationalization of values and constant movement attention on strengthening language in the one's regions wherein it's miles maximum probably to be carried out effectively. ACT asks human beings to step returned from lifestyle's regular issues and study what offers meaning to their lives. Values are decided on attributes of actions that could in no way be acquired as an entity. However, they may be instantiated in acts of being and doing second with the aid of using the latter. These are versions of verbs and adverbs, now no longer nouns (e.g., To lovingly connect or truly participate). ACT uses several techniques to assist people in choosing dependent lifestyle paths in one-of-a-kind domain (e.g., families, task, spirituality), even disrupting behavioral mechanisms that might contribute to experiential evasion, social conformity, or cognitive fusion established decisions. So in the ACT context, none of those assertions mirror authentic values: "I must experience responsible if I didn't admire Q," "I respect Z if my mom desires me," "I might appreciate X," and "A precise character must admire Y." The first is evasive, the second one is obedient, and the remaining are fused. Valuations are options. Values are the solution to the question, "What might you pick in an international wherein you may pick to have your lifestyles be about something?"

204

Values are ACT's linchpin, so ACT's honesty and effectiveness depend on them. Through ACT, recognition, defusion, being a gift, and the different essential resilience mechanisms aren't ended via themselves. Instead, they clean the route for a lifestyle; this is greater critical, well suited with principles.

ACT takes a role in opposition to the fact primarily based totally on a particular shape of relational philosophy known as practical contextualism. Reality is described on the idea of workability, and in impact, workability is associated with the values selected. Fact is a shape of verbal exchange in the greater conventional, mechanistic worldview. Using a map metaphor, if the marks at the map imply precisely wherein matters are in the actual international on every different subject, then the plan is authentic. Pragmatic fact seeks its validity most straightforward in some instances, relying on the viability of something being examined in that context. So even as a paper map of the sector should work (be authentic) to discern out the way to sail around the industry, locating your manner around New York City may be quite useless (now no longer genuine). You'd want a metropolis or kingdom map for that. In the general correspondence established context, is one map much less legitimate than the opposite? No. No. Yet one map of route works pleasant while looking for your manner around New York City. This relational method explains how ACT determines fact. ACT forgets the fact that comes from an authentic experience (i.e., correspondence) in choosing truth diagnosed with the aid of using what's useful in motivating human beings to stay prosperous, meaningful lives led with the help of using their beliefs.

In opposition to fact, this modern method facilitates ACT therapists to stay clear of usual mental pitfalls for people who get caught in debates about whether their personal reports are proper or wrong or whether their view of the sector is correct or inaccurate. Truth is nearby in terms of people and is decided in phrases of whether or not a positive manner of questioning or appearing is useful or unhelpful in searching for a pleasant lifestyle. For example, consider a purchaser believes that he's fundamentally unlikeable, that his lifestyles have long passed down the tubes, and that he's going to in no way be capable of having a lifestyle of loving relationships and a family, even though he feels that is deeply critical for him. An ACT therapist might now no longer attend to the rational or irrational nature of proof for and in

205

opposition to those minds. Alternatively, the psychiatrist must focus on what those emotions are at the disposal of and the way enjoy and suggests them to be useful in transferring the character toward a lifestyle that represents the values he has decided on. The problem in the room will probably be whether or not the patron is inclined to have those minds once they arise and nonetheless flow in the route of his selected values, now no longer what the mind purport to suggest about the kingdom of the sector, the patron, or the questioning itself.

Values studies are regularly socially associated with our subculture due to how critical social interplay and teamwork are. Only aesthetic beliefs (for example, introducing splendor into the sector) commonly contain acts of collaboration and generosity (for instance, assisting others to recognize brilliance).

Committed Action

Finally, ACT encourages clients to construct larger and large styles of powerful movement related to the values selected. The Latin roots of the phrase "commitment" suggest an experience of wearing ahead something with (com) a "send" or a "mission" (mittere). Committed practice, in a manner, manner surely embracing a value-primarily based lifestyle as a venture wherein the advent of large and large styles of conduct related to described beliefs is itself respected.

The "how" of making behaviors can then be a topic that has meaning inside that mission. When a slip happens, human beings have the choice to make a brand-new choice: do they construct a sample of gratitude, slipping, after which leaving the venture, or will they build an example of appreciation, sliding, and returning to the challenge again? Planning for those moments and organizing one's surroundings in such moments to foster value-primarily based selections is what engaged movement appears like. In this practice, ACT clinicians must benefit from any proof-primarily based totally system regarded to sell alternate in conduct: verbal exchange, obtaining skills, influencing techniques, placing dreams, or something else. Furthermore, variation mechanisms had been proven to boom the impact of those kinds of alternate in conduct.

206

Unlike values that are continuously instantiated; however, concrete dreams constant with benefits may be attained in no way found out as an object. ACT protocols nearly regularly contain homework related to hopes for alternate in short-, medium-, and long-time period conduct. In flip, other behavioral efforts result in touch with mental barriers addressed via different approaches of flexibility (e.g., popularity, defusion).

When socially expanded, engaged movement includes assisting different human beings' commitments. As a result, ACT research gravitated closer to work in social justice-associated regions, in component due to the fact seeing the misery in others needs a solution.

Chapter 4: What Is the Best: ACT Or CBT?

Envision a remedy that doesn't undertake to reduce facet outcomes anyhow, as a facet-impact, receives indication lower. A solution firmly rooted in the culture of empirical science, but with great emphasis on values, forgiveness, acceptance, compassion, dwelling in the gift second, and gaining access to a transcendent feel of oneself. A remedy so tough to outline that it's been described as an "existential-humanistic cognitive-behavioral remedy."

ACT is a behavioral remedy centered on attention that contradicts maximum Traditional psychology's floor rules. It uses a numerous combination of talents in analogy, Catch-22, and care, along with a great show-off of experiential sports and qualities, drove behavior mediations.

ACT has been proven to achieve success with some psychiatric conditions: insomnia, ADHD, occupational tension, continual pain, terminal most cancers trauma, anxiety, PTSD, anorexia, opioid addiction, drug misuse, or even schizophrenia.1 A record through Bach & Hayes2 determined that with the most beneficial 4 hours of ACT, medical institution reentry degrees amongst schizophrenic sufferers fell through 50 percent over the following six months.

ACT's Objectives

ACT's purpose is to create a colorful and significant lifestyle while at the equal time acknowledging the struggle that, in the long run, follows it. "ACT" is a superb abbreviation; due to the fact this remedy is ready to take powerful motion, this is guided through our values and wherein we're completely involved. We can most effectively construct a significant lifestyle through conscientious practice. Of course, while we strive to create such an existence, we will face all types of obstacles in the shape of uncomfortable and unwelcome "personal encounters" (thought, picture, emotion, feeling, desire, and memory). ACT acquires attention competencies as a powerful manner of managing those personal studies.

What Is Mindfulness?

At the factor, after I speak with clients about care, I represent it as: "Deliberately sporting interest for you enjoy at this very second with

208

transparency, intrigue, and receptivity. There are several factors to care about: remembering dwelling for the prevailing minute; connecting absolutely in what you do, instead of "getting lost" for your considerations; and allowing your feelings to be as they appear to be, letting them journey each which manner, instead of trying to govern them. Indeed, even the maximum terrible opinions, observations, improvements, and snapshots can appear much less frightening or overpowering while we see our studies with trustworthiness and responsiveness. Mindfulness could, as a result, be capable of helping us with converting our collaboration with lousy contemplations and feelings in a way that decreases their impact and effect on our lives.

ACT vs. Other Approaches Focused on Mindfulness

ACT is one of the supposed "third waves" of conventional treatments—along with Dialectical Behavior Therapy (DBT), Mindfulness-Based Cognitive Therapy (MBCT), and Mindfulness-Based Stress Reduction (MBSR) — all of which location tremendous accentuation at the development of care talents.

Introduced through Steve Hayes in 1986, ACT becomes the primary of such "third wave" interventions and now has a complete series of medical statistics to aid its efficacy. In the fifties and sixties, the "first phase" of healing remedy targeting specific behavioral strategies and used techniques associated with operational and conventional conditioning concepts.

In many respects, ACT differs from DBT, MBCT, and MBSR. For example, MBSR and MBCT have essentially manualized remedy procedures to be used with pressure and melancholy care units. DBT is often a combination of social competencies, schooling, and character remedy, mainly designed to deal with borderline personality disorder in a population. Interestingly, ACT may be applied in an extensive scope of scientific populaces with people, couples, and gatherings, each as a short remedy or a long-haul remedy. In fact, rather than adopting a manualized technique, ACT encourages the practitioner to construct and individualize their mindfulness techniques or maybe co-create them for clients. ACT is the most effective Modern psychotherapy produced according to its original human language and belief that looks at the project.

Another important distinction is that ACT sees formal attention meditation as the most effective, indeed considered one among many approaches to train attention competencies.

Mindfulness talents are "divided" into four sub-sets:

- *Acceptance*

- *Cognitive defusion*

- *Communication with the prevailing second*

- *The Observing Self*

The spectrum of ACT methods to enhance those competencies is extensive and keeps growing, spanning from traditional breath mediation to cognitive defusion.

What's Unique in the ACT?

ACT is the most effective Western psychotherapy based in tandem with its primary human language and belief studies program-Relational Framework Theory (RFT). Nonetheless, searching through RFT extensive is past the attain of this paper.

As a conspicuous distinction to maximum Western psychotherapy, ACT has no lower manifestations as an objective. ACT has no lower indications as an objective. This way relies upon the view that the progressing undertaking to free "manifestations" anyhow honestly makes a scientific issue. When a person is marked as a "manifestation," a battle is made with the "facet impact."

An "indication" is something "obsessive" through definition and something we must be trying to dispose of. In the ACT, the factor is to strategize our courting with our tough contemplations and sentiments, so we in no way once more see them as "facet outcomes." Instead, we discern out the form to see them as risk-free intellectual occasions, no matter whether they're awkward and transient. Amusingly, it is thru this technique that ACT honestly accomplishes a lower facet outcome—but as a result and now no longer as an objective.

210

Chapter 5: Advantages of ACT Over Traditional CBT

This remedy is an empirical query in the cease. Having taken into consideration that during a theoretical sense, we will have a take a observe the viable advantages. A handful of research, proper now, is regarded at once and that they tend to be medium to small. Only some are posted. One of these rarely mentions final results as it changed into a chunk about the alternate procedure. In this manner, we've got some distance to head earlier than this inquiry is precisely replied.

Here are the examinations which have been performed as such some distance: Rob Zettle, who organized with Beck, did little randomized preliminaries for wretchedness on the ACT as opposed to CT–one making use of singular ACT and CT, and the opposite making use of bunch ACT and CT remedy. Right now, a bigger randomized multi-web trial is underway. He located Cohen's d's at publishing among ACT and CT of 1.23 (in my view brought) and 0.53 (organization) in his research (see the ACT Handout), observed through 0.92 and 0.75. Yet the N changed into very small. In the man or woman, have a take a watch, the ACT organization transformed into the handiest an N of six, and about ten or so in the organization have a take a find.

The different four research are present-day and haven't begun to be posted. Ann Branstetter finished a randomized end-stage most cancers misery trial. Ann changed into conventional CBT and used CBT procedures, which she notion could assist (together with cognitive restructuring). There turned into no comply with-up because the individuals had most cancers on the cease of the stage; however, at week 12, ACT had a Cohen's d of 0.9 compared to conventional CBT on death ache. It is possible to electronic mail to her; she is at the State University of Southwest, Missouri.

Jennifer Block's dissertation at Albany (simply employed as a school member at LaSalle) compared ACT and CBGT in social phobia and located a Cohen's d of .45 in prefer of ACT as in comparison to conventional CBT on behavioral (status up and speaking) degree.

Carmen Luciano's crew at Almeria University simply did a smoking trial evaluating ACT and a CBT package deal utilized by a Spanish most cancers society and located a Cohen's d of .42 at a one-year smoking cessation comply with up.

In a feasibility experiment, Raimo Lappalainen and his colleagues at the University of Tampere offer proof contrasting ACT and popular CBT (the usage of CBT tactics associated with behavioral studying, together with abilities schooling or publicity) in a clinic. One ACT and one conventional CBT customer have been randomly assigned to starting scholar therapists (N= 14 every condition). Problems ranged throughout the same old spectrum of outpatients however have been mainly tension and depression. On the SCL 90, the publish Cohen's d changed into .62 amongst ACT and CBT. The final results were given extra noteworthy at improvement. Lappalainen, R., Lehtonen, T., Skarp, E., Taubert, E., Ojanen, M., and Hayes, S. C. (2015). (2007). Effect of CBT and ACT fashions using mind studies learner specialists: A essential managed initial of adequacy. Change of practices, 31, 488-511. There changed into more reputation of ACT individuals at segment level; extremely good self-assurance for sufferers with CBT. Both correlated with outcomes. However, the handiest status nonetheless pertains to issues while partial correlations are calculated. Accidentally, the result changed into now no longer protected in the document yet, in self-assurance, ACT changed into soon notably higher compliance with-up than CBT.

At Drexel University, Evan Foreman and James Herbert pronounced comparable facts from their clinic: Forman, E. M., Herbert, J. D., Moitra, E., Yeomans, P. D. Geller and P. A. (2015). (2007). A randomized managed initial of acknowledgment and duty remedy and mental remedy for uneasiness and despondency for adequacy.

Alteration of conduct, 31(6), 772–799. In this study, one zero one heterogeneous outpatients have been randomly assigned both to conventional CT or to ACT reporting mild to excessive stages of tension or depression. It hired 23 junior therapists. Members getting CT and ACT confirmed vital and similar upgrades in gloom, anxiety, operating challenges, non-public satisfaction, existence fulfillment, and clinician-evaluated managing. "Observing" and "describing" one's interactions triggered effects for those in the CT network as in comparison to those in the ACT category, and those in the ACT organization, "experiential evasion," "performing with sensitivity," and "reputation" produced performance.

Likewise, it is recognized that ACT strategies can empower behavioral approach (which, through the manner, also are a part of the ACT version... Thus, this locating is an affirmation of the text itself in essences). Consider this study, for instance: Levitt, J. T., Brown, T. A., Orsillo, S. M. & Barlow, D. H. (2015). (2004). The effect of tolerance and repression of anger at the chance of carbon dioxide in sufferers with panic ailments mental and psychophysiological reactions. Compliance Treatment, 35, 747-766. In it, reputation strategies (at once drawn from the ACT book) did a higher process than manipulate techniques in selling a successful CO_2 fuel online publicity in sufferers with panic ailment.

In Campbell-Sills, L., Barlow, D. H., Brown, T. A., & Hofmann, S. G., a similar locating changed into accounted for. (2015). (2006). Impacts of concealment and acknowledgment of human beings with anxiety and a nation of thoughts trouble with passionate reactions. Research and Therapy in Behavior, 44, 1251-1263. Similarly, as with the above investigation, quick acknowledgment strategies precipitated decreased pulse in the course of advent to an aversive movie and other useful effects in the course of the publish-movie healing length that managed methodologies in on side and temperament cluttered human beings.

So, some distance, it seems like ACT might also have a small benefit over conventional CBT strategies in effects. There's a one-of-a-kind set of tactics worried in an alternate, and ACT strategies might also empower traditional behavioral plans.

Theoretically, these are the ACT version's strengths in comparison to CBT.

· The version is scalable and broadly applicable. When you have a take a observe the whole final results studies that have been posted thus far (RCTs, regulated time collection designs, and case research), the recognized troubles form a reasonably vast list: PTSD, hysteria, insomnia, racial bias, burnout, addiction, OCD, stress, paranoia, disease, diabetes, a couple of sclerosis, sports activities psychology, pharmacotherapy behaviors, pores, and skin selection, studying new strategies at work, opioid psychology.

· The putative tactics of alternate are correctly described in maximum regions with at the least marginally ok measures available. Such transition mechanisms are a small set and do now no longer range wildly from ailment to ailment.

• This fact appears the mediational analyzes are useful. Our depend has already pronounced or finished sixteen effective systematic mediational analyzes. The outcomes thus far are genuinely helpful. The mechanisms that have been examined drastically encompass recognition, defusion, beliefs, decided intervention, and mental resilience so that the maximum of the principle ACTs has a few proofs in mediational trials.

• When examined inductively, unique additives appear to work. ACT methods are impactful in each case and work in a theoretically coherent manner. These encompass all 6 Hexagon idea stages.

• The simple concept is intricately tied to generation and appears to work itself. For instance, we're coming near 10 RFT research in the ACT, which can be connected to the three senses of self; RFT work is approaching values; and so on.

For folks that agree with the handiest in guide RCTs, a whole lot of that solution might be rejected. But technological know-how records indicate you couldn't create innovative technological know-how using the most convenient outcomes research. In the Scientist-Practitioner, I (SCH) defined why (Hayes, Barlow, & Nelson-Gray, 1999). Nevertheless, in a nutshell, it's miles this. Without a desirable concept, the query of technological improvement is centered on principles of not unusual place sense, and it turns into empirically and theoretically daunting.

This way has to no longer be heard as "ACT adherents say RCTs aren't essential." Nearly 30 RCTs of ACT strategies have been posted through ACT folks. But they don't suffice! Development in technological know-how philosophy, simple principles, implemented concept, procedure specification of alternate, and efficacy is simply as essential (and extra indispensable in the lengthy-time period) as generation efficacy tests.

The clinical sport performed through the ACT / RFT / Contextual Psychology organization is this: to create a merely innovative psychology technological know-how that can extra effectively cope with the human condition. Yes, that's daring; however, why don't they have got assured objectives? Does the ACT organization stand or fall on RCTs as a degree of success? In the cease, indeed. But we need and declare but some other, even extra tough criteria: the outcome is to peer an extra simply beneficial psychology surface. That consists of principles, ideas, materials, basics, efficacy, preparation, distribution, etc.

We agree with its miles handiest honest to insist that ACT be measured towards its own, very tough criteria after thinking about the development of this effort. Examining ACT without inspecting RFT, for instance, is like searching at most cancers drug without searching on the physiology.

Like hare and tortoise, ACT follows a gradual and consistent course. We agree that conventional CBT hopped beforehand right into a lay cognition concept— which produced speedy development, however lengthy-time period issues. We'd take the gradual course of descriptive behavioral technological know-how, one step at a time. Which one is going the farthest? Let's have a feel. Let's be cautious and feature a peek.

The possibilities are you've heard in a single manner or some other about cognitive behavioral remedy (CBT). CBT is a gift moment, proof-primarily based solution that has been around because of the 1950s (in its maximum punctual structure) with interest in supporting people tasks and other ruinous concept examples and conduct.

Acceptance and Commitment Therapy (ACT –stated because the word ' act' instead of the letters) can be much less acquainted to you–for no different purpose than that it has now no longer been around for therefore lengthy. ACT is considered a "third wave" remedy–remedies that move past the extra conventional cognitive treatments and include different abilities into the mix (e.g., focus, visualization, non-public values, etc.) CBT and ACT are each conduct-primarily based remedies; however, they fluctuate in general from the factor of view of wondering. While CBT works through supporting you to perceive an alternate terrible or unfavorable mind, ACT continues that ache and soreness are a reality of existence–something we want to be snug

215

with if we need a happy, fulfilled life to live. That's why ACT encourages you to just accept all minds instead of looking to alternate them–each the best and the bad.

We're going to dig a touch more in-depth into each tactic and what units them aside to get a higher knowledge of ways this appears in remedy.

What is the simple meaning of the ACT remedy?

Consider if she could much like just to accept existence as it's miles–the best and the bad–as opposed to resisting it? That's precisely the factor of this sort of remedy.

At its core, the ACT is a mindfulness-primarily based remedy with the number one goal of improving mental flexibility and supporting you to construct an existence that suits your values and authentically feels you.

Using reputation, commitment, focus abilities, and conduct-converting techniques, ACT's consciousness supports you to receive existence's realities and accept mind for what they are–simply mind.

This sort of remedy is particularly useful if you are willing to shrink back from the issues of existence or keep away from them. That is considering that it urges you to attract in together along with your troubles head-on and draw closer to difficult emotions instead of trying to get them away from them.

How Does that Look in Practice?

ACT teaches you a way to make your mind extra inquisitive, in addition to strategies for a way to diffuse them.

Different strategies will encompass: time and again announcing a tough notion until its meaning disappears and handiest the sound remains.

To attempt to just accept a sense for what it's miles. For starters, shifting "No one likes me" to "I'm feeling..." teaches you a way to increase a dating with the troubles you're dealing with, as opposed to combating towards, together with depression.

The commitment to do so and convey effective adjustments to your existence is another essential component of ACT. ACT remedy will assist you in recognizing the matters that remember to you and create a plan that suits your values–and in the long run, brings extra meaning and motive into your existence.

CBT Therapy; what Does it Mean?

"Men are disturbed now no longer through matters, and however through the view, they take of them" –Epictetus CBT is a brief-time period remedy (ACT may be brought each in the brief and lengthy-time period) that facilities at the concept that it isn't the activities of existence itself that reason us issues, however as a substitute the manner we interpret them. In different words, the method we consider the arena impacts our conduct and, in the long run, how we feel.

One instance should be: if you usually expect the worst (as opposed to focusing on the effective), you may emerge as very careful in existence. This sort of wondering is restricting because you're in all likelihood to be held again from attaining your goals. This way, in turn, will, in all probability, go away, you feeling unhappy and unfulfilled.

Thoughts that appear to start as harmless can effortlessly get ingrained, distorting our international view.

CBT pursuits to perceive and update those distortions with other useful and rational methods of wondering. And while the mind alternate, generally conducts and emotions comply with suit.

Because of the character of this remedy style, it=-'s miles anticipated that you might play an energetic position for the duration of your periods, together with homework, studying, and abilities schooling, etc. This way may also encompass monitoring temper adjustments in a manner that will help you perceive tricky styles of notion and conduct.

Goal-orientated in its approach, you'll go away with your preliminary evaluation with a hard and fast plan and an explicit knowledge of what number of periods it'll take you to attain your goals (everywhere among 6–20 periods).

217

CBT + DBT + ACT

Both ACT and CBT, extra or much less, are amazing, proof-primarily based remedies that can reap enormous existence adjustments. At last, it's the whole lot about locating a method that resounds maximum with you.

Chapter 6: Developing psychological flexibility

Letting yourself experience adverse occasions is broken down into the six core procedures of ACT. Consider a few instances of psychological flexibility in practice and recognize that you have just a single life to live. The essential aim of Acceptance and Commitment Therapy (ACT) is to assist you with living your life with transparency, essentialness, and meaning. To do this, build your psychological flexibility. The first engineers of ACT, Steve Hayes, Kirk Strosahl, and Kelly Wilson, characterized psychological flexibility by; contacting the current minute completely as a conscious human being, all things considered, not as what it says it seems to be, and dependent on what the circumstance manages, changing or continuing in conduct in the service of picked values. Psychological flexibility in this manner implies being available to and accepting of every one of your thoughts and feelings while continuing ahead with what you need to do in life. That may sound clear, but it ends up being very difficult! This section presents psychological flexibility and its different parts. We depict the ideas of acceptance, defusion, contact with the current minute, self as setting, and committed action, which educates the ACT to take on psychological health and wellbeing.

Accepting Negative Thoughts and Feelings

While accepting positive thoughts, feelings, and memories is simple, accepting negative ones is a lot harder. Nobody needs to experience unwanted thoughts and feelings. The problem is that a reluctance to experience negative thoughts, feelings, or physical sensations can lead to counterproductive at-entices to change or maintain a strategic distance from them. ACT terms this evasion conduct experiential shirking. It is massively problematic because it brings you down a fruitless way. You sit around and vitality attempting to control things that can't be controlled. Consistently you may experience a scope of difficult psychological experiences that you'd preferably not have.

For example:

- *Unkind or basic thoughts ('I'm a disappointment')*

- *Low self-regard ('I'm dumb')*

- *Disturbing memories.*

219

- *Negative feelings (sadness, nervousness, weariness)*

- *Physical pain.*

These psychological experiences are, by definition, horrendous, and it's anything but difficult to perceive any reason you'd need to dodge, change, or limit them.

The problem is that you have almost no power over your thoughts and feelings for the accompanying reasons:

- You connect your thoughts to signs and occasions occurring around you. You have next to zero control, which implies managing or controlling what you believe is difficult, if workable.

- How you feel or what you recollect relies upon what's befallen you beforehand, which implies that you can no more change your emotions and memories than you can change your past. Your endeavors to control, limit, or dispose of unwanted thoughts, feelings, memories, or sensations will, in this way, just ever have constrained success. Undoubtedly, proof proposes that efforts to lessen or maintain a strategic distance from negative thoughts and feelings exacerbate them, notwithstanding aggravating them. Another problem with endeavoring to control or change your thoughts and feelings is that it occupies valuable time and vitality that is better spent concentrating on esteem-based living, living a life shaped by doing things essential to you. If you redirect your time and vitality into impacting your thoughts and feelings, your life can become smaller and progressively inflexible, and at last, you can head into a negative descending winding.

Your endeavors to change or desist from negative psychological experiences meddled with your capacity to do the things that you truly needed to do. And doing less of what makes a difference regularly leads to negative thoughts and feelings in the more drawn-out term.

Understand that pain is unavoidable

Even when you're doing things that you appreciate and care about, you, despite everything, experience negative minutes.

If you don't accept these negative experiences, you face a significant hindrance to getting on with the life you need to be living. For instance, as a significant aspect of a drive to be healthier, you may practice more and begin cycling to work. But cycling up slopes or vulnerable and wet will unavoidably lead to somewhat of physical discomfort. If you're not set up to experience such discomfort, you'll probably not be going to jump on your bicycle each morning — although you may truly need to be healthier! Psychologically flexibility is connected to being willing to experience the intermittent discomfort (mental and physical) that accompanies life. Doing so implies that your life is characterized emphatically by your values and not adversely by endeavors to dodge unsavory thoughts, feelings, and sensations. Weight reduction gives a genuine case of using psychological flexibility to lead a life as per your values.

Applying psychological flexibility to weight loss

A 2013 review of weight watchers in the UK found that 10 percent endured a day, 40 percent seven days, 30 percent a month, and a negligible 20 percent made it to a quarter of a year. The greater part of these said that the physical discomfort related to dieting — yearning, weariness, and desires — made them abandon their arrangement to get thinner. Individuals additionally re-ported, finding the social strain to eat challenging to stand up to. These 'effects' of dieting are altogether negative experiences. If you can't figure out how to accept them, dieting gets inconceivable. Developing an examination is showing exactly how basic acceptance is to esteem-based living. A 2014 US study separated understudies into two groups. It showed one acceptance-based strategy (for instance, acceptance of yearnings) and the other group traditional weight reduction strategies (checking calories, gauging every day, and working out). Following the mediation, the main group of understudies lost 1.57 kg each and figured out how to keep up that weight reduction for as long as a year; the benchmark group — poor fiends! — increased over 1 kg each. Brief acceptance-based intercession was more powerful than traditional approaches. One key to successful dieting (and surely significantly more in life) is to figure out how to live with and accept its complex parts. Concentrate on your aim of being slimmer instead of on the amount you detest feeling hungry.

Presenting the Six Core Processes of ACT

ACT centers on six core forms related to psychological flexibility. Although they're set out as particular procedures, loads of cover exists between them. And, while it can apply only to them, ACT is pretty much every one of the six procedures happening together as one.

The six core forms are;

•　　　Values: Recognizing what makes a difference most to you in life and what you need your life to be about.

•　　　Committed action: Doing those things that carry your values to life.

•　　　Acceptance: Noticing, accepting, and embracing all your experiences, even undesirable or negative ones.

•　　　Defusion: Noticing your thoughts and thinking forms, without getting excessive, got up to speed in them, or attempting to adjust or control them.

•　　　Contact the current minute: Being mindful of your experiences as they're happening in the present time and place.

•　　　Self as the context: Getting in contact with your profound sense of self; the 'you' who sits behind your eyes, who watches and experiences, and yet is particular from your thoughts, feelings, and memories. To remind you of the interconnectedness of these six procedures, they're placed together in a Hexaflex, a term by Steven Hayes, Kirk Strosahl, and Kelly Wilson in 1999 to portray the six focuses related to psychological flexibility;

From the outset sight, the Hexaflex can show up very perplexing and difficult to understand. However, at its heart is a basic thought — to carry on with your day-by-day life with purpose and poise according to what is essential to you. The accompanying segments look at each of the six core forms in more detail.

Values

Values are vital to ACT because they speak to what you need your life to be about and stand for. They outline how you need to carry on a progressing premise and give your life meaning and purpose. ACT characterizes values as uninhibitedly picked verbal articulations about what is important to you. Identifying your values is basic because they furnish the inspiration to manage the difficult things in life. They're the reason you're set up to battle to conquer the difficulties you experience as you endeavor to achieve your goals. They dignify your life. For example, if you esteem being imaginative and learning new aptitudes, you may join a night stoneware class. This class will mean the consumption of time, cash, and vitality and may infrequently lead to a scope of negative thoughts and feelings. You may think, 'Would I be able to do it?' or 'Do I have sufficient opportunity?' and you may feel on edge or reluctant. However, the explanation you're set up to have these negative experiences is because you could then do the things that issue to you. From an ACT viewpoint, you're taking committed actions (that is, acting) in the service of your values.

This is the reason values are so essential to life. They remind you of what's significant and assist you with remaining on course with committed actions. Identifying your values is a significant early undertaking in the ACT. When you comprehend what you need your life to be about, you could then move in those ways. Evaluate the short exercise beneath to help identify your values. Envision you're 80 years of age and just have a few days or weeks left to live. You're sitting in a comfortable seat, maybe looking out of a window, looking back on your life and what you've finished with it. Record your answers to the accompanying questions. I wish I'd invested more energy.

- *I wish I'd invested less energy.*

- *I wish I'd been more.*

- *I wish I'd been less*

- *I invested too little energy concentrated on it.*

- *I invested a lot of energy stressing over it.*

- *I wish I could have been a little.*

- *If I could carry on with my life once more, I would.*

I lament the one thing I might want to have done is expecting yourself forward in time; you allow yourself to think about how you've carried on with your life as of recently and what's essential to you. If this activity uncovers something you'd prefer to do or change in your life, right now is an ideal opportunity to take care of business. From an ACT perspective, your values are those personal characteristics that you most need to discuss in your actions. If, for instance, being a helpful person is essential to you, this activity can assist you with perceiving conditions in which you haven't been useful and can address later on. You can build what you have to do to embody this personal quality in your actions. Your values give your life meaning and purpose and make it worth living. Your test is to be clear about what your values are and then to act reliably with them. And you do this by taking part in committed action.

Committed action, a definitive point of ACT, is to assist you with living your life in reality — and this implies getting things done. It includes placing one foot before the different as you move in esteemed life headings. From multiple points of view, all ACT forms exist to help committed action.

Committed action is the procedure whereby you manufacture bigger and more significant examples of activities connected with your values. Instead of permitting your life to function by the shirking of pain or discomfort, committed action is how you step forward decidedly into the life you need to be living. At the point when you've clarified your values and where you need your life to head, the following stage is to define goals that take you toward that path. ACT uses expressions, for example, 'esteem-based goals' to remind you you're not picking any old aim, but something that depends on the main thing to you. Defining esteem based goals includes three phases:

1. Choosing and clarifying the worth you need to work on.

2. Developing goals that speak to this worth.

3. Taking action.

For instance, if in the wake of finishing the activity in the former area you identify that you wish you'd invested more energy with your family, the subsequent stage is to ask what you can do that speaks to this worth.

You could, for example, think of certain goals that you can achieve tonight, like perusing a book or playing a game with your kids, or setting up a most loved dinner for, or truly tuning in to your partner. Have a go at the accompanying activity to assist you with defining some worth-based goals. **Follow this means:**

• Choose and clarify as unequivocally as you can the esteem you need to work on. The worth that I need to work on is, for instance: "the worth that I need to work on is being an old buddy.'"

• Develop goals that speak to this worth.

Shockingly, not all goals are 'acceptable' goals because some are unpredictable, remote, or essentially unachievable. Thus, set SMART goals, specific, quantifiable, achievable, reasonable, and time-surrounded. The goal I need to achieve is, for instance: "The goal I need to achieve is to call two companions tonight to perceive how they are."

This aim is a SMART aim because of it:

• Specifies what to do.

• Is quantifiable, as you'll know when you've achieved it.

• Is workable and achievable.

• Is significant to the picked esteem — being an old buddy.

• Is time-surrounded — it specifies when to achieve it.

• Take action.

Get that telephone! Making a move step may show up simple, but it very well may be shockingly difficult. The following segment clarifies why doing the things you need to do can be hard and the way out.

Acceptance

Acceptance includes being available to every one of your experiences and embracing them for what they are (and not what your mind may reveal to you

225

they are). Acceptance is something contrary to evasion. Acceptance is a significant and complex psycho-legitimate procedure, seen with empathy and pardoning. Acceptance is significant because it can let loose your vitality to do the things you truly need to do. Battling against things you can't change — for example, attempting to control or maintain a strategic distance from specific thoughts and feelings — is pointless. You don't have the vital command over what you think and feel to make this a beneficial procedure. Faced with this the truth, you're in an ideal situation accepting such thoughts and feelings for what they are when they're disagreeable. Acceptance includes more than the capacity to endure negative experiences, however. It implies being open to them, practically inviting them — not because you appreciate cynicism but because any battle with pessimism is pointless. What follows is a short acceptance workout; give it a go! This activity takes around five minutes. You need an ice 3D square (you can use anything solidified, but an ice 3D square is most straightforward) and a hand towel (because your hands will get wet!). Follow this means:

•   Place an ice 3D shape in the palm of your hand and leave it there for around 60 seconds. If you can, close your fingers and hold them firmly. A little while later, the cold of the ice block will make your hand ache, and you'll most likely have thoughts like "My hand feels numb" or "That harm."

•   Be mindful of your physical discomfort and any negative thoughts you're having, but keep on holding the ice 3D shape for whatever length of time that you can. This somewhat painful exercise encourages you to find out about and practice acceptance. It's a worth-based action in that you uninhibitedly hold the ice 3D shape because, in doing such, you find how you experience and react to discomfort. This activity is a microcosm of the difficulties you face in your regular daily existence. Eventually, each day, you'll most likely experience negative occasions, difficulties, and discomfort. These experiences are inescapable, and endeavors to maintain a strategic distance from or oppose them which will fail. Rather, your best alternative when facing occasions or experiences that you can't change or control is to accept them for what they are. Doing so may not be fantastic, but, similar to all things, they'll pass. Acceptance isn't accommodation or resilience; rather, it's receptiveness to encountering the occasion, regardless of whether it's terrible, so you can push your life ahead in manners that issue to you.

Acceptance and human happiness

Happiness is something everybody makes progress toward. Acceptance has all the earmarks of being a significant factor in achieving that aim because happiness isn't only the nonappearance of terrible stuff but additionally the nearness of good stuff. Opposing or staying away from terrible things may bode well (and can be something worth being thankful for in the correct conditions, for example, when facing an eager lion). Still, if you invest an excess of time and vitality attempting to control or maintain a strategic distance from awful experiences, you'll possess less energy for taking part in the positive things that can fulfill you. As the essayist George Orwell stated, "Happiness can exist just in acceptance."

Defusion

Defusion is something contrary to the combination. The combination is your commitment to or faith in the strict substance of your thoughts. At the point when you accept your thoughts to be valid — you intertwine with them — they can apply an impressive impact on what you do. The problem with accepting your thoughts is that they're frequently off-base or inaccurate! And when they're accurate, they may not be a practical manual for the proper behavior. If you combine with the idea 'I can't do it,' you're bound to surrender or not attempt. Regardless of whether that contemplation is accurate, accepting that the idea is genuine can hinder figuring out how to do whatever it is.

Conversely, defusion is the procedure by which you increase some good ways from your thoughts and cognitions (counting memories and mental pictures). It includes being mindful of your thoughts (and thinking forms) and not being stuck inside them. It implies looking at your thoughts as opposed to your thoughts. Defusing from your thoughts is difficult because they're so prompt, private, and steady that they can slip into your mindfulness unnoticed and unchallenged. As an outcome, it's anything but difficult to identify with their substance as an accurate impression of how things truly

227

are, as opposed to similar to a thought you're having. ACT looks to undermine the egotism of 'words' and considers being an only thought.

But what are your thoughts? From an ACT perspective, thoughts are close to a private language — words, pictures, and memories that you experience inside your head. Opinions might be valuable, but they can likewise not be right and unhelpful. The test is to work out when they fill a helpful need and when they're impeding worth-based living. ACT uses a scope of defusion procedures to assist you with seeing your thoughts and increasing a little detachment from them along these lines. This sense of detachment decreases the acceptability of your thoughts. You can settle on choices dependent on your values and not on what is experiencing your mind at a specific point in time. The following is a short defusion practice for you to attempt.

This is an especially active exercise, and to receive the best in return, you need to truly put it all on the line. Try not to stress if you feel somewhat self-cognizant or senseless — everybody does. Notice these thoughts and do it, at any rate. Locate a calm area where you won't be angry for a few minutes and a clock that estimates seconds. Consider a glass of milk. Picture it in your mind — the white milk in a glass. Now envision getting the glass and drinking from it. What does it pose a flavor like? Is it cold or warm? Swallow the milk and then picture holding the glass before you.

Picture a glass of milk in your mind's eye. With that picture crisp in your mind, begin saying the word 'milk' for all to hear. Start gradually and then, bit by bit, develop your speed until you're saying the word rapidly, again and again: 'milk, milk, milk, milk.' Increment your volume as you speed up. Now and again, you'll falter and lurch; don't stress, stay with it. Attempt to keep it awake for 45 seconds.

At the point when you finish, pause for a minute to think about the experience and ask yourself:

- *How did it feel?*

- *What happened to my mental picture of the glass of milk?*

- *Did I battle to create the sound 'milk'?*

- *What did the word 'milk' sound like?*

228

When individuals do this activity, they frequently report that they stop hearing the word 'milk' and rather feel they're making clever-sounding clamors. Albeit a touch of vocal twisting occurs, in fact, you're despite everything making the sound' milk.' You never again interface it with 'milk,' however. You're, despite everything, hearing the actual sound, 'milk,' but deprived of its representative meaning. Individuals additionally regularly report that the picture also vanishes. Once more, this happens because rehashing the word 'milk' decontextualizes the picture and, in this manner, strips away its meaning. You can use this procedure to strip away or change the meaning of any word or expression. Because you identify the meaning of a word with the setting in which it happens when you change the specific situation, you also change its meaning. Changing the setting in which a word or expression happens is the premise of defusion. Because of changing the setting of a word, you can consider it to be only a sound with meanings attached. And, critically, these meanings can change. Never again are they fixed or exact portrayals of the real world; rather, you come to consider them to sound individuals make to communicate with each other. At the point when you notice this, words have less significance in your life. Language and words stay significant and valuable, but because you realize that the meaning of words can change, so your commitment to their strict substance winds down.

This variability is especially helpful when you have negative or unhelpful thoughts because, as opposed to seeing them as factually accurate or clear, you rather consider them to be simple words or bits of language experiencing your head. You may believe that sounds very straightforward, but it's shockingly difficult. Regularly, you become involved with your thoughts and overlook your prompt experiences. Consider regularly announced a case of driving someplace and then having no memory of the subtleties of the excursion. In like manner, you can nearly drift through life without a re-partner seeing it. You go on the programmed pilot when you're so wrapped up in your thoughts you don't see what you're doing or what's happening in the more extensive world around you. For what reason does this lack of contact matter? Being detached from your general surroundings can make esteem based on living increasingly difficult because you aren't in contact with the main thing — your prompt world. Rather, you're away in your thoughts — arranging, stressing, recollecting, evaluating, and so on.

229

These mental procedures aren't all terrible, obviously. Still, an excess of time spent on them can meddle with your capacity to do the things you need life to be about. The current minute is all you have — don't pass it up!

ACT uses a scope of systems, for example, mindfulness, to assist you with reaching the current minute. The accompanying mindful strolling exercise is only one model from mindfulness that assists with associating you to the current minute. You can do this mindfulness practice anyplace, but discovering someplace calm, where you will not be angry, is most likely fit for your first endeavor. Center on the act of strolling, seeing each sensation and development as you place one foot before the other. While you can do this activity in a little space, it's simpler if you can discover a region where you can move around uninhibitedly around without haggling many obstacles. You can do it in-side or outside, with your shoes on or off, and it takes around ten minutes. Follow this means:

1.   Find a spot and standstill, with the two feet flat on the ground. Concentrate on your breathing and notice the progression of air as you take in profoundly through your nose and out through your mouth. Know about how your chest and shoulders rise and fall with each breath.

2.   Focus your consideration on your feet. Feel the heaviness of your body through your feet on the ground. Notice any sensations as you delicately influence back and forward.

3.   Stroll forward, gradually and purposely. Feel how development courses through your body while you place one foot before the other. Know about the vibe of placing each foot on the ground. Notice how your arms and legs move as you stroll forward.

4.   Look down at your feet as you keep on strolling gradually and with full mindfulness. Now and then, your consideration may wander — your mind may concentrate on different things, for example, thoughts, sounds, or different sensations. At the point when this occurs, know that your consideration has drifted and, tenderly and without self-analysis, concentrate back on your feet and each progression that you take.

5.   Contact the current minute by mindfully and purposely seeing each progression you take. Strolling is something you've accomplished for the vast majority of your life; it's so recognizable you barely notice it.

6.   Continue strolling for ten minutes or somewhere in the vicinity. At the point when you finish, do so deliberately and stand still for a minute. Thank your feet for the excursion you've recently finished and for all the excursions you've assumed control of throughout the years.

Self as a Setting

The self as the setting process is difficult to clarify because it's an experience instead of an idea. Like swimming, we could clarify the procedure, but you wouldn't understand it until you get in the water.

Self as a setting (sometimes called the spectator self) alludes to your experience that exists past your prompt thoughts and feelings — it's your remarkable and continuous point of view on life. Experientially self as the setting is the sense of being 'I' or 'me' in the present time and place.

Self as a setting is significant because it empowers you to know about your own experiences as they happen without being legitimately associated with them. This mindfulness is valuable because you can watch your thoughts and feelings travel every which way without feeling attached to them from a self as a set point of view.

This detachment empowers you to see that you are more than those while you experience your thoughts and feelings. You are an entire human being. One illustration frequently used in the ACT to help understand the self as the setting is a chessboard loosening up interminably toward each path, as appeared in Figure 3-3. Envision that everywhere throughout the chessboard are black and white chess pieces. Some are grouped together, and others are not. What you see is an immense war zone, with black and white chess pieces pitched against each other.

Envision yourself as a chessboard. Envision that your positive thoughts and feelings are the black pieces, and your negative thoughts and feelings are the white pieces. They're doing combating against each other, and you trust that

231

the black pieces will win. You trust that you can load your mind with constructive thoughts ("I'm a decent person") instead of pessimistic thoughts ("I'm idiotic"). To achieve this result, you enter the quarrel and attempt to free the leading group of the white pieces. You get the black pieces and endeavor to crush or push the white pieces away.

Similarly, each time you have a negative idea about yourself, you counter it with a positive idea. You can envision sending forward the black chess piece speaking to the idea' 'I'm a decent/great/loveable person" each time you experience a contrary idea, for example, "I'm moronic/appalling/hopeless."

It's near as if disposing of one terrible thought only makes space for another. The system doesn't free the chessboard from the white pieces. This technique likewise has another, more serious issue. By attempting to dispose of your undesirable thoughts, you're announcing war on your own experiences. An enormous piece of yourself is your foe. And here's the rub: you can always lose this fight without additionally wrecking a piece of what your identity is. Living in a combat area is unpleasant. It's hard, it's awful, and it's ceaseless. So what are your alternatives? You can continue with this war against yourself, or you can attempt something else — and radical!

Rather than partner yourself with the pieces, you can be the chessboard — you're the space that holds the pieces. You're still in contact with every one of your thoughts and feelings as the pieces lay on the board. They're despite everything part of your experience — but you become a spectator and have less enthusiasm for the result of the fight. You become the place where these occasions and experiences happen without getting included. This activity permits you to segregate yourself (as the chessboard) from your thoughts and feelings (the chess pieces). Simultaneously, you can perceive how you are in the specific situation, the setting for cognitions and emotions, but are likewise more than this. And that is the root as a setting.

Chapter 7: Overcoming Barriers to Living a Pleasant Life

Understanding and Then Dealing

These barriers can assist you with remaining on course to do what makes a difference in life. Understand how to defeat the obstacles to taking part in steady actions in line with your picked values. You investigate a portion of the run-of-the-mill courses in which combination with unpleasant thoughts and feelings can lead to carrying on such that is conflicting with the life you truly need to show. We also offer some diffusion exercises to attempt, which help you disentangle yourself from such undesirable thoughts.

Beating Psychological Barriers to Change

One offered clarification for why you neglect to achieve your goals because you don't want the result enough. According to this view, disappointments speak to a lack of willpower or even lethargy. If you can be progressively engaged or self-trained, you'll succeed. While inspiration is significant, other psychological barriers can disrupt the general flow. ACT identifies four essential psycho-consistent obstacles that, if left unaddressed, will probably undermine your capacity to achieve your goals; shortened with the acronym FEAR (initially authored by Steve Hayes, Kirk Strosahl, and Kelly Wilson):

- *F- Fusion with your thoughts.*

- *E-Evaluation of your experience.*

- *A-Avoidance of your experience.*

- *R-Reason-giving for your conduct.*

The accompanying areas portray each obstruction.

Fusion with your thoughts

Thoughts Fusion implies getting attached to and accepting of your thoughts' strict substance (arrangements with its inverse — diffusion — and we additionally talk about distribution in the later area, 'Replacing FEAR with DARE').

At the point when you intertwine with your thoughts, you look at the world from those thoughts. It's as if you're inside your ideas and can't separate from them. Your thoughts characterize you. The combination isn't entirely terrible, as language works excellent because of its strict substance. By tuning in to the importance of what others say, you could then react to it accordingly.

If a parent says, "It's coming down outside, so put your jacket on," the kid can respond adequately to the circumstance (that is, put her jacket on and remain dry) because she tunes in to exacting substance.

However, problems emerge when you become excessively combined with your thoughts because they aren't always accurate. And when they are, they're not still helpful. For example, connecting with ideas, "I can't do it" or "I'm excessively monstrous" implies that you're bound to carry on just as they're valid. You may not enlist on a photography course because you accept you're not wise enough or abstain from going out on the town if you're disturbed when you look in the mirror. Conflicting with what you get to be 'the fact of the matter' is problematic. ACT urges you to have a progressively adaptable relationship with your thoughts and your cognitive procedures when you say and do all. Being psycho-legitimately adaptable empowers you to react to your ideas and cognitions' strict substance. Doing so is valuable to perceive the truth about them — just words, pictures, and bits of language experiencing your head. We call this procedure diffusion.

Evaluation of Your Experience.

Assessment is an essential psychological procedure, and you do it regularly. Like every other person, you're continually deciding about everything that is going on around you. That is fine, aside from the fact that a considerable number of your assessments are negative. Nobody's exactly sure why this is the situation. Still, one clarification is that the transformative past has prepared humans (like all creatures) to be profoundly delicate to potential

234

dangers—these predispositions you to see life's negatives before life's positives. Being mindful of potential risks and dangers encourages you to make a sly move and make it due to living one more day. While you may have filtered the environment for predators, today, you might attract your consideration to an elusive floor, a flimsy stepping stool, or social dangers and pressures. Assessing risks in the environment, as endurance directs, is a specific something, but problems emerge when you evaluate yourself. At the point when you assess portions of your own experience (that is, your thoughts, feelings, and real sensations) as unfavorable, you can come to consider them to be something to be maintained. It is a strategic distance from similarly as you'd attempt to stay away from adverse occasions outside your body (fleeing from a predator, for instance). This approach may appear to be a smart thought initially, but evading what's going on inside your own body ends up being difficult. You are endeavoring to do so.

Avoidance of your experience.

Experiential evasion depicts your conduct when you're reluctant to stay in contact with difficult thoughts, feelings, and real sensations and instead take part in what are eventually counterproductive endeavors to limit or dispose of them. Experiential evasion happens because you attempt to control your inner private emotions and thoughts similarly as you endeavor to hold outside occasions. At the point when you experience outside adverse events, you can make a move to improve things. If your shoe rubs, you can evacuate it or quit strolling; if your child is crying, you can take care of her or put her to sleep. To put it plainly, you can take action steadily with your values (the benefit of being a loving, caring guardian, for instance). When you don't care for something in the outer world, you "change it or leave it." However, this method doesn't work with your thoughts and feelings. The more you attempt to control, keep away from, or limit them, the more prevailing they become. You don't have a similar authority level over your inside private thoughts and emotions as you do over occasions in the outside world. While you can think specific thoughts for a brief timeframe, more often than not, your thoughts (and related cognitions, for example, memories or mental pictures) are in connection with exterior upgrades through a scope of personal relationships over which you have practically zero control.

235

Therefore, your thoughts can be activated by occasions occurring around you in unstable and diverse manners. For instance, if you experience agoraphobia (the dread of open or public places), you may feel on edge and apprehensive in occupied or swarmed circumstances. But you may likewise get on edge about things related to swarms, for example, shops, football coordinates, or even noticing the words "individuals" and "outside."

Staying away from all relationships with things you don't care for is difficult to achieve. The primary way you can do so is to constrain your contact with the world to a little scope of unsurprising occasions (individuals with public square phobia regularly keep themselves to a single space for quite a long time). While you can't completely control your thoughts, you may feel that you can transform them or clear out or don' care about these things. Unluckily, you can't. Research has exhibited that the more you attempt to smother or control unwanted thoughts, the more you experience them. The very act of trying to control something implies that you're concentrating on it, and it, in this way, becomes a piece of your life.

The circumstance is a lot of the equivalent for your emotions, however, for a different explanation. Your feelings are what you feel in your body, and rely upon what's befallen you. You can't attempt to change how you feel right now because you can't change your past. Your only alternative is to do things now that make another history that will empower you to reach all the more psychologically deftly to difficult emotions later on.

Reason-giving for your conduct.

Human beings are adept at giving motivations to why they act as they do. In reality, we ask youngsters to clarify their conduct from a young age, so we're all around practiced when we find a good pace. However, the need to give clarifications urges you to allude to the thoughts, feelings, physical sensations, and memories that happen as you act as reasons for your conduct. And this leads to a related problem — because the two regularly happens together, it's anything but difficult to expect that great conduct results from positive emotions and cognitions and awful conduct from negative emotions and cognitions. A kid may say, "I'm too frightened even to consider going to class," how we introduce how she feels denote the reason for her refusal to go to class. For example, I also hit him because I was irate' and "I got her blossoms because I love her," allude to emotions as the reason for those actions. These statements can seem to clarify the reasons for your conduct, but actually, they're words. So profound in Western culture is the possibility that thoughts and feelings cause human behavior that from the start sight, it can appear to be ludicrous to address it, but that is precisely what ACT requests you do. From an ACT point of view, 'reasons are not causes.' Regardless of whether you think them to yourself or say them for all to hear, reasons are words — bits of language. What you think and say are significant, but they don't cause what you do.

If you don't trust us, attempt these:

•   Say for all to hear or ponder internally, "Contact my nose," but then do nothing.

•   Say for all to hear or ponder internally, "Don't say green," and at that point, say "green" for all to hear.

Most likely, you figured out how to do something contrary to what you thought or said. How is this conceivable if your thoughts and statements control what you do? When your reasons allude to your emotions, they're as yet not causal.

Clarifications, for example, "I ran because I was terrified" or "I was so happy, I hopped for bliss" are regularly acceptable in ordinary discourse but rapidly self-destruct under nearer investigation. Have you been in any of these circumstances?

•   Feeling sad but grinning and claiming to be all right? And a lousy habit verse?

•   Being furious, but holding your tongue?

•   Feeling tired but remaining alert?

•   Being hungry but not eating? And the other way around?

Everybody's experienced inclination one way and carrying on in another. But if your feelings control your conduct, this shouldn't be conceivable.

How you feel is significant, but the proof shows that your emotions don't cause your behavior. So, what's happening? According to ACT, the clarification is that you act and feel in specific manners because of something. It's on those occasions that you should look for the reasons for your conduct. Because your feelings ordinarily occur together, your actions are anything but difficult to infer that they're causal. However, your experience lets you know differently. You can behave in manners that differ based on what you're thinking or how you're feeling. Without a doubt, the whole acting calling depends on that reason and reality; the causes you attribute to your conduct are frequently minimal more than pardons for why you or didn't do something. And you most likely realize that!

Chapter 8: Overview of anxiety disorders

Despite some nuances, anxiety disorders are omnipresent and can be found in every ethnic group, country, and culture. Indeed, anxiety disorders are among the most prevalent psychological disorders, affecting at some point in their lifetime up to 25 percent of the general population. The core processes that contribute to such conditions— avoidance, escape, and other tendencies for controlling unpleasant emotions— are particularly common in Westernized nations. Of starters, most of us learned early so as not to approach a red-hot stove because it hurts. Some of us have learned this the hard way, and others warn us about the consequences by listening to our parents or caregivers. We also learn how to deal with physical pain when it comes. We are socialized to use physical and psychological pain and suffering as reasonable reasons for our and others' behavior. It's acceptable, for example, to miss a day at work or school for feeling ill, but it's not acceptable to miss a working day or education for feeling full of life.

We also learn to apply the same control strategies to our feelings, experiences, and emotions from multiple examples, particularly those uncomfortable or painful.

Anxiety and fear are much like the hot stove, and we must somehow control our actions against them. But, as applied to our thoughts and emotions, the sensible strategy of discussing potential sources of real pain and hurt never works in the same way. We can't switch them on or off just as we can move our hands on or off the hot stove. Wherever we go, our thoughts and feelings are with us. We can't escape them or prevent them. They are a part of us.

Anxiety Disorders Are Expensive

Nevertheless, individuals with panic disorder are more likely than those with any other psychiatric diagnosis (including schizophrenia) to seek help for their condition.

Also, individuals with anxiety disorders are the highest users of emergency room services compared to people with other emotional problems.

However, when left untreated, most anxiety disorders tend not to go down by themselves. Alternatively, they tend to remain the same or get worse over time before people reach their fifties, with a growing negative impact on the quality of life for the individuals and their families affected.

It is no wonder with high prevalence and chronicity that anxiety disorders are linked with significant personal and social impacts and substantial economic costs. In fact, as Barlow aptly noted, "real expenses dwarf even the most pessimistic estimates... anxiety disorders accounted for 31 percent of total mental health care costs in recent years, compared with 22 percent for mood disorders and 20 percent for schizophrenia".

Counting both the direct costs of care and the loss of productivity, the total annual costs of anxiety disorders in the United States are calculated at around $45 billion, with clinical and medical medication accounting for only 30 percent of that figure. Besides, over 50 percent of the expenses are attributed to the inappropriate (mostly unnecessary) use of primary health facilities. Several studies have documented the cost savings in treating anxiety disorders successfully greatly outweigh the cost of treatment. In the end, it is more expensive not to treat an anxiety disorder than to provide appropriate treatment.

NATURE AND FUNCTION OF FEAR AND ANXIETY

The essence and role of fear and anxiety teach us a lot about the central mechanisms of an "abnormal" or disordered anxiety involved. In trying to understand the plight of people with anxiety disorders, understanding the intense and primarily adaptive desire to flee from circumstances that cause fear is fundamental.

Fear—The Present-Oriented Basic Emotion

Fear is a present-oriented condition that occurs in response to real or imagined threats or danger. Some of these warnings occur in the here and now (e.g., a dangerous or distressing situation). Others respond to what is happening inside the person (e.g., a troubling physical feeling, a thought, or a past memory). Some are a mix of these.

240

Typically, fear is characterized by an abrupt and acute surge of the sympathetic branch of the autonomic nervous system, accompanied by intense physiological changes (e.g., increased suddenness, rapid heartbeat, breathlessness, increased blood pressure) and a powerful tendency for action to fight or flee from signs of danger. Fear is also associated with increased caution and stress management so that the attention of the victim is concentrated on the incident that causes fear.

Fear is perfectly adaptive under most circumstances because it serves an important function: it motivates and mobilizes the individual to take defensive action. Both the physiological and psychological changes associated with anxiety are meant to improve the individual's interpersonal capacity to avert the threatening occurrence.

The Function of Normal Fear and Anxiety

Fear is a warning reaction that prompts us to take some preventive measure when our life or wellbeing seems to be in danger. In some cases, these kinds of actions are reflexive and occur on an unconditioned (unlearned) basis. When we close our eyes and turn our heads sideways in response to an object flying toward us. In other cases, these actions take place on a learned (conditioned) basis, often with language assistance. So, as we take evasive action and leap on our left because somebody screams "risk on your right," we do so partially because of language learning. It may even be helpful and resilient to anxiety and worry about some future event that could affect our lives. A bout of anxiety, for example, will help us bring together an action plan to respond more quickly to potential threats to our family's health, jobs, protection, or welfare. In some cases, these preparations need to be quite detailed so that when faced with an actual threat, we can respond effectively. An excellent example of such arrangements would be a team that will develop a plan in case of a house fire.

Avoidance Makes Anxiety Problematic or "Disordered"

Thus, in many instances, experiencing fear and anxiety is healthy and adaptive. All emotions have one function, namely to keep us alive and away from danger. It, by the way, is also an important fact to relay before beginning a treatment program to customers.

Any irregular or disordered bodily feelings, emotions, and behaviors can cause fear and anxiety per se. This is true even where there is a great intensity of fear and anxiety. It is true even if the fear and anxiety in response to trauma occur on a learned basis. Consider, for example, a client that has been bitten by a pit bull and subsequently experiences a strong response of fear when they encounter the same or similar dogs. Here the tendency would be to describe the client's problems as a particular type of phobia— animal.

Nevertheless, avoiding these dogs is not disordered or abnormal— it is a sensible response designed to prevent any assault or accident and protect the person's physical health. Similarly, it is natural and resilient for a woman who has been sexually assaulted to feel a response of terror when she eventually meets her attacker. This anxiety could lead to a rapid escape or other protective responses to defend herself if she met the man again. Also, it can be adaptive and valuable for her safety to think of that man and worry about what could happen if she met him again. It may encourage her to formulate an action plan for what she wants to do to defend herself and how she can best avoid potential victimization. Such learned responses to the alarm are natural and adaptive.

On the other hand, too much uncertainty or anxiety may deter one from taking constructive and effective action. Even under extreme fear, animals aren't doing well. They uncontrollably freeze, shake, try to escape, or struggle to get away from the source of fear. In this way, humans are similar to other species.

For example, false alarms, such as panic attacks, seem to appear in awkward or uncomfortable circumstances (e.g., when getting ready to give a speech) for no good reason— out of the blue. We are pretty often intimidating and noisy. Over time, some individuals seem to learn how to be with such attacks and experience them while others do not. The answer variance is a critical point.

False alarms are often not clinical problems that warrant clinical attention. What could allow us to consider how fear and anxiety can get disordered is to investigate the far larger number of people in the general population who have panic attacks and no panic disorder. Epidemiological studies generally put the prevalence of panic disorder at about 3 to 5 percent in the general population. Several studies have shown that about 35 percent of presumably normal young adults have had one or more panic attacks in a given year. The distinction between these "natural panickers" and panic disordered individuals is not mainly the severity or duration of panic attacks. Instead, people in these two groups appear to react differently to their experiences of panic attacks. Most people who experience a panic attack from time to time learn to wait for it and hang in until it subsides.

They're not trying to escape the panic. Instead, "nonclinical" panickers pick up from where they were before the attack and keep on living their lives without spending too much time worrying about future panic attacks; most importantly, without doing things to avoid the panic experience and the places where they had panic attacks.

We believe that this acceptance and non-evasion posture are key preventive mechanisms that protect many of these nonclinical panickers from developing a panic disorder or social phobia. Only when people desperately and rigidly try to avoid the occurrence of panic attacks, and dedicate increasingly more significant portions of their life energy and resources to that mission, are they at high risk of developing genuine panic disorder.

Both the DSM and anxiety researchers have long stressed that what turns nonclinical panic into clinical panic is fear of future attacks and associated behavioral changes (e.g., activity restriction, avoidance behavior) to reduce the likelihood of another attack.

Some of this preparatory planning is done by non-human animals too. For example, when a tone-shocked animal hears the sound again, the animal changes its action and turns its head and eyes toward the tone.

We could say that this animal is concerned with a real threat (that is, the possibility of being shocked again). In contrast, humans can go much further in terms of both the time frame and what could happen to them.

That is so partially because, unlike other species, humans can think, visualize, and communicate. These otherwise functional abilities often allow humans to get wrapped up in a fight with their own feelings in an attempt not to have them. In turn, this struggle can feed on itself in a self-perpetuating cycle, paradoxically creating more of the very unwanted emotions.

Most specifically, it takes effort in the war itself. Any activity directed at reducing or avoiding anxiety and fear is no longer available resources and time to pursue more important tasks in life. Most importantly, this fight for control is really a war against one's own perceptions. It is a war which can't be won, quite paradoxically.

Overview of Anxiety Disorders

This section is intended to give a brief overview of the core symptoms of the major anxiety conditions as currently defined by the DSM.

Panic Attacks

Barlow noted that in panic attacks, the most prominent clinical manifestation of the basic emotion of fear is. Besides a powerful autonomic outburst that usually reaches its peak within ten minutes, individuals having a panic attack experience intense fear and terror, fears of death and losing control, and an overwhelming desire to run and get away from wherever they are.

Such fear responses are reactions to emergencies or to alarms. They serve to plan for action by humans and other mammals. Typically, such activities aim to prevent the potential impact of a threatening stimulus or event on the environment. Therefore, the center of that answer at its most basic level is an inclination towards combat-or-flight behavior.

Classifying panic as an acute response to fear and an inclination towards action implies an emotional response to the alarm: it helps to evoke motion. A strong urge to escape leads people to avoid places where it might be difficult to escape (e.g., movie theatres, large shopping malls, formal social gatherings). If the tendency to take action is actually blocked, the intensity of fear increases.

Panic Disorder and Agoraphobia

Panic disorder (PD) is characterized by frequent panic attacks, avoidance of body sensations consistent with autonomic arousal, and paranoia over possible panic attack possibilities. Current diagnostic criteria for a PD diagnosis require a person to suffer frequent and unexplained attacks. At least one of the attacks must be followed by at least one month of constant concern about future attacks, concerns about the effects of the attacks, or a change in actions related to the attacks (e.g., a form of avoidance). Panic disorder at its heart is a fear of feeling terror, where people literally fear panic attacks and the potential consequences of such attacks.

Agoraphobic fear occurs when people avoid areas where they may have had a panic attack (e.g., malls, movie theaters, grocery stores) and where recovery can be impossible if they have another stroke.

Remember that agoraphobia is simply a fear of having a single panic attack, not a fear of those locations as was previously thought. Accordingly, agoraphobia can also be seen as a symptom of panic disorder. Individuals try to avoid potential panic attacks by remaining in "safe" environments and ignoring fear-associated triggers and locations previously.

After first experiencing panic attacks, nearly all people who develop agoraphobia do so; in fact, only 1 percent of people with agoraphobia do not experience a panic attack.

The onset of PD typically occurs in the mid to late 20's. The onset of the disorder is often preceded by stressful life events. Nonetheless, the total severity of negative life experiences does not consistently separate people with PD from those with or without other anxiety disorders. Nevertheless, people with PD do mention witnessing negative events in life as more distressing than others. Individuals with PD often show a high level of concern regarding their health status, particularly regarding changes associated with body states. The PD path is often persistent without professional intervention, with an increase in the number and severity of assaults during periods of stress.

PD is twice as typical in women as in men. This gender difference is consistently found in studies worldwide. It is largely due to socio-cultural factors that moderate the emotional expression and males and females experience differently. For example, responding to fear by engaging in agoraphobic avoidance behavior is more socially acceptable for women. At the same time, men may alleviate fear and anxiety by using alcohol and other drugs ("self-medication").

Specific Phobias

A particular phobia is marked, recurring, and irrational or unfounded anxiety on a specific object or circumstance. Exposure to the dreaded entity typically produces an acute and extreme terror response (i.e., a panic attack). This reaction to the warning is followed by a strong urge to escape from the target or circumstance. It can be accompanied by severe disability and anxiety discomfort. Persons suffering from specific phobias often act as much as possible to avoid future encounters with the feared object. They will make great efforts to do so. We typically understand, however, that their anxiety is irrational or unfounded. However, this awareness does not impair the desire to run and stop dreaded stimuli or control emotional and physiological reactions that result.

Specific phobias, together with other anxiety disorders, are typically defined as involving changes in three loosely connected "response systems": motor behavior (e.g., avoidance or escape); elevated physiological activity (e.g., increased heart rate, transpiration, respiration, and muscle tension); and verbal-cognitive activity such as preceding, accompanying, or apprehensive reports of distress and apprehension.

Some specific phobias are situational (e.g., closed spaces, heights, or aircraft). In contrast, others focus on the natural environment (e.g., heights, storms, lightning, or water), animals (e.g., snakes, rats, or spiders), or bodily harm (e.g., diseases, injuries, or blood vision). In the general population, specific phobias are quite common, with extensive surveys showing a lifetime prevalence of 11 percent. Fear of rodents, heights, confined rooms, blood and injury, earthquakes and lightning, and flight are the most common phobias (in descending order).

246

Given this high prevalence, most people with severe phobias rarely seek treatment. Antony and Barlow report that only 5 to 6 percent of patients with a specific phobia present as their major complaint in their anxiety clinics.

Nonetheless, as a secondary issue, 26 percent of people diagnosed with other anxiety disorders often suffer from a common phobia. Many people with a specific phobia do not seek treatment because of their anxiety, in part because they are quite good at escaping the subjects of their fear and/or because interaction with fearful objects is not a concern in their daily lives (e.g., seeing a snake in midtown Manhattan). This avoidance is possible because the stimuli that elicit anxiety is clearly known and discernible. Yet even the "effective" avoidance often comes at a high personal or social cost.

Many particular anxieties can serve an evolutionary function. Studies also found that the most prevalent fears involve harm-related threats and endangered lives (e.g., rats, mice, thunderstorms, heights).

Through time, we've been "biologically trained" to respond to such triggers in a hyper-vigilant, frightening way to secure our safety. Many studies, including several in our own lab, have shown that fears of evolutionarily prepared objects are acquired more quickly than fears of other equally hazardous objects of more recent origin (e.g., electrical outlets, weapons).

Social Phobia

Individuals with such problems tend to be particularly concerned about being adversely judged by others, show increased personal knowledge of independent behavior in social situations, and report real or perceived social inadequacy. They also worry about other people detecting their social discomforts. Such fears are often viewed as irrational and as sources of disruption to life.

It's not surprising that people with social phobia usually fear to flee social situations as much as possible. These circumstances include, but are not limited to, public speaking, interpersonal communication with opposite-sex people, group meetings, telephone-based correspondence, social gatherings, and sometimes quasi-social activities such as using public toilets or public transport.

247

Nearly 90 percent of all people diagnosed with fear of social phobia and stop more than one social activity.

Scholars also discern a distrust of unique or isolated social situations (e.g., public speaking) from widespread social phobia.

The latter of these are marked by anxiety, and most social situations are avoided. Compared with specific social phobia, the generalized type is associated with a greater degree of psychological suffering.

The problems people have with social phobia usually go far beyond the anxiety of the actual social situation. Recall that those with agoraphobia, panic disorder, and other phobias are not necessarily afraid of public spaces, panic attack-related environments, or actual items per se. We avoid witnessing extreme emotional and psychological events in those situations. The same applies to people with social phobia, where anxiety sometimes depends on having a panic attack, struggling somewhere in front of others, or being insulted or ashamed while in a social situation. Thus, as with the other anxiety disorders, the core issue for individuals with social phobia seems to revolve around avoiding the negative impact experience.

We know social phobia prevalence is much more prevalent than previously thought, with recent data finding a median prevalence of 13.3 percent. This makes social phobia the most common anxiety disorder after major depression, alcohol dependence, and the third most common psychological disorder. Statistics consistently show that about 70 percent of people with social phobia are female and that social phobia slowly develops over time.

Few individuals report a traumatic experience that precipitates the disorder. Nevertheless, many socially anxious people report that they "have always had the problem."

This is confirmed by other epidemiological data suggesting that the mean age of onset begins on or about puberty (i.e., twelve years of age). More than 90 percent of people experience the condition by age twenty-five.

Post-Traumatic Stress Disorder

Post-Traumatic Stress Disorder (PTSD) 's core psychological manifestations fall into three large clusters: re-experiencing the traumatic event, resisting trauma-related stimuli, and consistently heightened body anticipation. Significant concerns about personal safety hazards (e.g., death) are central to the disorder.

The first cluster is also PTSD's most personally distressing feature, involving re-experiencing aspects of traumatic events through flashbacks, nightmares, intrusive thoughts, and emotional distress in response to internal or external indications that serve as trauma reminders.

Trauma-related stimuli often trigger a trauma re-experience, increased somatic activity, and extreme terror-like behavioral manifestations, such as immobility. Individuals with PTSD will vividly relive traumatic experiences through hallucinations and dreams in a manner that seems very believable to them.

The second class concerns the actions of avoidance. For example, people with PTSD typically go to great lengths to avoid thinking about the traumatic event or any indications or situations that may serve as event reminders. The core role of such avoidance is to eliminate the negative effect and psychological pain involved with the incident from being felt again.

As with other anxiety disorders, avoidance can range from very restricted and limited to extremely complex and comprehensive. As avoidance becomes extensive, it tends to limit the functioning of life to such a degree that sufferers with PTSD are no longer engaged in routine activities. For example, certain perpetrators of PTSD abuse reduce interaction only with certain categories of males (e.g., males of the same ethnicity as the perpetrator), while others cease communication with all males. Another common form of PTSD emotional isolation is numbing, which refers to separation from others and reduced impact area. For example, despite experiencing an equivalent number of orgasms, some rape victims with PTSD show a reduced degree of pleasure of sexual activity relative to others women. Many others simply report being unable to experience pleasure in life and being unable to trust and be close to others.

249

Ultimately, the third PTSD class consists of reports with increased body arousal or alarm response. Arousal-related psychiatric characteristics include sleep disturbances, high startle reflex, irritability, outbursts of anger, and hypervigilance. Many rape victims, for example, continuously search their surroundings for signs associated with the attacker and the traumatic event. Spiraling up into a full-blown panic attack is quite common for this elevated bodily excitement.

PTSD is the only psychological problem with a specific label on the etiology, including one or more traumatic events. Although problem reactions may manifest after the trauma in a relatively short time (e.g., within three to six months), they may also arise years after a traumatic event. Jaycox and Foa rightly termed the prevalence of traumatic experiences and alarming clinical PTSD.

Around 39 percent of the U.S. population in their lifespan would experience at least one traumatic event. Yet, only 24 percent of those people will continue to develop PTSD, representing a lifetime prevalence of PTSD in the general population of 9 percent. These numbers are certainly high, especially considering that subclinical PTSD affects up to 15 percent of the population. Furthermore, we learn from such research that around two-thirds of victims of abuse do not experience PTSD. Again we have to wonder, why do most people recover from physically relatively unscathed traumatic experiences? Why do some people experience just acute psychological symptoms that dissipate after a few months on their own? Why do problem behaviors occur in other situations so grow into the illness we call PTSD? Examining the central aspect of static negative impact avoidance will hold the key to answering these and other critical issues.

Obsessive-Compulsive Disorder

Obsessions are repetitive, recurrent emotions, urges, or images associated with substantial agitation and perceived as distracting, irrational, and distressing. On the other hand, compulsions are repetitive actions (e.g., testing, hand washing) and behavioral activities (e.g., counting, praying) that involve people rigidly and constantly to relieve anxiety caused by obsessions.

Ritualistic thoughts or acts are directed at eliminating, neutralizing, or otherwise manipulating troubling obsessional content. The behavioral or mental acts serve to restore safety, decrease anxiety, and prevent the event from occurring.

Obsessions and compulsive behaviors induce pronounced agitation and interact more profoundly with the daily routines and social functioning than any other major anxiety disorder

Nonetheless, when people are treated due to anxiety, they usually suffer from obsessive-compulsive disorder (OCD). Hospitalization also signifies the start of the relentless downward cycle of compulsions and repetitive routines. Both tend to place so many constraints on people's lives while consuming so much time each day that some people literally run out of time to do what they really need to do. In such situations, hospitalization usually constitutes a last resort to break this cycle.

Unlike GAD-related cognitions, the intrusive thoughts and fears experienced by people with OCD are not necessarily unnecessary concerns over actual, everyday life problems. Alternatively, OCD is characterized by irrational fears, unfounded and often weird. At some point, the majority of human beings had such intrusive and bizarre concerns. However, intrusive thoughts and images tend to give rise to more anxiety and are more difficult to cast off in OCD sufferers than others). Also, these impulses often culminate in a panic-like response and are usually avoided and prevented. This is why Steketee and Barlow define an individual's response to OCD as another form of phobic reaction. This reaction is similar to that seen in panic disorder, except that in OCD, the phobic objects are cognitions, not sensations of the body.

Many individuals with OCD understand the repetitive and irrational essence of their behaviors.

Yet they're still engaging in behaviors designed to control or reduce unwanted thoughts. Certainly, OCD sufferers can engage in such control behavior as obsessive intrusions cause more anxiety than in others. Moreover, the very desire to neutralize and monitor intrusions that unwittingly lead to elevated anxiety, too.

251

Empirical evidence for the negative and backfiring consequences of attempts to suppress or control unwanted thoughts and images is indeed mounting. Although the age of onset for OCD is typically mid to late adolescence, problems can begin as young as five to six years of age in children. There are more males in childhood and adolescence than females suffering from OCD (sex ratio 2:1). Still, the gender distribution is roughly equal by adulthood. OCD never occurs after age fifty. If untreated, the OCD prognosis is bad.

Anxiety Disorders Have Much in Common

The variations between anxiety disorders have been the subject of scholars and clinicians in the past. These discrepancies are apparent at the phenomenological level, particularly when one reflects on events that cause fear and anxiety through anxiety disorders. For example, in basic phobias, we centered on a particular object, occurrence, or circumstance. They have been focusing on social situations in social phobia. They concentrated on distinct periods of intense fear triggered by body sensations of panic disorder. In PTSD, we focused on past traumatic events and memories associated with them.

We also differentiate cued or expected fear responses, where we know the fear-causing stimuli (e.g., in specific and social phobias and PTSD), from uncued or unexpected types of fear responses that appear to occur out of the blue (e.g., in panic disorder), where we often don't have a clear understanding of the stimuli that produce them.

We have also focused on variations in reaction duration and intensity. For example, fear and the resulting physical changes in panic disorder are severe but relatively short-lived, whereas GAD's agitation and physiological responses are less extreme and appear over much longer periods.

Phenomenological Overlap

Despite these differences among the different anxiety disorders, some striking commonalities have been extensively studied. For example, while panic attacks occur most often in people with PD, they can and do occur in people with all other anxiety disorders, too. At least 50 percent of people with social phobia and at least 30% of people with GAD and OCD suffer sporadic or regular panic attacks, for example.

Furthermore, we have known for some time that there is little difference between a panic attack that occurs in the context of panic disorder and panic attacks cued (situationally bound) that occur in the presence of specific stimuli.

Most importantly, it is characteristic of just about every individual diagnosed with an anxiety-related disorder that tends to avoid and escape fear and anxiety.

At a phenomenological level, the specific types of escape and avoidance activity vary. However, the basic function of these behaviors is the same: they serve to remove fear and anxiety and get the person out of the situation where they experience anxiety and fear. Anxiety disorders and major mood disorders such as major depression and dysthymia also overlap significantly. Barlow and colleagues report that 55 percent of patients with a major anxiety or mood disorder had at least one additional anxiety or depressive disorder at the time of assessment. When considering additional lifetime diagnoses, this rate increased to 76 percent.

Panic attacks are actually common occurrences in people with significant emotional disorders. For example, 25 to 50% of people with major depression and as many as 35 to 60% of people with somatization disorder or hypochondriasis suffer panic attacks. Brown and Barlow analyze multiple large-scale studies indicating that major depression in people with a primary anxiety disorder is by far the most frequent concurrent lifelong condition. A surprising result was that the overwhelming majority of mood disorder patients had a current or past anxiety disorder, too.

In fact, only 5 percent of 670 patients who had major depression or dysthymia throughout their lifetime did not have a current or past anxiety disorder. In most forms of anxiety and depression that coexisted, anxiety disorders accompanied the onset of mood disorders rather than pursued.

Chapter 9: Role of practicing mindfulness and self-compassion

What is Mindful Self-Compassion?

Mindful Self-Compassion (MSC) combines the skills developed through attention with the self-compassion emotional practice. While the two may be strongly similar at first glance, there's a distinction to make. It's important to describe each term to really grasp how the two work together.

Definition of Mindfulness

According to the American Psychological Association, mindfulness is "A moment-to-moment awareness of one's reality without any judgment. Awareness in that sense is a condition and not a characteristic.

While it may be encouraged by specific techniques or exercises, such as yoga, it is not identical to or interchangeable with them."

Definition of Self-Compassion

Most of us find it easy to show compassion for a friend or loved one when they are going through a difficult time in life. But when we encounter challenges ourselves, we are less capable of applying the same consideration to ourselves that we would expect others to. Sometimes we are overly critical and judgmental, thinking inwardly destructive thoughts about who we are and how we act.

"Self-compassion requires the ability to console and soothe ourselves and to inspire ourselves with motivation when we feel inadequate, disappointed, or hurt. Self-compassion is gained in part from communicating with our inherent compassion for others. Self-compassion also helps to cultivate and maintain our compassion for others. "Thus, self-compassion is about focusing on how to turn the idea of compassion inward, to promote your own emotional development and acceptance.

Also, mindfulness allows us to pay attention to any interaction or subjective feeling–optimistic, negative, or neutral–with tolerance and without structures attached. In general, self-compassion is more embedded in developing an understanding and acceptance of only negative experiences or emotions.

Mindfulness inside self-compassion is about using mindfulness in a more targeted way, helping emotional development manage personal pain feelings.

Mindful Self-Compassion has us take and integrating both of these concepts, so we use the sense of awareness and presence formed through awareness and use it to help our self-compassion emotional development.

Mindfulness and Self-Compassion

If you want to strengthen your self-compassion, it could be an excellent place to start practicing your mindfulness skills.

While the two are different activities in their own right, their fusion will lead to excellent personal outcomes. In more general practice in mindfulness, the emphasis is on the experience-thoughts, perceptions, physical sensations, and how to channel or build the emotions around the experience.

For starters, if the condition is chronic pain, you should concentrate by mindfulness on recognizing the physical aspects of the situation and directing the thoughts from pessimistic–" this is terrible pain"–to a constructive analysis of what is occurring in your body.

Nevertheless, in the focused practice of self-compassion mindfulness, the focus is on the patient as much as the experiencer. In the case of chronic pain, in the sense of self-compassion, mindfulness shifts from physical sensations to inward-turning feelings about the situation, redirecting negative thoughts of 'this is my fault' to a more neutral or positive outlook.

Self-compassion centers on the self and on calming the victim when there are distressing circumstances. By consciousness, the person may change his or her field of perception as an entity and divert or transform negative thinking.

Mindfulness can also help build an understanding of negative or painful experiences, feelings, or thoughts in the sense of self-compassion, in ways that allow self-acceptance without rumination.

While trying to create self-compassion, it can be a tricky balancing act to ensure you concentrate on embracing the trauma versus reviving the negative story repeatedly. This was focused attentiveness, which puts emphasis on tolerance, will help the journey of self-compassion.

How to Best Practice Mindful Self-Compassion

Also embedded and difficult to overcome are the negative thoughts or impulses that can occupy our heads and hinder us from genuinely developing a strong self-compassion practice. It takes time to build a solid practice of Mindful Self-Compassion, and requires a lot of compassion, as you might guess.

To begin developing a Practice of Mindful Self-Compassion, you must first identify and appreciate the obstacles you may have that keep you from self-compassion. That will depend entirely on the perceptions and values of your individual life. Another way to do that is to focus on the main (usually negative) views that you retain about yourself at present.

Write down these and then ask yourself:

- How do you feel once you've written it down?

- When did you develop your belief first? What perceptions do you equate with it?

- What specific events or circumstances cause your belief about yourself?

- Who encourages your belief in yourself?

- What would your life look like if you didn't believe it on yourself?

Now you have your Mindful Self-Compassion exercise as its starting point. Meeting these values can take patience, but sticking with them can create a great deal of positive change for your personal development.

257

The following steps of your journey might include: develop a triggered awareness. When negative self-beliefs arise, try to identify what caused them. What was said about where you were, who were you with? This exercise aims not to know how to prevent stimuli but rather to gain a greater understanding of what they are.

Practice Mindfulness-Incorporate a daily practice of mindfulness focused specifically on or around the causes. Discover what happens to feelings or inner thoughts. In these moments, how would you prefer to think or feel? Which phrases can help to turn your emotional reactions into triggers?

Discuss troublesome feelings or sentiments–Similar to how you wrote down your core beliefs as they surface, put the mind back to those questions. By linking them to their roots, develop your awareness and understanding of judgmental or derogatory feelings about yourself.

Embrace what you have avoided-we often avoid or attempt to remove negative triggers from our lives. Identify how or when you could do that, and recognize that as part of who you are. That is a tactic of self-preservation. Then, try to allow yourself space to understand what you've been denying and embrace it.

Be your own best friend–Ask yourself how you would respond to a best friend who thought or felt this way about themselves when you feel negative thoughts of judgment for the self-beginning to come up again? Would you be harsh and aggressive or caring and gentle? Use this on yourself.

Chapter 10: Being Genuine, the Key to Success

When we decide to be authentic, the person we become will likely leave behind beliefs, dreams, relationships, places to rescue others. Deciding to take action, especially in what makes us happy, is courageous on our part and our responsibility.

A decision like this is the starting point of a path that begins and lasts a lifetime. Maybe at some point, we feel lost without knowing very well which option is the best or if it is the one we want. We find it hard to be sure about what we want. Although, in addition to being wrong and judging us, we can also be afraid of not accepting ourselves.

And what does it mean to be genuine?

Being ourselves is when we laugh at what makes us grace when we cry to what makes us sad when we exploit in anger at a situation that takes us out of our boxes. We live our circumstances accordingly to what we want, feel and think, moment by moment, regardless of what everyone else thinks, that is, to be genuine.

People live in a community. We tend to build our image based on the experiences we have in interactions with others. Thus, social context influences us. Although we have to consider that we live with more people, preserving or establishing a criterion (always from respect for others) is critical if we want to be genuine.

As we have already said, to be genuine, we have to get rid of habits, thoughts, or people that have become part of our identity or our life. To choose ourselves is to say goodbye to certain elements, although this means being tangent to the loneliness curve.

Feeling alone is not the same as being alone. If we manage it properly, emotions can help us have a personal scenario in which to exercise our freedom and take the steps towards what we understand as a success.

The Expectations of Others

In exposing ourselves to others' opinion, we have to face each of the filters that make up our social support structure:

Our closest circle is those who have seen us grow, with whom we enjoy privacy. People may think that they know entirely who we are, what we want, and what is best for us.

Those who are part of our professional circle would be the ones who, with their feedback, lead us to reaffirm ourselves as good or bad professionals.

We also have all those with whom we have a little relationship or have had it. They are not usually the most important people in our lives, but we typically give them that role. They end up becoming a mirror of a perverse reflection in which we look.

Last but not least, ourselves. It's funny, but we end up being our biggest and most feared enemy and the main culprit of our insecurities and misfortunes.

When Being Genuine Goes to the Background: The Fear of Being Oneself

The primary source of learning is observation, as evidenced by Albert Bandura's studies on social learning. Observing the behavior of others and the consequences that result from it, we learn: establishing associations.

Sometimes, the anticipation of valuable information makes us look more outwards than towards ourselves, especially in cases where insecurity and fear are the helms that guide us.

For example, Steve Hayes, within the framework of Acceptance and Commitment Therapy, works with patients from the idea that being genuine is the key to achieving goals. On certain occasions, dissociating ourselves from ourselves is the price to pay for living the dreams of others; acting disconnected from what we want and feel leads to a disconnection with the intimate, with the owner. This defense mechanism is common in people who do not act according to their wishes or values.

Another typical behavior pattern that derives from not being genuine is experiential avoidance. Many people avoid what frightens them and create anxiety, even sensing that what they escape is the same as what they want.

Live with meaning, the path to success

But what is success? Each one has its definition. Well, being genuine is also finishing specifying these semantics and acting in line with it. On the other hand, from Acceptance and Commitment Therapy, it is proposed that clarifying values is essential to build a life that is worth living, and these are the fundamental pillars that give meaning to who we are.

We focus on what others expect from us, what they want. To be genuine, we must focus on ourselves, especially on knowing ourselves in depth. It would be a question of tolerating - even wanting - a necessary solitude, which will not lead us to anything at all but will open the doors of our particular paradise.

Important ACT Exercises

This section is a handy guide, a rough exercise for mental health professionals to permit their clients to look at how counterproductive evasion may be. You will end up this hobby in the accompanying advances: bring your consumer a chunk of paper and a pen and technique them on the occasion that they may be organized for composed guidelines.

Before the purchaser composes something, pose an obstruction that obstructs the ability of the consumer to look at the paper and pen (e.g., a sheet of cardboard, a mask with a significantly confined vision, etc.) Ask the consumer if they may be disturbed via means of this and if they are as a substitute see how they type. Inform them that the barrier might live; however, they must nevertheless attempt to work across the impediment, which will write the sentence. Let them fail for 20-30 seconds to look across the obstacle. At this stage, they, in all likelihood, won't have written something comprehensible Tell the consumer about their revel in (i.e., "How became it? Was it hard? Are you capable of writing the sentence? Could we apprehend it?")

Propose that the consumer forestall seeking to see across the barrier simply agrees that it's miles there and writes the sentence anyway.

Applying Mindfulness to Your Therapeutic Practice

There is a significant distinction in the sentence they write while specializing in writing (as opposed to warding off); this may, in all likelihood, be greater readable. Please factor that out and assist in finding the link between stopping the bodily barrier and warding off the emotional ache and the terrible outcomes of every.

These exercises may be carried out on your own or guided via the means of a therapist. Taking those measures will permit you or your consumer to understand that ache is an inevitable part of life.

Follow those methods to strive for this routine:

Locate a critical motion or courting which you have pulled lower back from as of late;

Take out a document card or a chunk of paper. From one viewpoint, file what you esteem about that movement or courting or what you propose to reap or end up thru it;

then again, file the problematic issues and sentiments that once in a while transpire while you make a pass to choose up the well worth or accomplishments composed on the alternative facet;

Put the cardboard for your pocket, wallet, or sack.

Take it out all through the subsequent week, take a gander at the two facets, and ask yourself whether or not you're inclined to have that card, with each splendid and awful.

It is feasible that you could avoid the well worth and the soreness or draw close to each.

What Carol Vivyan says about Exposure to Emotions?

This way is a process of mindfulness that could defuse a substantial, terrible feeling. Follow the method to recharge your emphasis on tolerating your features and creating an active pass: take a seat down without difficulty in a relaxed zone.

Carry your attention concerning your frame, revel in the respiratory sentiments without endeavoring to govern the breath, observe the sensation(s) which you sense, and what it appears like; name the impression. Perceive what it's miles and what phrase exceptional portrays the way you sense; apprehend feeling as a hallmark and normal reaction to conditions. Don't tolerate or decide it; simply allow it to pass through you; look at the emotion via way of asking questions, including: how intensely do I sense this emotion? Did my respiratory change? What are the sensations which accompany my frame? What is my posture like? Do I revel in heightened muscle tension? What is my modern-day facial expression? How does that look on my face? Note the following feelings or conclusions; however, allow them to pass. When you locate your self-targeting any of them, lightly convey lower back your mind to re-centering your respiratory, then discover the sensation again. This method should yield exceptional consequences while you begin small and work your manner as much as greater excessive feelings.

This method is an unusual preliminary step to start rehearsing ACT approaches for absolutely everyone trying to. Qualities are a vital little bit of acknowledgment and obligation treatment, as referenced before.

The worksheet Valued Directions affords ten hobby regions for the scholar to take into account which might be indexed below:

- *Work/career;*
- *Intimate relationships;*
- *Parenting;*
- *Education/learning/non-public growth;*
- *Friends/social life;*
- *Health/bodily self-care;*
- *Family of birthplace (or connections apart from marriage or child-rearing)*
- *Spirituality Community life/condition/nature;*

- *Recreation*

The hobby at that factor requests that the per-user charge the importance of every well worth place to (giant) on a length of zero (under no circumstances giant). There's not anything incorrect with a greater fee of sure fields than others.

In every field, readers are then rating their pride in their lives on a scale from zero (now no longer glad at all) to (very glad).

When the determinations of value had been finished, the routine requests that per user survey any an incentive on the dimensions of essentialness evaluated as one and to compose the objectives for future years there. In different words, write down what you need to reap, retain, or end up in each critical place of the fee.

These aren't goals that may be finished and "checked off," however, as a substitute aspiration, which might be actionable and match the manner you need to behavior your day-by-day life.

This exercise can assist provide an explanation for what's critical for your life, what desires to be prioritized. It's higher when you have a medical doctor or an educated expert to proportionate the results and expectancies that may be actioned. Whether you're really present process counseling or now no longer, it's miles nevertheless a hit exercise.

Metaphors additionally play a critical position in attractiveness and commitment therapy. They supply clients with an honest approach to see how their sentiments and musings affect their activities, allowing them to understand how our practices are encouraged via means of converting our issues.

Here are 3 of our desired giant analogies for the ACT.

The Metaphor Sailing Boat

This analogy uses the putting off a bit cruising pontoon with "you" as a mariner. At instances, waves ship water over the floor and into the boats, allowing moist toes to disturb you. The ship has a bailer to spare the water to determine how to make use of that gas.

So, one day, you start bailing while a mainly massive wave breaks over the facet and leaves water for your boat. You might also additionally hold The Sailing Boat Metaphor performing to bail lightly or attentively; however, you could finally locate your self-bailing frantically or violently to get out of all this water.

Have you observed what occurs for your boat at the same time as you had been bailing? Where are they headed? Where did it float to? Would it's truthful to mention which you bailed up more significant than simply sailing?

Then believe taking a have a take a observe the bailer and seeing it's only a sieve, complete of holes? Which is it you will do?

The implicit cause of bailing water right here is to get your boat lower back on track— when you eliminate the water boat. But in case your tool doesn't match the mission, you'll locate yourself seeking to get out of any water, not to mention steer your ships.

The query is, might you as a substitute be on a ship that handiest has a bit water in the backside, however, is drifting without route, or on a boat which could have pretty a chunk of water in the backside, yet, heads in the way you need to go?

This illustration can assist you or your people in well-known matters: the techniques we use to control our disenchanted musings and feelings are devices just like the bailer and the sifter. A few are advanced to different human beings. At instances running frantically to live away from moist toes (or different hard or awkward sentiments) makes us so, of course, the "moist toes" interruption and conflict will become our squares to perform our objectives, now no longer the waves.

The Mind Bully Metaphor

This metaphor is meant for human beings who have a selected emotion or illness, including frustration, fear, or depression.

The thought bully is our specific hassle on this metaphor: it's miles a huge and effective bully. We are pulling from side to side on a rope on inverse facets of a pit because the Mind Bully tries to make us fall into the hole.

While we pull at the rope, track in, and consciousness at the beast, or maybe consider it, we're in reality looking after it. Like any bully, as we interact with it, the Mind Bully can do the handiest harm to us and accept as true the terrible matters it tells. To placed it every other manner, do now no longer allow your thoughts to bully your frame.

What do you believe you studied might manifest if we dropped it instead of pulling at the rope? The Mind Bully would possibly nevertheless be there, hurling its insults and meanness; however, it couldn't pick us to the pit anymore.

The much less we feed the Mind Bully, the littler it's going to get, and the calmer it's going to. Maybe, in the lengthy run, we can even increase compassion for this depressing animal and miracle why it says imply issues like that.

By seeing and spotting it, we end looking after the Mind Bully but transferring our attention away from it in preference to accepting what it says. Focusing on a brief exercise in mindfulness may be an exceptional approach to do this.

The Quicksand Metaphor

Quicksand is a loose, moist sand patch that couldn't preserve weight like dry sand can. Instead of searching for a stable footing, you begin sinking as you stroll into quicksand.

Basic statistics is that struggling with sand lure simply expands the charge, and it sucks you down into its profundities. At the factor, while you placed greater weight on one foot to try to raise the opposite, you, without a doubt, sink into the pit further. The decrease you fall, the greater you endure. Wonderment! Wonder!

The technique of surviving quicksand is to unfold your frame weight and pass slowly over a huge floor place.

Rather than trying to combat the sand lure, dismiss your struggling with impulses and, as a substitute, rests to your lower back.

It is nonsensical, but the much less you conflict, and the less complicated it's miles to get away, the greater you well known your gift condition and draw close weakness.

A comparable rule applies to soreness, enduring, and knowing while to request and assist. The greater we combat and combat in opposition to it, the greater we drag ourselves down deeper in place of accepting our situation.

When we agree that the ache is imminent, we're much more likely to live to tell the tale and pop out quicker and with higher efficiency from the opposite facet.

Conclusion

Many Psychological therapies have been proposed in the recent few decades. Acceptance and commitment therapy, also known as ACT, is one of such relatively new therapies. It has its roots in the behaviorism school of thought of Psychology. It is considered to be a third-wave behavioral therapy with many potent previous treatments like cognitive behavioral therapy lying in its foundation.

Acceptance and Commitment Therapy (ACT) offers skills such as mindfulness to help people live and act in ways that are genuinely compatible with personal values while improving their psychological resilience or flexibility. Using professionals, ACT helps individuals understand how their attempts to suppress, handle, and control emotional experiences pose challenges. By identifying and solving these issues, individuals can make way for decisions focused on values that promote well-being. Acceptance and commitment therapy helps deal with many mental health issues like stress, depression, anxiety, and eating disorders.

To fully take advantage of ACT, it is essential to understand the very core principles of the therapy. All the core principles can be incorporated in life through the use of different interventions for different individuals. Some of the ACT techniques, activities, and exercises can be practiced by the individual himself. However, in case of a complicated issue, an individual may seek the help of a professional therapist. ACT practices include the use of metaphors since the human brain prefers to learn through examples or stories. Other techniques include different mindfulness and acceptance activities. The methods can be applied in a one-on-one session; however, some people may be suggested to participate in group therapy. Participating in group therapy helps individuals to understand the perspective of other members and may provide better clarity.

The use of ACT has been proven to be effective in different aspects of life. ACT therapy techniques are used by the marital or couple counselors to help resolve the issues between the couple by encouraging them to develop acceptance, mindfulness, and psychological flexibility. ACT interventions have been equally valuable for the treatment of children with anxiety and an autism spectrum disorder.

Many researchers are suggesting applying the ACT techniques in schools to help kids with mental health well-being. ACT techniques are excelling at coping with workplace stress too. Studies suggest the employers abstain from creating constant stress and burden for the employees.

Similarly, it is suggested that the organizations provide employees with the opportunity to learn ACT skills like mindfulness to cope better with everyday work-related stress and live a life according to personal values. Acceptance and commitment therapy is clinically practiced in dealing with a wide range of mental health issues like eating disorders, depression, OCD, and anxiety. No matter what aspect of life ACT is used in, therapy aims to make room for accepting the life situations and committing to take a valued action to live a better life.

POLYVAGAL THEORY AND VAGUS NERVE

__^

Introduction

The Polyvagal Theory is a theory that axioms interconnection between the brain and the vagus nerves, which causes sensitive influences in the general body balance. The vagus nerve is an essential segment of the autonomic nervous system. Polyvagal theory lists the structure and capacity of the two unique parts of the vagus, the two of which start in the medulla. More explicitly, each branch is related to an alternate versatile conduct procedure, the two of which are inhibitory through the parasympathetic nervous system. The vagal framework is contrary to the sympathetic adrenal framework, which is engaged with assembly practices. As per the polyvagal theory, these contrasting systems are phylogenetically arranged.

The vagus, or tenth cranial nerve, serves to point out the connection between intuitive encounters and the vagus nerve's parasympathetic control of the heart, lungs, and stomach-related tract. The theory was presented in 1994 by a Scientist. As indicated by the theory and its expanding proof base, the autonomic nervous system is interconnected with and delicate to impacts that stream from the body toward the mind, called afferent impacts.

These capacities follow a phylogenetic chain of importance. The crudest frameworks are enacted just when the more developed capacities come up short. These neural pathways direct the autonomic state and the outflow of passion and social conduct. Hence, as per this theory, the physiological state directs the scope of conduct and mental experience. The polyvagal theory has numerous ramifications for investigating stress, feeling, and social conduct, which has customarily used increasingly peripheral files of excitement, for example, pulse and cortisol level. The estimation of vagal tone in people has become a novel record of pressure powerlessness and reactivity in numerous investigations of populaces with full of feeling issue.

Chapter 1. What Is a Polyvagal Theory?

The entire nervous system works in the wheel with the brain and may take over our emotional expertise, even when we don't need it. The polyvagal theory is based on the neurophysiological and neuroanatomical distinction between the two branches of the vagus, proposes that every branch supports a particular accommodative behavioral strategy. The idea relies on understanding the accommodative behaviors supported by three neural circuits, each representing a special phyletic stage of the autonomic nervous system. The polyvagal theory explains three different components of our nervous system and their responses to trying things. Once we perceive those three components, we can see why and how we tend to react to high amounts of stress. If polyvagal theory sounds as exciting as observing the paint dry, stick around, trust me. It's a desirable rationalization; however, our body handles emotional stress and how we can use different therapies to rewrite the impact of trauma. As polyvagal theory revolves around the vagus nerves that are an area of our nervous system that's thus complexed. We must have an idea about the types of systems, responses, and nerves running in our nervous system to better understand the polyvagal theory.

Before we can get too much into the Polyvagal system, we need to take a quick look at the autonomic nervous system or the ANS. This will be the system in the body that will take care of the visceral internal organs, including the lungs, stomach, heart, and intestine. It can also take control over a few of the other muscles, including the diaphragm, to help us control our rate of breathing.

The reason that it was given this name is that it will function without us consciously controlling it. For example, how often do you really need to think about your breathing (though you can hold your breath and control it a bit), about digesting your food, or about your heartbeat and how that is doing. They are going to happen automatically without you needing to think about it.

Most of the functions in this system are going to engage with two essential reactive systems. These will include the sympathetic nervous system and the parasympathetic nervous system, which we will call the ventral vagal response in the Polyvagal Theory.

This will be the system that can stimulate a series of calming responses and encourage interaction and social interaction. We will explore these in more detail as we go through the process, but for now, we need to go more into our nervous system and look at how it is meant to work.

The Peripheral and Central Nervous Systems

The nervous system is often known as either part of the central system or the peripheral system. We can start with the central region because this will comprise parts like the brain and the spinal cord. It is central because it is the part that controls all of our bodily functions along the way. Then we have the peripheral nervous system, which will be made up of all the nerves that go out of the body and out of the spinal cord and will control all of the organs and muscles.

The central nervous system is going to be in charge of it all. The brain will decide which actions will happen and will send that information down the spinal cord. It will then be translated over to the peripheral nervous system to control the actual body movements and actions that we rely on. The peripheral nervous system will help with most of the activities we do, including breathing, movements, digesting, seeing, hearing, and more.

The Sympathetic Nervous System

The next thing that we need to take a look at is going to be known as the sympathetic nervous system. This was a system that developed as a method that helped us to survive throughout the years. The reactions that we had, the ones that made us more intelligent, resilient, and able to react to the threats and dangers that came after us thousands of years ago, are commonly referred to as the fight or flight response and are part o the sympathetic system.

Long ago, these threats were tangible because they were real dangers of survival against wild animals, other humans, and even natural emergencies. Being able to run fast, swing more, hump high, and other defensive actions were necessary to make sure that we could survive.

273

These instant reactions with solid surges of energy were not really voluntary. Most of the time, they were not going to be thought through because we would not have the time to handle this. This is why the SNS< or the sympathetic nervous system came into play.

Today, the SNS is going to work in a slightly different manner. We may see it show up when someone raises their voice in anger when we hear a car horn blare, when a vicious dog comes our way, or something else that startles us. Today, it could even show up when we are anticipating something or feeling stressed out. This could be something like an interview, an exam, or something else.

Let's look more at how the SNS system is going to happen. When it is activated, we will see that it is going to initiate an immediate surge of hormones. One of these will be adrenaline, which will raise the rate of our heart and deliver more oxygen to the cells of the muscles. The lungs will then breathe faster and put more oxygen into the blood to increase the muscles' energy and increase the brain's alertness.

Another thing that will happen is that there will be a surge of glucose that enters the blood to help boost our responsiveness and energy. This action will take place in just seconds, without the awareness of the individual at all.

As all of this is going on, the vagus nerve will come in and trigger the digestive system to slow down and sometimes even stop so. That way, the energy that comes with doing this action can be used in other locations in the body. When all of this is done, the body will be at its peak performance and ready to take on any dangers that may be heading its way, whether these dangers are real or not.

The Parasympathetic Nervous System

While many of the ANS systems will be engaged to help start up the response that we see in the SNS, a different process has to also take place behind the scenes. Otherwise, when we got in that heightened state, we would never be able to get out of it and would be high on adrenaline and other issues all of the time. And that is where the PNS or parasympathetic nervous system is going to show up.

This is a system that will be mediated by the ventral vagus nerves and is set up to help deactivate and even counteract what we are going to see with some of those extreme reactions of the SNS. This is often called the rest and digest phase because our heart rate and our blood pressure will slow down, digestion will resume, and breathing will slow as well. Basically, when the PNS starts to work, we are going to enter into a state of homeostasis again.

We need to have the PNS show up, or we are never going to be able to slow down and relax. But for some people, the SNS Is going to be strong, and the PNS is not going to be as developed as it should. And when this happens, we stay at an elevated stress level and overstimulation for far too long. While this is a good state to occasionally help us succeed and get through more complex and stressful situations, if we stay at this level for too long, it can cause damage to our bodies, and it is never a good thing.

We will learn more about this system and how it works, figure out ways to limit the SNS (outside of situations where it is really needed), and increase what the PNS can do. This can improve our overall health and well-being in ways that you may not be able to imagine in the past.

The vagus nerve

When talking about the vagus nerve, it is more important to get the concept off neuroception first. As a part of our involuntary nervous system, this method is going on while not even aware that it's happening. Even if we tend to be ready to breathe while not telling ourselves to require a breath, we are ready to scan the environment for cues while not telling ourselves to try and do so. The vagus nerve is of specific interest throughout this method of neuroception. Within the method of neuroception, either side of our vagus nerve can be stimulated. Either side (ventral and dorsal) has been found to retort in distinct ways. We tend to scan and process information from the environment and social interactions.

The vagus nerve is the 10th cranial nerve, a long and vagus nerve that begins at the medulla. This part of the brain, the medulla, is found within the lower part of the brain, sitting simply on top of wherever the brain connects with our spine.

The vagus nerve is a primary element of the involuntary nervous system. Polyvagal theory outlines the structure and performance of the two distinct branches of the vagus, which originate within the medulla. Additionally, every branch is related to a unique adjustive behavioral strategy, each of which is restrictive via the parasympathetic nervous system. The vagus nerve system is opposite to the sympathetic system, which is concerned with mobilization behaviors. In line with the polyvagal theory, these opposing systems are phylogenetically organized.

There are two sides to the current vagus nerve, the dorsal (back) and the ventral (front). From there, the two sides of the vagus nerve run down throughout our body to own the widest distribution of all the nerves inside the body.

The ventral (front) aspect of the vagus nerve responds to safety cues in the environment and interactions. It supports feelings of physical safety and being safely showing emotion connected to others in our social surroundings.

The dorsal (back) aspect of the vagus nerve responds to cues of danger. It pulls us off from association, out of awareness, and into a state of self-defense.

Within his polyvagal theory, Porges describes three evolutionary stages concerned with the development of our autonomic nervous system.

Instead of merely suggesting that there's a balance between our sympathetic and parasympathetic nervous system, Porges describes that there's truly a hierarchy of responses designed into our autonomic nervous system.

Immobilization: It is represented as the oldest pathway. This involves an associate immobilization response. As you may keep in mind, the dorsal (back) aspect of the vagus nerve responds to cues of maximum danger, inflicting us to become immobile. This suggests that we might reply to our concern by changing into frozen, numb, and shut down. Nearly as our parasympathetic nervous system is kicking into overdrive, our response truly ends up in our shutting and freezing down. Shutdown, or freeze-or-faint, happens through the dorsal branch of the cranial nerve. This reaction will feel like muscle fatigue or lightheadedness of nasty influenza. Once the dorsal vagus nerve shuts down the body, it will move us into immobility or dissociation. Additionally, to move the center and lungs, the dorsal branch affects the body functioning below the diaphragm and is concerned with biological process problems.

Mobilization: Inside this response, we tend to are into our sympathetic nervous system because the system helps us mobilize within the face of a danger cue. We tend to spring into action with our Adrenalin rush to urge off from danger or defend our threat.

Polyvagal theory suggests that this pathway was next to develop within the evolutionary process hierarchy. The fight-or-flight response plays a crucial role in managing stress and danger in the environment. The response prepares the body to either fight or turn tail the threat. In response to acute stress, the body's sympathetic nervous system is activated due to the release of hormones. The sympathetic nervous systems stimulate the adrenal glands triggering the discharge of catecholamines, including Adrenalin and Noradrenaline. This ends up in a rise in pulse, B.P, and respiratory rate too when the threat is gone, and it takes between 20 to 60 hours for the body to come back to its pre-arousal levels.

Social engagement: It is the most recent addition to the hierarchy of responses. This is primarily based on our ventral (front) aspect of the vagus nerve. Keeping in mind that this part of the vagus nerve responds to feelings of safety and association, social engagement permits us to feel anchored and is expedited by that ventral vagus pathway. During this area, we feel safe, calm, connected, and engaged. The ventral branch of the vagus nerve affects the body functioning on top of the diaphragm. This is the branch that provides the social engagement system. The ventral cranial nerve dampens the body's frequently active state.

The polyvagal theory provides many insights into the adjustive nature of the physiological condition.

First, speculation emphasizes that physiological states support completely different categories of behavior. For example, a physiological condition characterized by a vagus nerve withdrawal would support the mobilization behaviors of fight and flight. In distinction, a physiological condition characterized by elevated vagus influence on the heart would support spontaneous social engagement behaviors.

277

Second, the speculation emphasizes the formation of an integrated social engagement system through purposeful and structural links between the neural management of the face's striated muscles and the sleek muscles. Third, the polyvagal theory proposes a mechanism of neuroception to trigger or inhibit defense methods. Through this approach, the theory provides a plausible rationalization for the reportable covariation between atypical involuntary regulation (e.g., reduced vagus nerve and enlarged sympathetic influences to the heart) and medical specialty and behavioral disorders that involve difficulties in regulation applicable social, emotional, and communication behaviors.

Chapter 2. The Physiological Regulation of Emotion

When we experience something upsetting, we react emotionally and physically. The emotional reaction may be anger, or anxiety, or stress. Or it may be fear. Our body may quickly prepare for action in the sympathetic nervous system's fight or flight response in more stressful or fearful situations. Our emotional reactions may trigger more moderate responses in less threatening conditions, such as a slightly elevated heart rate, marginally faster breathing, no real impact on our digestive system. Our pupils may dilate slightly in the facial zone, our hearing may become slightly more acute, our facial expressions may show only a small degree of frustration or disappointment.

But whether the reactions are extreme or moderate, they may be brought under control, bringing us back to a state of normalcy or homeostasis. According to Polyvagal Theory, the control may be mediated physiologically. Bodily actions affecting emotions, which, in turn, affect the physiological reactions or overreactions to stress. In other words, emotional responses first trigger physical reactions. Physical activities calm the emotional responses, bringing everything back to normal.

Managing Stress

Stress. Everyone knows—or thinks they know—what stress is, and the result is a variety of definitions. Some mix stress with anxiety; others think stress is tension due to anticipation of difficult challenges. Still, others perceive stress on a more physiological basis, including an elevated cardiovascular and respiratory state. Whatever the cause, and whatever the definition, there seems to be general agreement that stress is an undesirable and potentially destructive event that should be avoided or neutralized when it does occur. The goal of stress-avoidance or stress-elimination is to achieve a state of calm relaxation, that being the antithesis of stress.

279

Before the emergence of the Polyvagal Theory, the autonomous nervous system was understood to embrace two physiological stress response mechanisms:

The sympathetic response, which is the well-known call to immediate action when danger or high risk creates a high stress level. This leads either to fear, panic, and preparation for escape or evasion, leading to anger, rage, and preparation for aggression.

The parasympathetic response deactivates the sympathetic responses elevated levels to calm and cool things down, lowering elevated heart rate and slowing rapid breathing, returning the digestive system to normal and the person to an overall peaceful, relaxed state of mind. This response is mediated by the ventral vagus nerve, meaning it is located towards the front of the body.

But when Dr. Porges introduced the Polyvagal theory, he added a third level of reaction, the most extreme, when the parasympathetic nervous system causes a near-total shutdown of vital bodily functions:

This third level is called the dorsal vagal, meaning it is found in the rear part of the body. This response may cause an animal to play dead or a person to become immobilized, incapable of movement or rational thought. A person may become speechless, enter deep depression, faint, or go into shock. In the most extreme situations, cardiac arrest may occur, leading to death if not reversed immediately.

In almost all stressful situations we may encounter in our daily lives, the stress levels are perceptible, perhaps somewhat debilitating, with our sympathetic responses causing moderately elevated heart and breathing rates, some sweating, and a feeling of nervousness or anxiety. Suppose the event or situation causing the stress can be completed in the near term. In that case, the interview is over, the test completed, the dangerous road safely crossed, the steep hill easily skied down—the calming parasympathetic response will automatically bring you down, cool you off, put you in a state of relaxation, possibly elation if the challenge overcome was formidable.

But if the stress cannot be neutralized quickly by resolving its cause, can it be brought down consciously and deliberately?

A state of relaxation can be achieved through specific practices that have become better understood through the Polyvagal Theory.

The objective of stress reduction is called the relaxation response. The body's physical actions, mediated by the ventral vagus nerve, stop the surges of adrenaline, slow heart rate, lower respiration, and induce a state of calm.

Most techniques to induce the relaxation response center on the control of breathing. When under stress, our breathing becomes more rapid and more shallow. This is an involuntary sympathetic response, but it can be reversed, bringing down the sympathetic response and swapping in the calming parasympathetic response.

Polyvagal Theory originator, Dr. Steven Porges, recommends tricking the body by assuming deliberate control of the breathing process. Find a quiet place where there are minimal distractions. You may sit or stand, and in either case, be comfortable:

Begin by telling yourself it is time to become at peace with yourself.

Consciously become aware of your breathing.

Begin to take slow, deep breaths, pausing for a moment, or two between each inhale and each exhale.

Your breaths should be deliberately deeper than usual as you inhale, extend the diaphragm outward, and exhale fully, pulling in the diaphragm. Remember to pause briefly at each cycle.

Count the inhales, starting from one. Alternatively, count backward from 10. Repeat after each ten-count. Options: count exhales, or count both inhales and exhales.

Keep your mind on your breathing and nothing else. As other thoughts try to intrude, do not become angry but gently refocus your thoughts on breathing in deeply, pausing, breathing out deeply.

Remain conscious of your efforts to force the diaphragm outward on each inhale and inward, toward your spine, on each exhale. Be aware of the pauses and be aware of the count of each breath.

Continue the deep, deliberate breathing for a minute or two, ideally for five to ten minutes if time and patience permit.

When you resume normal breathing, keep a positive outlook and do not allow yourself to return to stress-inducing thoughts and worries. The best way to keep the stressful thoughts away is to tell yourself you are calm, in control, at peace. Smile, as smiling is a ventral vagus nerve response and will further induce a warmer, more relaxed physical and mental state.

Traditional meditation is a more formal method of achieving the relaxation response. Functional Magnetic Resonance Imaging (fMRI) studies of brain activities and responses confirm that mediation practiced over time can induce physiological changes in brain function; long-term meditation practitioners believe they have gained control of their emotions and have significantly reduced the onset of stress and its bodily reactions. The fMRI tests show increases in blood flow to parts of the brain activated by the meditation, confirming the onset and continuation of the relaxation response mediated by the ventral vagus nerve system.

Meditation may be performed like the above breathing exercises, but with the person seated comfortably in a quiet environment, eyes closed, and full focus on either the breathing or a mantra, a humming sound issued on each exhale. To some people, the mantra helps clear away extraneous, distracting thoughts.

Mindful meditation is a Buddhist-inspired variation in which the individual, while in the relaxed pose, remains conscious of the moment, aware of every feeling, every sound, every other sensation. It is a continuous, dispassionate, and non-evaluative state of mind. Mindful meditation followers believe their awareness of their total incoming environment, attention to the present moment, keep their minds clear of other thoughts, leading to more profound relaxation and elimination of stress and anxiety.

There are apps available online, free or at low cost, that can help the meditative process, providing soft, peace-inducing words and suggestions, and either restful music or sound effects, like waves crashing, gentle rain, crickets chirping, and wind blowing.

What about Yoga? While Yoga incorporates a range of physical activities that stimulating toning of the vagus nerve, the deep, deliberate breathing exercises.

Overcoming Depression

Depression is a state of mind. It is mental, yet it is also a physically affected disorder. The Polyvagal Theory establishes that depression is caused by malfunctions of the vegetative nervous system.

The action-directing sympathetic nervous system is keeping the depressed individual in a continuing state of low-level stress. The calming parasympathetic nervous system may be functioning but not sufficiently to fully counteract the sympathetic responses. The depressed individual falls into a state often characterized by apathy, lack of drive and motivation, and a general lack of energy. Yet, despite the lack of energy and drive, the condition inhibits the ability to rest, and sleep becomes lengthy but not restful. The agitating results of stress remain behind the scenes, keeping the action impulses from fully slowing down and dissipating since the parasympathetic response is only partially successful in its calming effects. Heart rate and breathing rate are only partially slowed. The result is a limbo between action and inaction, expending energy while not allowing relaxation to be achieved. Depression can worsen as the situation appears endless, hopeless, with further weakening of resolve as energy reserves continue to be dissipated. There is little interest in social activity and empathy toward other people.

As we have just seen with the management of stress, breathing may play an important role in reducing or eliminating depression. Breathing can be so influential due to the vagus nerve, which plays a key role in our breathing rates and depths. When the sympathetic nervous system causes the heart rate to increase and breathing rates to increase while making breaths more shallow, these vagus nerve-instigated reactions to stress can be managed. Instead of allowing the vagus nerve to affect breathing, we can use breathing to affect the vagus nerve, inducing it to switch modes sympathetic to parasympathetic. This is referred to as putting on the vagal brake. The two phases of breathing, inhaling and exhaling, are involved.

As with stress reduction, the technique to manage depression involves taking deeper, slower, more deliberate breaths. A deep inhale signals the parasympathetic vagal system to engage and stimulate relaxation. It also increases the amount of oxygen inhaled and delivered via the hemoglobin in the blood to the cells, where its metabolism results in greater energy output. There is also a purely psychological effect, as the deliberate, forceful deep breath gives feelings of strength and resolve, building self-esteem and trust.

Forceful, the exhales continue the relaxation response, exerting an influence on the vagus nerve to further slow things down, getting the sympathetic reaction to back off. Psychologists believe that the slow, forceful exhale adds a sense of accepting life and feeling better overall.

There can be immediate results within minutes of practicing deep, slow, deliberate inhales and exhales. This procedure may be further enhanced with the meditative and mindfulness procedures cited for stress management. Depression may also respond to Yoga and other activities that combine physical efforts in harmony with the deep managed breathing exercises.

Importantly, depression is a serious disorder that may require extensive psychotherapy and medication and should only be diagnosed and treated by qualified medical personnel. Further, the effectiveness of the breathing exercises described here depends mainly on long-term continued practice, as one brief session of deep breathing may bring momentary relief of depression. Still, daily repetition, over time, is necessary for a longer-term diminishment of symptoms.

Depression, epilepsy, Alzheimer's disease, cluster headaches, and irritable bowel disease are also being treated by electrical stimulation of the left vagus nerve. A device is implanted subcutaneously, connected to the vagus nerve by a thin wire. Signals are sent through the vagus nerve to its point of origin in the brainstem and on to the parts of the brain affecting depression or other diseases. Impulses may be triggered when disturbances are detected. Results of electrical stimulation for depression, epilepsy, and other diseases have been partially successful so far. The recent introduction of non-invasive electrical vagal stimulators encourages expectations for wider applications.

Asperger's Spectrum and Autism

Application of the Polyvagal Theory is based on the professional observation that patients, especially children affected by sensory-processing disorders that fall under the Asperger's Spectrum, are frequently characterized by a lack of eye contact with others and general failure to communicate. Polyvagal Theory connects facial expressions, including eye contact, with actions mediated by the vagus nerve.

Polyvagal Theory states that the social or myelinated part of the vagus nerve connects with the heart, lungs, and digestive system—this is well-known and to the facial muscles, the eyes, and the ears. These facial region functions comprise the elements of facial expressions, which turn out to be vital in reaching and motivating Asperger's Spectrum patients.

It was observed that these patients, especially children, could not process sounds, resulting in covering their ears or turning away when spoken to. Another observation was the expressionless facial poses that are typical of Asperger's children. It was determined that stimulation of the children's social vagus nerve could help them receive sounds more normally and express themselves facially. Also, many Asperger's Spectrum patients have difficulty controlling their breathing.

Work to apply the Polyvagal Theory to improving Asperger's patients has been performed by chiropractors, who, contrary to many misconceptions, are nerve system doctors whose specialty is helping nerve systems to rewire themselves. They are at the forefront of helping patients, from those with mild Asperger's symptoms all the way through the spectrum to autism. Chiropractors follow a salutogenic healthcare model; the goal is to optimize performance and increase the state of healthiness.

Chiropractic doctors working with Asperger's patients recognized that Polyvagal Theory is compatible with their salutogenic healthcare model. Specifically, it supports the concept that the body can self-regulate itself and self-heal under the right conditions. This inspired recognition that the Polyvagal can enable the doctors to tap into the healing potential. They apply neurological exercises that stimulate vagal tone in their patients. This gives the Asperger's Spectrum patients new ways to hear, perceive, respond to people and situations, smile, speak, and maintain eye contact.

One form of neurological exercise is atlas adjustments, or Vertebral Subluxation, manipulating the spine to correct vertebrae that have become misaligned. This procedure benefits from the close proximity of this part of the spine with the vagus nerve.

The other form is manipulating the vagus nerve in the neck, accessible as it exits the jugular foramen, which is an aperture, or opening, at the base of the skull.

Patients on the spectrum report achieving a greater awareness of their bodies due to Polyvagal Theory-inspired manipulative exercises. This work is early in its development but shows promise for continued progress.

According to Polyvagal Theory author Dr. Porges, there is a direct, positive link between the autonomic nervous system, which controls our organs' responses to danger and stress, and challenges in learning and socialization. This is most evident with Autism patients. Porges has postulated that we are social creatures and look to each other for comfort, security, a sense of belonging. But autistic people cannot perceive or recognize these safety cues and are therefore unable to relate easily to others.

Trauma, PTSD, and the Vagus Nerve

Much of the reason for these sorts of symptoms is that the sympathetic nervous system can never adequately shut off after the trauma. You wind up getting caught up in this loop in which you cannot escape the trauma that you went through, no matter how hard you try. Your body will not allow you to relax, and because of that, memories are not being processed properly. You are on high alert for just about anything around you. You struggle to deal with your responses to the world around you because you can very easily be triggered back into that fight or flight response.

Of course, this will wear on you after a while. You will feel like you cannot possibly cope with what is happening. You will try your best but ultimately find that you are entirely overwhelmed by it. When you do find that you are suffering from PTSD, you need some degree of treatment. Something has to happen, or you will not be able to get yourself out of that response.

286

You need to figure out what you can do, how you can do it, and why it needs to happen so you can protect yourself, those around you, and those that you care about.

Essentially, in some situations, your body has attempted to protect you from the trauma—but it did so in a very maladaptive way. Instead of helping you escape it, you are now going to struggle more with it. Your responses are meant to be adaptive, but they are still hurting you. The good news, however, is that you can begin to alleviate those symptoms. You can learn how to defeat those flashbacks when they arise. You can figure out how you can get yourself back to relative calmness to begin to focus on how you can protect yourself otherwise. You will be able to do this all through the activation of the vagus nerve. Let's take a look at two ways to sort of ground yourself, triggering your vagus nerve to activate and creating that sort of calming sensation that will help you take back control of your life.

Treating Trauma and PTSD With Salivation

When you suffer from flashbacks or anxiety, you probably feel like you are terrified. You need to escape somehow—but you do not know how. That is okay. You can begin to calm yourself down to avoid falling into this cycle in which your anxiety gets worse and worse, and you cannot cope with it. All you have to do is work with your bottom-up methods of engagement.

One such way of doing so involves using saliva to help yourself begin to settle down and calm down. You can make good use of this with relative ease—the next time you feel stressed out, overwhelmed or triggered, try using this technique to help yourself settle back down and avoid all of those painful feelings.

• Take a deep breath: Start by taking in a big, deep breath. Remember your diaphragmatic breathing. Do this once or twice before moving forward.

• Visualize: Now, you will want to take a moment to think about your favorite food. It could be anything—imagine it in your mouth. Think about the taste of the food, the texture, the spiciness, or anything else. Imagine that you are eating the food and really savoring it. The more realistic you can make your visualization, the better.

287

•   Feel the saliva: Now, you should notice that you are salivating—and that is precisely what you want right now. Allow that saliva to really pool up in your mouth. You want a sort of bath that you can use for your tongue, and this is exactly how you make it happen. Continue to visualize the food until you have a complete mouth full of saliva, and then dip your tongue into it.

•   Focus on the saliva: Remind yourself that you could not actually be in serious danger because you are salivating. You are safe; otherwise, you would not be able to do this in the first place. Reiterate this to yourself as you immerse your tongue in the saliva. Remember, the vagus nerve does innervate part of the tongue, and because of that, you will be sending feedback with it.

If you are not very good at salivating, you can do this in other ways, too. Perhaps you decide that you are going to eat a piece of candy or chew some gum. Both of those will allow you to trigger the production of saliva that you can then take advantage of to trigger your vagus nerve.

Chapter 3. The benefits of polyvagal theory

• We tend to consider our emotions as ethereal, complex, and troublesome to reason and establish. The reality is that emotions are responses to information (internal or external). Typically, they happen out of our awareness, particularly if we tend to be out of the bit or incongruent with our inner emotional lives. Our primal want to remain alive is necessary to our body rather than even our ability to place confidence in staying alive. That's wherever polyvagal theory comes in to play.

• The nervous system is usually running within the background, dominant over our body functions; thus, we can place confidence in different things like what dinner or dessert we'd prefer to order or how to get that A+ in master's degree college. The whole nervous system works in a wheel with the brain and might take over our emotional expertise, although we tend to don't need it. Polyvagal Theory is the best explanation of how are vagus nerves work in coordination with our nervous system. The polyvagal theory is of great benefit to every age group.

It suggests the way we react and build connections to our environments.

• For therapists and psychology experts, understanding the polyvagal theory help them understandings the following

• Understanding trauma and PTSD

• Understanding the attacks and withdrawal in relationships

• Understanding however extreme stress ends up in dissociation or shut down

• Understanding to deal with mental health

• Understanding the way to learn through body language

• Further benefits include:

• The Clinical applications of polyvagal theory and vagal nerve tone that has been employed in medical and psychological analysis to higher perceive the physiological underpinnings of various disorders' clinical applications.

289

•   Clinical applications within the human fetus have high variability in vital signs, and the vagus nerve mediates that. On the opposite hand, vital sign decelerations, which are mediated by the vagus nerves, are signals of distress. Additionally, specifically, prolonged withdrawal of vagal nerve influence on the guts creates a physiological vulnerability to the impact of the Dorsal vagal nerve management, which successively produces a very low heart rate. However, the onset of this slowing is usually preceded by tachycardia, which is reflective of the immediate effects of Ventral vagal nerve management withdrawal.

•   The theory has molded each human physiology and behavior. The human nervous system is a result of evolution. Via these processes, the nervous system has emerged with specific neural and behavioral options that react to challenge to take care of the visceral physiological state.

•   The Polyvagal Theory says that the phyletic origins of brain structures regulate defensive and social behaviors, domains compromised in people with syndromes, and several other psychiatric disorders.

•   The theory links the evolution of the autonomic system to experience emotions, gestures, communication, and social behavior. Thus, the speculation provides a plausible rationalization of many social, emotional, and communication behaviors and disorders.

•   The Polyvagal Theory provides a specific biological science model of how problems in spontaneous social behavior are linked to every facial expression and regulation of visceral state and how social behavior could function as a regulator of physiological activity.

•   The theory proposes a possible mechanism to clarify; however, these difficulties may form a core domain of many medical specialty profiles. Relevant to this focus psychiatric disorders are the specific deficits related to many diagnoses in each somatomotor (e.g., poor gaze, low facial effect, lack of prosody, and difficulties indigestion) and visceromotor (difficulties in involuntary regulation leading to an internal organ and biological process issues. This phyletic mechanical phenomenon leads to additional advanced neural structures being concerned with regulating behavior, particularly the social communication behaviors required to interact with others. Moreover, these phylogenetically more modern systems do not solely give mechanisms

290

for social communication; however, they are also concerned with visceral control organs to calm states.

•   The Polyvagal Theory provides a biological science model to justify how social behavior, positive support, and affectional states may support growth and health. In distinction to the health-connected states related to prosocial behavior, withdrawal of this new neural system would promote mobilization behaviors like fight and flight furthermore as different physiological responses that will probably be damaging if maintained for prolonged periods. Thus, it's attainable that people with specific psychiatric disorders, within which compromised social behavior may be a diagnostic feature, are experiencing neuroscience states that foster defensive and nonsocial behaviors. These phyletic principles give a basis for theories regarding the physiological and behavioral responses concerning psychiatric disorders.

•   The Polyvagal Theory provides us with a better understanding of danger and safety. One supports a better interaction between the primitive experiences of our bodies and the voices and faces of the individuals around us.

•   It explains why a form face or a soothing tone of voice will dramatically alter the approach we tend to feel. It clarifies why knowing that we are seen and detected by the important ones in our lives will make us feel calm and safe and why being unheeded or unemployed will precipitate rage reactions or mental collapse.

•   It helps us perceive why attuning with another person will shift us out of scrambled and fearful states. In short, Porges's theory makes us look on the far side of the consequences of fight or flight and place social relationships in the center in understanding trauma. It conjointly advised new approaches to heal that specializes in strengthening the body's system for control arousal.

Chapter 4. What does the Nervous System do for us?

The Polyvagal Theory describes the autonomic nervous system as having different functions to do this. But what can the nervous system do for us? What's the purpose of the nervous system, and how can it benefit us? Well, read on to find out about the importance of our nervous system and how autonomic functions will impact our bodies.

a.   The Nervous System at the Core

The basic model of your nervous system is essentially this: you've got two parts: one that you can control and the other that functions without you even realizing this. The one that controls the unconscious efforts is called our autonomic nervous system. This is the body temperature, respiration, everything. All of this mediated by the ANS is important since it'll push through the sympathetic nervous system and conserve our energy via the parasympathetic nervous system.

If you're anxious, you're automatically tapping into the sympathetic nervous system, and if you're stressed, you feel this way too. The parasympathetic is mostly involved with relaxation, so if you're feeling relaxed, you're much slower in movement, and you are engaging in the process of cell regeneration.

That's how our nervous system works, and they need to work in a balance. One being more prevalent than the other isn't good for anyone. The polyvagal theory essentially offers an understanding of how the autonomic nervous system is working and how the vagus nerve plays a role in this. If you have a healthy vagus nerve, you have a healthy autonomic nervous system.

Mammals actually have two of these vagal circuits. If one of them isn't working, it can lead to other physical issues. The vagus nerve primarily focuses only on the parasympathetic nervous system, so it focuses mostly on relaxing and regulation. But, if you're unsafe or worried about something, the vagus nerve will start to dampen over time. When you're safe, your vagus nerve works, and your parasympathetic nervous system is in place.

The thing is, this system should work perfectly.

After all, it seems unflawed, right?

b.   The Autonomic Nervous System

The autonomic nervous system involves the body's automatic processes, from the regulation of the heartbeat to respiration to even how your body digests different foods. Digestion, heartbeat, and respiration are all things none of us think about. In fact, it happens on its own. We don't control any of this.

The brain communicates with these parts of the body by automatic functions. It will control the different regulatory factors as well.

The vagus nerve does play into our nervous system. After all, it controls all of these automatic processes. This area is part of the brainstem, which is responsible for our respiration and other automatic functions.

There are two areas of our body: those above and below the diaphragm. Those that are unmyelinated are below, and usually, this is on a more freeze response basis. When our body is overstimulated, our nervous system will immediately send responses to go into survival mode. So, our digestive processes stop, our respiration slows down immensely, and our heart rate directly goes to a very low rate. This is almost vegetative and automatic in a sense.

This part of our nervous system is automatic, but it has little brain control. But the other part of our brains has more control and is based more on social cues.

c.   Vagal Tone and the Nervous System

The nervous system and vagal tones are one and the same. Vagal tone is actually a clear indicator of the stress on the body and how the nervous system is reacting.

Rather than using the heart rate variability that's typically used, if you look at the sinus arrhythmia, you'll see the outflow of the vagus to the heart and how your nervous system is performing with these functions.

293

This is a measurement of the vagal regulation of this part of our body. It'll help provide more sensitive feedback to the body and help understand precisely what's going on between the neural and nonneural mechanisms in the body.

When you look at this, you can extract the amplitude of your respiratory arrhythmia. It will tell the vagal activity. Heart rate patterns do discuss a vagal activity. While this isn't something new, it does prove that vagal tone has a big bearing on the body's overall state.

The vagal blockade is actually a big problem for a lot of people. When the respiratory sinus arrhythmia is too low, it can cause some significant issues in the body, both in heart rate and respiration.

What happens to the Nervous System when the Vagus Nerve Is not Active?

As we've said before, the vagus nerve regulates the parasympathetic functions of the body for the most part. But what happens to the nervous system when it's not fully activated?

Well, think of it as a communication system. The vagus nervous is communicating out towards the body. If it's not correctly communicating, it will cause significant issues.

The heart, which is an autonomic function in the body, is one of the main parts that's affected. If you can't activate your vagus nerve to control your heart, or maybe when you're in a situation where you're stressed all the time, you'll start to, over time, feel overstimulated. This can cause brachycardia in some cases, but most of the time, it causes tachycardia. Your vagus nerve is the natural brake on the heart. Your heart will beat too fast. When not accurately communicating, it will lead to a heart overworking and lead to elevated blood pressure and even heart attacks or a stroke over time. It does happen.

When the respiratory rhythm is too low, it can also cause breathing issues. The air isn't getting to the lungs fast enough, or it is getting there too quickly. If it's not properly working, it can lead to vagal syncope in some people, which is basically fainting because you're breathing too fast.

294

When your autonomic nervous system isn't correctly working, it can create issues. The sympathetic and the parasympathetic nervous systems need to be in balance. Too much of one or the other isn't healthy for everyone. Changing your shifts from one to the other may elicit a much healthier response.

The Polyvagal Theory plays a big part in our nervous system and understands why that is critical to your own personal health and happiness.

Chapter 5. Vagus Nerve Stimulation Therapy (VNS)

The positive effects of certain forms of massage, exercise, yoga stretches and poses, and managed deep breathing are subject to considerable discussion, debate, agreement, and disagreement about the actual effectiveness of these activities and maneuvers. Now, there is empirical proof that at least some of the actions do have tangible results. In particular, actions that stimulate the vagus nerve are increasingly accepted as effective and are being recommended as noninvasive, drug-free solutions to physical and emotional challenges.

Given that the vagus nerve intervenes with or passes close to parts of the face, the lungs, the gastroesophageal digestive system, the diaphragm, exercises and actions that engage these parts of the body can stimulate and tone the vagus nerve, providing a physical adjunct to thoughtful, emotional calming efforts.

d.   Massage Therapy

Massage of certain body areas can be effective in stimulating the vagus nerve and bringing about vagal tone; these may be performed by another person, such as a masseuse, or self-applied in some cases. For example, a cluster of nerves is called the carotid sinus, located on the right side of the neck and passed by the right side vagus nerve. Gently applied massage to this sinus is reported to reduce the likelihood of seizures because it causes vagal toning.

Foot massages have long been considered to be relaxing, and now it is understood that nerves in the foot interact with and can calm the vagus nerve.

Exercise And Breathing Maneuvers You Can Use

Easy to learn and practice breathing exercises involve slow, thoughtful, deep breathing that extends and contracts the diaphragm. It is believed that consciously engaging the diaphragm induces vagal toning, leading to relaxation, shifting the vagal response from the active, sympathetic nervous response to the calming parasympathetic state. This is achieved by toning the vagus nerve.

296

Managed deep breathing exercises: Normally, we take about 12-14 breaths per minute; practice slowing it down to half that rate by taking long, slow inhales while extending the diaphragm outward, pushing it forward. Pause for a few seconds, then exhale slowly, taking about eight seconds to exhale fully, and while pulling the diaphragm forcefully inward. Pause for several seconds, then repeat the cycle. A series of 10 to 20 repetitions can bring about a renewed sense of calm: the combined deep breathing and extensions and contractions of the diaphragm work to effectively tone the vagus nerve.

Meditative breathing: An adjunct to the deep, slow breathing and forceful diaphragm extensions and contractions includes thoughtful meditation. This is performed with eyes closed, in a quiet setting, seated comfortably. With each inhale, think the words, "inner peace," then, on the next inhale, "inner calm," then continue inhaling to "spiritual peace," then "spiritual calm," then "inner Zen," then "spiritual Zen." You may repeat the cycle or continue with other calming, peaceful words of your own.

Importantly, in addition to calming thoughts, try to remain conscious of your slow, deep breaths and forceful contractions and expansions of your diaphragm so your mind is fully distracted. The objective is to prevent outside thoughts from intruding upon your meditation. You may begin with five-minute meditation and deep breathing, and over time extend to up to 20 minutes. Try to do this at least once a day. With practice, you will experience what psychologists call the relaxation response; it's the serenity and sense of renewal that the toned vagal nerve induces.

An alternative to thinking meditative words to accompany the breathing, alternatively each breath can be counted, one, two, three, four, then repeating the sequence. Another option is to acknowledge the breaths consciously: breathe in, breathe out; breathe in, breathe out.

Yoga stretches & poses: Yoga has been practiced for centuries, and its followers strongly believe in its mental and physical benefits. It is now recognized that certain Yoga movements and positions tone the vagus nerve and bring the parasympathetic nervous system into dominance. There is an extensive range of Yoga poses (called 'asanas'), stretches, and movements, which can be seen and learned online, or in Yoga-themed books and magazines. For more practical learning, a Yoga class is an excellent way to get started; look for beginner-level classes if you start out.

With all Yoga exercises and poses, it is important to remember to perform the deep, slow inhales and exhales and diaphragm extension and contractions to move effectively stimulate the vagus nerve. Try not to be distracted (especially if in a Yoga class); keep your mind focused on the movements, the tensions of the stretches, and the breathing and diaphragm actions.

As a first step, here are four popular Yoga poses that can be learned and practiced easily:

•   Cobra is achieved by lying face down, hands next to shoulders. Push the head and upper body upward to arch your back as far as you can, without straining. Hold the position for 20 to 30 seconds, conscious of your deep, slow breathing and diaphragm movements. Lower to the ground and then assume the next position, downward-facing dog, by pushing your entire body up and then "walking your hands" back toward your feet.

•   Downward-facing dog is like bending over to touch your toes, but your fingers are on the ground about 24 inches in front of your feet. Work into the position from cobra (above). Feel the stretch in your legs, arms, and shoulders while practicing the slow, deep breathing and diaphragm extensions and contractions.

•   Pose of the child is performed on your back. While lying on a soft surface, lift both legs while keeping them straight and roll back so that your toes point toward the floor behind your head. It may take practice, but eventually, you can extend the stretch so that your toes may touch the floor.

•   Warrior is a popular pose in which you place one leg forward, the other leg to the rear, and crouch down so the forward leg's thigh is parallel to the ground. Extend the arm that is opposite to the forward leg, so your fingers are pointing straight ahead; extend the other arm to the rear in the same manner. Try to hold this pose for 30 seconds, then come to a standing position, and reverse the move, forward leg now to the rear, and so on.

Exposure to cold: While in the extreme, a nearly instant toning effect may be achieved by plunging your face into a bowl of ice water can activate vagus nerve pathways and may rapidly bring down the fight or flight response and induce calm. Alternatively, in the shower, turn the temperature to cold for the last few seconds, up to a minute, can tone the vagus nerve along multiple pathways. Walking outside in cold weather, wearing limited protective clothing can be practiced, but with caution and for a brief period only. Scandinavian's practice heating themselves in a sauna, then stepping outside and rolling in the snow; an extreme but apparently effective vagal toning technique.

Vocal expressions: Given the activity of the vagus nerve in the head region, including sending and receiving impulses to and from the throat, vocal cords, tongue, and ears, stimulating the vagus nerve may be achieved by humming, singing, and even audibly gargling.

In all methods of stimulating the vagus nerve initiates the parasympathetic nervous system and provides a calming of the fight or flight response and its resultant tension, elevated heart rate and blood pressure levels, anxiety, and fear. The results are enhanced when managed breathing is applied, consciously and deliberately. This increases the vagal toning effects and further enhances calming because concentrating on the breathing and diaphragmatic action helps trigger the relaxation response usually associated with meditation.

Chapter 6. Vagus Nerve and Anxiety Disorder

Anxiety Disorder has been misunderstood. First, it is produced from the body. Preconditions are first set by the body, and then the mind can enforce it. Of course, a trained mind can make it easier to cope with an anxiety disorder in an out-of-balance state. The body cannot find the equilibrium between the relaxation and stress modes.

The anxiety caused by the mind will continue by itself for a month because the body and mind will get used to the new psychological fears. A healthy body will find a way to go into relaxation mode. I would emphasize a healthy or well-functioning body because only when the body is healthy will it find the way. It is designed to go into relaxation mode. No help is needed. And body-induced anxiety will keep it longer, maybe years. The easiest way to treat it is to treat the body.

Many say that anxiety disorder-caused symptoms are the effect of the anxiety itself. Phrased differently, mind-triggered anxiety is the cause, and the body symptoms are the effect. But it is not so with body-triggered anxiety disorder. It is both the anxiety and body symptoms caused by the body not being able to find equilibrium. Anxiety and body symptoms are both effects of something else, which is the cause.

For instance, a simple example is a small hiatal hernia (in the stomach) which irritates the vagus nerve. Thus, the body is the cause, and the mind follows. The other way is also accurate that psychological stresses will bring physiological symptoms. But it will not go for long. It will be stabilized soon.

The nervous system that maintains the balance between anxiety (fight or flight) and relaxation can be considered a loop.

Most of the organs are connected to this loop and are guided to operate into two modes:

1) fight or flight and

2) relaxation.

This loop is comprised of the vagus nerve and the nerves coming from the spinal cord. The vagus nerve comprises two branches: the dorsal branch and the ventral one (polyvagal theory).

Mind-driven anxiety is a broken balance in mind due to psychological causes. And body-induced anxiety is a broken balance in the periphery (spinal and vagus nerves). The nerves can be disturbed in their path. They can be pinched. The vagus nerve travels a long path from the medulla, located in the brainstem, to all the organs. It is the longest cranial nerve. Thus, it is logical that some muscular-skeletal pressure can affect the vagus nerve along its path.

Based on experiences of osteopaths and physiotherapists, the most vulnerable places where the mechanical pressure can happen to the vagus nerve are two:

1) atlas-axis joint and

2) hiatus in the diaphragm (hiatal hernia).

Atlas is the upper cervical vertebrae, also known as C1. The misalignment of the atlas can put pressure on the part of the vagus nerve that is located there. When the suboccipital muscles are stiff or tense, the atlas-axis joint can't function properly. A well-qualified osteopath or chiropractor may address the misalignment of an atlas.

In this case, the stomach puts pressure on the vagus while it goes through hiatus. A well-qualified osteopath or chiropractor may address the hiatal hernia.

The symptoms of a compressed or pinched vagus nerve are too many and manifest differently in different persons. The most common symptoms are anxiety, nausea, heartburn, tachycardia, vertigo, headache, a lump in the throat, cold hands and cold feet, diarrhea, constipation, sweating, and many others.

The vagus nerve can be compressed or irritated at the diaphragm area. The diaphragm can be tensed or become tender. Abnormal breathing or a slouched position may contribute to the creation of trigger points in the diaphragm. Trigger point therapy or osteopathic diaphragm release may help

301

to release the tension and eliminate the trigger points located in the diaphragm.

First, observe if your anxiety depends on your postural changes in the body. Notice how your anxiety behaves when you are sitting or standing up and slouched. Try to notice if changing your neck position can decrease anxiety. Most anxiety disorder cases are due to mechanical causes which may compress or pinch certain nerves. Nerves play an essential role in blood supply by dilating the blood capillaries.

It is important to stress that many people have bodily symptoms without anxiety. In such case, the vagus nerve is not involved in these symptoms. When the anxiety follows the physical symptoms, the chances are high that the vagus nerve is involved directly in the scenario where the vagus is responsible for all. It would be normal to have mind-induced anxiety directly following some new symptoms but not continuously all the year. The person will get used to the symptoms after some time. Thus, if the anxiety repeats continuously following the bodily symptoms, it is body-induced anxiety where the vagus nerve is involved.

The first step to help the body recover is to do some gentle exercises. It is better to begin for the first 3 months with the Ping Shuai gong three times a day to then combine with or switch to the Zhan Zhuang exercise. Zhan Zhuang is the big secret.

Biking is also a very helpful exercise for anxiety but should be associated with an internal qigong exercise. External exercises are good to burn stress, but after doing them, they leave us exhausted. In contrast, internal exercise leaves us refreshed and energized.

We wanted to say that if you know that the cause of the symptoms is the neck, you must treat the neck. If the problem is located in the abdomen, you have to focus on the abdominal massage to treat the abdominal trigger points. But when you don't know the cause, then it is better to exercise the Zhan Zhuang. Moreover, it is typical with the anxiety disorder then, usually, the symptoms are located elsewhere different from the cause. The pain is here in a part of the body, but the cause of the pain is far away. The symptoms of anxiety disorder are tricky by misleading the sufferer and the doctor.

The Zhan Zhuang will enable the body to build new neural pathways by giving the body new ways of communicating information through the electromagnetic medium. Start the exercise for as few as 15 seconds in the beginning as you are not used to it. And then gradually increase the time to at least 15 minutes. 15 minutes is the minimum for seeing noticeable improvements. 20 minutes is better. The healing process starts at 15 minutes, and the max time to practice is 40 minutes. Keep in mind not to exert the body too much. The upper body must remain relaxed.

Whenever you experience new symptoms, your body is experimenting with new neural pathways for achieving equilibrium. So, the setbacks and the new symptoms are indications of healing. The healing process is not linear. It goes back and forth. Further, the healing effect is accumulative, which means the results seem to be nonexistent initially. Still, after some time, the healing appears instantly.

Vagus nerve and anxiety: exercises to tone and reduce stress

The vagus nerve is one of those responsible for relaxing your body. Among its functions is to reduce the heart rate, relax your breathing, improve your digestion, among other things. The good news that I want to share with you is that it is in your hands to make your vagus nerve healthy and strong so that it can fulfill this function of relaxing your body every time you need it.

The vagus nerve activates your parasympathetic system

The vagus nerve is a very important component of our body. For this reason, I recommend you get to know and recognize it because you can even know how to help your body reactivate its functions of the parasympathetic system (which is what relaxes us and restore) and thus maintain your balance.

As on other occasions, I have told you, your nervous system is responsible for regulating virtually all the sensations involved in stress and anxiety. The nervous system starts from your brain, sending signals to the different parts of your body that perform functions automatically, including your heartbeat, breathing, digestion, and so on.

It is also up to the nervous system to activate your body when faced with stressful situations and relax it once the dangerous situation has passed.

To relax, we will need to activate our parasympathetic system. It turns out that most of the functions performed during this activation are performed by your vagus nerve.

The vague nerve "wanders" throughout your body and is the longest of all

From your head, specifically from the brain, 12 pairs of cranial nerves, which will go to the rest of your body to transmit or receive different information, is the way we have to connect the brain to the body. And the tenth of these cranial nerves is the vagus nerve.

They are cranial nerves because it is divided into two, the right and left vagus nerve. Between them, they are responsible for 75% of the functions of the parasympathetic system. In other words, it is the vagus nerve that is responsible for relaxing.

Your vagus nerve is the longest of all cranial nerves. It travels your body practically from the anus to your brain. And from my point of view, we are most interested in learning about stress and anxiety.

Among the multiple functions of the vagus nerve, we find the following:

· Regulates the motor functions of the larynx, diaphragm, stomach, and heart.

· It generates the sensory functions of the tongue, ears and visceral organs (stomach, intestine, kidneys, and liver)

In other words, it is in charge of reducing the intensity of your heart rate, calming your breathing, regulating your digestion, expressing sensations of your throat, tongue, and ear, regulating the activity of the kidneys and liver, thus helping to improve your immune system too.

As you can see, there are too many functions in which the vagus nerve is involved; it also performs motor functions, which means that it gives movement to certain parts of the body. On the other hand, it makes you aware of the different sensations you have in your body.

Fun fact: humming or cooing activates the vague nerve of the mother who practices it and, at the same time, helps activate and relax your child's.

How do I know that I need to tone my vagus nerve?

If you perceive any of the following sensations, it will be of great benefit to pay attention to your vagus nerve:

- *Rare sensations in the tongue*

- *Difficulty to swallow*

- *Feeling of having something stuck in the throat*

- *Irregularities in your digestion*

- *Sudden changes in your heart rate*

- *Difficulty tasting food*

- *Tension in the muscles of your face*

- *Feeling of not being able to talk when you feel stressed*

- *Sudden onset of nausea*

- *Difficulty feeling connected to other people*

- *Excess empathy or affection for bad news*

- *Difficulty to socialize*

You may also have rare sensations in the ear, so giving tone to the vagus nerve can also help reduce tinnitus.

Vague nerve, empathy, and socialization

Something interesting about the vagus nerve is that it is also stimulated through socialization. Many of its functions have to do with regulating facial expressions and the tone of your voice. That is why the way you feel can be reflected in how you are speaking and in the expressions of your face, thus sending a message to the other about your current state.

305

It is also involved in generating oxytocin, which is the attachment hormone that we secrete from when we are breastfeeding until we have sex. That is why positive socialization and connection ties with other people will help lower stress levels. It is scientifically proven that it also prevents degenerative neuronal diseases.

Simultaneously, the vagus nerve is activated when facing another person, and we need to regulate facial expressions. That is why one way to stimulate our vagus nerve is through specific facial movements, in addition to healthy socialization.

Do you have trouble talking or opening up with other people when you feel bad?

When we have a history that has caused post-traumatic stress, we probably also have the need to work with our vagus nerve because precisely a feature that arises after experiencing trauma is the difficulty of speaking or approaching other people in times of stress emotional. At the same time, you are likely to feel an excess of empathy concerning the problems of others; all this has to do with the same, and stimulating your vagus nerve can help you.

Many times we disconnect to protect ourselves, avoid socialization so as not to feel in danger. Still, if we learn to give a positive tone to our vagus nerve, it can even help us feel connected to others healthily and positively. Some scientists also link the vagus nerve with feelings such as gratitude and compassion for oneself and others.

How to tone our vagus nerve?

Until now, we have understood that the need to give tone to our vagus nerve is born that the better it is, the better our ability to relax. That is the easier and faster we can get to do it.

There are many things we can do to tone our vagus nerve; what I recommend is that you do not abuse them or do them with the intention of "urging me to relax my body." Remember that the intention is to offer help to your body, but with love and living it with awareness.

Wash your face with cold water - bath with fresh water

Instinctively when we feel bad, we go to the bathroom to wet our faces, right? Well, it is precisely because the freshwater on the face, forehead, and neck will help tone your vagus nerve. Hence also that baths with fresh water are recommended.

Sings

Has it happened to you, or do you know someone who, after taking singing lessons, changed his life in many ways? As it turns out, singing will also tone your vague nerve, so put your favorite songs and sing.

Gargle

When you gargle, you will stimulate the vagus nerve, but as I tell you, do not overdo this activity. You can do a gargle session once a day.

Deep breathing

Deep breathing at the diaphragm level will tone your vagus nerve; oxygenation is key to reducing stress in the body.

Massages

Dare to give yourself the pleasure of a therapeutic massage a month, with someone with whom you feel comfortable, to help you relax the muscles of your face and your back. This helps a lot to keep the vagus nerve healthy.

Improve your posture

As I explain in this other article, improving your posture will align your vagus nerve. That will immediately make it perform its functions correctly; hence practices like yoga help a lot.

Consume probiotics

The vagus nerve controls many of your stomach functions, so if you try to take care of your stomach, you will help your vagus nerve; the connection is bidirectional. It is scientifically proven that consuming probiotics will help you with that. In this other article, you find examples of probiotics along with my favorite foods to lower anxiety.

307

Socialize in trust

If you have a person in your life with whom you feel confident, go out more often with that person, talk to him on the phone, and try to connect with more. Positive socialization is key to this whole process. If you feel very disconnected from others, I share this article.

Respect the natural rhythms of your body

By this, I mean that if you are sleepy, you sleep... if you are hungry, eat... if you are thirsty, drink water ... And so, respect your body, listen to its needs and adapt your day to what your body is asking you what it needs.

I tell you some of the main points that your body needs to balance, check, and share with us which one you will start.

When we lose the inner balance, the existence of anxiety in our lives is facilitated. We should not pretend to remain in a static state always the same; that is not balance. Balance is learning to move within your changes without getting too far from your center.

Now, I share some of the balance your body needs to be healthy and stop generating so much stress or anxiety.

Balance between being alert and relaxed

Your body needs you to be in a balance between moments of alertness and moments of relaxation, the moments of alertness being the least in your day. Alert is when you tense, when you squeeze, when you activate attitudes of apprehension, control, resistance, demand, and relaxation. It is when you are in the present, focused, and with your body relaxed.

Constant food

Your body needs that at least every 4 hours you give it some healthy food, which contains healthy calories, healthy fats, fiber, and nutrients as natural as possible.

Constant hydration

Of the same importance that food has, water has it; you need to be constantly hydrated. When you are thirsty, it is because your body is already stressed. It sends you the signal that you need it. The idea is that you drink at least 2 liters of water a day but distributed.

Aerobic exercise

Your body also needs aerobic exercise that leads you to sweat a little, and sweating is one of the best ways to release toxins from stress; walking, swimming, and doing yoga or Chi Kun are excellent exercises for this.

Balance between tension and relaxation

Muscularly you need to be relaxed; this can be done by stretching in the mornings, going to massages, entering hot tubs, through osteopathy, or muscle relaxation techniques. This allows your body to function better because the muscles are not generating tension.

Breathing - oxygenation

It is really important that you breathe effectively, with your stomach relaxed, bringing oxygen to your diaphragm or stomach, so that the oxygen that enters actually relaxes your body.

Needs covered

Your body needs you to listen to it in its needs. Do not crush it for a long time, such as going to the bathroom, drinking water, eating, or resting before you feel that your body is going to ask for it.

Hours of work and concentration controlled

In balance, you also need to alternate your work hours or concentration with moments of healthy recreation, such as stopping to walk or drink water every hour. Is more than 1 hour sitting doing the same activity exhausts your body and mind.

Mental relaxation

Your mind is also part of your body, specifically your brain. Your brain can get tired from being over-activated for a long time, so meditation is to the mind like exercise to the body. You just need to close your eyes and feel your breathing for at least 1 minute a day. With that, you will allow your brain to rest for a few moments.

Emotional release

In the same way, your emotions live in your body, that's where they feel, and that's where they have an influence on your body muscularly, that's why for your body to be in balance, you need to focus on having your emotions in balance (this we will continue seeing in March).

Don't try to change everything at once

If you feel that it is a lot to do, do not try to change everything from one moment to another, focus on going to include activities that you feel are more necessary for your body than others, and little by little, your body will respond and restore its inner balance. It is not about "stop doing this or that," but "start doing this that does me good."

Cover your physical needs and allow your body to do the rest

Once you cover your needs, that you are rested with relaxation and physical activation exercises, with your emotions off the hook ... then, leave your body the rest and allow it to recover its balance on its own, without pressing it, without hurrying it, just watch it how it achieves it while you are in charge of not leaving your balance ranges.

Chapter 7. How to Stimulate your Vagus Nerve through meditation?

Stimulating the social nervous system and activating these features takes a while for some people. Thankfully, there are a few things you can do to properly do this, and we'll discuss a few how-to aspects that'll help you with stimulating this and using the Polyvagal Theory to better your life.

e.   Trust and the Polyvagal Theory

The first thing to understand is you need to have a trust-based relationship. Find someone you can trust. Whether it be a partner, a therapist, or someone else, when tackling this issue, you need to first and foremost learn to trust others again.

The problem with tackling trauma and stimulating the social engagement system, and learning to come out of shutdown when facing these traumatic moments, is that if you aren't working with someone you fully trust, it'll cause you to re-traumatize, which is definitely not a good thing.

When seeking a therapist, when tackling these traumatic instances, you want someone who you can trust. Otherwise, you'll get traumatized once again, which isn't fun whatsoever. It will make even the hardest traumatic moments ten times harder.

You want to express your feelings with this person that you can't with other people. Shameful feelings, anger, issues with sexual response, and in essence, you want to be able to say what you need to say. If you can't do that, the sad thing is, you'll never heal, and you need a trusting relationship. This is very hard for some people, especially those with PTSD or even C-PTSD, but by learning to find someone you can say this to, you'll feel secure.

By having this safe person, you'll be able to activate your social regulation system. After all, it works when you're safe and sound, right? By having that safe person to go to, you'll be so much happier, and you won't feel bogged down by the stressful situations.

f.   Your Calm Center

This is another personal thing you can do. A lot of people who have distress struggle with calming and finding their center.

Often, staying in the moment when talking with someone and trying to understand and handle your distress will help you improve your social engagement.

When you start to dissociate, try fighting this. I know it's hard. Fighting this urge feels like an impossible task, but the thing is, no matter how hard the subject matter is, you need to fight this, and you need to ensure you don't try to dissociate.

The reason why you do this is because you want to run away. But, when working with a therapist that handles heavy trauma, you need to work to re-engage with it, and get that support to help you face it and overcome it.

The easy solution is to run away. That's what our bodies naturally do. We either fight or flight, and when we can't do that, we freeze in the moment. Every time we freeze, though, it keeps us in that moment, never letting us escape it, which means that we're not fully running away from this moment, and instead, we are frozen in time. We'll always bounce back to that moment frozen in time if we can't come out of it.

But, when you safely re-engage with that trauma with someone who has the experience to take care of this, it'll change you. You'll be able to face the moment, and re-write everything that's in your brain, and help you build better support within your mind.

Remember when we touched upon the neuroplasticity of the brain? That the brain will re-write and change over time, that it's never just one specific instance? Well, that applies here, and you need to work to re-write this so you can change your response to it.

Stay calm, and when facing the moment, learn to understand and fully grip the emotions and work to make it, so your body's response is fine and not overdone.

g.   Be More Assertive

When you're facing these moments and stimulating your vagus nerve, you're properly able to face the trauma. You need to understand that an emotional shutdown occurs when you aren't fully communicating and discussing this out.

You need to practice assertiveness and work on trying to be more in control. This takes time. Not every person will be able to face this right away. Sometimes, they'll feel angry at the moment since they're facing this on purpose, and they need to stay in control. But, by working out the anger and working out how to properly understand and attain what you need from this, you'll be happier.

Assertiveness isn't necessarily a bad thing. A lot of people think when you're assertive, that's bad. But for those who don't have the proper social regulation, they immediately succumb to the freezing aspects of this. But, by learning the power of asserting yourself, you'll be happier, and you'll be able to move towards a healthier relationship pattern over time. You'll be much better off as well. For most people, there are a lot of fears that come from being assertive. They might never have done this. Being assertive, being able to face your emotions, and getting through this will help you feel better and let you stay in the moment. It will change your life, and understand that you'll be happy to truly make a change if you take some time to truly be yourself.

h.   Attentional Control: A Valid Mechanism

This is a mechanism some PTSD survivors will use. Essentially, it's the ability to choose what to pay attention to and what you choose to ignore. It's also called executive attention control. This can essentially be a voluntary means to concentrate. Most of the time, this is mediated by the frontal parts of the brain. It is closely related to working memory and other executive functions.

Our attention works on three different networks. The first is alertness, orientation, and executive control, which is where you resolve conflict. These are usually all working in different ways.

313

When we perceive threats, at first, we'll be on the alert, and we'll look at information, and then, we'll use executive control. The research from this shows some MRIs depict attention, and of course, different interactions between the alertness, other orienting, and of course, executive controls.

When our attention isn't actually controlled properly, one of these usually is overstimulated. For example, the conflicts are never resolved, but instead, they just hang there, and our attention is always on it. We are focused too much on one thing or another. If there is something that reminds us of traumatic experiences, we tend to immediately focus on this.

This can actually relate to the vagus nerve. The vagus nerve and the polyvagal theory say that each of these different parts, when not in balance, will cause various issues. Often, our attention immediately focuses on the other parts of this, which means that we're not fully resolving the conflicts and determining which and which doesn't get our full attention.

Those who have autism, anxiety, or ADHD tend to have issues with attentional control, either too much power on one part of their life or not enough control on something. Many times, this can develop early on in childhood, but sometimes it may show up later.

Disrupted attentional control can also cause disruption in executive functions, including working memory across many different disorder group groups. How does this all show itself, though? Well, there is still some research being done about it.

Learning to better control your attention can help offset the effects of disruptions in your polyvagal system.

If you have low attentional control, you may experience other attentional conditions, especially with ADHD, hyperactivity, and then impulsivity, which can cause impairment in activities in life. It can also happen in those with schizophrenia and also in other problems too.

If you have social anxiety, anxiety that's generalized, and depression, it can cause issues with attentional control too.

Those who respond better and have better control over their executive functions will have lower levels of depression and anxiety.

314

There is also a chance you may develop psychopathology because the ability to shift your focus from the threat information is very important in processing these emotions. Many researchers are also accounting for attentional control and might not always focus on the attention and how the attention shifts from the different stimuli and the relation to the threat.

Improving your attentional control and working to better this is a good way to improve your life. This does play a part in your polyvagal system, and we'll discuss how you can improve this here.

i.   Attentional Control and Polyvagal Theory

When we experience trauma, our brains immediately will focus on that trauma and how it stimulates us instead of learning to overcome it. This can cause us to have trouble processing the emotions of the moment and the situation at hand.

When this happens, and our other vagal systems take over, we suddenly will think it's a bad thing to do anything or see everything as a threat. That's what we'll perceive, and from there, we won't be able to improve or overcome the trauma. But, by learning to physically control our attention in a voluntary state and not hyper-focus on the things we can't do anything about, we'll be much better off.

Our polyvagal system works in a balanced matter. Homeostasis is achieved through balance. When one of these is imbalanced, the trouble occurs there, whether in a sympathetic or a parasympathetic system. It can cause issues with how we process emotions.

This is why trauma sticks around. It's because our mind starts to focus only on this instead of moving forward and overcoming the struggles.

Those with PTDS especially have a lot of trouble with attention control. That's because when they give this a bias, they'll immediately process only negative information over positive information. It can hurt our own personal attentional control, which means we don't have good control over our thoughts. Instead, we feel anxiety over the whole mess.

How can we overcome this? The best way to do it is via mindfulness and learning how to shift our control and work to process these emotions.

315

Therapy to tackle the trauma and face it is ideal. Still, there are a few things you can do on your own to help improve your ability to keep a better, more balanced life so you're not disrupted by these negative thoughts.

When we know how to use this, we'll better approach these cognitive processes, and from there, understand how the control occurs.

But the biggest thing you can do is mindfulness. Even just four days of mindfulness will change your working memory, along with your executive functions as well.

However, you won't be able to act involuntarily. This will just help you control the problems manually so that you're not hurt either. If you try to manually inhibit, switch, or detect different objects and practice mindfulness, it can help reduce the stress. It doesn't directly affect your natural intentional control. Still, it influences your general emotional well-being, which is why more and more people see praise mindfulness as one of the best things for you to do. Finally, another way to tackle this is, of course, to learn about it. You should become versed in the different cognitive faculties you use to better yourself and understand how this works for you.

Chapter 8. Simple Exercises to Activate the Vagus Nerve

There are three techniques you can use to activate your vagus nerve. The techniques are pretty simple and also involve some ancient medicinal processes which activate the vagus nerve. The first is an exercise you can perform pretty much anywhere, so let's look at this first.

Twisting the Trapezius

The trapezius muscle is something all of us use extensively when we're babies. When babies crawl around, they use all points of the trapezius to support their weight on their shoulder blades, lift themselves, and move forward. Once babies learn to walk, the trapezius is used unevenly, and as a result imbalance develop.

The exercises I will highlight should ideally be done multiple times during the day to revitalize yourself and to readjust your posture to prevent it from going bad. Those who suffer from their heads leaning forward will also benefit from this. The result of carrying out these exercises is usually instant revitalization and energy. You won't start doing jumping jacks, but your energy levels will be higher than what they just were, that's for sure.

Steps

There are three ways of performing this exercise, so you can choose whichever one suits you the best. Ideally, you should perform all three of them. To begin, sit on a comfortable surface or stand if that feels better. Take a few deep breaths and keep your eyes open. Now, bring your arms out in front of you and cross them. Let your palms rest on top of your elbows.

With your face looking forward, twist your torso towards one side. Don't think of this as turning from the hips. Instead, move your elbows out to one side and then to the other briskly. Do not stop in these movements or rest in between. Keep the moves brisk and twist thrice on either side. This activates the trapezius muscle fibers.

The second way of performing this is pretty much the same as the first, but instead of crossing your arms in front of you, cross them and hold them higher than your chest. Now twist from side to side while keeping your face as forward-facing as possible. Remember to not rotate from the hips. Keep your hips stationary and only move your elbows from side to side.

The third way has you raising your arms above your head while still being crossed. Twist from side to side thrice and keep the movement brisk. Do not stop in between. Once the exercise is complete, you will feel your head becoming lighter and moving back in line with your spine. You might feel taller thanks to this.

Acupuncture Techniques

Acupuncture has been shown to stimulate the vagus nerve effectively. The technique relies on stimulating specific points throughout the body. The techniques I will be highlighting here have to do with stimulating the facial muscles. Remember, the vagus nerve innervates portions of your face along with other cranial nerves, namely CN V and CN VII. These techniques have the following benefits:

- *Improves blood circulation in your face*

- *Makes your skin look fresh and vibrant*

- *Refreshes the corners of your eyes and mouth*

- *Relaxes the muscles that help you smile*

- *Loosens up the muscles in your face and opens you to deliver more expressions in social interactions*

When performing this technique, look into a mirror. Perform them on one side of the face before moving on to the other side. You will notice your muscles relaxing on one side when you're finished with it.

Steps

The preliminary step for you to take is to find the LI 20 point on your face. This is an acupuncture point and is where the endpoint of the large intestine is. No, your large intestine does not run up to your face. This is simply the meridian of the large intestine, and it exists on this axis which happens to end on your face. In addition to this, the spot also lies directly over a joint

318

between two bones. These bones are together referred to as the Maxilla. Still, in infants, they used to be two, namely the pre-maxilla and the Maxilla.

This spot is referred to as the beauty triangle in acupuncture and other eastern forms of massage. The spot lies about an eighth of an inch to the side, above the fold between the cheek and the upper lip. This point is usually more sensitive to touch with your finger, so take the time to explore this area. Alternatively, you can refer to an acupuncture chart to get a fair idea of where this spot is.

With a finger, lightly brush the area. Apply pressure but so little that you can barely detect it. Your fingertip and the skin underneath should seem fused together. Slide the skin over this point up and down and note which direction provides more significant resistance. Move the skin in that direction and hold it there until it releases. Now move the skin from side to side and again note which direction provides the greatest resistance.

Hold the skin against that side until it gives way. Remember to keep your pressure light. This is not a massage. Now, increase your pressure ever so slightly. The objective is to stimulate the first layer of muscles underneath the skin. Once you become better at this technique, you will feel the first layer moving against the second layer.

Move your finger around in circles and feel which direction has the more excellent resistance to it. Hold your finger in that direction for a short while until it gives way. Keep circling the spot until you feel almost no resistance. Now, increase your pressure until you can feel the bone underneath the skin.

Move your finger up and down and side to side and feel for increased resistance. Hold your finger in that direction until it releases. Remember to keep your push firm but not hard. You should feel the bone but don't press down hard on it.

You will find that the muscles around the corners of your mouth will relax immensely, and you'll be able to smile a lot wider. This is because the cranial nerves V and VII have been stimulated along with the vagus nerve. Over time, you will notice wrinkles decreasing as well. Relaxing the muscles underneath your face will give you a friendly and more gentle demeanor.

All of this will contribute to your social engagement, and you'll find your interactions becoming more pleasant.

Technique #2

The second technique works in the same way as the first, but its focal point is different. In this exercise, you will be focusing on the area around your eyes. This is referred to as acupuncture point B2, and it exists on the inside of your eyes, just in the area between your eyes and the top of your nose. Most of us rub this area when we're stressed naturally. If you're having problems finding this spot, you can refer to an acupuncture chart.

The muscles here are very thin, and for this reason, it is best to use your thumb. Again, you want to feel the skin, then the muscle underneath, and then the bone. The technique is the same. Begin by lightly running your thumb from side to side and look for the direction of greater resistance and lightly push against that until you spot a release.

Then move it up and down and look for a release in the direction where the more excellent resistance lies. Once this is done, press harder until you can feel the bone and move the skin up and down and side to side, looking for a release in the direction that offers the greatest resistance. Remember that while your press should be firm, you don't want to be pressing as hard as you would during a massage.

This pressure point directly stimulates the thin muscle that surrounds the eye called the orbicularis oculi. This controls the opening and shutting of the eye, and if imbalanced, your eye might be open too wide or simply not enough. The massage balances it out. Also, massage stimulates the lacrimal bone, which plays a role in producing tears within the eye. While you don't need to be crying buckets, some level of moisture in your eyes gives them a twinkling look that is particularly alluring to others.

The goal of both the massages or facelifts, if you will, is to leave you looking refreshed and to present your best face to those around you. This will improve your social engagement, and you will automatically stimulate your ventral circuit further.

When carrying out these actions, you might feel like you aren't doing too much but resist the thought. The fact is that you don't need massive or forceful stimulation to engage the vagus nerve. The exercises also seem simple at first, but the longer you perform them, the better your quality of life will be. Ultimately, this is a marker of how well you are stimulating your ventral circuit.

Meditation and the Vagus Nerve

Increasing Parasympathetic Responses Through Meditation

Meditation is a mental exercise that exercises the mind through relaxation, heightened focus, and creating awareness. Meditation is similar to physical exercise, but for our minds rather than our bodies. Meditation enables us to exercise our minds and purify our thoughts.

Meditation is based on the following techniques;

• Concentration; this is achieved by focusing on a particular object that can be external or internal.

• Observation; this is where you concentrate on the sensations, feelings, and thoughts present in your body at that moment.

• Awareness; this is where you remain consciously aware of your own thoughts and feelings, but without getting distracted or engaged physically or mentally.

Regardless of the type or technique of meditation, the primary goals of meditation are;

• Improving mental awareness and clarity.

• Reducing stress and anxiety.

• Raising our level of self-awareness when it comes to our bodies, emotions, and thoughts.

• Relieving pain.

• Achieving inner peace and calmness.

All these benefits of meditation soothe our bodies and activate the parasympathetic vagus nerve responses, which helps us fight inflammation, irregular brain activity, depression, high blood pressure, and digestive disorders.

Meditation Techniques

Mindfulness Meditation

In mindful meditation, the goal is to concentrate your mind on the thoughts, sensations, and emotions that you are experiencing in the present or current moment. It normally involves the regulation of breathing, muscle and body relaxation, mental visualization, and a heightened awareness of the body and mind.

Mindfulness meditation is effective in stress reduction, cognitive therapy, and the treatment of depression symptoms. The basic technique involved is easy to learn and can easily be done for about 10 minutes daily to obtain the benefits in terms of increasing your vagal tone.

A simple mindful meditation technique for beginners is described below;

• Find a quiet and well-aerated room to practice your meditation in.

• Sit comfortably on a chair, or you can sit on the floor

• Ensure that your posture is relaxed and that your shoulder and neck muscles are not tense.

• Your head, neck, and spine should be aligned but not tense or stiff.

• Bring your mind to the present by pulling all your focus to the here and now.

• Concentrate on your breathing, feel the breath enter your body as you inhale, and feel the air exit your body as you exhale.

• Take deep breaths all the time, focusing on the sensation of the rising and falling of your diaphragm.

• To make it easier to focus on your breathing, you can place one hand on your upper chest and the other above your navel. This will aid you in engaging your diaphragm when breathing in and out.

• Breath in slowly through your nose; as you inhale, the hand on your navel area should feel your stomach rise gradually as the air enters your body.

• On the exhale, let the breath out through your mouth with your lips slightly pursed. As you exhale, the hand on the navel area should feel the stomach relax and fall back into the starting position.

• As thoughts pop up in your mind, do not quash or try to suppress them. Simply turn your attention back to your breathing and focus on the inhale and exhale motions of rising and falling.

• Stay in this state for at least 10 minutes, always pulling your focus back to the present and away from thoughts and emotions by simply focusing on your breathing.

• At the end of the 10 minutes, rise slowly from your position and allow your mind to become gradually aware of your surroundings.

Mindful meditation is effective in reducing inflammation and improving stress resilience. More benefits of mindful meditation include;

• Increased self-awareness

• Improved concentration and cognitive aptitude

• Better emotional regulation and management

• The overall reduction in stress and anxiety.

Breath Awareness Meditation

Breath awareness meditation is similar to mindfulness meditation. It encourages you to focus on your breathing as a way of soothing and calming your body.

The goal of breath awareness meditation is to concentrate on the breathing motions and sensations and ignore any thought that may crop up in your mind.

A simple technique to follow for this type of meditation involves following the steps outlined below;

• This meditation can be done in an upright or sitting position or even laying down on your back

• You can do this with your eyes closed, or you can leave them open, but your gaze should be down and not looking at anything in particular.

• Feel the muscles on your shoulders, the back of your head, and neck area. Focus your attention on these three areas.

• Breath in slowly through your nostrils and feel the rise of your shoulders as the air is getting into your body.

• Exhale slowly, and this time focus on the falling of your shoulders as the breath leaves your body.

• With each inhaling and exhaling action, feel your jaw, shoulders, and neck beginning to loosen up and relax.

• After a few breaths in and out, begin to think I am breathing in on the inhale, and I am breathing out on the exhale. Again, the point of this is to ensure that your mind is entirely focused on your breathing.

• Continue to monitor your breathing for about ten minutes.

• As you come towards the end of the ten minutes, you can stop thinking I am breathing out with the inhale, and I am breathing out with the exhale. Allow your mind to stray from the concentration on the breathing

• While you are exiting this focused concentration on the breathing, ask yourself, "What do I want?" on the inhale and listen to the response from your mind on the exhale.

• Then, on the next inhale, ask yourself, "What am I thankful for?' and listen for the answer in your mind as you exhale.

• Acknowledge what you are feeling at that moment, open your eyes, or bring your gaze back up and rise from your meditation position.

Transcendental Meditation

Transcendental meditation is a spiritual meditation that is mostly spiritually based and focuses on bringing an individual's awareness past their physical being or state. It involves the repetition of particular mantras and the use of particular postures to enhance the feeling of inner peace and calmness. Transcendental meditation differs from mindful meditation. While mindful meditation is geared towards bringing attention to the present, transcendental meditation aims to transcend or go past thought itself.

In transcendental meditation, you use the repetition of a mantra to settle your mind and remove all thoughts. It does not involve concentration or focusing on a particular object. Transcendental meditation is typically learned from certified teachers because it requires a precise technique to achieve a transcendental state.

The ultimate result of consistent transcendental meditation is an increased awareness of our existence as part of a large cosmos. It thus helps in shifting thoughts from our own person to our surroundings and those around us. It is effective in stress and anxiety reduction and creates a high level of cognitive and thought clarity.

Body Scan Meditation

Stress manifests itself in our bodies in tense muscles, shallow breathing, irregular heartbeat, and overall physical discomfort. It is hard to be always aware of how we feel each and every time and what is triggering us to feel a certain way.

Body scan meditation primarily involves examining or scanning your body for areas of tension. The aim is to identify areas where your muscles are tensed or where you have tension knots and essentially relax them to release the tension. The general technique in body scan meditation involves scanning your body from one end to another; for instance, you can start from toe to head. The following steps can help you in practicing body scan meditation;

• Sit in a comfortable position and relax your body.

• Slow your breathing drown, and focus on deep breathing, breathing from your stomach, not your chest.

• To help you breathe from the belly, you can create a mental image of a balloon inflating and deflating in your stomach as you breathe in and out.

• Focus on each part of your body and feel for signs of tension, start from your head, and work yourself down systematically through the neck, chest, abdomen, and limbs.

• During this systematic scanning process, keep doing your deep breathing as it will heighten your awareness and ability to detect tension in your muscles.

• Notice the general feeling and sensations in different parts of your body, for instance, if you have soreness, tightness, or tense muscles in any part of your body.

• Once you come across the areas on the tense or uncomfortable body, focus on this area as you breathe in and out. You can accompany this focus by gently massaging the area of tension and concentrate on feeling the tension leave your body as you exhale.

• Do this process throughout your entire body, paying special attention to the tense and sore areas until you start feeling relaxed in those areas.

Body scan meditation is very important in increasing your body awareness and your ability to recognize when things are going wrong or not working as they should. This type of meditation is a tool that you can use when you feel stressed or anxious, and it will help you release tension and become more relaxed.

Like in the other types of meditation, our vagus nerve functions best when we are relaxed, so any type of meditation that helps you relax and get into a peaceful state of mind will be instrumental in activating and stimulating your vagus nerve.

Kundalini Meditation

Kundalini meditation is practiced as part of a type of yoga that focuses on releasing the energy present at the base of the spine. This energy is referred to as kundalini energy. In Kundalini meditation, the chief goal is to unleash this power at the base of the spine and using its energy to cleanse your body of ailments, mental and emotional disorders and essentially purify your system.

For this type of meditation;

• Increase your awareness and prepare your mind to receive the kundalini energy

• Dress in loose, comfortable clothing and find a quiet, comfortable place for your meditation.

• Cover your head using a shawl or scarf

• Sit with your legs folded and ensure that your spine, head, and neck are aligned but relaxed

• Close your eyes.

• Practice deep breathing and focus on the inhale and exhale process

• Break down your inhaling with gaps, i.e., breath in, hold, continue breathing in, hold, and continue. Inhale this way with four pauses and do not exhale during this step

• Once you have done the above process, you can exhale using the same technique, exhale-hold, then continue exhaling again. Do these four times.

• Do this staggered inhale and exhale process for about four minutes.

• At the end of the four minutes, inhale deeply, bringing your palms together and holding them together for approximately ten seconds.

• Then exhale deeply and feel your body relax as you exhale.

• As you continue increasing your breathing rate and feeling the breath in your body, you will gradually control your rate and flow of breath.

As you go deeper and deeper into these breathing techniques, you should start to uncover the energy at the base of your spine.

The Wim Hof Method

The vagus nerve is connected to many parts of our bodies. As such, it has been found that we can activate it naturally using these parts of our bodies to stimulate it. An active Vagus nerve means that our bodies can achieve a state of equilibrium between the parasympathetic and sympathetic nervous systems. When either system is not balanced out by the actions of the other, we tend to develop physical and psychological disorders that impact our quality of life.

The Wim hof method of stimulating the vagus nerve is chiefly based on three main principles, i.e.;

• *Cold Exposure*

• *Breathing*

• *Commitment*

Cold Therapy

Cold therapy, also referred to as cryotherapy, is one of the Wim Hof method pillars. Have you ever wondered why a cold compress applied to a bruise or swelling helps in reducing pain and speeds up healing? Applying a cold compress reduces blood flow to a particular area, regulates nerve activity, and reduces inflammation and swelling.

In the same way, cold exposure has multiple health benefits to the body. It has been found to increase weight loss through fat loss, reduce inflammation, and stimulate the secretion and release of feel-good hormones or endorphins in the body. There are several ways you can expose your body to cold therapy. These include;

• Cold showers- these are an easy way to get cold therapy. You can start off by turning the water to cold when taking your normal shower.

328

As you build up your cold resistance, you can then go for fully cold showers. Not only is a cold show invigorating, but it will also get your vagus nerve activated and energize your mind.

• Ice baths – once you get accustomed to cold showers, you can then graduate to ice baths. The rule of thumb here is to not subject your body to extremes without first building up your stamina. So, start with the cold showers, and once your body has adjusted and can cope with that level of cold exposure, you can then gradually move on to ice baths.

Using about 3 bags of ice, put these in a half-full tub. And wait until most of the ice is melted and the bathwater temperature is approximately 59 F degrees.

You can start with limited exposure from 5 to 10 minutes, then build up your exposure as your body gets accustomed to the ice water baths. If you notice your body is getting uncomfortable or is in distress at any point during the bath, simply get out as you do not want to cause harm to your body.

After the bath, a hot beverage such as some hot cocoa will help you to warm up. You can also go for a short walk to stimulate blood flow. It is important to remember that cold exposure should be done sensibly. People with pre-existing conditions should not attempt this kind of therapy to avoid causing complications.

Breathing Techniques

Breathing exercises are a tried and tested method of bringing your body and control. From taking deep breaths when you are about to lose it and punch someone in the face to women in labor trying to cope with labor pains, breathing exercises are useful in combating stress and anxiety, minimizing and controlling pain, and restoring your body to a rested or relaxed state. It is, therefore, no surprise that controlled breathing is one of the pillars of the Wim hof method.

Breathing correctly can help in increasing your oxygen levels, slowing down the heart rate, and boosting your body's natural immunity.

The basic breathing technique in the Wim hof method can be achieved by following the steps outlined below;

• Sit in a meditation posture with your head, neck, and spine aligned and relaxed

• Inhale deeply, and as you do, focus on the sensation of air entering your body.

• Hold the breath for a moment

• Exhale deeply, feeling the air leaving your body.

• Inhale again deeply, hold and then deep exhale.

• Repeat this breathing technique 14 more times

• After this, you move on to power breaths.

• Breathe in deeply through your nose and exhale through your mouth in short bursts as if you inflate a balloon.

• Repeat this breathing technique 30 times.

• While doing the 30 inhale-exhale repetitions, practice the body scan meditation technique of going over your body and identifying areas of tension and try and focus your energy on those areas that feel tired or tense,

• After the 30 breaths, inhale deeply until you fill your lungs completely, then again exhale completely until all the air is pushed out. After the exhale, hold your breath long as you can and focus on feeling the energy in your body as you hold

• After your hold for as long as you can, inhale deeply, feeling your chest expand in the process, and hold again for about 15 seconds.

• During this hold, try to direct your energy to your tension areas and mentally picture the tension ebbing away and the negative energy being released.

• Exhale after the 15 seconds hold.

• You can start this technique with one or two rounds of this sequence and then build up to more rounds as you get more practice with time.

Commitment

Consistency in following your breathing techniques and cold exposure therapies will determine your level of success in improving your mental and physical health.

Results in any technique or method require consistency and commitment to following through on the process. Just like dieting for a day and expecting to lose weight would be unrealistic, following a meditation technique for a couple of days and expecting it to reverse your mental and physical health is unrealistic.

Settle on a method that suits your lifestyle and that you can commit to regularly.

Chapter 9. The Healing Power of Vagal Tone

The vagus nerve is the most significant nerve you likely didn't have any acquaintance with you had. In contrast to different Vegas, what occurs in this vagus doesn't remain there. The vagus nerve is a long wandering heap of the engine and tangible strands that connections the cerebrum stem to the heart, lungs, and gut. It additionally stretches out to contact and connect with the liver, spleen, gallbladder, ureter, female richness organs, neck, ears, tongue, and kidneys. It controls up our automatic operational hub—the parasympathetic sensory system—and controls oblivious body capacities, just as everything from keeping our pulse consistent and nourishment assimilation to breathing and perspiring. It also manages circulatory strain, blood glucose balance, advances general kidney work, helps discharge bile and testosterone, animates the emission of spit, helps with controlling taste and discharging tears, and assumes a significant job in ripeness issues and climaxes in ladies.

The vagus nerve has strands that innervate practically the entirety of our inside organs. The administration and preparing of feelings occur through the vagal nerve between the heart, mind, and gut, which is why we have a solid gut response to extreme mental and enthusiastic states.

Enthusiastic processing Emotional handling happens through the vagal nerve between the heart, mind, and gut.

Vagus nerve brokenness can bring about an entire host of issues, including weight, bradycardia (strangely moderate heartbeat), trouble gulping, gastrointestinal illnesses, blacking out, disposition issue, B12 inadequacy, constant aggravation, debilitated hack, and seizures.

A Closer Look At This Super Nerve

The vagus nerve is the longest of our 12 cranial nerves. Just the spinal section is a bigger nerve framework. Around 80 percent of its nerve strands—or four of its five 'paths'— drive data from the body to the cerebrum. Its fifth path runs the other way, moving signs from the cerebrum all through the body. Tied down in the mind stem, the vagus goes through the neck and into the chest, parting into the left vagus and the correct vagus.

Every one of these streets is made out of many nerve strands that branch into the heart, lungs, stomach, pancreas, and almost every other organ in the guts.

The vagus nerve utilizes the synapse acetylcholine, which invigorates muscle compressions in the parasympathetic sensory system. A synapse is a sort of synthetic errand person discharged toward the finish of a nerve fiber that considers signs to be moved along from point to point, which animate different organs. For instance, if our cerebrum couldn't speak with our stomach by means of the arrival of acetylcholine from the vagus nerve, at that point, we would quit relaxing.

Longest cranial nerve

The vagus nerve is the longest of our 12 cranial nerves.

A few substances, for example, botox and the overwhelming metal mercury, can meddle with acetylcholine creation. Botox has been known to close down the vagus nerve, which causes demise. Mercury hinders the activity of acetylcholine. When mercury connects to the thiol protein in the heart muscle receptors, the heart muscle can't get the vagus nerve electrical motivation for withdrawal. Cardiovascular issues typically pursue. Mercury utilized in fillings just creeps from the mind just as the 3,000 tons of mercury put into the air can meddle with acetylcholine generation. Mercury-loaded immunizations may likewise assume a job in vagus nerve-related chemical imbalance in kids.

Hoffman says:

Hypothetically, anything that improves the nearness and capacity of acetylcholine will likewise direct the wellbeing of our vagus nerve. It suggests normal nootropics hyperfine and galantine for improving the affectability of acetylcholine receptors.

Vagus nerve harm can likewise be brought about by diabetes, liquor addiction, upper respiratory viral diseases, or having some portion of the nerve cut off unintentionally during an activity. Stress can kindle the nerve, alongside exhaustion and nervousness. In any event, something as basic as an awful stance can contrarily affect the vagus nerve.

333

The effect of stress can kindle the vagus nerve, alongside exhaustion and tension.

A Feeling in Your Gut

When individuals state they feel it in their gut, that is not only a creative mind, as per Dr. Imprint Sircus, acupuncturist and specialist of Oriental and peaceful drug.

Our gut impulses are not dreams yet a genuine anxious sign that guides quite a bit of our lives.

This is because the enteric sensory system (ENS), which oversees the capacity of the gastrointestinal tract, speaks with the focal sensory system (the mind) through the vagus nerve. This is known as the gut-cerebrum pivot. The ENS is now and again alluded to as the subsequent mind or reinforcement cerebrum focused in our sunlight-based plexus. Sircus proceeds:

We presently realize that the ENS isn't only fit for independence yet additionally impacts the cerebrum. Truth be told, around 90 percent of the signs going along the vagus nerve come not from above, however from the ENS.

Keeping the gut and vagus nerve passage solid affects our emotional wellbeing. An ongoing report shows how anti-microbial can make us forceful when they upset the microbiome balance in our gut. A significant examination a year ago by McMaster University in Hamilton, Ontario, Canada, found that specific helpful gut organisms can really forestall PTSD. Probiotics can help keep the gut and vagus nerve flag in a more advantageous state, as indicated by a National Center for Biotechnology Information (NCBI).

Emotional wellbeing and the vagus nerve Keeping the gut and vagus nerve passage sound impact our psychological wellness.

Dr. Abby Kramer, an all-encompassing professional and chiropractor in Glenview, Illinois, clarifies: Probiotics help advance vagal action because of its association with the gut and stomach-related capacities. Zinc is an extraordinary enhancement for anybody with stress or emotional wellbeing issues, which likewise interfaces back to the vagus nerve.

Boosting With Electricity

Specialists have since quite a while ago misused the nerve's impact on the cerebrum. Electrical incitement of the vagus nerve, called vagus nerve incitement (VNS), is now and then used to treat individuals with epilepsy or gloom. VNS is intended to counteract seizures by sending standard, mellow beats of electrical vitality to the mind through the vagus nerve.

These heartbeats are provided by a gadget, something like a pacemaker. It is set under the skin on the chest divider, and a wire runs from it to the vagus nerve in the neck. Specialists concentrating on the impacts of vagus incitement on epilepsy saw that patients encountered a second advantage inconsequential to seizure decrease: their states of mind additionally improved.

A recent report distributed in the Proceedings of the National Academy of Sciences (PNAS) indicated how animating the vagus nerve with a bioelectronics gadget "fundamentally improved proportions of malady movement in patients with rheumatoid joint pain," a ceaseless fiery illness that influences 1.3 million individuals in the United States and costs several billions of dollars yearly to treat.

Electrical incitement of the vagus nerve incitement (VNS) is utilized to treat epilepsy, despondency, and joint pain.

Chapter 10. The Polyvagal Theory And PTSD (Post-Traumatic Stress Disorder)

PTSD, or post-traumatic stress disorder, has gained considerable attention in recent years due to its occurrence among military veterans, especially those returning from the long, ongoing conflicts in the Middle East. These traumatized individuals may have experienced severe physical injuries. Still, their injuries are psychological in many cases, resulting from their overwhelming reactions to their battlefield experiences. In earlier wars, mentally traumatized veterans were suffering from shell shock, the result of seeing and feeling the consequences of war. We now recognize this condition as PTSD.

Typical symptoms of PTSD include flashbacks of the traumatic event or the inability to stop thinking about it obsessively, anxiety, depression, sleeplessness, and recurring nightmares. Beyond the discomforts of experiencing PTSD, it is now known that it can lead to suicidal thoughts and suicidal behavior. In many cases, PTSD can lead to continuing deep depression and anxiety and eating disorders, and substance abuse, notably drugs and alcohol.

Apart from veterans, people in all walks of life may have had terrifying, traumatic experiences, either themselves or as witnesses, that trigger PTSD, like an automobile accident, sexual or other physical assault, a severe fall at home, or loss of a loved one. Any of these extremely distressing experiences may initiate the PTSD response. Victims of PTSD may have been told to shape up or get over it. Still, today, PTSD is a recognized, psychological, severe condition requiring professional assistance to resolve. It may affect children as well as adults.

Based on the Polyvagal Theory, many psychologists now believe that PTSD has its roots in the dorsal vagal response of the parasympathetic nervous system. This is the primitive freezing or shutting down mechanism triggered when the person or animal faces an insurmountable or overwhelming immediate threat. When this dorsal vagal response is initiated, it can cause immobility, speechlessness, fainting, and even severe shock. PTSD appears to be an ongoing form of dorsal vagal reaction.

The Polyvagal Theory's potential treatments for overcoming dorsal vagal-caused PTSD, an understanding of the human brain's evolution and functions are presented for perspective.

The Three-Part Brain

The human brain, with its complexity of 100 billion or so neurons and perhaps 100 trillion neural connections, is generally known to be organized into two hemispheres, the left, recognized for controlling rational, logical, organizational thoughts, and the right, associated with creative, imaginative and unstructured thinking. We also know that the functioning nervous system is comprised of the brain, spinal cord, and between them, the brainstem.

The brain is where all the conscious and unconscious action occurs, from managing our cardiovascular, respiratory, and digestive functions to feelings, senses, and sensations and embracing all thought, memory, and decision-making.

The spinal cord is the central cable that receives all nerve impulses from the extremities and forwards these impulses to the brain. It returns the brain's reactions to the impulses with the appropriate reaction.

The brainstem is where 10 of the 12 cranial nerves originate and extend to the organs and other vital areas, including number 10, the longest, most diverse neuron, the vagus nerve.

But we know today that the evolution of the human brain has been built upon a sequential three-part structure, beginning with the earliest, most primitive part, called the reptilian brain, then continuing to evolve an early old or paleomammalian brain, and concluding with a more sophisticated new or neo-mammalian brain. This concept of a three-part evolution-driven brain structure was first identified in the 1960s by a neuroscientist, Dr. Paul MaLean, who called it the triune brain and postulated that these three parts of the brain still struggle to coexist. Each part has specific functions to perform:

The early reptilian brain is responsible for primary, involuntary reflex actions, including reproduction urges, arousal to a range of stimuli, and maintaining a balanced, normal state or homeostasis.

337

It can be considered a fundamental survival mechanism. One of its continuing characteristics is compulsiveness.

The old mammalian, or paleomammalian brain, is positioned to surround the reptilian brain. It manages emotions, learning, and memory functions. It enabled early mammals to remember and act upon favorable and unfavorable experiences, for example.

The new-mammalian, or neo-mammalian brain, is responsible for conscious thought and self-awareness and is positioned atop the two early brain parts. All of our reasoning, decision-making, and rationalizations occur here.

But one may ask if we really evolved from reptiles? The concept of our brains evolving from reptiles comes as a surprise. We understand that we evolved from mammals since we are mammals. Okay, but reptiles? Over the long course of evolution, the earliest mammals evolved from, yes, reptiles, and not from the dinosaurs that became extinct 66 million years ago or the dinosaurs that grew feathers and evolved into birds. Our reptilian ancestors were small and obviously smarter than the giant dinosaurs, which gave them an edge in natural selection. They had strong survival skills built into their small but highly functional reptilian brains. Some of these hardy reptiles evolved into small mammals. In their turn, these early mammals evolved more complex brains, the paleomammalian brain, with its added values of learning, memory, and emotion. As mammals further evolved as primates, the third neo-mammalian brain component developed, giving Homo Sapiens the ability to think consciously and with increasing complexity.

The three parts of our current triune brain correspond, approximately, to the brainstem and cerebellum (reptilian), limbic brain, which includes the hippocampus, amygdala, and hypothalamus (paleo mammalian), and the neocortex (neo-mammalian). Because the reptilian-originated brainstem reacts completely unconsciously and immediately for survival, historically, it tends to dominate in many situations when the brain perceives danger or other need for prompt action. The conflict between the purely instinctive reptilian brain and the two more advanced components is considered by some to be represented by Freud's ongoing battles between the conscious and the subconscious.

The complexity of brain functioning begins to become clear. These aspects include the two-hemisphere structure, vertical networks connecting the layers and departments of the brain, and a near-infinite number of interacting neurons and variations in brain structure due to gender, genetic and environmental influences.

In recent times, the precise sequential evolution and functioning of the triune brain and its exclusivity among humans have been questioned by some animal behaviorists since complex brains have developed among non-mammal species, including certain birds. Also, new studies demonstrate that in humans, the prefrontal cortex performs complex functions apart from the functions of the neocortex.

Post-Traumatic Brain Reeducation

Separate from the psychological disorders associated with PTSD, physical brain injuries are resulting in serious trauma. About 10 million people worldwide suffer traumatic brain injury (TBI) each year. Many cases are fatal, and most who survive the injury experience some degree of cognitive impairment. This trauma may occur in many circumstances, including vehicular accidents, sports injuries, falls inside and outside the home, acts of conflict or violence, even being struck by falling objects.

There is a range of treatments to reverse the impairment. The type and duration of treatment depend on the type and severity of the trauma. Generally, a multidisciplinary set of treatments is required, involving psychiatric and neurologic medical practices, as well as pharmacotherapy.

Classifying TBI as mild, moderate, or severe depends on several key factors: Degree of post-traumatic consciousness, duration of the coma if experienced by the patient, and the degree and duration of post-traumatic amnesia. Generally, TBI patients whose symptoms continue for one month or more are classified as either moderate or severe and whose full recovery takes years. At the same time, those showing marked improvement within a few weeks are considered mild cases and often return to full cognitive function within two months.

There are several impairments to the cognitive functions following TBI. These are the most commonly treated:

- *Decreased ability to concentrate*

- *Impaired attentiveness*

- *Reduced visual-spatial cognizance*

- *Tendency to be easily distracted*

- *Memory lapses and impairments*

- *Loss of executive ability (decision-making)*

- *Disrupted communications skills*

- *Judgmental lapses and dysfunctions*

Reeducation of TBI patients begins with assessments based on standardized testing protocols, including visual and auditory attentiveness, visual and verbal measurements, language comprehension and understanding, executive function (decisiveness), overall mental and intellectual function, and motor function.

Post-traumatic brain reeducation is undertaken primarily through cognitive rehabilitation, which increases the injured person's abilities in the processing and interpreting of information and the overall performance of mental functions. Cognitive rehabilitation is most effective in mild or moderate levels of TBI and with persons who have a high level of motivation to succeed in the recovery. The multidisciplinary group that collaborates with brain educational therapy may include doctors, speech and language specialists, and physical and occupational therapists. However, it is recognized that each patient's treatment will be unique, prescribed, and tailored to each individual, based on the specific injuries suffered and resultant trauma.

One important approach that has wide application is attention process training (ATP), which is based on mental skills training, gradually increasing the complexity of the exercises, from simple initially and subsequently increasing in complexity, forcing the brain to retrain itself.

340

The activities include selective attention, focused attentiveness, alternating attention, divided attentiveness, and sustained attentiveness.

The Parasympathetic Recovery

The Polyvagal Theory links PTSD to one dimension of the parasympathetic nervous system (PNS), the early-evolved dorsal vagal freeze survival mechanism. The dorsal vagal mechanism may protect an animal by allowing it to play dead until the coast is clear. Still, in a human being, it can lead to inaction, inability to think or speak, or worse, passing out or fainting, shock, or even cardiac arrest. With the linking of PTSD to the dorsal vagal mechanism, the unrecognized cause may now be open to evaluation and potentially alleviate the symptoms of PTSD.

Precisely, the other, more recently evolved PNS response, the calming, relaxing, socially engaging ventral vagal response, may be applied to reduce the emotional and physical symptoms of PTSD. The methods used to achieve vagal tone and lower heart rates and breathing rates, reactivate the digestive system, and induce an all-encompassing state of calm and relaxation may be applied by the individual, easily, every day. These methods include meditation, yoga stretches and poses, and managed deep and conscious breathing. The practice of deep, slow breathing, with a forceful extension of the diaphragm to tone the vagus nerve, is applicable as part of meditation or Yoga or simply done without other techniques.

It can also include auricular and facial massage, massage of the vagus nerve as it passes next to the right and left carotid artery in the neck, and cold facial therapy. The practice of mindfulness or being in the moment in which all outside thoughts are prevented from intruding, can also be beneficial. The person concentrates on every external sound, every feeling, every awareness of things in the environment. Vocal stimulation of the vagus nerve can be done easily by singing, gargling, or reciting a mantra while performing mantra and transcendental meditation.

Another application of Polyvagal Theory to treating PTSD is for the individual to recognize that the symptoms of PTSD are biological in nature, caused by the body's primitive instincts and reflexes to protect itself and that

341

the body can be taught to relax, get over it, rejoin and socially engage with those who are living active, normal lifestyles. This is called somatic awareness. It trains the individual to become aware of essential bodily functions like heart rate and breathing and consciously try to slow them down. The deep breathing exercises may help achieve a sense of bodily control.

The reduction or elimination of PTSD symptoms can further be achieved by practicing a series of mental exercises called attentional control, a conscious effort to recognize the cues that may trigger PTSD reactions, and gently but firmly cancel them out by acknowledging that there is no danger, nothing to fear, and all is well. This form of body awareness is called cognitive behavior therapy (CBT). It encourages the individual to be aware that an unneeded fight or flight response is continuing and can be shut down by conscious thought, replacing disturbing thoughts and memories with relaxing, peaceful thoughts. Over time and with practice, replacing bad thoughts with positive ones will make the cooling down of the dorsal vagal action-orientation easier.

Chapter 11. Music Therapy, Trauma, and the Polyvagal Theory

Music is a documented feature of civilizations. Cultures have incorporated music into the educational procedure, strict and tribal rituals, and patriotic articulations. Through the two verses and song, vocal music has been used both as a new vehicle and an archival mechanism to transmit important cultural, moral, spiritual, and historical occasions and values. Music has been used to calm, enable sentiments of safety, construct a feeling of a network, and decrease the social distance between individuals.

Music is an important part of the human experience. Music is interwoven with feeling, affect regulation, interpersonal social behavior, and other psychological procedures related to personal reactions to environmental, interpersonal, and intrapersonal challenges. Sorts of music have been exceptionally associated with distinct sentiments, encounters, and social interactions. These psychological procedures shape our feeling of self, add to our abilities to frame relationships, and decide if we have a sense of security in various settings or with specific individuals. Although these procedures can be impartially watched and abstractly depicted, they speak to a mind-boggling interplay between our psychological experience and physiology.

More than listening to music, singing, or playing a musical instrument, music therapy includes the dynamic interactions among three features:

(1) therapist

(2) customer

(3) music.

The polyvagal hypothesis is used to introduce a plausible model to explain how and why music therapy is useful in supporting physical health and enhancing capacity during compromised states associated with mental and physical sickness, including trauma. The polyvagal hypothesis gives a strategy to understand the mechanisms and procedures that enable music and music therapy to improve social engagement behaviors and to facilitate the regulation of natural and behavioral states.

343

The hypothesis further gives bits of knowledge that connect music therapy to the sensory system and to health results and is used to deconstruct music therapy into two parts: (1) the interpersonal relationship among therapist and customer, and (2) the acoustic features of music used in the therapeutic setting as it pertains to clinical treatment.

How music and prosodic vocalizations trigger the social engagement system

As vertebrates advanced from reptiles to mammals, the structures at the finish of the mandible (i.e., jaw bone) characterize the center ear bones became detached. For humans and different mammals, sound in nature encroaches on the eardrum. It is transduced from the eardrum to the internal ear via the small bones in the center ear known as ossicles. When the stapedius (regulated by a branch of the facial nerve) and the tensor tympani (regulated by an extension of the trigeminal nerve) muscles are innervated, the acicular chain becomes progressively inflexible. It dampens the amplitude of the low-frequency acoustic stimulation from the earth, reaching the inward ear. This procedure is similar to fixing the skin on a kettledrum. When the skin is fixed, the pitch of the drum is higher. When the acicular chain is set, similar to the extended skin, just higher frequencies bobbing against the eardrum are transmitted to the inward ear and to the auditory preparing areas of the brain. This functional relation is depicted and illustrated in a Scientific American article by Borg and Counter.

The advancement of the human center ear enabled low-amplitude, relatively high-frequency airborne sounds matching the frequency of the human voice to be heard, in any event, when the acoustic condition was dominated by low-frequency sounds, for example, sounds made by large predators. Detached center ear bones were a phylogenetic innovation that enabled mammals to communicate in a frequency band that couldn't be distinguished by reptiles. Reptiles have difficulties in hearing higher frequencies since their hearing is reliant on bone conduction.

Studies have demonstrated that this critical neural regulation of center ear muscles, a necessary mechanism to extract the soft hints of the human voice from the uproarious hints of low-frequency background noise, is inadequate

344

in individuals with language delays, learning disabilities, and autistic range disorders. Additionally, center ear contamination (i.e., otitis media) may bring about a total inability to inspire the reflexive contraction of the stapedius muscles. Disorders that impact the neural capacity of the facial nerve (i.e., Bell's palsy) impact the stapedius reflex; however, they may also affect the patient's ability to discriminate discourse. The watched difficulties that individuals with various physical and mental disorders have in extracting human voice from background sounds may be reliant on the same neural system that regulates facial demeanor. In this way, deficiencies in the social engagement system would compromise feeling and social awareness and language improvement.

Music therapy, trauma, and the social engagement system

The frequency content of melodies in most musical creations duplicates the frequency band of a human voice. Functionally, acoustic properties of melodies, typically encompassing center C and the two octaves above center C, easily pass through the center ear structures regardless of the neural tone to the center ear muscles. When the frequencies pass through the center ear, they trigger a neural feedback mechanism to tense the ossicle chain. Vocal music duplicates the impact of vocal prosody. It triggers neural mechanisms that regulate the whole social engagement system with the resultant changes in facial affect and autonomic state. Basically, we start to look and feel better when we listen to melodies. Along these lines, while social engagement is a shared objective in music therapy practice, incorporating the polyvagal hypothesis gives a plausible scientific justification to how music therapy may provide chances to exercise the social engagement system.

Consistent with the parallel between music and social communication, the same frequency band that characterizes melodies characterizes in the human voice, the frequency band in which all information (i.e., verbal content) is communicated. When this frequency band is weighted to enhance the understanding of voice, it is known as the "record of articulation" and, all the more, as late as the "discourse understandability list." These lists emphasize the relative importance of specific frequencies in passing on the information installed in human discourse.

345

In the normal ear, acoustic vitality inside the primary frequencies of these lists is not attenuated as it passes through the center ear structures to the internal ear. The frequency band characterizing the articulation list is similar to the frequency band that authors have historically chosen to communicate melodies. It is also the frequency band that moms have used to calm their infants by singing lullabies.

Trauma can kill the social engagement system. Attempts to engage an individual with a trauma history, rather than evoking spontaneous social behavior, may trigger guarded and aggressive behaviors. From a clinical perspective, traumatized individuals often present gaze aversion and flat facial affect features

If we were to screen the physiological state of these individuals, we would watch an ANS that is poised to battle or escape (i.e., high heart rate and low vagal regulation of the heart).

The traumatic experience functionally retunes neuroception to conservatively distinguish risk when there is no risk. Most therapeutic strategies attempt to engage with a direct face-to-face eye to eye connection.

Working with traumatized individuals creates a great challenge to therapists since the normal social engagement behaviors of the therapist may trigger fear and reactive guarded strategies. Music therapy gives a special portal to reengage the social engagement system that doesn't require an initial face-to-face interaction. Music can be used to stimulate the social engagement system without expecting face-to-face correspondence. Since melodic music contains acoustic properties similar to vocal prosody, music may be used to select the social engagement system by challenging and modulating the neural regulation of the center ear muscles. Suppose the social engagement system is adequately selected. In that case, positive facial articulations will develop, eye stare will spontaneously be aimed at the therapist, and the traumatized individual will shift to an increasingly calm and positive physiological state.

Chapter 12. Yoga Therapy and Polyvagal Theory

Yoga therapy is a recently developing, automatic correlative and integrative human service (CIH) practice. It is growing in its professionalization, acknowledgment & use with a showed responsibility to setting practice principles, instructive & accreditation norms, and elevating exploration to help its viability for different populaces and conditions.

In any case, heterogeneity of training, poor detailing principles, and absence of an extensively acknowledged comprehension of the neurophysiological systems associated with yoga treatment restrain the organizing of testable speculations and clinical applications.

The currently proposed structures of yoga-themed practices center with respect to combining base up neurophysiological and top-down neurocognitive components. It has been suggested that phenomenology and first individual moral request can give a focal point. Yoga treatment is seen as a procedure that contributes towards eudaimonic prosperity in the experience of torment, sickness, or incapacity. In this article, we expand on these systems and propose a model of yoga treatment that merges with Polyvagal Theory (PVT).

PVT joins the development of the autonomic sensory system to the rise of prosocial practices and states that the neural stages supporting social conduct are engaged with looking after wellbeing, development, and reclamation. This logical model that associates neurophysiological examples of autonomic guidelines and articulation of enthusiastic and social behavior is progressively used to understand human conduct, stress, and disease.

In particular, we portray how PVT can be conceptualized as a neurophysiological partner to the yogic ideal of the gunas or characteristics of nature. Like the neural stages portrayed in PVT, the gunas give the establishment from which conduct, passionate and physical traits rise. We depict how these two distinct yet closely resembling structures - one situated in neurophysiology and the other in an old intelligence convention - feature yoga treatment's advancement of physical, mental, and social prosperity for self-guideline and strength. This parallel between the neural foundation of PVT and the gunas of yoga is instrumental in making a translational structure

347

for yoga treatment to line up with its philosophical establishments. This way, yoga treatment can work as a particular practice instead of fitting into an outside model for its usage in inquires about its clinical settings.

Mind-body treatments, including yoga treatment, are proposed to profit wellbeing and prosperity by reconciling top-down and base-up forms that encourage bidirectional correspondence between the cerebrum and body. Top-down procedures, such as the guideline of consideration and setting of expectation, have been shown to diminish mental worry just as hypothalamic-pituitary pivot (HPA) and thoughtful sensory system movement (SNS) balance insusceptible capacity and irritation. Base-up forms, advanced by breathing procedures and development rehearsals, have been appeared to impact the musculoskeletal, cardiovascular and sensory system work and furthermore influence HPA and SNS movement with frequent changes in resistant capacity and passionate prosperity.

The top-down and base-up forms utilized at the top of the body treatment priorities list may control autonomic, neuroendocrine, enthusiastic, and conduct actuation and bolster a person's reaction to challenges. Self-guideline, a cognizant capacity to keep up the framework's security by overseeing or modifying reactions to risk or misfortune, may diminish the side effects of differing conditions. For example, peevish inside disorder, neurodegenerative diseases, interminable agony, wretchedness, and PTSD through the moderation of allosteric load with a move in the autonomic state have proposed such a model of top-down and base up self-administrative components of yoga for mental wellbeing.

Versatility may give another advantage of mind-body treatments as it incorporates the capacity of a person to "ricochet back" and adjust in light of affliction and unpleasant conditions in an opportune manner to such an extent psychophysiological assets are rationed. High strength is related to faster cardiovascular recuperation following abstract passionate encounters, less seen pressure, more noteworthy recuperation from ailment or injury, and better administration of dementia and incessant agony. Traded off versatility is connected to dysregulation of the autonomic sensory system through proportions of vagal guidelines (respiratory sinus arrhythmia. Yoga is related to both improvements in ratios of mental strength and improved vagal guidelines.

348

This article investigates the mix of top-down and base-up forms for self-guideline and versatility through Polyvagal Theory and yoga treatment. PVT will be portrayed in connection to contemporary understandings of interception as the biobehavioral hypothesis of the "preliminary set," which will be characterized later. This will help spread out an incorporated framework to see which mind-body treatments encourage the development of physiological, enthusiastic, and social qualities for the advancement of self-guideline and strength.

PVT, and other rising hypotheses, for example, neurovascular combination, help explain associations between the frameworks of the body, the cerebrum, and the procedures of the mind offering expanded understanding into complex models of incorporated top-down and base up forms that are natural to mind-body treatments. PVT portrays three particular neural stages in light of apparent hazard (i.e., wellbeing, peril, and life-risk) in the conditions that work in a phylogenetically decided chain of command, steadily with the Jacksonian guideline of disintegration. PVT acquaints the idea of neuroception with depicting the subliminal recognition of wellbeing or peril in nature through base up forms including vagal afferents, tangible info identified with outside difficulties, and endocrine components that recognize and assess ecological hazard before the cognizant elaboration by higher mind focuses.

The three polyvagal neural stages, as portrayed underneath, are connected to the practices of social correspondence, guarded procedure of activation, and protective immobilization:

• The ventral vagal complex (VVC) gives the neural structures that intervene in the "social commitment framework." At the point when wellbeing is recognized in the interior and outside condition, the VVC gives a neural stage to help prosocial conduct and social association by connecting the neural guideline of instinctive states supporting homeostasis and reclamation to facial expressivity and the open and expressive areas of correspondence (e.g., prosodic vocalizations and upgraded capacity to tune in to voice). The engine segment of the VVC, which starts in the core ambiguous (NA), manages and organizes the muscles of the face and head with the bronchi and heart.

349

These associations help arrange the individual towards human association and commitment in prosocial connections and give increasingly adaptable and versatile reactions to ecological difficulties, including social communications.

•   The SNS is often connected with battle/flight practices. Battle/flight practices require initiation of the SNS. They are the underlying and essential guard procedures enlisted by warm-blooded creatures. This safeguard technique requires expanded metabolic yield to help activation practices. Inside PVT, the enlistment of SNS on guard pursues the Jacksonian guideline of disintegration. It mirrors the versatile responses of a phylogenetically requested reaction progressively in which the VVC has neglected to alleviate risk. When the SNS circuit is selected, monstrous physiological changes are remembering an expansion for muscle tone, shunting of blood from the fringe, restraint of gastrointestinal capacity, an enlargement of the bronchi, increments in pulse and respiratory rate, and the arrival of catecholamines.

This assembly of physiological assets makes way for reacting to genuine or accepted peril in the earth and towards the ultimate objectives of security and endurance. When the SNS turns into the predominant neural stage, the VVC impact might be repressed for activating assets for a quick activity. Though prosocial practices and social association are related to the VVC, the SNS is related to practices and feelings, for example, dread or outrage, that helps to prepare the earth for security or wellbeing.

•   The dorsal vagal complex (DVC) emerges from the dorsal core of the vagus (DNX). It gives the essential vagal engine filaments to organs situated beneath the stomach. This circuit is intended to adaptably react to massive peril or dread. It is the crudest (i.e., developmentally most established) reaction to stretch. Initiation of the DVC in resistance brings about an uninvolved response portrayed by diminished muscle tone, and emotional decrease of heart yield to save metabolic assets, and modification in gut and bladder work through reflexive poop and pee to lessen metabolic requests required by processing.

PVT states that specific physiological states, mental traits, and social procedures are associated, developed and made open through these neural stages.

350

The physiological state built up by these neural stages in light of risk or security (as decided through the coordinated procedures of neuroception) considers or limits the scope of passionate and social attributes that are open to the person.

A center part of PVT is that examples of physiological state, feeling, and conduct are specific to each neural stage. For instance, the neural foundation of the VVC is proposed to associate instinctive homeostasis with passionate qualities and prosocial practices. These contradict the neurophysiological states, enthusiastic attributes, or social practices that show in the neural foundation of protective procedures found in SNS or DVC initiation. When the VVC is predominant, the vagal brake is executed, and prosocial practices and enthusiastic states, for example, association and love, can possibly develop.

When the SNS is the essential guarded system, the NA kills the inhibitory activity of the ventral vagal pathway to the heart to empower thoughtful enactment, and in turn, social and passionate procedures of assembly are bolstered. On the off chance, the DVC idleness reaction is the cautious system. The dorsal engine core is initiated as a defensive component from agony or potential demise, which means dynamic reaction methodologies are not accessible.

It is imperative to note that the VVC has different qualities that empower mixed states with the SNS (e.g., play) or with the DVC (e.g., closeness). Be that as it may, in these mixed states, the VVC remains effectively available and practically contains the subordinate circuits. When the VVC is pulled back, it advances the availability of the SNS as a guard battle/flight framework. Also, the SNS practically restrains access to the DVC immobilization shutdown reaction. In this way, the significant shutdown response that may prompt demise turns out to be neurophysiological available just when the SNS is reflexively repressed.

a. Vagal Activity, Interception, Regulation, and Resilience

Vagal movement, via ventral vagal pathways, is recommended to be an intelligent guideline for the versatility of the framework where high heart vagal tone is associated with increasingly versatile top-down and base up procedures; for example, consideration guidelines, full of feeling preparation and adaptability of physiological frameworks to adjust and react to the earth.

Vagal control has additionally been shown to relate with differential actuation in mind locales that manage reactions to risk evaluation, interception, feeling guidelines, and the advancement of more noteworthy adaptability in light of challenge. On the other hand, the low vagal guideline has been related to maladaptive base up.

Top-down handling brings about poor self-guideline, less social adaptability, discouragement, conclusive uneasiness issues, and antagonistic wellbeing results remembering expanded mortality for conditions, such as lupus rheumatoid joint pain and injury.

The vagus nerve is involved in 80% of afferent filaments. It fills in as a significant conductor for interceptive correspondence about the condition of the viscera and inside milieu to cerebrum structures. Interception has been investigated as basic to the connecting of top-down and base up preparation and examining the connections between sensations, feelings, sentiments, and sympathovagal. The backing has been found to join interceptive info, feeling. A guideline of sympathovagal balance in the separate and cingulate cortices, encouraging a bonded reaction within the person to body, mind, or natural (BME) wonders.

Self-guideline is proposed to be subject to the precision we decipher and react to interceptive data, with more prominent exactness prompting upgraded versatility and self-guideline. This way, interception is viewed as significant in torment, habit, enthusiastic guideline, and solid, versatile practices, including social commitment. Furthermore, interception has been proposed as key to versatility as the precise preparation of substantial interior states advancing a brisk rebuilding of homeostatic parity.

It has been suggested that mind-body treatments are a successful device for the guideline of vagal capacity, with results encouraging towards of versatile capacities including the alleviation of unfavorable impacts related to social difficulty, the decrease of allosteric load, and the assistance of self-administrative abilities and strength of the ANS crosswise over different patient populaces and conditions.

Conclusion

Congratulations! You have made it to the end of Polyvagal Theory. Hopefully, it was a book full of information that was useful and relevant to you while delivered in a method that was readily understood. With the utmost hope of being useful for you, the reader, this book was crafted. If it has succeeded, you should now be aware of several different aspects of the polyvagal theory.

You should be well aware that the polyvagal theory believes that there are three different activations of the vagus nerve. There is the primitive freeze response to fear. Your entire body freezes up because it does not believe that it can get away and actually live. There is the modern fight or flight response, in which the body sees some sort of stressor and is convinced that it can fend it off in some way, shape, or form, either in fighting or running away. This is why you get afraid or angry when you are stressed out. Finally, the state of mind you are calm and ready to socialize is known as the connection state of mind. This is where you can make meaningful interactions and connections with other people.

The polyvagal point of view is an endeavor to apply, construct and derive from the Polyvagal Theory to comprehend the inconsistencies in writing identified with strategy for measurement, neurophysiological and neuroanatomical components, and versatile function of vagal efferent pathways. The methodology underlines that predispositions or order discipline myths happen when information and investigation are limited to mental or physiological degrees of inquiry.

The polyvagal point of view recommends that it is essential, not exclusively, to comprehend the vagal efferent activities on the heart from a neurophysiological degree of request. Yet, the versatile capacity of neural regulation of the heart must be interpreted inside the setting of the phylogeny of the autonomic nervous system. A few control discipline myths have been deconstructed and interpreted in the areas over, depending on the inquiry level. These centers outline detailed explanations to stimulate further logical experiments and challenges using well-designed structured investigations.

With an accentuation on sensory system regulation, the polyvagal theory is a significant shift for psychophysiological scientists, who generally have not credited mechanism to pulse or Heart Rate. What is more, this point of view drives the specialist to create new questions, including such uncomplicated issues as establishing information collection parameters, the techniques designed to evaluate different components of the pulse rate patterns, and even the procedures used to address any artifact.

• The polyvagal point of view empowers experts intrigued by autonomic-social relations to extend their exploration and expand their research plan to incorporate questions listed

• Features of the source nuclei in the core ambiguous, and the dorsal motor core of the vagus

• Impacts of the afferent vagus through the nucleus tractus solitarius on the source nuclei of the two vagi

• The effect of ascending pathways from the nucleus tractus solitarius on mind regions directing cognition and attraction

• The practical contrasts between the vagal efferent pathways portrayed by preganglionic nicotinic and muscarinic acetylcholine receptors

• The useful differences in the impact of myelinated and unmyelinated vagal efferent channels on the sino-atrial node

• The collaboration between the regulation of the exceptional instinctive efferent and myelinated vagal pathways

• The effect of peripheral and central structures and pathways on modulating the output of the vagal efferent pathways

By examining the inconsistency between techniques used to calculate RSA, we can perceive how different research questions and presumptions lead to various strategies and ideal models. When investigation systems depend on a peripheral physiological degree of demand, at that point, cardiac vagal tone is assumed to speak to a unitary development.

In any case, when research techniques depend on a neurophysiological degree of inquiry, at that point, the mission for a component of cardiac vagal tone is refined to concentrate on strategies that individually measure every one of the two vagal systems. The last methodology ought to be expressing to physiologists since the two vagal systems advanced to help various types of behavior.

Vagal activity starting in the nucleus ambiguous is neurophysiological and neuroanatomical connected to regulating the striated muscles of the face and head, structures that are engaged with social communication and emotions. Hypothetically, RSA should intently resemble individual and intra-singular varieties in emotion connection, social interaction, and behavioral status.

Interestingly, vagal action beginning in the DMX ought to reflect tonic impacts to the visceral organs (i.e., basically subdiaphragmatic). The quick and immense increase in the output of the DMX that may deliver bradycardia, apnea, or defecation would happen as a defense procedure to decrease metabolic demands. Maybe, the negative feature of stress and wellbeing defenselessness being related to the slower rhythms may have driven researchers to accept that these rhythms were affected by the sympathetic sensory system.

The polyvagal perspective shifts the research from a theoretical technique towards hypothesis-driven ideal models subordinates upon specific neural mechanisms. Preeminent, the polyvagal theory accentuates the significance of phylogenetic changes in the neural structures controlling the autonomic nervous system. The phylogenetic technique gives experiences into the versatile capacity and the neural regulation of the two vagal systems. Without having constructs from the Polyvagal Theory to depict versatile abilities and to decide the estimation details of the two vagal systems.

 One related with calm states and social commitment manners and the other a minimal defense system that is conceivably bad to warm-blooded animals. It would not be conceivable to explain the methods and components of the segments of cardiovascular vagal tone.

355

COMPLEX PTSD

Introduction

This book will shed light on the topic of trauma. Trauma is a disorder, which makes a person depressed and agitated about specific events.

Trauma can be of many types. It can be psychological trauma, physical trauma, and physiological trauma. Trauma has symptoms as well, and it can be cured through proper medication and a flexible routine of exercises.

A World Mental Health overview led by the World Health Organization found that 33% of the 125,000 individuals studied in 26 unique nations had encountered injury in any event.

Regular Responses and Symptoms of Trauma

The reaction to a bad accident mainly changes from person to person.

Enthusiastic signs include:

Bitterness.

Outrage.

Forswearing.

Dread.

Disgrace.

These may prompt:

Bad dreams.

A sleeping disorder.

The trouble with connections.

Emotional upheavals.

357

Expected physical side effects:

Sickness.

Discombobulation.

I changed the rest designs.

Changes in hunger.

Migraines.

Gastrointestinal issues.

The mental issue may consist of:

PTSD.

Sorrow.

Uneasiness.

Dissociative issue.

Substance misuse issues.

Some people develop specific side effects like those mentioned above; these usually disappear after 10-15 days. This is called the intense pressure problem (ASD).

Some individuals after a traumatic event do not show PTSD symptoms for a long time. The signs of post-traumatic stress disorder can make anxiety attacks, sadness, and depression worse.

Chapter 1: Defining Depression

Many people all over the world suffer from some form of depression. Many disorders fall under the category of depression. In this chapter, we will discuss what depression exactly is, as well as who it affects the most. We will also outline the various types of depression and the process of how depression is diagnosed.

What is Depression?

Depression is a common mood disorder. It is perhaps the most common mental illness. However, although it is common, it can also be quite serious. Depression can affect a person's daily life - how one thinks, feels, and even how one goes about their daily activities in life. Even the most mundane of daily activities such as eating, sleeping, and going to work or school can be affected by depression.

Depression can be diagnosed as clinical depression or, more seriously, as depressive disorder. Still, these are just the two broadest terms used in the world of psychiatry in diagnosing depressive disorders. To receive a diagnosis of depression, the symptoms a person experiences must be persistent, nearly daily, for most of the day, for a minimum of two weeks. Symptoms and signs that may point to depression include constant anxiety or feelings of sadness or emptiness. This can include feelings of loneliness, low self-worth, and apathy.

Feelings of intense pessimism or lingering hopelessness can also be a part of depression. A person who suffers from depression may lose interest in activities that they previously enjoyed. A depressed person may find that he or she is struggling with feelings of guilt, has become more irritable than usual, or feels helpless or worthless. A patient with depression may begin to talk and move in a slower way than he or she did previously. This could be because of fatigue or because of decreased levels of energy that have occurred. This can be related to the fact that many people suffering from depression have difficulties associated with sleep.

These patients may experience insomnia, often wake in the early morning hours, and often oversleep past the time they need to be up. On the other hand, a person who is experiencing depression might have difficulty sitting still or feel restless and move about much more than what is normal for him or her. A mental fog causes the person to have trouble remembering things, often losing their train of thought in conversations, having difficulty concentrating, and unable to make even the most inconsequential decisions.

A person with a depressive disorder often experiences changes in their appetite and, therefore, can have weight gains or weight losses. Some people lose their appetite altogether and find that they are only picking at their food if they even remember to eat and may experience weight loss, while others might eat more out of emotion or feelings of anxiety and so will see an increase in their weight. Although at extreme opposite ends of the spectrum, both instances can be seen in people with depression. Achiness and different pains such as cramps, headaches, and digestive system issues are often complaints of depressed patients. These pains often occur with no apparent cause in a physical sense and usually are not successfully treatable. Some of the most troubling concerns that may emerge in patients with depression include uncontrollable thoughts of suicide and death that, in some cases, can even lead to attempts of suicide.

Major depressive disorder or clinical depression is a diagnosis given when the symptoms discussed above cause distress to the person or cause significant impairment in occupational or social functioning.

The symptoms cannot have a relationship to the use or abuse of drugs and alcohol. There is a high mortality rate associated with major depressive disorder.

The majority of these deaths are a result of suicide. It is of the utmost importance that anyone who thinks that they may have symptoms of depression is seen by a doctor, therapist, or psychiatrist to receive treatment for their condition.

Depressive disorders are one of the most common mental illnesses and, in most cases, are highly or entirely treatable.

Cognitive-behavioral therapy is a short-term treatment that is highly effective when utilized to treat depressive disorders. The tools and strategies developed and learned in therapy can help people manage their mental conditions for a lifetime.

Depression in Daily Life

Over 15 million people suffer from depressive disorders worldwide. Depression has been cited as one of the most common disabilities. Sadly, only approximately 10 percent of the millions of people who suffer from depression will receive adequate treatment.

One-quarter of adults in the United States live with a diagnosis of clinical depression, also known as a major depressive disorder. Although depression is a disorder that affects mental wellness, it can also take a toll on physical health. The cardiovascular system is especially vulnerable to the added stress placed upon it as a result of depression.

The risk of suffering cardiovascular issues increases with a diagnosis of depression. This is mainly because depression causes the blood vessels to constrict, making the heart work harder. People who have depression are also more likely to die due to a heart attack than their counterparts who do not have depression.

Depression can have a direct impact on nutrition, especially in the form of fluctuations in appetite. Some people with depression do not eat enough. However, it may seem an unpleasant side effect; it can contribute to anorexia nervosa. This eating disorder can often be quite severe. People who experience depression also have deficiencies in at least one of the following categories: B vitamins, amino acids, minerals, and omega-3 fatty acids. Without adequate amounts of these nutrients, the brain is unable to work as it is supposed to. In other cases, people with depressive disorders tend to overeat, even binging. This can lead to extreme weight gain and other physical health disorders such as the onset of type II diabetes, high blood pressure, and other illnesses resulting from obesity.

It may be difficult, but for these reasons, it is essential to maintain a healthy and nutritious diet while experiencing depression and while undergoing treatment for depressive disorders.

Many factors lead to worse overall health in those people who have a depressive disorder. These include poor sleeping patterns, poor eating habits, and a lowered immune system. It is just as important to receive treatment for one's physical health as for one's mental health when suffering from a depressive disorder.

Depression has an impact on every aspect of an individual's daily life. It affects your ability to eat and sleep. You may not be able to sleep well, you may have insomnia, or you may sleep away your entire day. All of these can be symptoms of depression. As far as eating goes, a person with a depressive disorder may eat too much or too little. Depression can rob a person of the ability to understand when they need to eat. Due to these factors and the suppression of a person's immune system, depression can also harm your health.

Depression can also take its toll on your relationships. The correlation between your moods and emotions and the health of your relationships is vital. When dealing with a mental health disorder such as chronic depression, it can be difficult to manage relationships. When your mood is often low, your behaviors can cause distance to occur between you and those with whom you have relationships. You may not even realize that you are behaving in a manner that can cause your relationship issues.

This is one-way learning replacement behaviors through cognitive-behavioral therapy can significantly benefit people suffering from depressive disorders.

There are many ways that depression can affect a person that may not be visible to others. One of the most common and extreme feelings that a person with depression may experience is guilt. Too often, a person with depression just does not feel the ability to do what needs to be done. This includes showering, eating, cleaning his or her home, walking his or her dog, and more. A person with depression knows that these are things that should be done but may not have the ability to complete them. The resounding feeling that follows the inability to complete these daily tasks is often guilt. Studies

362

have shown that due to variances in the brain, people with depression feel shame in a much more intense way than people who are not depressed.

Some people with depression have a much more difficult time dealing with their lives in the morning than at any other time of day. This is when it can be a tremendous struggle just to make it out of bed. Frustration, fatigue, anger, and extreme sadness are some of the feelings that can compound so-called morning depression when the mornings contain the most severe depression symptoms.

People with depression are often good at hiding things from the outside world. This can be due to the guilt that they feel. A person with a depressive disorder may actually be totally exhausted at any time yet be able to pull himself or herself together to prevent causing distress to others. Some people experiencing depression might be great at acting like they are alright, even when they are not. This is why it is not always possible to look at a person and decide if they are depressed.

A behavior that is often displayed by people dealing with depression is canceling plans. This is especially common in cases of bipolar disorder. Many times a person feels that they can go through with the past when the time comes. However, when dealing with depression, the person cannot participate or even leave their house once the time comes. Just the thought of preparing for a scheduled activity can be too much to deal with. Entering the outside world, where it seems that everyone else can easily function, can be highly stressful for a person struggling to deal with the side effects of a depressive disorder.

One of the most challenging things for a person with depression to understand is that they know logically that their lives are excellent.

They think that they should be happy and grateful because it is impossible to use logic in feelings. Even if a person does not believe that there is any reason to feel depressed, the feelings are not necessarily on board. Feelings are not something that can be controlled. This can be one of the most frustrating circumstances a person with a depressive disorder must endure.

What Causes a Person to be Depressed?

In the United States, depression remains one of the most diagnosed mental conditions. There are many factors at play in how a person can have a diagnosis of depression. These factors can be singular in nature or occur in a combination of the cause of depression in any one individual person. Depression can be genetic, meaning that it can be found in a person's DNA to have a higher risk of developing a depressive disorder. In many cases, a diagnosis of major depressive disorder is not merely a psychological effect. Still, it may be linked with biological factors as well. In some of these cases, a biochemical background of higher depression risk can help develop the disease of depression. Environmental factors can also be at play in the onset of depression. This is most commonly seen in seasonal affective disorder cases, including divorce or a family member's death. Lastly, psychological reasons may be the cause of depression in some cases. In this case, pessimists and people who already carry conditions such as having low self-esteem may develop depression.

Some people develop depression as a comorbid diagnosis, along with another serious physical or mental medical condition. It is not uncommon for patients who experience cancer, diabetes, heart disease, or Parkinson's disease to develop depression. Any of the previously listed diagnoses can completely change a person's life and limit daily activities, which, in turn, can lead to depression.

Some people carry higher risk factors for developing depression than the rest of the general population. As stated above, experiencing significant life changes can predispose a person to be at a higher risk of developing depression. This can include anything from a job change to a loved one's death or going through a divorce. Trauma and stress can also cause depression to occur more easily in some people. Even high levels of pressure on the job can contribute to a diagnosis of depression. People who experience post-traumatic stress disorder have a very much increased likelihood of depression. Post-traumatic stress disorder is often seen in soldiers who have been on active duty. It can also occur in other situations, such as after an abduction, assault, or car wreck. Depression and post-traumatic stress disorder are often co-diagnosed in individuals.

A patient with a personal history of depression is more likely to have concurrent relapses of the disease, especially when medication or therapy has been discontinued. Likewise, a family history of depression allows for a higher incidence of depression to occur in an individual with this background.

Many medications carry potential side effects that include the possibility of predisposing a patient to become depressed. As discussed previously, specific diagnoses of physical illnesses can cause a person to more likely develop depression. Sadly, in many cases, the disease itself lends a higher incidence of depression. Still, the medication prescribed to treat or control it can carry depression as a potential side effect.

Depression often coexists with the abuse of substances such as alcohol or illegal drugs. Propensity substance abuse is quite similar to that of depression. There can be a genetic link, as both depression and substance abuse are generationally in families. Issues with mental health can, at times, be found as the reason that a person began to abuse substances. Conversely, substance abuse can be a cause for later mental health issues to develop. Both depression and the abuse of alcohol or other illegal substances influence the human brain. They both affect the same portion of the brain, which is the one that oversees a person's response to stress.

This combination of depression and addiction is often referred to as a dual diagnosis. A dual diagnosis can be any form of mental illness that coexists in combination with any form of addiction. The instances of dual diagnoses in the U.S. are rising in number. Another worrying fact is that both mental illnesses and substance abuse can down a person's immunity, causing them to become more susceptible to illnesses.

One safety measure that can be taken is to avoid alcohol and medications that have not been prescribed for you.

Depression can become so severe that it can be considered a disability. Depending on how well a person with a depressive disorder continues to function in daily life or how much impairment it creates will determine whether it is an actual disability. Major depressive disorder (or clinical depression) and bipolar disorder are considered disabilities by the social security administration.

Types of Disorders Found Under the Umbrella Term of Depression

Anyone can potentially have a depressive disorder. Depression is not a disease that occurs only at a typical age, to a standard stereotype. Age, fitness level, wealth, race, or religion make no difference in developing a depressive disorder. Depression can be mild or major. Mild depression typically has less severe symptoms, and it mostly interferes with motivation. Major depressive disorders, as previously stated, are also called clinical depression, are the most commonly diagnosed form of depression. It interferes in a person's daily life and with his or her daily activities.

Some types of depression may be slightly different from each other, while others will develop only under certain unique circumstances. In addition to clinical depression and major depressive disorder, we will discuss five other forms of depression that exist under the umbrella of the depression diagnosis.

The first type of disorder we will look at is persistent depressive disorder. This is also termed dysthymia. A persistent depressive disorder is a mood of depression that persistently lasts for at least two years. This is a continuous, chronic, and long-term type of depression. The critical component of persistent depressive disorder is the length of time it lasts. Similarly, to clinical depression, the patient may experience inadequacy, hopelessness, and a lack of productivity.

The person may lose interest in their typical daily activities and even complete personal hygiene tasks regularly. People diagnosed with this disorder often feel gloomy and down, finding it difficult to be happy even in circumstances and occasions that would typically warrant higher spirits. This particular depressive disorder can cause impairments that range from mild to severe. Next, we will discuss postpartum depression. This is a type of depression limited only to women who have experienced pregnancy or delivered a child.

Postpartum depression is viewed as a complication of giving birth. It is a separate phenomenon from the typical "baby blues" that many women experience in the first few weeks after giving birth, including difficulty sleeping and mood swings.

366

Women who experience postpartum depression have full symptoms of a major depressive disorder that begins at any point during the pregnancy or after the delivery has occurred. The woman may experience anxiety, severe feelings of sadness, and extreme exhaustion.

Many women who experience postpartum depression have a difficult time bonding with their new baby. Due to these symptoms, the women experiencing postpartum depression may find it challenging to care for themselves or complete daily care for their newborn babies. Many women with postpartum depression feel intense emotions of anger, sadness, and irritability.

They may think that they are not or are unable to be a good mother to their child. In some of the most severe cases, the new mother can have recurring fantasies of hurting either herself or her baby. This can include uncontrollable thoughts of suicide and death. There are cases of postpartum depression that can occur in new fathers as well as new mothers. Men experience the same symptoms as women, but they are typically focused on the lack of sleep they now endure, feelings of being unworthy as a father, and a lack of energy. Other symptoms may include insomnia, difficulty bonding with the baby, and withdrawal from friends and family members.

The third disorder we will outline is psychotic depression. This term is used when a form of psychosis is present in addition to the diagnosis of severe depression. It can also be referred to as major depression with psychotic features. Depression with accompanying hallucinations or delusions qualifies for this diagnosis. A delusion is defined as holding a false, disturbing fixed belief. Hallucinations can be auditory or visual in nature.

Auditory hallucinations occur when a person hears things that are disturbing that no one else can listen to. Likewise, visual hallucinations occur when a person sees upsetting things that are not seen by anyone else. Typically, the theme of the hallucinations and delusions is of a depressive nature.

An example of this is a person with depression who experiences delusions of illness, poverty, or guiltiness. This is what occurs when the psychotic features are mood congruent. This means that they comply with typical depressive features. When the psychotic features are termed mood-incongruent, it is considered more dangerous for the patient and the other

367

people in their lives. With these hallucinations and delusions, the risk of suicide, harm to others, and self-harm are much increased.

The hallucinations and delusions cause people to hear and see things that are not real and believe in them. Approximately one out of every five people diagnosed with depression also has a psychotic diagnosis, making this disorder far from uncommon. This type of depressive disorder is more serious than some other types. Behavior, mood, sleep, and appetite are among the many areas of a person's life that this depressive disorder can affect. It typically requires immediate attention from a doctor and immediate medical treatment.

Seasonal affective disorder is a type of environmental depression commonly experienced by many people, particularly in the northern hemisphere. There are prolonged seasonal periods of darkness. This disorder is most characterized by depression symptoms that have an onset in the winter months while lifting in the spring and summer months.

The onset generally occurs due to the lessened availability of natural sunlight. The seasonal affective disorder symptoms include an increased amount of sleeping, a withdrawal from social activities, and weight gain. The seasonal affective disorder usually has a predictable return each year as the months grow colder and darker. Some reasons that may potentially be behind the cause of this disorder include a disruption of the body's natural rhythm and an imbalance in the hormone melatonin, which is caused by the decrease of natural sunlight.

The last type of depressive disorder that we will discuss in this chapter is bipolar disorder. This illness was previously named manic-depressive disorder, referring to the extreme highs and extreme lows that the patient could reach.

People who experience bipolar disorder have extreme shifts in mood. At the End of the spectrum, dark moods meet the diagnosis criteria of major depressive disorder. These low moods are labeled as bipolar depression. On the other hand, patients with bipolar disorder also go through periods of extreme highs, called mania. These moods are unstable and can cause the patient to feel either irritable or euphoric.

Manic episodes of lesser severity are called hypomania. Some of the symptoms that people with bipolar disorder experience include changes in activity levels and sleep patterns, unusual behaviors, and intense emotions. While displaying signs of depression or mania, the moods and actions are quite different from what would typically be expected.

Manic episodes can consist of high energy, difficulty sleeping, difficulty staying on topic, being and irritable, risky behaviors, and thinking that many things can be handled simultaneously. Periods of depression can consist of decreased energy levels, feelings of hopelessness, sleeping too much or too little, difficulty concentrating, and thoughts of suicide or death. Bipolar disorder is actually able to be divided into four distinct subcategories.

All four categories have a commonality in that mood, activity, and energy levels are variable. The first of the subcategories is bipolar I disorder. Manic episodes lasting for at least one week are a characteristic of this category. Sometimes the manic symptoms can be so intense that the person will require hospital care immediately.

The time frame for depressive episodes can last as many as 14 days. Some patients with this diagnosis can experience mixed features during their depressive episodes, which means that manic and depressive symptoms can exist at the same time. Bipolar II disorder is quite similar to bipolar I disorder. The main difference is that instead of reaching the intensity of the manic period experienced in bipolar I, bipolar II consists of hypomanic periods and periods of depression. Cyclothymia which is also known as the cyclothymic disorder, is quite an interesting category.

With this diagnosis, symptoms must last for a period of a minimum of at least two years. There are depressive and hypomanic symptoms present, but they are not at a level of severity as to be diagnosed as either bipolar I disorder or bipolar II disorder.

This is because the diagnostic requirements have not been met to see the episodes as truly depressive or hypomanic. The last category of bipolar disorder is labeled "other specified and unspecified bipolar and related disorders." This serves as a category for people whose symptoms of bipolar disorder do not meet the requirements to be diagnosed as any of the other three categories.

In some cases, having switched from depression to mania may not notice the shifts themselves. Still, they can be picked up by family members or friends.

Bipolar disorder is famously challenging to diagnose due to the similarities of symptoms it shares with types of psychosis and other mental conditions.

Depression can take on many forms. A similarity among each type of depressive disorder is the theme of feeling low, sad, empty, or sad.

Due to the similarities of symptoms and the number of diagnoses that fall under the umbrella term of depression, finding the correct diagnosis and treatment option can be difficult.

However, in most cases, if a person has a diagnosis of depression, cognitive behavioral therapy can be a key to successful treatment.

At this point, you can skip ahead to chapter four if you wish to find out how cognitive behavioral therapy can help you to overcome your depression.

Chapter 2: How to Avoid Becoming Part of the Problem

Working with clients reporting memories of abuse and trauma is a potential minefield for the client and the therapist. The False Memory Syndrome Foundation (FMSF) formation in the United States in 1992 led to a political and legal storm across the trauma and abuse field.

Many lawsuits resulted against alleged perpetrators and the therapists of alleged victims. Clients faced additional stress and trauma due to sensationalized media stories about sexual and ritual abuse, child pornography, and sex rings.

These stories frequently alleged that high-ranking public officials, including politicians, judges, lawyers, police, doctors, teachers, and others with access to children, were among the perpetrators. The media's predominant position, often without any conclusive evidence that a crime had or had not been committed, was that alleged victims' claims were false. Furthermore, according to the media, such memories resulted from charlatan therapists' suggestions and questionable therapy on vulnerable clients.

The term Recovered Memory Therapy [RMT} was coined by the media. While there is no doubt that there have been questionable therapeutic practices that harmed clients, there is no actual therapy called RMT.

Some clients present reporting continuous recall or partial recall of abuse. Others may seek therapy due to everyday life experiences, such as disappointing relationships, addictions, generalized depression, or disappointment with life. A major life-changing event, such as a birth, death, marriage, separation, job loss, or a severe accident or illness, may be the precursor to entering therapy.

While these events can be experienced as traumatic in and of themselves, they may also be the catalyst for dissociated memories to begin to surface.

Clients may have diverse reactions to the veracity of their memories of abuse, which may change throughout the initial phases of therapy, including during the processing of traumatic material.

This can occur regardless of whether the memories have always been intact, partially conscious, or have surfaced years after the events.

371

Some clients are convinced of the truth and accuracy of their memories. Others are racked with doubt, erring on the side of disbelief. They prefer to believe they have a "mental illness" or, for some inexplicable reason, are simply making it up.

At some point during therapy, a client may seek from the therapist, directly or indirectly, validation of her memories. This is the "Do you believe me?" question. It is a question asked at a time of

great confusion, uncertainty, and vulnerability and out of a need for something or someone to hold onto. Depending on how the therapist answers this question, it can have far-reaching consequences for the client and therapy progress.

Pre-empting the question by educating the client about the principle of therapeutic neutrality can avert a great deal of misunderstanding and polarizing with her therapist help keep therapy on track.

The Principle of Therapeutic Neutrality

As therapists, we identify ourselves as people with a great capacity for compassion and empathy. Indeed, these are essential traits in our work, as well as life in general. This is why the word "neutrality" in reference to therapy can sound counterintuitive. Neutrality seems to conjure a lack of empathy, even indifference. To be non-empathic and indifferent would be damaging to the client and limit the potentials of therapy. The essence of therapeutic neutrality is "supporting the client through ambivalence, conflicts, and intense emotions about her memories and the alleged perpetrator.

Transference describes the process whereby a client project conflicts about himself and significant people in his life. The issues he is in therapy to address, the therapist and therapy process, onto the therapist. Countertransference describes the therapist's reactions to her client's projections, as well as responses toward the client's personality, behavior, and the material he brings into therapy. During therapy, both client and therapist may have genuine reasons to be upset, angry, or hurt by others' behavior.

372

However, it is always the therapist's responsibility to manage these reactions with a clear understanding of the unequal power relations and the context, boundaries, and triangle dynamics in operation.

In any therapy situation, the possibilities of transference are limitless. The nature of trauma, abuse, and dissociation amplifies the potential for complicated transference reactions. It can be almost guaranteed that, in varying degrees, two of the biggest internal conflicts are the "reality" of his memories and his relationship to the alleged perpetrator. This is true even when a client is high functioning and has a clear understanding of attachment dynamics to the perpetrator and the locus of control shift.

Understanding concepts does not immediately translate into a shift in the emotional "reality" of the client.

Believing" or "Not Believing" Memories

FACTORS INFLUENCING CLIENT RESPONSES TO MEMORIES OF ABUSE

Attachment to the Perpetrator

Locus of Control Shift

Age and duration of abuse

Intervention and support

Level of functioning and stability

Most adults who report a history of abuse do not have independent corroboration, such as police, hospital, school reports, or verification from a witness. It is for this reason we often refer to the "alleged perpetrator." This term may seem cumbersome and as if we are casting doubt on clients' reports of abuse. The intention is to assist clinicians in approaching clients' uncorroborated abuse reports with an open mind and avoid the risks of making assumptions about actual or false memories.

Taking the position of believing or not believing a client's memories, where there is no corroboration, sets the client up for more significant conflict. For example, suppose the therapist says she believes her client.

In that case, she takes away the possibility of disbelieving, which is an essential avenue for him to leave open as he works through painful and conflicting feelings. If the therapist disbelieves the client, he will feel limited in his ability to explore all the issues he needs to deal with, whatever the truth of his experience may be.

Lacking corroboration, it is possible that the client's memories may not be accurate in part or totality. The client needs to explore what is coming up for him and what it means for himself. If the therapist takes a position of believing or not believing, this process is hindered.

The memories are a source of great conflict and ambivalence. This is a struggle in which the client needs support to find his way through. The therapist who states a belief or disbelief in her client's memories becomes a player on the Victim-Rescuer-Perpetrator triangle.

The client will either feel rescued or victimized by the therapist's position. Whichever the client feels, the therapist has also become the perpetrator.

If the therapist believes and the client recants, or it becomes apparent the memories were in part or total not true. The therapist has contributed to his suffering by encouraging him to believe. If the therapist doesn't think she has hurt the client, whether the memories are ever found to be true or not. She has become another person who has let him down and not validated his experiences. Whatever the truth of the memories may be, the therapist who states a belief or disbelief has hindered the client in his own discovery journey and its potential for healing and growth.

In stating a belief or disbelief in the client's memories, the therapist is, in fact, "suggesting" that abuse did or did not occur.

REASONS TO REMAIN "NEUTRAL" ABOUT UNCORROBORATED REPORTS OF ABUSE

To minimize the client projecting the conflict of believing or disbelieving onto the therapist.

To not become part of the problem by taking on the polar position in the client's conflict.

To allow the client the space to work through conflict and ambivalence.

To keep off the Victim–Rescuer–Perpetrator triangle.

Where there is no corroboration of a client's accusations, the therapist can never know what did or did not happen. There will be exceptions, such as a client in a state of psychosis. For example, during a psychotic episode, a client claimed that she knew that there were tunnels underneath the therapist's office building. She had seen one of her therapist colleagues exit the building through these tunnels to secretly meet secret service agents in a nearby coffee shop.

Another client, who was not psychotic at the time, remembered that she had given birth to piglets. The therapist knew that neither of these events had occurred. However, it is important not to dismiss such claims as delusional and, therefore, meaningless.

The therapist may choose, depending on his knowledge of the client, to remain "neutral." It may also be equally valid for the therapist to state that these events didn't occur (in the first instance) or couldn't have occurred (in the second instance). Whichever approach the therapist takes, such material can be explored in the same way other memories and issues are brought to therapy.

Of course, a therapist will form opinions about a client's memories over time. These opinions may or may not be accurate. While it may appear to be supportive and empathic, stating an unequivocal belief or disbelief in memories will typically create more problems. As with many things in life, "never say never." There may be times, with some clients, when stating your beliefs may be helpful to therapy. We recommend that, if you have such a client, it might be beneficial to communicate your position to thoroughly explore this with your supervisor or case consultant.

"Taking Sides"—Conflicted Feelings Toward the Alleged Perpetrator(s)

Linked to the delicate issue of believing or not believing a client's memory manages your client's and your own feelings toward the alleged perpetrator. Ambivalent attachment to the perpetrator is to be expected. The client may primarily express idealized love, outrage, and hate, or seemingly total indifference.

It is common for an individual to oscillate among these states. When the client has DID or DDNOS, other parts will hold the polar position to the one expressed, creating additional internal conflicts.

Horror, disgust, anger, and outrage are some of the feelings as therapists we experience when we hear about the atrocities committed against others. These are normal and healthy reactions. When we are working with clients, we need to monitor these reactions in sessions. We are not suggesting that it is inappropriate to show or express any feelings in front of clients. It can be validating and a pivotal point in therapy for a client to witness another human being—their therapist—expressing sadness and anger on their behalf. The timing and degree of such expressions may either help or hinder a client's process.

Conflicted feelings about the perpetrator will be present throughout all stages of therapy, including the end stages. Clients generally need a great deal of assistance in learning how to manage and express their feelings in healthy ways. Learning to hold conflicting and intense feelings safely is an integral part of therapy. It will be discussed in a later chapter.

Our own feelings toward our client's experiences must not cloud our judgment or pressure clients to take a particular position toward their perpetrator. Clients have reported they were getting the message from their therapist, implicitly and explicitly, that they should or should not feel a particular emotion, such as anger, hate, or love. Clients have expressed feelings they were "wrong" to feel or not feel something. Similarly, we have consulted with therapists who were either pushing too hard in a specific direction or colluding with their clients to avoid unpleasant feelings and reactions. In general, the process the therapist was trying to initiate may have been correct. Still, the timing was inappropriate for the client.

When the therapist "takes sides," not only is he making a statement about the accuracy of the client's memory, he also becomes a player on the Victim-Rescuer-Perpetrator triangle. The client will either feel rescued or victimized by the therapist's position. As with the memory issue, whichever the client feels, the therapist has also become the perpetrator. When the client gets in touch with the therapist's polar position, she may feel she is "wrong" or "not allowed" to express these feelings. She may fear rejection or disapproval

376

from her therapist and hide what she is feeling, which will hinder her progress and create further conflicts.

When the therapist takes a one-sided stance toward the alleged perpetrator, it deprives the client of the critical process of learning to manage her conflicting feelings, eventually leading to a resolution.

The resolution does not mean "happily ever after," it means the client can make healthy choices about her actions and relationships. When the therapist is overwhelmed by his feelings and is left unaddressed, they interfere with therapy. It is important to take such feelings and reactions, which are part of the territory, to supervision or personal treatment.

HANDLING CLIENTS' FEELINGS TOWARD THE PERPETRATOR AND NON-PROTECTING PARENT

Clients typically have strong and ambivalent feelings toward their perpetrator and non-protecting parent.

It is common for therapists to have strong feelings about a client's perpetrator; these should be processed in supervision or the therapist's own therapy.

Allow the client to experience and express all feelings: anger, hate, fear, love, etc.

Be careful of explicit or implicit messages regarding contact, no contact, forgiveness, etc.

Communicating the Principle of Therapeutic Neutrality

A client may come into therapy reporting a history of abuse. Other memories may emerge or be recalled for the first-time during therapy. When your client raises a known or suspected abuse history, it is crucial to explain what he may expect to work with such issues. This includes information about the nature of memory, some of the difficulties he may experience and encounter along the way, and the principle of therapeutic neutrality. An outline of the concepts of attachment to the perpetrator and the locus of control shift can also help him understand your "neutral" position concerning his memories and relationship to his alleged perpetrator.

377

As well as providing a verbal explanation, it is also helpful to provide handouts and/or an informed consent form. As with any psychoeducation, timing is key to when and how much information you give in any particular session. These things will depend on your assessment of your client's emotional capacity and his current level of functioning.

PROVIDE INFORMATION TO HELP NORMALIZE FEELINGS AND REACTIONS

Information on memory, traumatic memory, and dissociation

Informed consent explaining some of the issues that will come up as part of working with a history of trauma and abuse.

Information on Attachment to the Perpetrator and the Locus of Control Shift Therapy is never clear sailing, and it generally does not run along the neat lines laid out in manuals and books! Other issues come up out of the blue that requires attention; the best therapy plans don't necessarily flow smoothly. For clients with a history of abuse, therapy is usually long-term, and the same ground is covered many times. A client may disclose abuse without your having any idea this is where he was heading. He may ask if you believe him or ask for your position before you have had the opportunity to explain the principles behind therapeutic neutrality—so be prepared!

Most clients are eager for any educational material you can give them to help them understand their experiences. Education about memory often eases the pressure clients place on themselves to believe or disbelieve their memories. Education can assist in developing a tolerance for ambivalence and uncertainty. It helps to prepare for some of the difficulties clients will encounter along the way.

However, providing information does not mean that clients will necessarily welcome this position during working with complex material or grappling with intense feelings toward their perpetrator. These are times when you may expect your client to express anger, frustration, and feeling that you are not supporting or validating him.

378

A "neutral" stance can be misinterpreted as you saying you do not believe. Remember, these are conflicts that your client needs to navigate with your help. Let him know you understand why he is angry; remain emotionally present and empathic. Your role is to help him work out what the cause of his distress is for himself. Remember that you are working "as if" his memories are accurate.

When It Is Important Not to Be "Neutral"

Therapeutic neutrality is a fundamental principle in Trauma Model Therapy. As explained above, therapeutic neutrality does not mean lacking empathy or warmth. Therapeutic neutrality is about "supporting the client through ambivalence, conflicts, and intense emotions about her memories and the alleged perpetrator." This requires the therapist to be empathically attuned to the struggles and conflicts within the client.

Explaining the principle of therapeutic neutrality to your client allows the therapist to be free to respond compassionately and validate her client's distress and feelings without compromising the therapy. Explain that you cannot believe or disbelieve memories but that you can see something has caused such great sorrow and difficulties. The client and therapists should remain open to all possibilities.

WHEN NOT TO BE NEUTRAL

Make clear statements that abuse of any kind is never OK.

Make clear statements that it is never the client's fault he/she was abused.

Follow professional guidelines regarding mandatory reporting.

Express concern if the client is in a current abusive situation; explain that working on safety is a priority.

Assess and take appropriate action regarding threats of violence toward others and suicide risk.

Equally crucial to humane and the ethical therapeutic practice is making clear statements that abuse of any kind—emotional, physical, sexual, or spiritual—and neglect are never OK and are never the client's fault. This will need to be reiterated throughout therapy as the client works through attachment issues to the perpetrator and the locus of control shift.

Suppose a client reports knowledge of the abuse of a child occurring in the present. In that case, therapists are required to follow their professional guidelines regarding mandatory reporting. Suppose your client is currently in an abusive situation.

In that case, it is essential to state that what is happening to her is not OK and that you are concerned for her current well-being and safety. Working with a client on how to increase her safety is crucial. Clients are rarely ready to immediately exit an abusive relationship or cease contact with a perpetrator who is still abusing them. However, stating concern about her safety, and reminding them that this needs to be a primary focus of therapy, is vital.

Therapists need to respond when a client makes threats of violence toward another person that they believe could be acted upon and when suicide is assessed to be an imminent risk. Seeking supervision or case consultation in such situations is recommended.

Finally, being compassionate and empathetic to a client's struggles with the long term and ongoing trauma impact is central to effective therapy. Similarly, offering encouragement, praise, and humor where appropriate are the golden threads that weave together the an intricate and complex tapestry of a solid therapeutic relationship.

While knowledge and skill in working with trauma provide the foundation of effective therapy, it is the "relationship" between client and therapist that offers the healing framework.

Chapter 3: Dealing with category D symptoms.

Good endurance conduct is a vital "endowment of nature." Humans have been genuinely effective in lessening the danger to life. All things considered, going across a road or driving a vehicle requires expanded readiness to endure. Cataclysmic events as war, fear-monger assaults, slaughtering, looting, sexual and physical maltreatment, and plane accidents show how helpless we are. In the wake of enduring such an occasion, individuals need nuts and bolts—nourishment, cover, therapeutic consideration, and encouragement. These days mental consideration has been added to this rundown of fundamental requirements for certain individuals.

Specialists should know whether and when mental assistance is vital. The new rule on overseeing post-horrible pressure issues in essential and auxiliary consideration from the National Institute for Clinical Excellence (NICE) fantastically outlines sufferers' and carers' encounters. It gives proof and exhortation on intercessions for grown-ups and children.1 The rule provides extraordinary thoughtfulness regarding "debacle arranging"; the requirements of ex-military staff, casualties of abusive behavior at home, and displaced people and refuge searchers; and the job of the non-statutory segment, underscoring the expansive effect of injury in present-day society. Giving more regard for the nature and importance of post-awful pressure issues in a social and recorded setting would have made the rules total.

When manifestations as flashbacks, rest issues, trouble in concentrating, and emotional lability are gentle, the rules suggest beginning attentive pausing. Behind this shrewd counsel lies the proof-based End that early mental intercession, frequently called questioning, has no impact in anticipating post-horrendous stress issues. 2-4 Clearly, the standard practice of questioning after debacles and fiascoes should end. In any case, for dealing with the bedlam, material misfortunes, misery, and outrage—for instance, after a fear-based oppressor assault—no indisputable proof is accessible yet on how a fiasco struck network recovers control.

According to the NICE rule, treatment is essential when the outcome of injury, post-horrible pressure, or dissociative issue emerges. The danger of creating post-horrendous pressure issues after an injury is 8-13% for men and

20-30% for women,5 with a year pervasiveness of 1.3% to 3.9%,6 making a colossal weight on society.

The post-horrendous pressure issue is essentially deregulation of the dread framework. Dread is an essential feeling on occasion of peril and is trailed by a stress reaction—battling, solidifying, or escaping.

This endurance framework relies upon evaluating dangers to start endurance behavior.7 Once the risk or injury is finished, the dread framework ordinarily quiets down following a couple of days or weeks. In a post-awful pressure issue, this framework neglects to reset to typical, keeping the sufferer hyperalert, filtering for hazardous signals as though the occasion may happen once more.

The turmoil is subsequently described by automatic, tireless recalling or remembering the awful accident in flashbacks, striking recollections, and intermittent dreams—the individual attempts to abstain from recalling the injury by dodging its area or T.V. programs about it. Diligent manifestations of expanded excitement, for example, hypervigilance, overstated frighten reaction, dozing issues, peevishness, and trouble concentrating are a piece of the turmoil. Like misery, substance misuse, and other nervousness, comorbidities are the standard instead of the exemption.

The NICE rule deliberately audits the proof for both mental and pharmacological mediations. As first-line treatment, NICE suggests injury-centered mental therapy.

NICE does not prescribe utilizing drugs as first-line treatment.

The best treatment for resetting the dread framework is psychological conduct therapy.8 By fanciful presentation to the horrendous accident, the dread response will diminish in time.

Ideas about the self that are provoked by the occasion, for example, feeling "frail," liable, or insusceptible, are supplanted by progressively sensible perceptions. The treatment with eye development desensitization reprocessing uses a distractive move of respective incitement after the presentation to diminish the passionate lability identified with the injury.

An unanswered inquiry remains whether the elevated feeling of dread in post-horrendous stress issues identifies with the occasion and animosity realized by the awful experience.9 Like Summerfield, we accept that more consideration ought to be paid to the significance of shocking encounters, breaking the sufferer's perspectives about life, 10 even though proof on this viewpoint is deficient. We also concur with the rule about focusing on the common comorbidities of post-awful pressure issues (for example, misery and uneasiness); however, the proof is still extremely limited.

Regardless of the presence of powerful psychosocial medications, 33% of patients won't recuperate fully. 11 Comorbidity, chronicity, and the aggregation of intense and ceaseless pressure may disclose the restricted reaction to treatment. Additionally, from a developmental perspective, one can perceive how "the endowment of nature" of recollecting and gaining from peril may confine what is achievable in treating post-horrendous pressure disorder. 12 We can't erase the memory of injury.

Chapter 4: How to deal with the Trauma.

It's normal to be apprehensive in the wake of something frightening or hazardous occurs. At the point when you feel you are at risk, your body reacts with a surge of synthetic compounds that make you increasingly alert. This is known as the "flight or battle" reaction. It causes us to endure perilous occasions.

Be that as it may, the cerebrum reaction to terrifying occasions can likewise prompt constant issues. This can incorporate the problem of being effectively alarmed, on edge, or jittery, having flashbacks, or maintaining a strategic distance from things that help you remember the occasion.

In some cases, these side effects leave the following half a month. However, now and again, they last any longer. On the off chance that indications stay over a month and become severe enough to meddle with connections or work, it might be an indication of a post-awful pressure issue or PTSD.

"There are genuine neurobiological results of injury that are related to PTSD," clarifies Dr. Farris Tuma, who directs the NIH awful pressure research program. NIH-supported scientists reveal the science behind these mind changes and search for approaches to counteract and treat PTSD.

What is Trauma?

"A great many people partner post-awful pressure side effects with veterans and battle circumstances," says Dr. Amit Etkin, an NIH-subsidized emotional wellness master at Stanford University. "Notwithstanding, a wide range of injury occur during one's life that can prompt post-horrible pressure issue and post-awful pressure issue like manifestations."

This incorporates individuals who have experienced a physical or rape, misuse, a mishap, a catastrophe, or numerous different genuine occasions.

Anybody can create PTSD at any age. As per the National Center for Post-Traumatic Stress Disorder, around 7 or 8 out of 100 individuals will encounter PTSD sooner or later in their lives.

"We don't have a blood test that would let you know or inquiry you can pose to someone to know whether they're in the most elevated hazard bunch for treating PTSD," Tuma says. "However, we do realize that there are a few things that expansion chance by and large and a few things that secure against it."

Science of Traumatic Stress

Analysts are investigating what puts individuals in danger of PTSD. One group, Dr. Samuel McLean, an injury master at the University of North Carolina, examines how post-horrible pressure side effects create in the cerebrum. They will pursue 5,000 injury survivors for one year.

"We're enlisting individuals who visit injury focuses following an injury since proof proposes that a great deal of the significant natural changes that lead to steady side effects occur in the early fallout of the injury," McLean says.

They're gathering data about existence history preceding injury, distinguishing post-awful side effects, gathering hereditary and different kinds of organic information, and performing mind filters. The examination is additionally utilizing keen watches and PDA applications to gauge the body's reaction to injury. These devices will help scientists reveal how damage influences individuals' daily lives, for example, their actions, rest, and state of mind.

"Our objective is that there will be when injury survivors come in for consideration and get screening and mediations to avert PTSD, just similarly that they would be screened with X-beams to set broken bones," McLean clarifies.

Adapting To Trauma

How you respond when something awful occurs, and in the blink of an eye a short time later, can help or defer your recuperation.

"It's imperative to have an adapting methodology for overcoming the awful sentiments of a horrible mishap," Tuma says. A decent adapting methodology, he clarifies, is discovering someone to converse with about your emotions. A terrible adapting system would turn liquor or medications.

Having a positive adapting procedure and taking in something from the circumstance can help you recuperate from a horrible accident. So, can looking for help from companions, family, or a care group.

Chatting with emotional well-being proficient can assist somebody with post-horrendous pressure side effects figure out how to adapt. It's significant for anybody with PTSD-like side effects to be treated by a psychological well-being proficient prepared in injury-centered treatment.

A self-improvement site and applications created by the U.S. Branch of Veterans Affairs can likewise offer help when you need it following an injury.

"For the individuals who start treatment and experience it, an enormous level of those will show signs of improvement and will get some help," Tuma says. A few drugs can help treat specific indications, as well.

PTSD influences individuals unexpectedly, so a treatment that works for one individual may not work for another. A few people with PTSD need to attempt various medications to discover what works for their manifestations.

Discovering Treatments

"While we right now analyze this as one issue in psychiatry, in truth, there's a great deal of variety among individuals and the sorts of side effects that they have," Etkin says.

These distinctions can make it hard to discover a treatment that works. Etkin's group attempts to comprehend why a few people's minds react to treatment, and others do not.

"PTSD is extremely normal. In any case, the assortment of ways that it shows in mind is huge," Etkin clarifies. "We don't have the foggiest idea what

386

number of fundamental conditions there are, or particular mind issues there are, that lead to PTSD. So, we're attempting to make sense of that part."

His group has recognized cerebrum circuits that show when treatment is working. They have discovered a different cerebrum circuit that can anticipate who will react to treatment.

His gathering is presently trying a noninvasive cerebrum incitement procedure for individuals who don't react to treatment. They trust that animating certain mind circuits will make treatment progressively compelling.

A great many people usually recoup from injury. Be that as it may, it can require significant investment. In case you have indications for a long time— or that are excessively extreme—chat with your medicinal services supplier or psychological wellness proficient. During an emergency, call the National Suicide Prevention Lifeline at 1-800-273-TALK (8255) or visit the crisis room.

"PTSD is genuine. This isn't a shortcoming in any capacity," Tuma clarifies. "Individuals shouldn't battle alone and peacefully."

Chapter 5: Trauma treatment Exercises for Self-Therapy

Suppose you feel your daily life is a blur, that you are not achieving your goals. In that case, it's time to change that attitude because the only thing that is stopping you from enjoying a fulfilling, successful, and worthwhile life is your negativity!

Yes, negative attitudes and mindsets are among the biggest obstacles that disable creative thinkers, movers, and shakers from achieving success beyond their wildest dreams. Suppose you want to change the way you look at the world. In that case, the first thing you need to do is change your perspective and outlook on how negative and positive emotions play different roles in our lives.

In this chapter, we look at the various exercises that therapists often use in trauma treatment and how you can employ some of these therapies on your own safely.

1. Journaling

Keeping a journal of thoughts and moods is one of the most fundamental aspects of trauma treatment exercises. In doing this, therapists look for specific dominant patterns that they can take appropriate steps to change.

2. Challenging thoughts

With trauma treatment, the primary goals are to find and change disruptive and negative thoughts.

Therapists specifically look for automatic thoughts. These thoughts are the ones that occur without any intention.

When the therapist finds these negative thoughts and patterns, they challenge them.

3. Changing behavior

This type of behavior is usually used for those suffering from OCD. For this type of exercise, therapy usually uses intentional exposure to situations in which they will respond negatively in repetitive ways. The therapist will also intentionally re-create a scenario and encourage the patient to react in a different or alternative method.

4. Introspective exposure

For this type of exercise, therapy is usually used for those who have panic attacks and anxiety.

In this situation, the therapist intentionally recreates bodily sensations that patients will respond negatively to. They then deliberately make the patient react in a different, new and healthier way. This exercise trains the patients' minds to stop reacting to sensations that would cause anxiety and panic.

5. Following Fear to the End

Most of the time, when a person feels fear, they stop all their thoughts or start thinking irrationally. For example, if patients fear heights, therapists usually help them push aside their feelings of fear. Using this exercise, therapists generally allow the anxiety to manifest and continue until it is over. They will then recreate a scenario that enables the patient to feel this fear and then helps them get on with life after the episode is over.

This will then train the patient to realize that things will probably not end up that bad as how they imagine it in their head, even if the worst happens.

6. Changing behavior experiment

For this exercise, therapists usually test how a patient's different and irrational thoughts and beliefs lead to other and foolish actions. For instance, if patients believe that being hard on themselves makes them work harder, the therapist will experiment with the opposite reaction. Patients will be encouraged to stress less and be a little kinder to themselves and see the kind of response they get and the results that come with it.

7. A change of perspective

With this type of exercise, therapists employ the technique of thinking the other way. Take, for example, a child that keeps getting bullied and then ends up failing their exams. They begin thinking that they are a failure and just stupid. What can this child do? The therapist will first ask the child to write down all the reasons or evidence that points out that they are failures.

389

Next, the child is asked to write down all the reasons or evidence of success. This gives this child a better and clearer perspective. They are now vividly aware of their shortcomings and acutely aware of their strengths too.

8. Looking for positives

This is a favored exercise among trauma treatment therapists. It has been proven that positivity makes people healthier. But how do you train your mind to be more positive?

You can:

Make a habit of scheduling positive events that you can look forward to

Always look at the positives from past experiences.

Always look at the positive aspects, even at the present time, and focus on all the good things around you.

Do all of those things above, just not one of them. These are all some of the small things you can do to object to a little bit of positivity.

9. Facing Fears

For this trauma treatment technique:

You need to write a list of your fears or of negative things that worry you.

Compile a list of events from the good ones to the bad ones.

Go through each event, beginning with the easiest and working towards the hardest. And actually, face those fears.

This will build your tolerance for unpleasant experiences and train the mind to overcome fear.

10. Turning negative to positive

For this trauma treatment technique, writing positive reasoning for every negative thought that comes out of the patient's mind is about writing a positive rationale. For example, when a patient thinks "I'm ugly" so adversely, they just write "I'm beautiful." This technique, it is all about remembering positive things that happened yesterday and even today.

11. I hate that, but I love that.

This final technique is about turning our negatives into our positives. Whenever a negative situation arises, we pinpoint and focus on the positives. So even if you are in a burning building, you focus your mind on looking at the positives. Is there an open window? Can you find the door? Is your phone with you? Can you call the fire department? Do you have a blanket that you can wet and cover yourself with? A bathtub, maybe?

Training our minds not to dwell on the negative enables us to see the positives and respond reactively.

Try These Mindfulness trauma treatment Exercises.

12. Three-Minute Breathing Space

The primary mindfulness trauma treatment exercises are called 'Three-Minute Breathing Space.' It is an easy and quick mindfulness-of-breath exercise. According to Zindel Segal, this breathing exercise is also called a practice for approaching experience from two intentional lenses, both narrow and wide'.

This three-minute exercise is broken down to:

The first minute is dedicated to observing how we feel, and we describe those feelings in words.

The second minute focuses on practicing the awareness of our breathing.

The third minute is the continuation of focusing on breathing and bringing awareness to the entire body.

13. Body Scan

The body scan meditation is a popular meditation technique. You have probably come across some YouTube videos or even meditation apps. This type of meditation has a great way of enhancing a person's happiness and, at the same time, reducing any symptoms related to depression and anxiety.

14. Mindful Stretching

Both body and mind health is crucial, and if the body can benefit from some stretching, indeed the mind can have those same benefits. Mindful stretching is exactly what it sounds like. It stretches the mind. There are different types to this technique, and this includes:

• Pandiculation: While sounding ridiculous, this technique refers to a type of stretching that we do when we yawn. To do this stretch, we do precisely what we do when we yawn, palms-on shoulders, elbows raised, mouth open.

• Proprioceptive Neuromuscular Facilitation: This technique is a stretch that is typically used by sportspersons, especially footballers who have cramps in their legs.

• Gomukhasana (cow-face pose): For this technique, which is sort of a yoga post, you sit cross-legged while interlocking your hands behind your back. This move expands the chest.

• Side-to-side neck stretch: You probably would have done this stretch a few times during gym class. You simply put your hand on one side of your head, tilting it to the right and left.

• Eka Pada Rajakapotasana (One-Legged King Pigeon Pose): For this technique, you place your hips to the mat, with one leg in front of you, perpendicular while your other leg stretches out straight behind you. This is a more complex pose that beginners may struggle with. For a more comprehensive guide, visit YogaOutlet guide.

• The Scorpion: This technique requires you to lie flat on the ground on your back and keep your arms on your side. Lift your right foot high up and press out your right hip. Next, stretch the right foot to the outside of the left leg. It's essential to keep your chest and the arms on the flow while doing this. This technique is a modified version of Vrischikasana (Scorpion Pose).

15. Trauma treatment Stop Techniques.

In this technique, you basically stop all negative thinking. Trauma treatment therapists use this technique to intercept evil thoughts when a patient starts thinking it and immediately aids them in changing them.

Here's how the stop technique is conducted:

Take note of when you have negative thoughts.

When this happens, STOP. Take a deep and mindful breath.

Make a mindful observation of the thoughts going through your mind.

Notice what elements or topics that you are focusing your thoughts on.

Notice any sensations in the body.

Pull back and examine the thoughts.

What is the overall picture of the thought?

What is another way of looking at the situation?

How critical is the thought?

What would you say to a friend who had this thought?

What is the first thing you could do right now to help yourself? Do it.

16. Trauma treatment Downward Arrow Technique

This downward arrow technique can be used to uncover core perceptions and beliefs that disrupt our everyday life. It is usually conducted with the help of a licensed therapist.

Here's how the trauma treatment Downward Arrow Technique is applied:

It starts with choosing one negative thought from the patient's journal. This could be anything from meeting people, swimming, or having to do a presentation.

The therapist asks the patient, "Why would it upset you if this happened?"

393

The patient answers the question. "If my presentation is bad, my boss will be angry."

The therapist then asks why that would matter, "If my boss is angry, I may lose my job."

This keeps going until the therapist and patient come to a core self-defeating belief: "Because if I lose my job, I won't be able to support my family."

17. Creative visualization

Creative visualization is a mental technique that harnesses our imagination to make our goals and dreams a reality. When used the right way, creative visualization has been proven to improve the lives of people who have used it. It also increases the success and prosperity rate of the individual.

Creative visualization unleashes a power that can alter your social and living environment and circumstances; it causes beneficial events to happen, attracts positivity in work, life, relationships, and goals. Creative visualization is not a magic potion.

It uses our mind's cognitive processes to purposely generate an array of visual mental imagery to create beneficial physiological, psychological, or social effects such as increasing wealth, healing wounds to the body, or alleviating psychological issues such as anxiety and sadness.

This method uses the mind's power to attract good energy, and really, it is the magic potion behind every success.

Mainly, a person needs to visualize an individual event or situation or object or desire to attract it into their lives. This is a process that is similar to daydreaming. It only uses the natural process of our mind's power to initiate positive thoughts and natural mental laws.

Successful people like Oprah and Tiger Woods, and Bill Gates use this technique, either consciously or unconsciously, attracting success and positive outcomes into their lives by visualizing their goals as already attained or accomplished.

The Power of Thoughts and Creative Visualization

So how does this work, and why is it so important to us?

Well, our mind is a powerful thing. With only the power of our mind, we can reach fantastic success, or we can also spiral out of control. It swings both ways. Our subconscious mind accepts the ideas and thoughts that we often repeat.

When our mind receives it, our mindset also changes accordingly, which influences our habits and actions. Again, a domino effect happens where you end up meeting new people or getting into situations or circumstances that lead you to your goal. Our thoughts come with a creative power that can mold our life and attract whatever we think about.

Remember the saying that goes 'mind over matter?' When we set our mind to do it, our body does what our mind tells us. Our thoughts travel from mind, body, and soul but believe it or not, they can travel from one reason to another. It is unconsciously picked up by the people you meet with every day. Usually, most of the people you end up meeting are the ones who can help you achieve your goals.

You probably think and repeat certain thoughts every day often, and you probably do this consciously or unconsciously. You likely have focused your thoughts on your current situation or environment and subsequently recreate the same events and circumstances regularly. While most of our lives are somewhat routine, we can always change these thoughts by visualizing different circumstances and creating a different reality to focus on.

Changing Your Reality

Honestly, though, you can change your reality by changing your thoughts and mental images. You are not creating magic here. All you are doing is harnessing the natural powers and laws that inhibit each and every one of us. The thing that separates ordinary, average folk from wildly successful people is that the successful ones have mastered their thoughts and mental images while the rest are still learning to cope. Changing your thoughts and attitude changes and reshapes your world.

395

Take, for example, you plan to move into a larger apartment. Instead of wallowing in self-pity, such as the lack of money, do this instead, alter your thoughts and attitude, and visualize yourself living in a larger apartment. It isn't challenging to do because it's precisely like daydreaming.

Overcoming Limited Thinking

You may think daydreaming about positive things, money, success, and great relationships are nothing but child's play. Still, in fact, creative visualization can do wonders. Though it may be hard for different individuals to immediately alter their thoughts. Limits to this positive thinking are within us and not the power of our mind. We control it.

It might sound like it's easy to change the way you think, but the truth is, it takes a lot of effort on your side to alter your thoughts, at least in the immediate future. But never for a second doubt that you can't. Anything that you put your mind to work on, it can be done.

We often limit ourselves due to our beliefs and our thoughts, and to life, we know. So, the need to be open-minded is an integral part of positive thinking. The bigger we dare to think, the more significant and greater our changes, possibilities, and opportunities. Limitations are created within our minds, and it is up to us to rise above all these obstacles.

Of course, it takes time to change the way we think and see things, but small demonstrations of changing our minds and the way we believe will yield more significant results in due time.

Concise Guidelines for Creative Visualization:

Step 1 - Define your goal.

Step 2 - Think, meditate, and listen to your instinct. Ensure that this is the goal you want to attain.

Step 3 - Ascertain that you only want good results from your visualization, for you and for others around you.

Step 4 - Be alone at a place that you will not be disturbed. Be alone with your thoughts.

Step 5 - Relax your body and your mind.

Step 6 - Rhythmically breathe deeply several times.

Step 7 - Visualize your goal by giving it a clear and detailed mental image.

Step 8 - Add desire and feelings into this mental image, how you would feel, etc.

Step 9 - Use all your five senses of sight, hearing, touch, taste, and smell.

Step 10 - Visualize this at least twice a day for at least 10 minutes each time.

Step 11 - Keep visualizing this day after day with patience, hope, and faith.

Step 12 - Always keep staying positive in your feelings, thoughts, and words.

Staying positive can be easy. It is all about training your mind. When you do feel doubts and negative thoughts arise, replace them with positive reviews. Remember to keep an open mind because opportunities come in various ways, so you can take advantage of them when you see them. Every morning, or each time you conclude your visualization session, always end it with this 'Let everything happen in a favorable way for everyone and everything involved.'

Creative visualization will open doors, but it takes time. Whenever you feel you are in a position of advantage, act. Do not be passive or wait for things to fall on your lap. Perhaps, you have met someone who can put you in a position of advantage to reach your goal or maybe, you've landed a job that has the possibility of enabling you to travel. All these things come into your life, and if you have an open mind, you can see the opportunities more vividly.

When you use the power of imagination for you and the people around you, always do it for good. Never try creative visualization to obtain something forcibly that belongs to others. Also, don't harm the environment.

Most visualized goals happen naturally and gradually, but it can be times that it can happen suddenly and expected manner too.

Be realistic with your goals, though. Do not visualize a unicorn and expect it to turn up. If money is what you desire, you know that it just will not drop from the sky. You may or may not win it in the lottery. But the chances or possibilities are higher when you go through life with a new job, or you get a promotion, or you end up making a business deal. It is always better to think and visualize what you actually want because you do not wish to attract negative situations.

Chapter 6: Trauma treatment and Mental Health

Trauma treatment might be a relatively new term to some, but too many commons. Cognitive-behavioral therapy is a type of mental therapy that helps or enables one to deal with their thoughts and balance their daily mental state. This involves one's surrounding in terms of their societal constraints and actions and how they affect them in one way or another or their feelings. This study will help you keep a profile of some of the things that trigger you emotionally and how to manage and contain them.

Just as the name entails, therapy is done to treat mental conditions caused by past experiences or situations that impacted one's wellbeing. That is, conditions or ailments such as depressions or even anxiety. Yes, depression is an ailment. As we all know that when someone is depressed beyond measures they can handle, they are prone to self-destruct or self-inflict injuries or mostly common abuse drugs. TRAUMA TREATMENT is not only for mental but also physical wellness as well.

This has always been a study under review, and many have benefited from it in society. Many people have mental or behavioral distortions unknowingly. Still, when addressed and carefully decrypted, you'll find that there's always one thing that can o does trigger a person not to be or act themselves. Trauma treatment helps improve and uplifts personal, emotional, social, or even physical regulation by providing lasting and long-term solutions.

The main aim of trauma treatment is to help an individual with previous problems upgrade and treat dysfunctional and wrecked emotions one may harbor. As we all know, emotions affect our every move and influence them in one way or another. That is, our behaviors, actions as well as thoughts. Trauma treatment is mainly rooted in providing and implementing practical solutions that will help individuals outgrow previous toxic habits and encourage them to change.

The thought of emotions influencing a person comes out strongly. We know that distinct circumstances or situations bring a rare and authentic part of us all raw, accurate, and original and either negative or positive.

So, trauma treatment identifies problems, possible roots of the issues, how logical or realistic they are, and how or what degree and extremity bring one to their breaking point.

Trauma treatment as well know, is a practice done on everyone that is all ages and races and has no limitations in terms of the level of mental advancement or development.

I mean, anyone can be depressed; anyone can feel extremely anxious due to haunting thoughts or even past negative experiences. It is an efficient task that can be carried or conducted around physically and mentally. Still, with that said, it requires one's devotion and consistency, and discipline levels to be checked. It is a practice for one's wellbeing. There is no better doctor than oneself since they know where the shoes pinch the most.

In trauma treatment, there are various tools used. These are not physical tools but rather ideologies that are believed to have worked over the years in successfully treating patients or clients. These include identifying and disputing unhelpful, toxic, or even unrealistic thoughts and coming up with problem-solving solutions. Trauma treatment is one of the most if not the only efficacious modes of verbal therapy if only inducted into our day-to-day lives. This form of interest brings out one's attention to insight into their behavioral and cognitive processes. It turns them into effective and constructive methods that incorporate gradual practice for success and complete recovery. If one fully cooperates and sticks to the course, they are most likely to have fewer sessions and more productive time.

Trauma treatment helps people moderate their thoughts. These people tend to overthink situations and tether them in the wrong direction; there are unhelpful ways or means that people direct their thoughts, leading to psychological problems. Our own thoughts either elevate our moods or send us on a roller-coaster of thoughts. The same behaviors and traits develop as a result of the toxic thoughts and emotions that manipulate us.

Psychological issues just don't originate out of nowhere. It starts as small ideas that grow in due time and develop roots in our day-to-day lives. As it becomes tailor-made in us, it also changes our personalities into darker and more mentally disturbed individuals.

When it comes to an individual's modes of thinking and reasoning out, they do according to previous experiences or how the norms of things oblige them. As we all know, our minds are weapons that could positively impact society in significant ways if used rightfully and effectively. However, inefficiency comes when one's moods are low, or feelings are no right, affecting a person's performance and output. Output in the sense of socializing or even interrelating with people and handling situations and responsibilities around them.

Trauma treatment introduces newer or rather older but more advanced ways that improve one's behaviors and thinking. The introduction or adaptation of new ideas and habits can significantly heal or relieve mental or physical symptoms.

How trauma treatment works

When followed and packaged correctly, trauma treatment can help get over overwhelming problems and make sense of them by segmenting them or breaking them **into small bits. It's primarily broken down into:**

Situations

These are the predicaments an individual finds themselves in that force them to yield mental instability. Situations may be the triggers that occur, probably an action that reminds someone of something or brings forth certain emotions or feelings. It may be out of our own creation or some that we just find ourselves in unknowingly.

Emotions

Emotions are triggered by thoughts. Emotions are also reflected by our physical states. That is, if we are sad, we frown or show in our facial expressions. Emotions in trauma treatment are a critical factor that leads towards the cause of many ailments. Trauma treatment focuses on emotions since emotions cannot be manipulated since they are always original and authentic.

Actions

Our actions reflect on our emotions and thoughts. What we do as reflex actions show or rather expresses our true intent and feelings towards things. Think about it, when you see something and immediately start trembling or shaking, it may be simply related to past experiences. As they say, actions speak louder than words than it is.

The genuine intent or motive generated in our mind comes out in the respective body parts or physically. It communicates what words could not have expressed. One's thoughts and feelings about specific things directly affect and influence how they feel and react emotionally and physically. Trauma treatment incorporates all these to help and provide quick diagnosis and arrest issues by finding quick or dominant pointers that tether or learn more on a specific aspect. It may seem more straightforward to read, but the real deal is quite more on the ground.

The difference between trauma treatment and other therapies

Since it is all under the same room of therapies, most people dismiss it to be as common as any other. They do not know that all this deals with different solutions and issues. As much as they are connected or related to the human body, they serve different purposes. Trauma treatment is unique in its own ways from other psychotherapies since it is:

Highly structured

This means that instead of narrating your life history to look for specific problem-causing issues, it helps your therapist focus on specific problems and set up achievable goals for the treatment journey.

Collaborative

If truly you are seeking help, you ought to be cooperative and disciplined. You don't expect your therapist to always be on your case, getting you to do regular self-responsible tasks. Remember, this interactive session requires you and your therapist to lock heads, brainstorm, and help each other come with solutions. In some cases, the therapists have consistency issues, but rarely will you find such a case. Since it's you who is in need, you're required to be collaborative and instrumental in this journey since it's all for your own good. Attend all sessions as supposed to. Observe the dos and don'ts; keep in mind that you are not doing it for anyone but yourself.

Tethered on current issues.

Trauma treatment may dig your past for a few pointers or root causes. Still, it never focuses on your then mental or emotional state. It focuses on the here and now state where your actions and reactions are fresh and under the current reign of emotions or feelings in play. The current issue is the one to be diagnosed and addressed as it affects your wellbeing and those surrounding you. Your past may be necessary, but what you felt and did back then can't be treated or worked on by real-time solutions.

Pragmatic

This is simply put as pointers that point directly to problems. You may be having all a thousand and one issues on your back, and some filled up in your head. Still, when zeroed in on, there are those specific ones that will help bring out the issue at hand and even point out which route to healing to take. Focusing the energies on one problem helps an individual to get the best of the therapy sessions and complete exposure to the solutions and what they have to offer to the full extent.

Stopping and reducing negative thoughts

Often, we take into serious considerations some of the things that happen to us due to our own doing. We take them as the final verdict of our happenings and even future possibilities of them happening again. Some of these things leave us sad, hopeless, helpless, depressed, or even tired of life. This traps someone in a negative cocoon that is filled with regret and a trail of loneliness. Instead on is supposed to learn from previous mistakes, and I think this is what becomes hard for a lot of people. Accepting failure and seeing it as a learning mode and a possible push to a higher pedestal in the future.

Trauma treatment aims to help individuals facing such issues break out from the negative cycles that keep on haunting them. This sheds more light on your problems and makes them more manageable.

Trauma treatment will arguably help you come out of the cycle, come to terms with your conditions or situation, change the negativity patterns, and uplift you as an individual and your wellbeing. In the first stages, it requires help from a specialist. Still, once you're out of the woods and capable enough, you can even get to much greater heights of self-care on your own as well as tackle issues without a therapist.

Trauma treatment sessions being the main form of appointments, can either be physical or online. The physical is best considered since there is a bond or relationship that is developed firsthand. It may be a one-on-one basis or just a group of people with the same issues and experiences seeking help.

The period taken to see a therapist in terms of personal or individual basis depends on your current problem and how cooperative you might be in the process. You can really count on time in group sessions because your understanding rate and abilities are all not yoked the same. However, trauma treatment is essential, and everyone deserves proper mental healthcare.

Chapter 7: Understanding anxiety and the anxious mind.

Historical Treatment of Anxiety

Reported that 300 million people worldwide suffer from depression. That is almost 1/5th of the world's population. Depression is also believed to be the No.1 contributing disability in the world. Anxiety disorders ranked at 6th. The US has one of the highest rates of anxiety. With 8 people in every 100 suffering anxiety disorders in some form WHO (2017).

Studies also show that common mental health disorders occur at a higher rate in the lower-income sectors. Even more disturbing is the fact that anxiety disorders are treatable. Why then are the figures so high? Is it a modern epidemic?

In medieval times treatment consisted of blood leeches and bathing in freezing water. It was a real breakthrough when psychologists such as Sigmund Freud started treating sufferers more like patients. Such patients began to undergo the "talking" therapy. It was not until as late as the 1980's that the American Psychiatric Association recognized "anxiety" as a mental health disorder. Before then, anxiety was simply classed as a "woman's problem." Sufferers became stigmatized and labeled as depressives. Women are twice as likely to suffer from anxiety disorders. Still, such conditions are by no means restricted to females only. Today, anxiety may be treated with medication as well as therapy.

What is Anxiety?

In days gone by, our ancestors risked their lives whenever they hunted live food. Luckily, these skills are no longer needed, but it brings us to how the body reacts when facing danger. This is a time when we instinctively make the decision of "fight, flight, or freeze." It's not a choice brought on by conscious thought. Instead, it is set in motion by releasing chemicals in the part of our brain known as the limbic system. The chemical is cortisol, which is a steroid hormone released through the adrenal glands. One of the side effects of raised levels of this hormone is anxiety. If you feel this type of anxiety too often, the high cortisol levels can damage cells in a part of the brain known as the hippocampus.

Symptoms of Anxiety

Anxiety is now separated from the condition of depression. Although many who suffer from depression also have anxiety issues. Patients who suffer from depression tend to dwell on the past and feel extremely negative about themselves and life in general. This is not typical in the case of patients suffering from anxiety. They will worry excessively about the here and now or the future. Their lives are full of "what ifs" in the eventuality of a disaster.

Symptoms of anxiety can vary in individuals, but here are a few to look out for:

Feeling tense for no reason, on edge, and almost nervous.

The sense of dread and impending doom.

Unable to sleep because of worry.

General restlessness and fidgeting, unable to relax.

Lack of concentration.

Irritable for no reason.

Breaking out in a cold sweat.

Shaking.

Feeling nauseous.

Digestive and intestinal upsets.

Panic attacks can come as a result of feeling one or many of these symptoms. When someone has frequent anxiety attacks, it inevitably leads to ill health. This is because the cortisol levels remain high too often and for too long. One of cortisol's roles is to increase blood sugars. Unbalanced, and this can result in insulin resistance. In turn, this may lead to late-onset or type 2 diabetes—Hackett et al. (2016) (2c).

In a modern, fast-paced society with access to social media, many people feel more and more anxious about the world around them.

This can start at an early age. If young people are not diagnosed and treated, their anxiety attacks will follow them into adulthood.

Various stages throughout life can lead to feeling overanxious:

Education

Learning and education should be enjoyable experiences. Too often, children are pressured to meet specific academic targets. Those who do not meet them may very well consider themselves a failure. The burden of being successful lays heavy on the shoulders of young people.

Family life

This is a worrying time, particularly if you have never had responsibilities. Women are expected to raise families and go out to work at the same time. Such pressures create considerable stress in their daily lives. With the increasing break up of marriages, the force of anxiety reflects on both parents and the children.

Materialism

People who live in wealthy industrialized countries are bombarded with a heavily capitalized culture. Advertising constantly prompts us to buy the newest and seemingly greatest ever products. Such deviant tactics imply that their goods will improve your life and make you happy. It seems we must keep up with all the latest gadgets to have an attractive home and wear the newest fashion labels to look good. All increasing the pressures of life as we attempt to earn more money to keep up.

The Anxious Mind

While it might seem to be stating the obvious, worry plays a crucial role in anxiety. People who suffer from anxiety attacks are likely big worriers. Often, the only way a worrier will stop panicking over a specific problem is to move on to a different one. Worry leads to anxiety until the released chemicals mean the person cannot reason. At this point, they will jump to conclusions of their own making. Unable to focus on reality because their minds are highly aroused, the problem is no longer solvable. They cannot see any solutions, which then leads deeper into anxiety.

Simple Coping Techniques

For those who experience the build-up of burdening pressures and suffer anxiety attacks, there is help available. We will look at this in more detail later in this book.

There are lifestyle changes that can be put into practice, using techniques to nip the bud's anxiety attacks. A sufferer may find that these techniques are all they need to alleviate the experience of anxiety.

Such as:

Discussing your anxiety issues with your doctor. Doctors can prescribe medication to help you initially and then refer you to a trauma treatment therapist. Look at the foods you eat and what you drink. Caffeine and alcohol can both affect anxiety levels negatively. Take the general advice and at the very least cut down on the intake of foods known to cause such effects.

Exercise is beneficial, but it doesn't mean you must work-out like crazy at a gym. Go on walks in calm and soothing vistas, if possible. Learn relaxation exercises that you can do sitting at a desk or watching TVs, such as breathing exercises and muscle relaxation. Try and keep active, so you tire yourself out naturally during the day. That way, sleep will come easier at night.

Stress and anxiety are closely related conditions. Though it is possible to suffer one without suffering the other. For both, you should seek help, but there are many self-help techniques that you can do to ease some of the immediate pressures. Anxiety can include phobias and is often only triggered in certain circumstances. Stress is more a build-up of worry because there is too much pressure in your life. Something has to give. We will look at ways of helping yourself to cope with anxiety. Many coping methods are ways to ease the pressures, which are similar to the stress self-help approach. It could be that stress is what has brought on your anxiety in the first place.

Deal with one, and the other may ease as well. Recognizing that you are suffering from anxiety is the early stage. Events such as employment interviews will naturally cause anxious feelings. These are normal. You should not worry about anxiety when associated with everyday stressful events. Having adrenaline coursing through your system when under such stress is how your body copes with the situation.

When you come out of the interview, the anxiety should lift to be replaced with relief. Of course, you may stress while you wait for the results but try not to be over-anxious in such situations.

When you are anxious over too many things, especially every day and maybe even all day. This is unhealthy as you will be producing those hormones we mentioned earlier in high amounts. If you find that stress is affecting your everyday life, then it is time to seek help. The pressure will mount up, causing triggers to anxiety attacks. Hopefully, you will recognize the dire situation before it gets to that point.

If you have suffered anxiety attacks for over 6 months, this is known as Generalized Anxiety Disorder (GAD). Our next chapter will help you to assess yourself and recognize if this is you.

Chapter 8: Developing your anxiety profile.

Matching Anxiety Types with Anxiety Programs

Self-diagnosis is not encouraged when it comes to health issues, but anxiety can be eased with self-control. To do this, you will need to think about "when, where, and what" triggers your own symptoms. Because there are various types of anxiety, it could help recognize which one you are suffering from. Learning the different kinds of anxiety and seeking the correct treatment for it is essential in self-help. We will go into detailed treatment options later in this book. This chapter will look at ways to identify your anxiety type and outline possible self-help treatment options.

Let's start with some of the more serious profiles for the onset of anxiety. Post-Traumatic Stress Disorder (PTSD) is not as prevalent as generalized anxiety. The rarer types are usually brought on from specific events. By learning the various anxiety types, it will help you categorize your own anxiety profile. Once you understand your own profile, you will be better able to know which treatments might help you.

PTSD

Situation:

This relates to people who have experienced a traumatic incident that is out of the ordinary. It is usually an event that is not considered the norm, such as:

Soldiers in combat.

Childhood abuse.

Rape or physical attack.

Witnessing a murder.

Natural disasters.

This list is only an example, but it shows the unusual circumstances that someone suffering from PTSD may have experienced.

410

Symptoms:

They will suffer symptoms such as:

Reliving the experience as if in a daydream. The event will play out in their minds with a feeling that the experience is happening right here and now.

Reliving the experience in a nightmare when they sleep.

Bad dreams will lead to broken sleep.

A broken sleepwalk leads to irritability.

Trigger points can set off the memory and lead to a panic attack.

They may begin to avoid places and people. This is because they become frightened of any reminders of the traumatic event.

Anger issues can set in as they are always on guard.

Sufferers may become easily startled and have difficulties concentrating.

PTSD sufferers may find their minds focusing on the traumatic memories more and more each day. This can lead to the inability to cope with the normality around them. Sadly, they may try to forget by taking drugs or alcohol.

The onset of PTSD symptoms can be delayed by months or even years after their experiences. It can be a gradual process before the patient finally breaks down. Anxiety symptoms may not be diagnosed until it comes in the form of panic attacks. They will likely suffer the symptoms of depression first. PTSD does not only affect victims of traumatic incidents. It can include anyone who witnesses such an event.

Treatment:

Self-help alone cannot treat the symptoms someone with PTSD will suffer. Only when a PTSD patient can control their maladaptive thought process can they begin their self-help process

411

Medication can be an essential first step and a valuable tool at the beginning of their treatment.

Attending group sessions with other PTSD can help them to talk about their experiences. Support groups will consist of fellow sufferers, so the patient can see that they are not alone.

Family counseling can be helpful to allow those closest to them to understand what they are going through. This also helps families to realize their loved one is suffering an illness. Then they too can provide that all necessary support.

Phobias

This is when a person feels afraid of a particular sight, smell, or situation.

Situation:

It could come in the form of seeing insects, blood, or even certain smells.

Or it could come from an experience of heights or being enclosed in an elevator.

Symptoms:

When in that situation, they begin to imagine extreme consequences; What if I fall and die and nobody finds me? What if the spiders go inside my body? What if the elevator gets stuck and no one knows?

Feelings will be a sense of dread, shallow breathing, dizziness, cold sweats, nausea.

It can bring on a panic attack.

They will begin to avoid any situation that might entail such fears. Someone with a fear of spiders may no longer enjoy working in a garden, even though they loved to before their phobia took hold.

Treatment:

It may be a combination of self-help exercises similar to stopping a panic attack.

Plus, there will be an element of exposure therapy which we cover in another chapter.

OCD

Situation:

Someone suffering from OCD may have spent many years with generalized stress and anxiety.

They may have suffered a terrible experience that brought on their anxieties in the first instance.

It could be a build-up of many situations as to why an OCD sufferer becomes obsessed.

Symptoms:

Everything around them is exaggerated and distressing in their minds.

They feel that the world around them is intruding upon them all the time. To overcome this, they may pray over and over or repeat certain words of comfort to themselves.

Other forms of OCD can lead to obsessive cleanliness, and everything must be orderly.

One OCD symptom is that of hoarding, in case they need it later.

They will probably be aware of their irrational behavior but cannot stop.

Some have intrusive and disturbing thoughts. Thoughts such as, if I do not spin around to the left 3 times, then someone in my family might come to harm. Or they may imagine they will get a disease if their home is not clean and tidy.

For some, everything must be placed in a particular order.

For others, they must carry out their rituals in a specific order.

OCD is how they relieve their anxieties.

When it takes an extended time to complete rituals, it can take over their lives and become debilitating.

Treatment:

Medication may be an option.

Support from family members will be encouraged.

Group therapy means sharing their worries and admitting their obsessive behavior.

Exposure therapy is a good option for those who avoid certain situations. Learning to confront their fear and seeing that all is still well in the world.

Panic Attacks

Situation:

This type of profile is more one of sudden intense fear.

A sufferer may, or may not, know the reason for the onset of sheer fear.

It is almost always a reaction to a bodily sensation, such as increased heartbeat or tightness in the chest.

Symptoms:

Heavy and fast breathing.

This can lead to a tingling sensation.

Dry mouth causing and you may have difficulty swallowing, or even feel like they are choking.

414

Hot and cold sweats.

Lightheadedness and dizziness, believing they might collapse.

The impending doom that something terrible is about to happen.

Imagining horrible scenarios, such as:

- "I'm going to die."

- "Someone is going to attack me; I don't feel safe."

- "There's going to be a disaster, and I won't be able to get away."

- "I've lost all control."

The sufferer has started to feel anxious for some reason, which has led to a full-blown panic attack.

For example, you are sat in your car on the freeway in a huge traffic jam. Usually, you are patient in such situations, but you have a meeting to get to. Already the stress is setting in because you have no control over the situation.

Then, you hear a car backfire, and it triggers off an anxious thought. You start thinking, "What if someone's running loose with a gun and we all think it's just a car backfiring?" Now you will not get out of the car because you imagine bad things. This makes you feel trapped, so your anxious thoughts take control of you. You cannot breathe, and you are all alone in the car. You start to imagine that you are going to have a heart attack.

You begin to breathe quick and shallow breaths, which leads to tingling in your fingers. That is it, now you know that today you are going to die. All the signs are right. You are currently in a full-blown panic attack.

Can you see how this happened?

- Clearly, this person is already suffering stress.

- They must get to the important meeting on time.

- Frustration is setting in as the delay increases their stress levels.

- This could play out in many ways. Perhaps, in the same scenario, the driver gets out of the vehicle and starts shouting and swearing at no one in particular. If someone responds, the driver abuses them as they have now become the focus of their target.

The entire scenario has been caused by stress.

- Do you recognize any of these feelings happening to you, whereby you blow a situation out of proportion?

- See how easy stress can lead to feeling anxious, which can bring on a full-blown panic attack?

Treatment:

- Self-help treatment will teach how to recognize and deal with the symptoms before they blow out of proportion.

- It may also involve medication initially to help with relaxation.

- Learning simple relaxation exercises, such as mindfulness and deep breathing.

Generalized Anxiety

Situation:

We have looked at many anxiety conditions. Yet, being over-anxious can happen to anyone who is overloaded with stress. The main problem with generalized anxiety is that it never goes away. Everyone has everyday worries to contend with.

Symptoms:

- The first sign you are not coping is when you are constantly worrying until the worry is on your mind all the time.

- It will be a build-up to lots of minor concerns, such as will you get somewhere on time? Who is doing the school run? How can you pay bills?

- You may find yourself not eating breakfast because you woke up worrying.

- Suffering constipation because your body is too tense.

- Constant headaches.

- The situation escalates until you feel physically ill.

Treatment:

- Recognize that you are suffering from anxiety.

- Self-help treatment begins with mindfulness. Recognizing; Acceptance; Setting out a plan of action to ease the stresses in your daily life.

Chapter 9: Why Some People Are More Prone to Depression Than Others

According to surveys, about 7% of the population experiences depression. With 7 billion people on the planet, that means 490 million people battle depression every year. Women are more likely to develop depression than men. In fact, about one and a half to three times more likely.

Why do you think that happens? Could it be attributed to the impossible standards that society sets upon women? Could females worry more about the house and caring for the family, and putting their own needs ahead? Men experience stress just as much as women do, but they are taught to keep their emotions inside and not show it.

Are we more depressed as a society than we were 50 years ago? Or is it that we are learning how to talk about it now where our parents and grandparents were not? It was not something you did back in the day to discuss your feelings. Many times, people dealt with their problems and depression behind closed doors. Now we have services to help us express ourselves, but it seems like we're becoming more depressed.

People don't have the same reactions when it pertains to stress and depression. Still, several factors do affect and cause depression. It may be a combination of two or more of the following factors that induce depression:

Neurotransmitter Defects

Neurotransmitters are mood-regulating chemicals in your body. Research says that it plays an important role as when these chemicals change in function and effect, it leads to depression.

Genetics

Unlike other genetic diseases, depression does not seem to have an exact explanation or link to why it exists in a person with a family history of depression.

Even if your family has a genetic predisposition towards depression, it does not guarantee that you will automatically have it. However, there may be a possibility that you are prone to it as it also includes other factors.

Hormones

You have more possibilities of depression if you are susceptible to hormonal changes or imbalance. People who undergo hormonal changes, like women who gave birth to children or those who have certain thyroid conditions experience symptoms of depression.

Abuse and Early Trauma: those who have experienced trauma and abuse at their early age are more prone to depression during their prime years or later part of their life.

Prescription Medication

Are you taking prescribed medications? Medicines such as sleeping pills, corticosteroids, Accutane, and interferon-alpha increase risks for depression.

Drug Abuse

It may be hard to determine why some people use drugs. Maybe they want to treat their depression with self-medication or have previously started using drugs abusively. It's the same with prescription drugs. Certain illegal drugs can also cause you to have depression symptoms, and their effects are seen.

Pain and Illnesses

There are two main reasons why pain and illnesses are related to depression. The sickness itself causes biochemical changes in the body that causes depression.

People with illnesses tend to be depressed as they experience prolonged pain, normal body function is limited or incapable, and sometimes face death. They become depressed because of their health.

Death and Loss

Don't be surprised if you see somebody depressed after experiencing extreme losses, whether it is in finances, properties, or even the lives of their loved ones. These events may have triggered their tendencies of depression.

419

Personality

Check this out if you have got some of these traits in your personality.

Overly dependent on others

Low self-esteem

Self-critical

Pessimism

If you have any of these traits, you are more prone to getting depressed.

Interpersonal Conflict

Family and friend conflicts also contribute to increased stress. Undergoing disputes such as these will tend you to develop depression.

Stress

You can have stress whether your life is uphill (getting married) or downhill (losing your job). When you are under attack by stress, your cortisol levels rise to the point that possibly affects serotonin transmission, a mood-regulating molecule.

In other words, depression is a complicated situation wherein certain factors are involved, e.g., biologically based differences in brain function. The more you are faced with various aspects, the more tendencies, and possibilities to develop depression.

Chapter 10: Cognitive Distortions

Whenever you feel stressed or worried, do you notice the kind of thoughts that occupy your mind? Usually, when we go through stress or sadness, worry or fear, our thoughts are filled with negativity.

What are Cognitive Distortions?

There is a strong relationship between what we feel and what we think. Whenever we feel challenged or unhappy, our thoughts become dramatic and absolute. It usually goes along the lines of feeling 'I am stupid and unworthy' or 'I don't fit in' or 'nobody likes me.' These types of thoughts are recognized as 'cognitive distortions.' It is a term in psychology that describes how we are thinking about something that does not match up to the extent of reality.

Why Are Cognitive Distortions So Important to Understand?

Cognitive distortions are extreme thinking elements, and they often lead a person into a negative cycle. This can make anyone spiral further and further down into a whole series of negativity until they feel there is no way out or no solution or end to their problems. Distorted thinking is quite common among people who suffer from negative issues such as low-self-esteem or mood swings, and anxiety.

When a thought affects your bodily sensations and your feelings, this combination then dictates your behavior. Your behavior then triggers your next idea, which then creates another cycle of negativity.

It is an ongoing loop that goes on and on, and each cycle leads to an even more destructive negative thought. For example, you go to a party and see the girl you want to talk to. Before you can even approach her to say hello, you are already processing the many different things that could go wrong. You start thinking, 'What if she doesn't like me' or 'What if she snubs me.' This negative thinking then makes you start feeling anxious and self-conscious (feelings). It makes your body react by excessively sweating and your heart beating fast (bodily sensations).

Because these negative feelings have overcome you, you abandon all desire to speak to that girl. You retreat to a quiet place and do not talk to anyone.

421

You feel left out of the party and alienated, which then produces another negative thought, "Is there something wrong with me? Why doesn't anyone like me?" (Behavior)

This starts the cycle all over again.

Cognitive distortions determine the number of trauma treatment therapists that work with you to change your moods and alter the way you think. Trauma treatment therapists help you recognize the moment when you think distorted thoughts. They also help train you to replace these thoughts with more balanced and positive thoughts. While this sounds simple, the process to get there is not. Negative thoughts are a strong habit. It is deeply rooted in a person's unconscious mind that it sometimes can be perceived as usual.

Changing negative thinking is a robust process of focused work and attention. Still, with the therapist's help, a patient is steered in the right direction.

How to Recognize Cognitive Distortions

It may be you or someone you know who has these distortions, so it would help to try to recognize these signs. Here are ten of the most common distortion traits:

Mental Filter

Mental filtering relates to how a person focuses, whether consciously or subconsciously, on the most hostile and upsetting feature in a situation. When they think this way, they filter out positive aspects of that situation. For example, you had a night out with friends and suffered from a hangover the very next day. Your entire mood goes downhill because you are too focused on your hangover even to think that it results from a fantastic night out with friends. You convince yourself that you feel too sick and that you will not participate in future events. This levels you not recognizing the fun times of last night and the enjoyment that you felt.

Disqualifying the positive

This happens when we continuously dismiss and discount positive experiences that we encounter and instead choose to dwell on negative details. We decide that the positive experiences are not necessary or do not count. For example, an acquaintance comes over to your worktable and compliments you on the sweater you wear. Instead of feeling good or pleasant, you decide that they are nice just to get something out of you.

Always or Nothing

This type of thinking is when we view things only in black and white. Everything you see is either good or bad or a failure. More often than not, it is usually the negative perception that is pushed forward. In contrast, everything in the gray area is discounted. For example, you score 90 percent on your driving test but get sad and think you are a terrible driver because you did not score 100 percent.

Over-generalization

Over-generalizing refers to how we often perceive a single unpleasant incident or event as proof that everything else will be the same awful and negative experience. Everything around will go wrong. For example, if you fail an exam, you immediately think that you will never pass. Or you might even go for a job interview and fail badly at it and think you are never going to get a job.

Jumping to Conclusions

A person that jumps to conclusions is very inclined to make a pessimistic prediction that the worst is yet to come even though there is no evidence to support their assumption. This thinking materializes from what we think others feel towards us. People like this often act like mind readers. They assume others' thoughts and intentions, or they also work like fortune tellers anticipating the worst.

For example, you are giving a pitch presentation, and you already know (fortune-telling) that you'll end up failing. Or you are going to a party and do not like the dress you are wearing because you think everyone will hate it (mind-reading).

Magnifying or Minimizing

Thinking either in a minimizing or magnifying way is thinking where we exaggerate the importance of adverse events and downplay the positive possibilities. People who are depressed often exaggerate other people's positive characteristics and the negative ones are downplayed. It is the reverse when we think of our own selves. When we exaggerate a situation, we cannot see other ways or outcomes except the worst one. For example, you wrongly sent an email out to a client, and you exaggerate the worst by thinking, 'I'm about to lose my job now. My house and car will not now be paid for. I am going to lose my house. I will no longer have a place to live.'

Personalization

Personalization in cognitive disorders refers to a situation when a person automatically thinks a bad thing or adverse event has happened because of him or her. They assume responsibility and blame for things above and beyond their control. They feel guilt, shame, and inadequacy. For example, there was a burglary in your house. You immediately assume responsibility because you did not install proper locks or cannot remember if you ever locked your gates and doors when you went out. You would probably be thinking 'if only I installed professional locks' or 'if only I subscribed to the neighborhood watch.'

Should Have, Must have or Ought to have thinking

Individuals who think this way often have a very rigid view that can arouse anger, frustration, guilt, and disappointment with their constant thinking of 'Should' 'Ought' and 'Must.'

For instance, your daughter does not like playing the piano. Still, you put her in classes anyway because you feel that she should learn it and when she makes mistakes, you think that her teacher 'ought' to be stricter on her.

Emotional Reasoning

This kind of thinking relates to when we assume that our feelings reflect their evidence. The basis of this is 'I feel it, which means it has to be true.' This kind of thinking often leads to self-fulfilling prophecies.

Our thoughts end up promoting the very behavior we predicted, all because we changed our behavior in line with that specific thought. For example, if you think, 'I feel stupid and useless; therefore, I must be stupid and useless.' This might cause you not to learn new things or read more books even though you are a bright person and very resourceful.

Labeling

An individual with this kind of thinking usually assigns a negative and very emotive label on themselves and even others, with no room of change. This label is automatically given the minute something goes wrong or is done wrong.

For example, you send out a newsletter, and there is a spelling error. Immediately, you think, 'I am so stupid and careless' instead of thinking, 'It is a mistake, and I will not let it happen again. This person can also label someone else automatically. For instance, your friend made an error in a computer program, and you quickly say, 'You are so incompetent.

Do you suffer from Cognitive Distortions?

Sometimes, we all become negative, especially when we are not focused or become too stressed. It is normal human behavior to experience these emotions. Still, people with cognitive distortions often exhibit these behaviors too often and are usually destructive to themselves and their people. If you feel you or someone you know has any of these thoughts, don't panic. Instead, realize that you can overcome this pattern of thinking. Realization is halfway to the path of change. It would be good for you to monitor when and how often you experience these distortions and the situations they occur.

Chapter 11: Common Mental Health Issues

Mental health has always been a vital topic of discussion in society. One's cognitive abilities and potentials are dependent on their wellness mentally and health. This is obvious because an insane mind cannot be trusted in judgment and in making decisions. However, mental health is not all about mental illnesses or ailments that require medical attention. Some of the issues that cause illnesses or problems in one's health commonly come about due to the things we engage ourselves or involve ourselves in our day-to-day lives. The people we interact with the impact our mental health significantly. You could be asking as to how your friend does this. Still, it's not really rocket science to understand that how they talk or treat us or rather relate to us affects us in one way or another.

Just as people have physical health and are greatly concerned about it, how does one's mental health prove necessary? We should look after ourselves we a lot of care and consideration to the things that affect or influence us either in terms of behaviors or even making decisions. We need to look after ourselves and glitter around what we bring in into our lives. I know that this might be hand; controlling things in our lives, but there's always something within our power. Some things happen because of our choices, and we end up facing the repercussions.

In contrast, some come about obviously and affect us the same way. At the end of the day, we cannot escape our mental responsibilities or try to suppress them or manipulate them. They will always come out as they are. The question is, are they going to be of positive impact to those around us, or we will be spreading out negative vibes.

Possessing a good and healthy mental state means that one can reason out, think, react and feel their surrounding as per how you'd want or desire to be living your life. Every day as you walk the streets, what you do not notice or have at your attention is the state of mentality or mental health of people around you. Once you interact or relate with them, you'll notice some of the things that could disturb an individual. Most times, people mask their feelings and mental ailments in a bid to look strong, brave, and indestructible were in a real sense, their inner self is crying for help.

Looking at yourself as an individual, there are points in your life that you have noticed a state of inferior or questionable mental state. These situations make you realize that your reactions to things or feelings towards specific aspects of your surroundings are becoming or instead seem impossible and difficult to get along with. Some react to the extent of even bringing about a physical effect of illness or even worse conditions.

You have seen people before becoming bedridden due to the stressful situations around them. Some end up sick and hospitalized in the same way. Mental issues are also a matter of concern in society that, if not handle at an early stage and effectively, could cripple one's wellbeing.

Mental issues arise about almost everything that we engage ourselves in. yes, everything. Don't you use your mind to think in situations? Making decisions? Speaking? Conducting and relating to people? Imagine if all that is compromised manipulated, and distorted, how life will be for an individual. That is what mental issues are all about. With such tragic results when an individual is unattended to, it leaves one with no choice but to seek help. Coming out and asking for assistance won't make an individual week. Instead, it makes them stronger than someone who is living in denial and pretending to be alright. Accepting your flaws and imperfections helps one go a long way to be a much better individual and puts them on a pedestal to advantageously influence others.

Mental issues vary and are brought about by many situations and causes. Some of the mental problems we all suffer from are anxiety and depression. Well, at least those are the most commonly experienced and dealt with in society. And no one can ever say they have never experienced them to some specific point in their lives. However, some rarer issues are also essential to note and be on the lookout for. These are bipolar disorders as well as schizophrenia. Having to understand the mental health spectrum could be rather a bit complex and confusing.

That is, you would not really know where you stand as an individual well unless you are examined or observed and later brought to attention. The experience could be frightening to some bits, especially during your denial stage, where you think that things are just temporary and will soon go away.

427

There is never anything like being weak when you accept your conditions. One might think they are losing their mind, but that is not the case. It's all normal to be unwell and fall into the unfortunate pits life has dug for us. The fears one develops overtime when their deteriorating thoughts are reinforced by the negative and unrealistic way people package mental health experiences and problems in society. Often at times, this stops individuals from opening up and seeking help or counsel. In the same isolating and solitude, one gets only much worse and an increment in their degree of distress and ailments. Looking at it from a medical point of view, for instance, having a wound not attended to for a long time only opens more doors of resultant illnesses or even infections.

In the same analogy, so does mental issues bask in. Ignoring a serious issue affecting you will only leave you vulnerable to more problems in the same way.

However, to treat such problems, one requires a combination of support and treatment that must be followed to the latter for a successful healing and sane wellbeing journey. Do not wait until you have breakdowns to consider yourself viable for help or wait until it's serious enough. The following are some of the mental issues explained and characterized by people's daily experiences and can as well be present simultaneously:

Anxiety

Depression goes hand in hand with anxiety. It is pretty unheard of to find some who are suffering from the latter lacking depression somewhere in their trail. Anxiety can come about due to several factors such as life events, constant thoughts, and genetics all the way to brain chemistry.

Anxiety is considered normal in society, and that is where people go wrong, self-diagnosis conditions. Whereas some may be temporary, some have a lasting effect on an individual and could affect their wellbeing. Being anxious in the same situations someone finds themselves in constantly should raise an eyebrow and prompt the subject to seek treatment. In treating anxiety, medication comes in handy but not self-medicating. Seek help from a specialist who'll know the problem and recommend the right drugs to use. A psychotherapist will effectively help in such conditions and help control and manage the situation or symptoms that come out strong.

Schizophrenia and psychoses

The name might be unheard of, but its actions and ripple effect are seen in the community at large. It is brought about by distortions in one's ways of thinking, their emotions, perceptions of things in their surroundings, their behavioral traits overall as well as their self-sense. The effect of such a condition is hallucinations as well as delusions. Interacting with such characters becomes more challenging, especially when they see you as a source of distress or even conflict. They will gradually create their own profile of you with added and exaggerated traits that could be negative.

People in society are often discriminated against and secluded since they are seen as "mad." This stigma leaves them in their own cocoons in which the exact condition will keep on deteriorating. In the discriminative community at large, you will notice that these people don't have access to social amenities and help diagnose and treat their disorders. And alteration of thoughts and manipulation of them is not something that should be taken lightly. Suppose you've ever been under some drug (prescribed or not) and experienced hallucinations. In that case, you now know what individual suffering from such must get along with daily.

Dementia

This is a chronic condition in nature and is all about the deterioration of one's cognitive functions beyond one average aging rate. This affects one's brain completely. That is from one's thinking, calculation, and reasoning out, comprehensions of things around them as well as their language at large. Unfortunately, there is no cure available for dementia patients. This has been sad since one's brain is impacted in ways that one cannot control or prevent. On the flip side, there might not be a cure in hand. Still, some palliative treatments have been designed and formulated to ease the confusion and suffering inflicted on the subject with the condition.

One with dementia should seek medical attention to arrest the situation early in its development stages and avoid further damage. This is a condition that does not have a specific age group or caliber that is attacks. One's memory deteriorating could start at any age, whether from school or even while you are working. All this affects one's social and emotional control and could affect you tremendously.

Anger

We all get angry at different times as we mind our business. This may be as a result of one thing or the other. Either people around us cause it or just something not working in our favor. I mean, it is all part of an average human. Its shows a firm stand and belief in principles or perspectives. It is something everyone must feel like an average emotionally healthy person. Anger can be managed and controlled, but it now becomes a problem when out of bounds and unleashed.

Anger becomes a dangerous problem when it now tends to harm people around us and offend them. We might get angry at every little irrelevant. Still, our anger goes overboard when we constantly express it in destructive or unhelpful behaviors. It is also considered a problem when it negatively impacts your physical and overall mental health. When someone always runs to their anger "protectorate," it blocks out all other emotions.

It makes one numb to different feelings that could be used or considered, or experienced in place of anger. So, find healthy and meaningful ways and means to be expressing your anger. Possible signs of severe anger issues are increased aggression, slamming of doors, banging, hitting, or even throwing things. Still, it also takes a much worse turn to self-hate and inflicting injuries to yourself, i.e., by cutting yourself or denying yourself essential in your life in a bid to punish.

Hearing voices

I don't know if you've heard voices before in your head or just heard someone call you out, yet you're alone. Well, you could be having a mental issue, or maybe just an ordinary day that you're tired.

This is, however, considered a problematic condition when it gets overboard. It might result in the form of hallucination brought about by anxiety or depression. People may find their "voices" distracting and quite irritable, whereas some don't mind them after all. To some extreme extent, some see them as intrusive and frightening, and this could lead to madness since it's only you who is hearing these strange voices.

You are rather distressed and fed up since you cannot mute or stop them. Such conditions, in the long run, lead to self-destruction.

Some of the causes of such like condition could be lack of sleep, hunger, abuse of drugs, stress, or even a series of traumatic experiences. All this, when combined, could bring out mental disorders. Other confuses instincts for a condition but at the same time distinguishing is not easy. If it persists and becomes a brother, one should seek help and at least some counseling.

Loneliness

Loneliness comes about as a form of missing something that gives you a sense of belonging and value. Experiencing loneliness is quite normal, but it could affect your wellbeing when it persists for a long time. It detracts from a person's rosy personality and even the radiant self that had remained faced away. Loneliness may come from losing a loved one or friend or even an item that used to occupy your time and gave you a sense of accomplishment. Feeling lonely and tolerating it for long affects one's mental health as well as productivity. Having a mental disorder or issues that separate you or make you want to seclude yourself from the public leaves you lonely and could bring about adverse effects.

Loneliness may require a specialist if it is an extreme condition, but this time can be self-treated. To cope with loneliness, one first must accept their current state and shun way denial that could be wrapped up in a word like "I'm laid back." We all have a social circle, no matter how small it is.

That social circle is the perfect treatment for this condition. But what happens when nothing happens, or we cannot connect with them? Develop new social contacts. Yes, it might be hard at times, but a little compromise would help you greatly.

First, get to know what makes you lonely, try and make new connections, and be open as you take the process slow. You should also be careful as you try to uplift by making comparisons and majorly getting some help. It never really hurts just to reach out and get you a helping hand and support.

431

Conclusion

After this workbook, you will have learned everything you need to know to create your own program, which should last for a minimum of two months and can last as long as half a year. This is probably one of the few anxiety disorder books that has covered this much information for a beginner interested in self-treatment.

The next thing for you is to take out your journal for one last exercise from this workbook. Write down how you feel about the information here. Does it relate to you in any sort of way? How did these principles make you think about yourself and your condition? Are you more confident of your ability to overcome depression and anxiety disorder?

Using a combination of these techniques, you can create a customized program that will help you overcome your own depression and anxiety disorder. You can either work with a licensed therapist to bounce your ideas or work alone and fully personalize your approach.

Note that this workbook is not a complete source of every technique and method used in trauma treatment. Over the years, trauma treatment has acquired many changes and adaptations that have made it a very flexible program today. It is a constantly improving method that is refined just as much as it is critiqued. As you conclude this book, walk away with the notion that this is not the end of your learning and self-practice. As with any other therapeutic approach, trauma treatment is not perfect and has its own list of flaws. In time, more developments will be made to trauma treatment to overcome these flaws and improve the program's overall effectiveness. As a practitioner, you should also be on the lookout for these developments.

Experts and therapists worldwide are constantly researching and experimenting on new ways to complement trauma treatment to make it better. An excellent place to start research next would be the hybrid form of trauma treatment mixed with heavy hypnotism principles. You should also remember that you are now a source of relief and comfort for other people suffering from the same afflictions as you walk away from this workbook.

As a human being, you have a calling to reach out to these people and share with them what you know. You never know who among your social networks could be in dire need of help.

EMDR THERAPY

Introduction

Frightening and trauma invoking experiences come in many forms; however, their impact can be devastating to human life if not addressed in time. Assume that you're involved in a near car accident as you drive towards the intersection of a busy road. Such an experience is more likely to leave you frozen and in a state of shock. As a trained somatic psychotherapist, you are more likely to move your body to centralize the awareness by taking deep breaths as you focus on releasing the fear that you are feeling at the moment. After several months, you might notice anxiety gripping your heart whenever you're approaching the intersection of a busy road as you drive, and you may notice your stomach tightening and your breath also quickening.The experience can lead to intense feelings of trauma and deep anxiety that can be immobilizing if not addressed.

This is just an example; however, there are numerous causes of trauma, depression, and PTSD. Somatic psychotherapy and EMDR therapy help address the conditions, identify the root causes, the emotional and behavioral impact, and treat the conditions effectively.

Somatic Psychotherapy and EMDR therapy offer a structured and comprehensive approach that effectively treats trauma, PTSD alongside the associated sensations, beliefs, and emotions. The synthesis of somatic psychotherapy and EMDR therapy provides such an advanced treatment to mental health and is considered per the various research findings as two of the best models of available trauma treatment. Integrating the two therapies helps with enhancing their level of effectiveness.

Somatic Psychotherapy and EMDR Therapy is a book that's fully packed with valuable insights, techniques, and strategies to address and treat trauma. The book provides an in-depth guide to mastering the two's integration and how both can be effectively used in addressing traumatic experiences and behavioral issues.

The effectiveness of somatic interventions can significantly improve the effectiveness and results of EMDR therapy. This book is ideal for therapists who desire to realize tremendous success in their engagements and individuals looking for ways to enhance their performance by learning how to stay centered and emotionally whole. Take your time and read the book all through to the end for a deeper understanding of how you can use the strategies to alleviate your own pain and trauma and gain some professional insight on how you can help others as well.

Chapter 1: Understanding Somatic Psychotherapy and EMDR Therapy

The body has several ways of manifesting the different types of trauma and fear that people face. Many opt for talk therapy to cope with the various symptoms of emotional distress. Talk therapy is a type of psychotherapy that's generally based on verbal processing of thoughts, experiences, and feelings. Somatic psychotherapy and EMDR therapy are quite different from talk therapy as they shift the paradigm from talking to feelings. The approach helps with providing a new way of healing trauma through engagement in body-centered techniques.

What is Somatic Psychotherapy?

Somatic psychotherapy, which is also referred to as body psychotherapy, mainly focuses on the powerful and complex connections between the mind and the body and how the bonds tend to affect processing and recovery from the various forms of emotional distress and trauma. In somatic psychotherapy, practitioners tend to use mind-body exercises alongside other physical techniques to help clients release the held-up tension that negatively affects their physical and emotional well-being.

Somatic psychotherapy stems from the fact that human beings tend to engage with others and the world through movement, expression, and sensations. When responding to any situation and stimuli, the core response network of the body gets activated. This network consists of the limbic system, autonomic nervous system, and other regulatory body functions. Those influence the organizing and generation of an immediate response to the challenges presented by the environment that one finds themselves in, like the fight, flight, or freeze way of response to the perceived dangers and stressors.

Somatic psychotherapy is ideal for those suffering from anxiety, stress, grief, addiction, and depression alongside abuse and trauma issues. Humans tend to struggle with recovery after undergoing a traumatic experience. Those who experience ongoing or sudden trauma alongside other distressing events lack ways to clear their arousal systems, survival, and the energy produced in response to such experiences.

The energy ends up lingering in the body. If it stays unresolved for long, it might lead to depression phobias, post-traumatic stress disorder (PTSD), muscle aches, insomnia, digestive issues, and autoimmune diseases.

The primary purpose of engaging in somatic psychotherapy is to resolve issues that trigger physical and emotional distress. Unlike cognitive behavioral therapy focuses on helping people talk about their experiences, somatic psychotherapy starts with the body. It identifies how the trauma is being experienced physically. It then progresses to finding ways of safely discharging the energy that's related to the trauma. While talk therapy encourages those with traumatic experiences to express their feelings in words, the somatic approach focuses on feeling the body sensations fully and the emotions that come with such feelings. People are then encouraged to engage with their bodies' responses to experiences, memories, and surroundings.

What is EMDR Therapy?

EMDR refers to Eye Movement Desensitization and Reprocessing. This is a form of therapy that enables people to heal from trauma or other conditions of distressing life experiences. It is an integrative psychotherapy approach that has been proven to be effective for trauma treatment. EMDR consists of a set of standardized protocols that entails elements from diverse treatment approaches and involves bilateral stimulation through tones, eye movements, or tapping.

The human brain has a natural way of recovering from traumatic events and memories. The process entails communication between the amygdala, which is like the alarm that signals the brain on stressful events; the hippocampus, which includes storage of memories in the prefrontal cortex, analyzes and controls human emotions and behavior. Several traumatic experiences can be solved or managed spontaneously; it's typically difficult for the condition to be processed without help.

Stress responses are generally part of the natural fight, flight, and freeze instincts. When one is stuck with some distressing experience, the upsetting thoughts, images, and emotions can create feelings of being overwhelmed or frozen in time or back in the moment.

EMDR therapy helps with processing such memories through the brain's engagement and allows for normal healing to resume. The person might still remember the experience, but it will not lead to the fight, flight, or freeze response once it's resolved.

EMDR, unlike other forms of therapies, doesn't require engagement in detailed talking about the distressing issue. It instead focuses on changing the thoughts, emotions, or behaviors that result from the painful issue and enables the brain to resume the natural healing process.

EMDR therapy is majorly designed to help with resolving the unprocessed traumatic memories within the brain. Part of the treatment entails the use of sounds, traps, and alternating eye movements.

EMDR therapy has helped millions of people relieve different psychological stress types and traumas. The model is based on adaptive information processing. This type of therapy is ideal for those struggling with mood disorders and depression, generalized anxiety disorders, panic attacks, PTSD, somatic problems such as image issues, gastrointestinal issues, chronic pain, vicarious trauma, performance enhancement, and more.

Basic Concepts of Somatic Psychotherapy and EMDR Therapy

Effective treatment of trauma requires a holistic way of addressing emotional, cognitive, and somatic symptoms. Traditional therapy majorly focuses on the traumatic experience's emotional elements, and the somatic experience is usually left out in most cases. EMDR uses a structured protocol to address post-traumatic stress and the related beliefs, emotions, and sensations. The therapy entails somatic awareness and interventions that help with enhancing body awareness during treatment.

Therapists trained in the effective use of EMDR and somatic psychotherapy as a combination have advanced tools that they can work with. Trauma is considered by somatic psychotherapists as an event in the whole body, so addressing psychological distress's physiological components alongside the cognitive part is quite vital when engaging in the therapeutic process.

Trauma experts believe that the human body can reflect on past traumas through body language, body posture, and physical manifestations, such as digestive problems, chronic pain, and immune dysfunction.

Somatic therapy integrates the mind and body by focusing on how the autonomic nervous system works. The nervous system controls the consciously directed body functions, such as heartbeat, breathing, digestive processes. It reflects traumas experienced in the past through the expression of instability. It also helps those traumatized to regain mastery when going through difficult experiences by regulating the nervous systems.

Somatic psychotherapy is a body-oriented therapy that helps with healing trauma and other related conditions. Those affected get to release survival energy that has remained stuck in the body.

Body awareness gets induced that enables those affected to tolerate some of the problematic bodily sensations and emotions through greater body awareness and touch.The physical, emotional, and cognitive processing are vital for working through trauma. The physical sensations get tracked as a step to recovery.

Somatic psychotherapy helps with the resolution of trauma and PTSD-related responses. Human beings can't think their way out of traumatic experiences. One is more likely to feel trapped with the physical and emotional states. Such feelings heighten the sense of anxiety and cause panic, making it difficult for the body to calm down. There are times when one just feels unmotivated and depressed without the ability to accomplish even simple tasks. The great thing about somatic psychotherapy is its ability to intervene directly by developing new neural behaviors that provide one with alternative ways of responding to the environment.

The synthesis of RMDR therapy and somatic psychotherapy is such an advancement in mental health. It is considered two of the best trauma treatment models available. Integrating the two therapies helps with enhancing the effectiveness of both of the therapies. Somatic psychotherapy focuses on body awareness as a way of intervention in psychotherapy.

Somatic interventions tend to address the connections between the brain, the mind, and the body's behavior. Therapists who only focus on talk therapy tend to appeal to the mind to influence psychological health. However, somatically oriented therapists tend to use knowledge of the nervous system's basic functions as a way of enhancing the therapeutic process.

Some of the basic concepts of somatic psychology include;

Grounding

This concept is based on all-body-based psychotherapy. The idea was introduced by Alexander Lowen, who was the developer of bioenergetics. Grounding refers to a human's ability to experience embodiment. It's where one gets to feel their feet as they step on the earth; they sense the body and calm the nervous system.

Cultivating Somatic Awareness

Somatic psychotherapy promotes body awareness. One can work with tension patterns and brain constrictions held beneath conscious awareness. It's achieved by simply bringing to the physical sensations that in turn creates change.

Staying Descriptive

As much as the early somatic psychotherapists made interpretations based on posture patterns and tension, the modern-day somatic psychotherapists are more focused on the client's somatic experience. This is a concept that you can try on your own as you take note of the sensations. Try making use of descriptive words such as tingly, hot, cold, sharp, or dull.

Deepening Awareness

Once you know the sensations or the tension pattern, you can gently amplify the experience by amplifying the senses. Focus your breath on the sensations by making some sound or even adding movements. The key is to deepen your knowledge at a pace that doesn't make you feel overwhelmed and honors your timing.

Resourcing

When helping clients to develop resourcing, you should focus on increasing safety and a sense of choice. Identify time, people, and places that reinforce a sense of safety, peace, and calm. How do they know when they are feeling relaxed and peaceful? How does their body feel?

Titration

When the attention is turned to traumatic events, the body's centered awareness enables one to become conscious of the physical tension patterns. Titration is the process of experiencing small amounts of distress and is done to discharge the tension. It's used in somatic psychotherapy and is typically achieved by pendulating or oscillating attention between feelings of distress and calm.

Sequencing

When somatic tension begins to release or discharge, therapists can report on the movement of sensations and emotions. When anxiety is experienced at the belly, it's more likely to move to the chest. It leads to tightness in the forehead and the throat. At times, you can see the hands or the legs shake or even tremble. The tension can then get released at times in tears or by breathing freely and a feeling of lightness.

Movement and Process

Somatic psychotherapy taps into the innate healing capacity and invites one to listen to the body's story. From the body postures to gestures and space use, therapists are provided with insight into what the client is experiencing. For example, a client who might experience an impulse to cower, hide or crouch should be led to mindfully engage in the defensive movements.

After doing that, you might notice a new impulse emerge that causes them to kick the legs or push the arms. As the client reengages intuitively, the protective movement resolutions may arise with some newfound sense of calm in the body.

Boundary Development

When you allow the somatic experience to guide your therapy process's pacing, you should consider working in the here and now. Focusing on the present moment makes it possible for you to stay responsive to the clients changing needs and makes it possible to develop clear boundaries. A boundary makes it easy for the client to recognize and speak your yes and no in a way that makes them feel stronger and protected.

Self-Regulation

Modern somatic therapies integrate the research obtained from neuroscience on how humans respond to trauma and stress. The research emphasizes the importance of mindfulness to the body while experiencing big emotions or sensations. When you create awareness of the body sensations, you get into a position where you can effectively respond and even regulate the emotional intensity. This helps one to stay connected and supported while experiencing the intensity of healing trauma.

By practicing mindfulness, the body gets to access the prefrontal cortex through interception as a way of recognizing what's taking place inside. Then it re-interprets the danger by either moving the body, synchronizing voices, or the respiratory systems. This can be done by singing or breathing together, which then activates the bidirectional communication system between the nervous system.

Discovery and Development of EMDR

Eye Movement Desensitization and Reprocessing (EMDR) is a therapeutic approach that's usually guided by an adaptive information process. It is an integrative psychotherapy approach where the dysfunctionally stored memories become the primary basis of clinical pathology. The processing of such memories and their integration within the larger adaptive networks creates room for transformation and reconsolidation.

Over the past 25 years, sufficient research has been gathered for EMDR therapy, which makes it widely considered effective for the treatment of trauma. The history of EMDR therapy, the AIP model, the clinical applications, and the procedural elements are clearly described.

EMDR is an integrative and therapeutic approach with procedural elements that are compatible with somatic psychotherapy and other procedures. The therapy is generally guided through the AIP model. It emphasizes the role of the brain's information processing system within human health development and pathology.

The AIP model focuses on the insufficiently processed memories of the traumatic or disturbing experiences as the primary source of all the psychopathology caused by an organic deficit. EMDR is an eight-phase treatment that focuses on;

The memories that exist beneath the current problem

The present situations alongside triggers must be addressed to bring the client to robust psychological health.

One of the critical characteristics that distinguish EMDR from other therapies is bilateral stimulations such as the alternating hand taps, auditory tones applied within the standardized procedures, side-to-side eye movements, and protocols that address all the facets of targeted memory networks.

History of Somatic Psychotherapy

Somatic psychotherapy originated in the 1940s with Wilhelm Reich. Reich perceived that the human's life force energy flowed through the body as primal expressions of human emotion and needs. He identified the body's holding patterns, which had emotional tension as the abdomen, pelvis, chest, diaphragm, neck, forehead, and jaw. He identified the habitual tension patterns that developed into symptoms such as the grinding of teeth, headaches, and sluggish digestion.

Mr. Reich identified that the needs that were left unmet all throughout early development stages became the root holding patterns. The approach he used to release the bound energy ranged from pushing, kicking, and screaming to release the physical tension and emotions from the body.

In the 1950s, Reich worked closely with Alexander Lowen and branched off into developing bioenergetics. Those could help resolve what was referred to as the body-mind conflict. This type of treatment is where the therapists observe and interpret the client's breathing, physical and muscular tension patterns. These patterns are referred to as character strategies and associated with core beliefs that are learned during childhood.

Bioenergetics brings clients into stress positions where the body gets to stay in long holds and even uncomfortable holds at times to evoke physical shaking and vulnerable emotions. This therapy's ultimate goal is to release both physical and emotional tension so that one can feel connected and grounded to self and the world.

History of EMDR Therapy

The development of EMDR started in 1987 when Shapiro recognized the effects that eye-movements had on disturbing memories. It led to her developing a treatment protocol referred to as Eye Movement Desensitization (EMD). Since she was coming from a behavioral background, she perceived eye movements' impact to be similar to systematic desensitization. She knew it was based on an innate relaxation response.

Shapiro's initial research assumed that the END process was to an extent related to Rapid Eye Movement (REM) sleep phenomenon and the effects. The initial study was more of a random one that showed promising results with the treatment of war veterans and sexual assault victims. She continued to develop and also refine the procedures that were used in EMD beyond the behavioral paradigm. In 1991, she changed the name to EMDR with the R meaning reprocessing. It came to the understanding that desensitization was just an outcome of the therapy. The broader aspects of the therapy would be understood better through information processing theory.

EMDR therapy has so far been proven to be an effective treatment leading to the realization of results much faster for many clients. Shapiro felt that it was her ethical obligation to teach other therapists and clinicians so that those struggling with PTSD could help find relief.

445

However, EMDR therapy was still experimental since it had not received any independent confirmation through the controlled studies. She opted for controlled training that was only focused on licensed clinicians.

She ensured that everyone who learned the EMDR approach did it within the institute and in the same model as that helped safeguard what was taught. By 1995, after publishing the controlled studies, the raining restrictions were then removed and textbooks published. Shapiro has been intensely criticized for her dissemination method and the restrictive way of training. However, critics tend to ignore the APA ethics code that mandated the responsibilities of an innovator to determine the training practices and the fact that there had not been effective treatments for PTSD that had been well established and well-validated.

Various studies have been published so far that have demonstrated the effectiveness of EMDR in the treatment of PTSD, and EMDR has been recognized as efficacious in treating PTSD. IN 1995, a professional association independent of Shapiro and the EMDR institute was established to help set the standards for EMDR training and practice. The EMDR International Association (EMDRIA), with the primary role of establishing, maintaining, and promoting the highest standards of excellence and integrity in EMDR practice, education, and research, was formed.

World View and the Values of EMDR and Somatic Psychotherapy

Substantial research studies have shown that adverse life experiences contribute to both biomedical and psychological pathology. EMDR therapy is a form of treatment for trauma that has been empirically validated. The positive therapeutic outcomes that have been achieved rapidly without detailed description provide the medical community with an efficient treatment approach alongside a wide range of applications.

EMDR can rapidly treat psychological trauma and other negative life experiences in such an effective way. The ability to treat unprocessed memories of diverse backgrounds tends to have significant implications for the medical fraternity. The clinical application of EMDR entails a wide variety of psychological problems that affect family members and patients.

446

The systematic way EMDR brings about substantial improvement within short periods has brought relevance to some of the major problems within the medical practice, such as an increase in patient load and the cost of medical care.

One of the key components that have been used during the reprocessing phases consists of dual attention to stimuli through bilateral eye-movements, tones, and taps. Eye movement is a subject that has generated great scrutiny and has been called into question previously as the studies evaluated treatment effects with and without the component.

EMDR therapy is guided by the adaptive information processing model, which was developed in the 1990s. This concept focuses on the fact that, apart from symptoms caused by injury, the toxicity of organic deficits, the critical foundation of mental disorders are the memories of earlier experiences that stay unprocessed. The high arousal level that arises from distressing life events causes the memories to be stored with the original emotions, beliefs, and physical sensations.

The nightmares, flashbacks, and intrusive thoughts of PTSD are examples of symptoms that result from the triggering of such memories. As shown in the AIP model, a wide range of traumatic life experiences can be stored in a dysfunctional manner. That provides the basis room for diverse symptoms to emerge, including the negative affective, somatic, and cognitive responses. Sufficient processing of the memories that have been accessed within EMDR therapy protocol brings about adaptive functioning and resolution.

Processing the targeted symptoms transfers them from being memories that are implicit and episodic to those that are episodic and semantic. The negative emotions experienced initially alongside beliefs and physical sensations get altered as the targeted memory gets integrated with some more adaptive information. Whatever that's useful gets learned and stored with the appropriate somatic interventions and makes the disturbing experience a source of resilience and strength. Clients that experience anxiety, hypervigilance, depression, frequent anger, and such emotions need to be evaluated for the adverse experiences that contribute to the current dysfunction that they are experiencing.

447

Two RCTs have demonstrated the effectiveness of EMDR in the treatment of distressing life experiences. Both the trials reported some positive results within three sessions. The ability of EMDR therapy towards the treatment of unprocessed memories has numerous applications within medical practice since such memories have been identified as the cause of diverse clinical symptoms. Exposure to various stressful events has always been linked to socioemotional behavioral problems and cognitive deficits. Before opting for EMDR therapy, a client should be evaluated for adverse life experiences. When treating children, the therapy should be focused on identifying interpersonal experiences, bullying, household dysfunction, humiliation, and other symptoms that might be contributing to the hard feelings. EMDR therapy can help alleviate the effects of experiential contributors and evaluate whether medication is necessary.

Conditions such as night terrors, traumas, and insomnia should be evaluated since the processing of memory alone is capable of improving sleep quality. Rehabilitation services can equally benefit from EMDR therapy to support the client and family members.

The use of such an approach can help with:

Facilitating the processing of traumatic events with the client and the whole family.

It can help establish an interpersonal context that's secure between the client and the caregiver by reducing the high arousal level.

It can help transform the health service into very effective support for the client and their family.

EMDR therapy can be used to provide support to family members that are dealing with the death of a loved one. There are trauma symptoms that come with the sudden death or prolonged debilitation of a loved one. It can make it difficult for the grieving family member to retrieve the deceased's positive memories, which can further complicate the grieving process.

Chapter 2: The Neurobiology of Stress and Trauma

The development period also tends to bring along a higher probability of the emergence of some mental health disorders. It can intensify childhood behavioral and emotional concerns. Neuroscientists are committed to understanding what takes place in the brain that increases the human's vulnerability to mental health challenges. Factors such as genetics, childhood adversity, and behavioral concerns are significant influences of mental conditions.

Chronic stress experienced during childhood and referred to as childhood adversity have been associated with being a factor that contributes to mental health difficulties in later adulthood. The brain areas that are notably involved in responding to traumatic experiences are the same ones that undergo significant developmentally based changes during the transition to adolescence and through the 20s.

Trauma is a word that's commonly used in describing a range of everyday experiences. However, not all stressful experiences tend to change an individual's neurobiology or ability to feel safe emotionally. Psychological trauma is a form of traumatic stress that's felt both physically and emotionally. It tends to affect the brain networks, including altering the stress response system. Traumatic experiences tend to differ with individuals and are influenced by a person's subjective perception of what's considered traumatic.

Some of the critical factors that influence such a variation include; prior traumatic experiences, the severity of exposure to traumatic experiences, and social stressors resulting from interpersonal relationships. Taking time to recognize the underpinnings of psychological stress and trauma can help identify what needs to be addressed. The traditional way humans respond when faced with perceived threats is the fight or flight, which is generally a reflective nervous phenomenon that has survival advantages typically.

However, the systems that lead to the trigger of reflexive survival behaviors can sometimes lead to functional impairment in some people who may get psychologically traumatized and, in turn, suffer from PTSD.

Numerous research studies have shown neurobiological abnormalities in those struggling with PTSD. Some of the studies have provided an insight into the pathophysiology of post-traumatic stress disorder and the biological vulnerabilities of some in developing PTSD. Psychological trauma can occur from having witnessed an event that might have been perceived as life-threatening or a situation that poses bodily injury to oneself and others.

Such experiences are generally accompanied by intense fear, a sense of helplessness, and horror that can lead to the development of PTSD. The response to trauma doesn't depend only on the stressor characteristics but also on certain specific factors to the individual. For the vast majority, a trauma that comes up due to some profound threat can be limited to an acute disturbance. Such reactions are typically characterized by reminders of the exposure to intrusive thoughts or nightmares, activation of an irritating or agitating experience, or deactivation that leads to withdrawal or a numbing experience.

As much as these reactions are self-limiting, they tend to provoke minimal functional impairment over a period of time. The psychological trauma that comes up due to such experiences often leads to a more prolonged syndrome; this has been defined and validated clinically as PTSD. Post-traumatic stress disorder is characterized by the presence of symptoms and signs that reflect a persistent abnormal adaptation of the neurobiological systems to stress related to a witnessed trauma.

The neurobiological systems that help regulate stress responses include neurotransmitter pathways, specific endocrine alongside a network of brain regions that help regulate fear behavior at both conscious and unconscious levels.

Various research studies have focused on exploring these systems in more detail. They have helped with addressing the changes that take place in clients that develop PTSD. There still are ongoing efforts that link neurobiological changes identified in the patients who suffer from PTSD to the clinical features that constitute PTSD, such as altered learning, heightened arousal, and intermittent dissociative behavior.

Neuroplasticity and Adaptive Coping Strategies

Neuroplasticity refers to the brain's ability to adapt or coping strategies that tend to emerge in response to some traumatic experience or adversity. It's rooted in the biological ability to survive life-threatening situations alongside the ability to cope with the consequences of traumatic experiences. As much as they are formed during childhood stages, these adaptation strategies are embedded in the neural networks that normally function outside of conscious human awareness.

The human brain tends to store traumatic memories as a protection strategy. When memories begin to intrude into the present moments through upsetting emotions, flashbacks, and bodily sensations, the original fear experienced during the past traumatic experience, and the survival strategies get activated. Adaptive behaviors such as spacing-out, aggression, distrust, and avoidance become automatic responses to any slightest cue of anger. For example, trauma survivors could be sensitive to loud noises, physical proximity to other people, and touch. Such experiences can activate adaptive reactions.

Neuroplasticity is vital for the healing and recovery from psychological trauma. The body and the mind can learn how to feel safe again after undergoing a traumatic experience.

When therapists identify traumatic stress responses as neurobiologically-embedded adaptations, they can successfully help their clients revise their coping strategies to better meet their current psychological needs.

The stress-response system referred to as hypothalamus-pituitary-adrenal (HPA) is initiated by an actual or perceived threat. The amygdala is usually the first responder that receives information from the incoming sensory information known as the thalamus, which rapidly screens for danger. The hippocampal memory system helps with the assessment by providing the amygdala with the information in the past threats database.

It works in tandem with the prefrontal cortex, which is quite critical for decision-making and hormone regulation. The memory storage structures, which is also referred to as the hippocampus, are also essential for deactivating the HPA axis when the threat subsides. Once the alarm gets triggered by the amygdala, the HPA axis releases a cascade of chemicals alongside hormones that enable the individual to face the traumatic experience to survive by either fighting or fleeing. When survival through mobilizing is impossible, automatic survival through immobilization gets triggered. It slows the individual's life-sustaining systems such as breathing and heart rate.

Such reactions take place instantly and usually bypass any of the thoughtful decision-making that one can engage in. Once the real or even perceived danger has passed, the HPA axis returns to the original pre-threat status. However, when their traumatic experience is ongoing, the HPA axis continues to flood the body with the stress hormones that get released from the adrenal glands. The overproduction of hormones creates a very toxic state of stress within the body, which changes the function and physical structure of other hormones.

As much as the brain's intention is to promote a higher survival possibility to be constantly vigilant, it can compromise other capacities such as the ability to manage feelings and think clearly. The release of high cortisol levels and the inability to emotionally regulate the overproduced hormones leads to engagement in risky behaviors and the onset of some physical health issues. Youths who have had traumatic childhood experiences are more likely to get stuck in the fight or flight mode. They tend to feel anxious, jumpy, hyper-vigilant, and even feel disconnected, numb, disconnected, and foggy.

Such feelings and the resulting behaviors can be confusing. They might also end up disrupting the daily activities and relationships of an individual.

How the Brain Works and the Impact of Trauma on Health

The brain areas implicated in stress response are the hippocampus, prefrontal cortex, and amygdala. Traumatic experiences can have a lasting impact on the brain areas and are generally associated with increased cortisol, norepinephrine responses, and other subsequent stressors. Through brain imaging techniques in research, various changes have been recognized in the brain structure that might be connected to the impaired functioning of those suffering from PTSD.

452

To understand how the traumatic stress that takes place at the different stages of life interacts with the developing brain, one must get a clear understanding of normal brain development. The average human brain typically undergoes changes in function and structure all through an individual's lifespan, right from childhood to the later stages of life. Understanding the various stages is critical in determining the difference between pathology and normal development alongside how both interact.

It's therefore understandable that trauma that happens at different stages in life can have adverse effects on the brain's development. Various studies have suggested that there are differences in the impact of trauma on neurobiology. That highly depends on the stage of development at which the trauma occurs. Symptoms of PTSD such as nightmares, sleep disturbances, and intrusive thoughts represent behavioral manifestations of the stress-induced changes in brain function and structure.

Stress arises from the acute and chronic changes within specific brain regions and neurochemical systems, leading to long-term changes in brain circuits that involve stress response. Trauma has such a powerful ability to shape the brain's physical, emotional, and intellectual development, especially when experienced at an early age. Traumatic experiences have the potential of altering an individual's life and ability to diminish their resilience.

Continual exposure to threatening situations can make a young person's brain prone to flight, fight and freeze response, which makes it difficult for one to build meaningful relationships or reach out for help.

Traumatic experiences tend to overwhelm an individual's coping capacity and have typically long-term effects on the individual's functioning and well-being. There is a connection between traumatic childhood experiences and the greater chance of experiencing physical and behavioral health challenges. Before children reach 5 years of age, their brain tends to be in a critical development stage.

Positive experiences are more likely to lead to healthy brain development; however, negative experiences can lead to unhealthy development.

Long traumatic experiences can impact the brain's cognitive functioning, such as having short-term memory, emotional regulation, and such.

Children with exposure to trauma tend to develop coping mechanisms that enable them to overcome the feelings of hurt due to the trauma. The strategy can, in most cases, evolve into health risk behaviors such as overeating, drug, and alcohol abuse. When childhood traumatic stress goes untreated, the coping mechanisms are more likely to lead to anxiety, social isolation, or even chronic diseases.

Chapter 3: The Principles Somatic Psychotherapy and EMDR Therapy for Trauma Treatment

The human body needs to process events that are stressful through movement and breath. When a therapist fails to include body awareness, conscious breathing, and move into trauma treatment, it limits the body's ability to work with the innate healing capacities. Somatic psychotherapy engages the awareness of the body as an intervention. Also, it addresses the connections that exist between the mind, brain, and behavior.

The field of somatic psychotherapy encompasses a broad range of treatment modalities that have evolved over time to a great extent. EMDR therapists who have training in somatic interventions use advanced tools to work with dysregulation of the nervous system associated with post-traumatic stress. Both somatic psychotherapy and EMDR therapy were endorsed as one of the best approaches for treating PTSD by Bessel Van der Kolk, a trauma treatment researcher.

Somatic psychotherapy has evolved through the years from the cathartic approaches. The early therapeutic modalities used some intense and even invasive methods such as deep pressure massage, stressful positions, primal screams, and deep pressure massage held over time. As much as the therapies created room for rapid change, they also, in a way, re-traumatized the client. As a result, modern-day somatic psychotherapy and EMDR therapy help incorporate mindfulness that helps with the somatic release in a safe and well-contained fashion.

As covered earlier, the brain is such a powerful organ that constructs human experiences from diverse sensory inputs, then regulates the responses through the thoughts and emotions of humans, and controls actions. Human beings should learn from their experiences to effectively adapt effectively and meet the challenges in our environments.

The human brain has a unique dual perspective. While the neuroscientists still grapple with the physical brain's workings, from an external viewpoint as they examine the brain's neural firings, the psychologists focus on their study from what is being in such a system feels like.

455

The dual view of the brain also applies to the body. While traditional medicine focuses on evaluating and objectively investigating the body's functions and treats them, somatic psychotherapy focuses on the subjective study from experience.

Understanding the biological nature of perception, thought, feeling, memory, learning, and consciousness has become such a central challenge in biological sciences. To approach psychotherapy more effectively, there is a need for a multifaceted paradigm. The body's neural memory is the ground on which the life experiences get imprinted. Psychotherapy treatment starts with tracking the experience.

A therapist should start treatment by investigating how a client experiences the world by focusing on the primary diagnostic inquiry and not asking how the client feels but how he perceives and comprehend the world. Memories get created by the neurons' physical firing, and therapists should focus on the emotional surface feelings first as they consider their biological cause and effect since the body's communication extend beyond the symbolic verbal expression.

People's belief is normally bound in body posture, breath, and movement. Simultaneously, the inner realities get masked, emphasized, or even betrayed by the facial expressions. Emotions, on the other hand, get revealed by the rate of breath. In somatic psychotherapy, facial expression, posture, movement, breath, and vocal tone tend to provide important clues about the congruence between the inner experience that has been embodied and the outer expression.

In somatic psychotherapy, the body is never separate from self and from the perspective of the body; therapeutic objectives seek to elicit a sensory dialogue that stirs up a meeting point and establishes conscious unity between the mind and body. The main focus of therapy should be on helping clients develop the ability to observe the bodily activities on the layers of sensory awareness, which might be challenging to express in words. Such can be said through diverse body experiences such as body heat, muscular contractions, skin sensitivity, and organ vibrations.

Body-centered approaches tend to focus on the sensory experiences as they rise from diverse realms. Somatic methods tend to use sensory tracking alongside recognition of the movement impulses to access interactive links or the lack that exists between behavior, sensation, affect, and cognition. Somatic psychotherapy encompasses the experiences processed in the neocortex and those experiences through the limbic and the mid and lower brain centers.

Sensorimotor Psychotherapy

This approach focuses on using the basic tools of body-mind integration such as movement, body awareness, and breath in providing a framework for understanding the fundamental connection between the mind and body about psychological development and growth.

Mind-Body Psychotherapy

The basis of body-mind psychotherapy lies in physiology and early motor development. The psychological forces tend to use physical energy. Mind and body care function in mutual feedback loops where the state of the body reflects that of the mind, with the mind's state also reflecting that of the body. This principle is vital towards integrating somatic and cognitive processing within a therapeutic context. The recognition of the connection between mind and body is also the basis for somatic self-discovery that focuses on exploring the relationship in posture, sensation, and movement to the emotional and mental states.

The early motor development forms the basis for the later development states and usually is nonverbal. The body, therefore, provides direct access to the early developmental and implicit behavioral issues. All human beings can read each other's signals; however, translating nonverbal bodily states into verbal consciousness can be challenging. With more evidence accumulating that supports the mind and body idea and how they are closely connected, therapists gradually embrace the different types of treatment alongside somatic psychotherapy.

Doctors understand the impact that mental health can have on the overall physical well-being. The body is linked quite closely to mental health, and both can be healed if complete victory is to be realized. The principles of somatic psychotherapy explain that the mind, body, and spirit together with emotions are all connected. Emotional events, therefore, impact the body in several lasting ways, including facial expressions, body posture, and body language. Therapists trained in somatic psychotherapy can recognize the physical changes and help with treatment for improved physical and mental health.

Benefits of Somatic Psychotherapy and EMDR Therapy

Various independent studies, including controlled ones, have shown that EMDR therapy effectively treats PTSD. The therapy is even used by the Department of Veterans Affairs and is strongly recommended for treating PTSD. The benefits of somatic psychotherapy and EMDR therapy are diverse; however, having knowledge of them can be of great help;

Therapeutic touch links the body and mind

As much as human beings are whole, they hardly operate as one. For example, when experiencing a panic attack, you might feel like just being in a body while unable to breathe. Combating fear with logic is never possible. It's also advisable to intellectually understand the impact that trauma can have on one's life.

Therapeutic touch helps with bridging the gap that exists between the mind and body. Through somatic psychotherapy, one can become increasingly aware of what's actually happening in mind and body. Engaging in top-down thinking helps one to even heal much faster.

Helps work through attachment issues

Most people have attachment issues emanating from their childhood experiences that repeatedly show all through their adult life.

458

Various methods can help with working through the issues; however, somatic psychotherapy and EMDR therapy have been proven to be some of the most effective tools. Therapeutic touch goes way back to the first attachment that was entirely nonverbal. The primary caregiver or mother conveyed emotions that were understood through strict, and the child understood senses.

Learn skills to rebalance the body

Somatic psychotherapy and EMDR therapy help with bringing back the body into balance. Trauma has a way of impacting the body. When the trauma lasts for a longer period of time, the remnants of that traumatic experience can get stuck in the body. Somatic psychotherapy incorporates a range of techniques that helps one to regain one physical and emotional health. Through the therapy, one can learn new methods to soothe self, get centered and grounded, and connect to the mind, body, and spirit.

The techniques are helpful whether one considers themselves to be a trauma survivor or not. Such people can reduce stress, increase mindful awareness, quell many anxieties and stress-related issues.

Helps improve resiliency for the future

Some of the skills that you get to learn during somatic psychotherapy and EMDR therapy may not help you immediately but are more likely to help you improve resiliency for the future. Regardless of what you get to face in the future, you will likely be in a much better state to work through the challenges. One of the techniques used in somatic psychotherapy is referred to as pendulation. It is a structured way of moving from stress within the body to that of calm and back again to a state of anxiety.

As you engage in pendulation, you will realize how the body feels like when in different states. You will also learn the process and how to bring the body back to that calm state. Learning this technique can be quite helpful for all of future experiences. As a result, you will be able to reach more significant goals, and you'll feel more confident about the potential to handle whatever life throws your way.

Re-empowers you

After taking time to study trauma responses across survivors of sexual abuse, war veterans, and others, Dr. Bessel van der Kolk realized that the most paralyzing aspect of trauma is the feeling of being completely powerless. The brain's amygdala tends to respond to danger with either fight or flight response. However, when the wires get crossed and instead of engaging in fight or flight, you get to freeze. It means that the brain becomes desperate to get out of danger, but it can't, leading to a feeling of being disempowered.

Through working with the mind and body system, it's possible to regain the feeling of empowerment that you might have lost in the past.

Increased engagement with life

When the mind and body are in a state of disconnect, it's possible to feel disengaged from life. One is more likely to feel as if they are just going through motions, and it feels as if you're present but not fully there. Somatic psychotherapy helps clients to regain that sense of engagement with all the areas of life. As one becomes free of physical, psychological, and emotional pain, they also get to increase their ability to feel freedom, joy, and an increased range of positive emotions.

Chapter 4: Embodiment in Trauma Treatment

Human beings live in a disembodied culture. More time is spent in entertaining the boredom with short attention spans given to information and media. Very little time is spent feeling and sensing the body's responses to what we actually spend time-consuming. In the process, humans get to lose that connection with embodied self-awareness. Embodiment is vital as it helps with reducing numbing that does occur.

When people are embodied, they tend to feel others. They can easily connect with others and become more active in showing empathy and protecting those perceived as vulnerable, including the surrounding environment. Getting into a disconnection state from our embodied self leads to interruption with the larger body and the world around us. Embodiment helps ensure survival and is the natural feeling of oneself without constant narration or the thinking mind's interpretation.

Traumatic experiences tend to defy all manner of subjectivity as it is with mind and body dualism. The physical traumas hardly keep to the boundaries of the body but also progress to impact the mind. In most cases, psychological traumas often manifest in the body. In most cases, events that just seem to be physical may not be, and even those that hardly leave any scars can, to an extent, manifest in physical symptoms. Trauma then reveals that actual issue to be foundationally embodied and one whose body and mind coexist in such a dynamic and interconnected relationship.

When dealing with an embodiment, the mind tends to be of great importance since it's the actual seat of the matter, and the body becomes the object. Which should be clearly observed and analyzed. If all you understand is the traumatic experience, then the mind becomes the framework for analyzing the human experience.

It then leads to systems based on the belief that it's only by intellectual reflection and detailed examination to gain access to the actual truth in such a scenario. The underlying principle is that the human condition highly depends on their reflection of the issue at hand rather than the issue's actual existence.

Instead of viewing life just as it, there should be an attempt to analyze the behavior to understand the context from which the trauma rose. The challenge, however, lies in the fact that the body can either perceive correctly or incorrectly. Hence, it takes working with a therapist if the truth is to be established. Embodiment entails focusing on your sensations. Awareness of the body works more like a guiding compass that enables people to feel more control of their lives.

Somatic psychotherapy creates a foundation for empathy and encourages people to make healthy decisions. They provide important feedback concerning their relationship with others.

How people think and feel tends to influence how we operate in the world. How humans work in the world also impacts how they feel and think. The representation, processing, and perception of bodily signals play such an integral role in human behavior. Several theories that embody cognition identify the fact that higher cognitive processes tend to operate on perceptual symbols. The conceptus entails the reactivation of sensory-motor states that takes place as we experience the world. This type of bi-directional loop, to a great extent, shapes the perceptions of people and how they experience the world.

It focuses on family, cultural and social norms as guiding patterns to an expression of emotional behavior. Therefore, the embodiment is culturally and socially determined and cultivated through engagement in reflective awareness of sensations within the present moment. Embodiment entails the integration of sensory feedback systems such as exteroception, interoception, and proprioception.

Exteroception

This is the sensory experience of the external environment that gets facilitated by the sensory neurons that generally travel from the body areas such as eyes, ears, nose, tongue, and skin all the way to the brain. The sensory experience may also include sounds, sights, smells, tastes, and the sensations of touch, such as having a feeling of clothing touching the skin.

Humans tend to perceive feelings from the body concerning the body's internal and external state, which provides the body with a sense of our physical and psychological condition. This is based on the fact that humans have a body that we are embodied in.

The familiar feelings often lead to the intuitive notion that bodily sensations are typically tied to life and represent the relevant signals for well-being and survival and beneath all that underlie the emotional state, mood, and the fundamental cognitive processes.As much as bodily response and perception are vital processes when constructing an emotional experience, physical processes might be of great importance for most psychological functions, including decision making or cognition, which is quite important.

For example, imagine experiencing a very frightening situation where you're left alone in a dark hall or park, and all of a sudden, you begin to hear footsteps coming towards you. The mental processes seem to be quite embodied when we are experiencing such situations. The strong emotions can turn out to be overwhelming.

The influence of bodily interior signals on experience and behavior has been investigated for over 100 years. It has, to a great extent, influenced how humans understand themselves.

Proprioception

Proprioception refers to sensory feedback about the position of the body about gravity. This form of awareness entails knowing how you are sitting, whether it's upright, maintaining balance while walking, standing, or leaning to the side. Proprioception gets facilitated from the body joints and inner ear all the way to the brain. The influence of bodily interior signals on behavior and experience has been investigated for over 100 years. It has, to a great extent, influenced the human understanding of self.

Interoception

Interoception entails the sensory experience of the inner body. It consists of feelings of sleepiness, pain, tension, and restlessness. It has two forms of perception such as proprioception and interoception. Emotions such as those of thirst, hunger, and other internal sensations are, to a great extent, less distinct and also less discriminated. This makes them different from those associated with the exteroceptive somatosensory system, such as temperature, itch, and pain. The foundation of emotional feelings depends on the neural representation of the body's physiological condition.

The somatic elements evoke emotions that influence behavior and feelings.

Interoception helps provide feedback about the sensory neurons' inner emotional experience that brings information from the organs, muscles, and the brain's connective tissues. Theories of embodied cognition tend to hold higher cognition processes that operate on perceptual symbols. The concept use involves reactivation of the sensory motor-states that generally occur during a person's experience with the world. The three sensory feedback systems tend to create a sense of self. With the help of somatic psychotherapy, the embodiment can be developed by engaging in mindfulness practices that include body awareness.

A central component of somatic psychotherapy is that a felt sense of embodiment brings awareness inside the body as the ever-changing energetic, sensory and emotional landscape gets evaluated. Embodiment removes the therapist's focus from the client's actions and other things in the outside world to the qualities of the client's present and internal experience. It focuses on sensations, textures, and colors.

Being in the body when undergoing trauma can be quite challenging. One has to be helped to re-learn how to stay present while also positively sensing some of the basic things.

Embodiment is such a powerful exercise that can help with recovery from PTSD. It helps with encountering hypervigilance and dissociation. When engaging in EMDR therapy or somatic psychotherapy, the client should develop the ability to be in tune with their mind.

464

Therapists should take caution when engaging in such an exercise. Suppose they encounter a traumatized part of the body. In that case, they should bring their awareness to a neutral or positive part or engage in an activity that brings resources to that same part.

Human beings have the habit of overriding their natural behaviors. Therefore, it means that the nervous system is more likely to become stuck on alert when experiencing a traumatic experience. To an extent, one becomes oriented to danger even if the traumatic experience has passed. The nervous system can remain stuck in that chronic state where the traumatic experience gets activated easily. It ends up draining one's energy and creating patterns of tension that become habitual within the body. Over time, one gets to construct their lives based on a very complex foundation of complex defenses designed to protect and keep them safe from danger.

Once the patterns are established within the body, the person may start avoiding people and situations that, to an extent, represent a potential threat. One can be found in a loop of some self-perpetuating stress without knowing how to break the cycle. Somatic psychotherapy contends that it's not actually the original events that normally cause traumatic symptoms to emerge. Still, the client's inability to discharge the fight/flight /freeze responses generated to cope with the crisis. Such an experience leaves the body in a state of suppressed high activation. It causes the chronic tension to keep appearing alongside other physical and psychological symptoms of ill health that the person might experience.

The aim of somatic psychotherapy is to help with bringing back the nervous system into regulation. One of the ways that this can be achieved is through felt sense which also means embodiment. It entails creating a deepening awareness of emotions and physical sensations as they continue to arise within the body, making it possible for one to navigate more skillfully as they go through high activation and stress states.

Somatic psychotherapy uses techniques referred to as titration, which is also commonly used for trauma treatment. The therapists use the method to dive straight to the heart of that traumatic experience during treatment. The client gets encouraged to work at a pace and level that they find to be manageable.

As the session progresses, the therapist gradually increases the client's capacity to bear the sensations and the feelings as they arise while also building safety and confidence as they progress. This, in turn, helps with integration; however, there are several somatic psychotherapy techniques or strategies that can be used.

The Phases of EMDR IN Trauma Treatment

EMDR (Eye Movement Desensitization and Reprocessing) is a therapeutic treatment method that initially addressed post-traumatic stress disorder (PTSD). It is presently being used in various therapeutic sessions, such as phobias, anxiety, pain disorders, and dermatological disorders. EMDR therapy enables clients to heal from symptoms and the emotional distress encountered by experiencing disturbing life experiences. It uses detailed procedures and protocols learned during EMDR therapy training sessions, and therapists can help clients by activating the process that allows for natural healing to occur.

Complex PTSD happens due to longtime exposure to some unrelenting stressors, attachment injuries, and repeated traumatic events that majorly take place during childhood. In most cases, the traumatic experience is interpersonal, which means that an individual might have experienced some chronic neglect, exposure to domestic violence, or abuse at an early age. It's also important to note that chronic trauma can also occur due to ongoing experiences such as bullying, undiagnosed or unsupported disability, or such. In all forms of PTSD, the injury usually is repetitive, cumulative, and prolonged. In most cases, trauma occurs when one is in vulnerable times, and the experiences tend to shape an individual's identity.

The purpose of engaging in EMDR therapy for trauma is so that clients can develop an embodied self that one can compassionately hold on to their emotions, including the vulnerable sensations. The embodiment process requires that the therapist develop skills on working with nonverbal and preverbal memories stored in the body and mind as motor patterns, affective states, sensations, and psychological arousal. The therapist should focus on the relational exchange.

EMDR therapy is an eight-phase treatment process where eye movements alongside other liberal stimulation are used during the treatment process. Once the therapist has determined the actual traumatic experience that should be targeted first, they can then ask the client to hold in view different aspects of the experience or thought in their mind as they use their eyes to track the therapist's hand. At the same time, it's being moved back and forth across the client's viewpoint. EMDR therapy is believed to be connected with biological mechanisms that are similar to Rapid Eye Movement sleep.

While engaging in the exercise, internal associations arise as the clients begin to process the memory of some of the disturbing feelings. EMDR therapy helps with transforming the painful and traumatic events on an emotional level. For example, a victim of rape can shift from feelings of self-disgust and horror to that of holding a firm belief that they survived the rape and, therefore, they are strong. Unlike engaging in talk therapy, the insights that the client gets to gain during EMDR therapy results not quite much from the therapist's interpretation but from the accelerated emotional and intellectual processes of the client.

Therefore, the client is more likely to conclude the therapy feeling empowered by the very same traumatic experience that debased them before. The natural outcome of EMDR therapy phases is that where the clients' thoughts, feelings, and behavior become the indicators of the resolution of emotional health. It all happens without engaging in speaking or engaging in homework as used in other therapies.

The EMDR Therapy Phases

EMDR therapy entails focusing attention on three time periods, the past, present, and future. Focus then goes towards the memories of the past that can be disturbing and the related events. It also focuses on the current situations that cause emotional distress and develop the attitudes and skills needed for positive future actions. With EMDR therapy, the specific items can be effectively addressed using an eight-phase approach of treatment.

Phase 1 – History Taking

This initial phase's primary purpose is to help the therapist gather a thorough history of the client's life, including both the joyous and traumatic life events. The first phase of EMDR therapy involved history taking and treatment planning. Having a detailed history helps the therapist identify how ready the client is and the secondary gains that might maintain the current problem. The therapist can analyze the behaviors that appear to be dysfunctional alongside symptoms and specific characteristics. They can decide on an ideal form of treatment that is suitable for the analyzed situation.

When identifying possible targets, the therapist should also focus on related traumatic incidents that might have happened in the past. Initial EMDR processing can also be directed towards childhood events instead of adult traumatic experiences. It can be realized in the process that the client might have had some problematic childhood. As clients continue to gain insight into their situations, the emotional distress gets resolved, and they are more likely to start changing their behaviors.

The length of EMDR treatment depends on the number of traumatic experiences and the period the client has experienced PTSD. Those who only have a single event of adult-onset trauma can be treated and free within 5 hours.

Those struggling with multiple trauma may require longer treatment times for the resolution of trauma. Therapists should be able to observe the capacity of the client for somatic awareness and also assess for dissociation. They can review the individual's early childhood history to understand how their somatic or core patterns and the pervasive negative cognitions are conceptualized.

Phase 2 - Preparation

The second phase is referred to as the preparation process. It's where the therapist and the client move towards creating that therapeutic relationship. The therapist helps the clients develop the necessary resources to help them face complex challenges or memories without feeling overwhelmed. The preparation process can be accomplished through engagement in resource development installation.

The client is encouraged to practice feeling and imagining being connected to a positive emotional state. As you commence the second phase of treatment, the therapist should ensure that the client has diverse ways of handling emotional distress.

They can train the client on some of the self-control techniques that they can use to close those sessions that appear incomplete and maintain stability between and during the treatment sessions. The therapist can also instruct the client on how they can use metaphors to enable them to stop signals and provide a sense of control during treatment sessions. The client can also be taught a range of imagery and stress reduction techniques that they can use during the treatment process. The goal of EMDR therapy is to produce effective and rapid change. At the same time, the client maintains some equilibrium elements between and during the treatment sessions.

Phase 3 - Assessment

The phase involves engaging in target development. The therapist helps the client identify some disturbing feelings, body sensations, images, and emotions associated with the traumatic experience. The client can then be instructed to recognize a salient image that's associated with the memory. The therapist can, in the process, help with eliciting negative beliefs that are associated with the memory to provide some insight into the irrationality of the specific event. Positive views that suit the target can also be introduced, especially those that contradict the client's emotional experience.

The therapist should evaluate the validity of the cognition scale and the subjective units of the disturbance scale. Such is usually assessed to understand how appropriate the client's positive cognition is to be true a true statement that addresses the target memory. Both of the assessments can be used by the therapist as baseline measures. In the assessment phase, the physical sensations and emotions associated with the traumatic memory also get noted down.

EMDR therapy gets modified when working with nonverbal and preverbal memories by targeting childhood events that might have unknown origin or some pervasive cognitions that don't resolve after traditional EMDR therapy.

Phase 4 - Desensitization

The fourth phase incorporates the use of a dual awareness state where the client maintains awareness of both the present moment experience while recalling at the same time memories of the traumatic event. The desensitization phase is when the disturbing event gets evaluated to change the trauma-related sensory experiences and their associations. This process helps with increasing the client's sense of self-efficacy and elicitation of insight. The client can be asked to focus on both the eye movement and the target image simultaneously as they get encouraged to be more open to whatever takes place.

After engaging in a set of eye movements, the client can be directed to take a deep breath as they blank out the material they were focusing on.

Depending on how the client responds, the therapist can then direct their focus of attention alongside the length of time, speed, and the type of stimulation that they get to use. Also, the client can identify a positive belief concerning the experience. They can then get asked to rate the positive belief and the intensity of the negative emotions. The client can be asked to focus on the negative thought, the image, and body sensations while engaging in EMDR processing through bilateral stimulation.

Dual attention stimulation gets amplified through bilateral eye-movements, tones, and pulsars that get alternated between the right and the left side of the body. EMDR therapy for complex traumatic experiences involves focusing careful attention on the dissociative symptoms during the treatment process. The emphasis should be on keeping the client regulated with tolerance while processing. This can be achieved through engagement in somatic psychotherapy interventions such as titration or pendulation.

Phase 5 - Installation

This is the installation phase that focuses on strengthening the positive beliefs to become more available after the process of desensitization is accomplished. The therapist attempts to intensify the strength of positive cognition, which is supposed to be used in replacing the negative experience.

Until the cognition scale's validity reaches about 7 or up to the desired ecological validity, some of the most enhancing positive cognition can be

470

paired with what was previously dysfunctional during this bilateral stimulation stage.

For example, once the client can no longer hold on to the misconception that they are not lovable, they can then start developing and integrating a new positive belief that they are worthy of being loved.

In most cases, there will be a new embodied experience where the client can attend to their emotional parts with great acceptance and compassion.

Phase 6 - Body Scan

This is the body scan phase, where the body is brought into the therapy process to assess any lingering tension or distress while also enhancing the good feelings that the client might be feeling after the completion of desensitization and installation phases. The client gets asked to be aware of any somatic response that can be considered as residues of the tension related to the traumatic event that's still remaining. If there is a residue, then the therapist should target the specific body sensation for some further processing.

Phase 7 - Closure

This closure phase is essential for successful treatment. It ensures that the client is entirely grounded before leaving the session. Self-control techniques that the client had already been taught are used whenever reprocessing is considered incomplete. It helps with bringing back the client to that state of equilibrium. The therapist can explain what they are likely to experience during the sessions and maintain a record of disturbances that are more likely to arise during the sessions through the use of the targets if necessary.

During this phase, the client can be asked to keep a log through the week to document any specific instance related to the process that might arise.

It also helps with reminding the client of the self-calming activities that they had mastered in phase 2. During the process, the therapist instructs the client that they can function in between sessions.

Phase 8 – Reevaluation phase

This phase entails reevaluation. A review of the process is carried out to attain optimal treatment while also checking out additional targets. During this phase, therapists can also examine the progress that has so far been made. It's important to note that all of the EMDR treatment processes are related to historical events. The current incidents tend to elicit feelings of distress and what is required if the future possibilities are different. During the reevaluation phase, the embodied EMDR therapist takes time to review the previous sessions. They also look for any lingering cognitive, somatic, and emotional distress that is likely to lead to other traumatic experiences. Early childhood and attachment trauma require ongoing therapeutic support. The psychological arousal can be integrated accordingly since such states as emotions, beliefs, and sensations have been in place for more extended periods.

Therapists should help clients develop an awareness of the body's various parts that hold memories of the early trauma. There are times when a part of the body may have some resistance to trauma work and sabotage therapeutic intervention in the process. There are also times when the part of self could be holding traumatic memories. So in EMDR therapy, vulnerable parts should be sourced together with the allies to create safety. Resourcing such parts may take time; however, when the client has ideal resources, processing the traumatic memories can be quite effective and much gentler.

When dealing with EMDR therapy, it's important to note that the process is not in any way linear. Early development of trauma is generally a process that might be slow and dies require ongoing stabilization alongside resource development. Therefore, successful treatment outcomes should focus on building tolerance for the emotions together with the body sensations that usually accompany traumatic experiences. The client should increasingly be able to access their whole wise self as they get to attend to their while also upholding the responsibilities that they get to experience.

The symptoms of PTSD that once seemed overwhelming can be resolved as the client learns how they can turn toward the parts of themselves that hold such pain and suffering as they experience greater compassion and awareness.

Chapter 5: Use of Somatic Psychotherapy and EMDR Therapy with Client

Several theories have emerged on how EMDR therapy works based on the observed clinical effects. It could be that it ignites stimulation of the brain's hemispheres which then causes the reprocessing impact to occur. There are also theories based on the fact that eye movements tend to be linked with the hippocampus, which is associated with the consolidation of memory. Another theory states that the dual attention that the client gets to maintain during somatic and EMDR therapy enables them to focus on their inner feelings. The eye movements make them more alert in the brain, which helps with metabolizing whatever they are witnessing.

Therapists use eye movements patterned with somatic psychotherapy techniques to help with clearing physical, emotional, and cognitive blockages. In theory, traumatic experiences tend to leave unprocessed feelings, thoughts, and emotions that can either be metabolized or processed through the engagement of eye movements and other techniques. In the same way, in which rapid eye movement or dream sleep works, the eye movements similarly help with processing the blocked information, allowing the mind and body to release it.

In some cases, the intense dreams that we get to experience with the past events are attempts made by the body-mind to heal the past trauma. The challenge lies in the fact that when one awakens during such disturbing dreams, they disrupt the eye movements and interfere with the recovery process. It's important to note that rapid eye movement alone cannot complete the trauma's task. Engaging a therapist that helps the clients maintain eye movements while also guiding them on how to focus on the traumatic experience is essential. It then allows for the traumatic event to be reprocessed and even integrated.

During the trauma treatment process, the therapist can engage in other acts such as tapping of hands or sending sound to the client's ears can also stimulate the reprocessing of the traumatic experience.

Trauma Treatment with Accelerated Information Processing

Traumatic experiences have the potential of causing one to develop beliefs that are erroneous about themselves or the world. For example, a child who has been molested may develop a negative view about themselves, that they are wrong, and that the world is always unsafe. Such experiences are more likely to become fixed in their body and in their minds in the form of blocked energy, irrational emotions, and physical symptoms. Traumas are in two states; some traumas assaults one's sense of self-efficacy and one's self-confidence.

Traumas are more likely a perceptual filter that keeps narrowing and also limiting one's views of self and the world. For example, you can come across a teased person as a child due to some attributes, such as being overweight. Such people may struggle with low self-esteem issues and with a deep irrational feeling that they are not good enough profoundly embedded into their psyche. Even if such a person claims that they are smarter than many people, they are still more likely to feel inferior.

If not well addressed, such false beliefs can dictate their self-concept and how they get to approach life. Traumas can affect a person in dramatic ways and have the potential of interfering with one's perspective on life while also making them question themselves and their world. Such traumas typically lead to debilitating symptoms of PTSD, such as having nightmares, flashbacks, phobias, anxieties, and fears, including difficulties at work and at home.

Traumas tend to lock into one's memory network what was actually experiences with the physical sensations, images, smells, tastes, sounds, and beliefs. That's why a person who has experienced a train crash will continue to have a fear of trains. He will end up panicking at the sight or even sound of a train since all the memories related to the accident are still lodged within their nervous system.

Both the traumatic memory's internal and external triggers bring the experience into their consciousness just as it took place in its original form.

As a recording, traumatic experiences are more like recording as they get trapped and form a perpetual blockage.

475

They keep repeating themselves in the body. Nightmares could be the mind's attempts to metabolize the trapped information; however, the traumatic experiences tend to last beyond the dream time. When engaging in therapy, a client might be asked to focus on the trauma's target, such as a dream, a memory, a person, a projected event, and an experience. While using the target, the therapist tries to stimulate the memory network where the traumatic experience is stored.

Simultaneously, other stimuli or eye movements can help with triggering a mechanism that stores the mind-body system's information processing capabilities to enable it to draw onto the information from a memory network that's different and that which will give the client insight and understanding. Accelerated information processing then occurs when there is a rapid free association of information between the memory networks. Each set of eye movements helps with further unlocking the disturbing information and accelerating it towards an adaptive path until those negative feelings, thoughts, pictures, and emotions have dissipated and replaced spontaneously with an overall positive attitude.

As shared, early somatic psychotherapy and EMDR therapy work quite successfully with clients who are motivated to change. The clients should show the willingness and readiness to detach themselves from their past as they get to experience life without previous problems. Secondary gains, if focused upon, can act as an impediment to the successful processing of therapy. Clients should be ready to experience disturbing thoughts and uncomfortable feelings. As the therapy process begins, the troubling memories can be intensified through engagement in eye movements and other techniques. The therapist can then instruct the client to stay with the feelings or refrain from doing anything to make the feelings go away.

Occasionally, the intense emotions and feelings can become overwhelming, which might cause the client to blackout or be in a state where they cannot proceed with the process. The therapist can then ease the client through such obstacles by helping them move to an adaptive resolution.

There are times when a client can fail to process memories, and that might be as a result of an existing neurological problem and some obsessive–compulsive disorder. A client might be very willing to engage in therapy.

476

CBT + DBT + ACT

Still, such conditions can, in a way, hinder them from connecting with their emotions and going past the blockages. There are also times when a clients traumatic experienced may not be possibly traced to a specific target. Clients with problems caused by deep conditioning of religious orders or punitive parents may have difficulty lowering their psychological defenses to allow EMDR and somatic psychotherapy.

Structure of EMDR therapy Processing Session

Therapy processing typically starts with the therapist taking a thorough history and establishing an alliance with the client. The step usually takes a few sessions. However, it can still last longer. The client needs to establish a feeling of connection with the therapist when the process can effectively begin. EMDR therapy can last for about 90 minutes, depending on the problem that the client could be faced with. For example, a client with traumatic child abuse issues can be advised to follow ninety minutes of EMDR session with fifty minutes of somatic psychotherapy within the same week.

It can help the client integrate the information raised within the first session well with that of the second session. There is a client who might also benefit from engaging in EMDR therapy in succession.

During therapy, the therapist acts more like a facilitator or a guide to the client's process. The therapist should help the client identify and focus on the target related to the trauma they are dealing with. For example, a person who has been involved in a traumatic car accident can picture being in their car and seeing another car hitting them from the side.

In the next step, the client can verbalize a life-limiting belief associated with the incident that the client might have carried over to the present time. The therapist can verbalize opinions such as "I'm not safe when driving at night". Since that negative belief is emotionally charged, it can affect the person in his/her everyday life. The therapist can then ask what the client desires to believe for themselves when such an image is evoked. A positive cognitive in such a case would be I am safe when driving any time.

477

The therapist can then question the physical sensations they feel when the image of the accident is recalled. The client might mention feelings such as stomach tension, a knot in the throat, or any other sensation type.

Lastly, the therapist can ask if any other thing also surfaces when the client thinks of the sensations. The client can report hearing the sound of the impact or gasoline smell. Remember, asking such is to aid stimulation of memory network where the actual memory is locked so that the various components of the memory can be reprocessed. Using subjective units of disturbance scale, the client can then report how disturbing the experience is on a scale of 0 – 10. The client should be encouraged to recall the disturbing image and its related sensations, sounds, and negative cognition.

The client should follow the therapist's finger with their eyes while allowing everything that comes up to the surface without censoring it. Clients may experience images, a range of emotions, insights, body sensations, and ordinary thoughts or even nothing much at all. Since everyone processes their experiences differently, the feelings revealed should not be labeled as wrong or right.

Therapists should pay close attention to the clients' experience as they keep moving the client's eyes until they obtain a clear indication that the client is through with processing the information.

Suppose in case the client is highly emotional. In that case, the therapist should ensure that the client's eyes are kept in motion until they can stay calm and have fully cleared the traumatic experience. However, a client can also signal the therapist to stop the process for some time. Each client may refer to a different number of eye movements that can either be 10 or 15, while others may continue to hundreds. After engaging in a few rounds of eye movements, the therapist can then ask the client, "What's happening now" or "what are you getting now." Once the client has answered, they can proceed with the eye movements.

During the eye movements, clients tend to go through a multidimensional free association of feelings, thoughts, and body sensations. People go through a range of experiences, including horrific images, intense sensations, and strong emotions such as overwhelming terror, homicidal rage, love, grief, forgiveness, and terror.

478

There are times when memories and descriptions that suggest prenatal, as well as infancy experiences, arise. Rich and detailed dream-like imagery alongside symbolism also occurs. Throughout the experiences, therapists can tell the client to stay with that, let it pass through, or even reassure that the experience is old.

Engaging in EMDR therapy has a way of evoking a thorough and immediate re-experiencing of the past just like it was locked within the mind and body.

A witness awareness can enable the client to let the unfolding experiences continue with minimal interference. The process of eye movements and the check-ins should continue until the session comes to an end. During this time, the initial image should be reassessed with SUDs.

For example, the therapist can ask the person with a traumatic car experience the following question; "when you bring up the accident picture, how disturbing is the image?" They can then respond on a scale of 0 to 10. When the client responds to being free of the emotional charge with a scale of 0, the therapist can then ask what it is that they believe to be accurate at the moment.

Eliciting a positive cognition towards the end of the process is an important step that should not be ignored. When the disturbance level is entirely reduced and the client is free from feelings of distress, the therapist can ask them to express their new way of understanding. The positive cognition should only come from the client and should also fit their subjective experience. The client can say that they are safe. The client can then install positive cognition by asking the client to join the statement and the distressing image, which might have changed by becoming dimmer, smaller, and less threatening.

As they combine the experience with positive cognition, they can also engage in a few sets of eye movements. It will make it possible for the client to experience a new orientation to the traumatic image. The therapist can then check if in case a new material has emerged that might require reprocessing. If there is a new material, it can be cleared during the same session or carried forward to the next session. When doing therapy, creating a sense of closure is quite vital for the client's well-being since engaging in therapy brings up highly charged materials and can leave one feeling vulnerable and open.

479

Suppose case clients don't arrive at a good closure. In that case, they can feel overwhelmed with emotions that can be depressing, making it difficult for them to function well both at work and home. They can also be scared of continuing with therapy. The processing material should be allowed to progress on its own during therapy sessions. The process should be facilitated naturally by recording the dreams and insights that come up in a journal and painting, drawing, or engaging in any kind of artwork.

Somatic Psychotherapy Approach

Somatic psychotherapy can be integrated easily with EMDR therapy or any intervention that one is already using. The critical aspect is that you have to inform and include clients in the decision that you are making when using such techniques.

 Somatic psychotherapy is a body-oriented therapy that's designed for the treatment of trauma and PTSD conditions. The focus is on physiology and instinctual biology regarding what happens when the body is exposed to an extreme threat. The approach is based on the knowledge that PTSD and trauma symptoms, in most cases, the result of the nervous system being overwhelmed by the speed and intensity of a threatening and violent event.

The nervous system cannot manage to process the traumatic experience, which makes the event get stuck in two patterns; hyper-arousal, the fight-flight response, or the immobility response. When the stuck energy isn't released, the traumatized person may end up experiencing all manner of symptoms such as nightmares, flashbacks, alongside physical symptoms such as chronic pain, tension in different parts of the body, and stiffness. Because of the neurological impact that trauma has, resolving it should also occur at the physiological level before the person starts processing the thoughts and emotions about that event. This is because the feelings of a traumatized person make it difficult for them to interact effectively at an emotional level or even to benefit from the empathy shown by a therapist until they can regain some self-regulation element to their nervous system.

Somatic psychotherapy focuses on regulating the nervous system where the client gets guided on how to become aware of and experience the bodily sensations. Traumatic experiences tend to trigger self-protective mechanisms within the body. However, a traumatic experience such as being involved in a car accident tends to interrupt the completion of self-protective mechanisms, leading to destabilization of the nervous system.

Through the use of the various body-oriented techniques, clients can regain pleasure in the body as they also reach the different stages of relaxation that allow for the progressive gentle releases of energy that in turn induces self-regulation to the nervous system in a great way.

Sensations of goodness can then get triggered in the client's body, which allows them to reconnect with the outside world and be able to regain a sense of independence in life until they reach that stage where they can process the trauma at a cognitive and emotional level.

Evaluation and Preparation

Here are some of the building blocks to somatic psychotherapy approach;

Create a relatively safe environment

Before getting started with therapy, ensure that the therapy room promotes calm and enables the therapist to stay present, centered, and calm. There are vital things that should be taken note of, such as the therapist's positioning in relation to that of the client. The therapist should assume a neutral stance that's easily acceptable to the client and not just at a cognitive and emotional level but also at a physical level.

Support the initial exploration and comfort with the bodily sensations

Since trauma survivors tend to view their body as the enemy, the therapist should help them make friends with the body again by assisting them to experience positive sensations.

Pendulation

This technique encourages coming into contact with an intrinsic rhythm in the body that keeps alternating between states of expansion and relative contraction. Those facing traumatic experiences are more likely to react with fear to the contractions they might be experiencing and stop them.

The somatic approach aims to help the client experience the rhythm so that they can learn through their body that the contraction is followed by an expansion. Such awareness provides the client with a tool that can help them feel relaxed.

Restore the active defensive responses

Human bodies tend to instinctively react to danger by trying to protect us. When traumatic experiences occur, the protective responses get thwarted, which causes the nervous system to get overwhelmed and, in turn, collapse. The completion of such protective reflexes helps in enabling the normalization of the traumatized body.

Titration

When working with traumatic experiences, you should get to work with one feeling or sensation at a time to avoid getting the nervous system overwhelmed. Since the client, the nervous system may not distinguish between the original traumatic experience and the feeling of being overwhelmed by re-experiencing the trauma again.

Uncoupling fear from immobility

The immobility response gets typically engaged when the fight-flight response fails to resolve the situation. The body collapses and becomes frozen, which causes the sensations perpetuated by fear to keep continuing.

This process helps the client experience the physical sensations associated with immobility when fear is absent, which causes the paralysis to dissolve.

Encourage energy discharge

The discharge of energy accumulated during the traumatic experience occurs through various reactions such as trembling, shaking, vibrating, or changes in breathing and temperature. This experience usually takes place in cycles and allows for hyper-arousal states to be brought right to equilibrium.

Restore balance and equilibrium through self-regulation

The discharge of energy in cycles helps with resetting the nervous system. Clients are then more likely to be calmer as they experience a sense of hope, goodness. At the same time, they feel more empowered to regulate themselves.

Reorient to here and now

The client's ability to re-engage with their environment gets to increase as their nervous system regulates. The therapist should encourage this orientation to the environment so that the client can get a sense of coming alive to what the outside world is like.

When engaging in somatic psychotherapy, the consent and also involvement of the client are very critical. You can begin by asking a client questions such as "Would you like to try out some experiment" "How about we try this exercise." Asking such questions is not just an expression of respect but also helps place the client into an experimental frame of mind and one that can be adjusted and improved upon for success.

Somatic psychotherapy entails engagement in experiments aimed at helping the client take time and find out for themselves what really works and what doesn't.

The therapist should be willing to explain what the practice of exercise is like to make them feel safe as they access the practice. The therapist should also be open to any suggestion made by the client in regards to the exercise. The majority of somatic techniques are typically aimed at increasing the client's self-awareness level as they get invited to discover what they can do differently for the traumatic conditions to change. Lasting and sustainable change or recovery usually occurs when the client reaches a state where they can discover for themselves what they need to do to realize the desired change.

To initiate a process with a client, a therapist can do the following;

Suggest the exercise to the client;

Get their consent to try something new;

Follow the process through by asking some questions;

Summarize the outcome to be realized.

As you incorporate somatic techniques, you can ask questions such as;

Would you like to try out this exercise?

How about if we try this other one?

Let's find out if we can help you try this out with this next exercise;

Are you ready to try out the following experiences?

As a therapist, when working with the body, you are working with how the mind perceives the body. So you should keep in mind the fact that the mind and the body are actually connected.

You should therefore be aware of the following principles about the body:

The human body tends to respond to a traumatic external experience with blockage, constriction, imbalance, and muscle tension. The body also tends to be drawn to unhealthy habits when physiologically and emotionally stressed, threatened, or misused.

The body tends to remember feelings, memories, and sensations implicitly when touched, triggered, vulnerable or emotional. It's also important to note that the body changes at all times; it's pretty flexible and moldable.

The body's experience is transient and therefore doesn't last, so even the traumatic pain can subside.

The body is capable of experiencing healing at any time. When the body is treated with kindness, curiosity, and patience, it yields wisdom on what it needs.

The body is also the most essential place where healing and transformation can take place.

Tools and Techniques

For successful delivery of somatic interventions, the therapist should have a clear understanding of how to assess for body cues and symptoms related to the traumatic experience. For example, you might hear a client claiming to be having severe shoulder pain due to sleeping in a bad posture, then brush it aside as the ideal truth. The therapist can instead respond by saying, "Let's pay attention to the shoulder right away to see what you can feel or sense in the process. It can bring forth some increased and meaningful level of body awareness.

Learning of a client's individual expression is such an important factor in regards to somatic psychotherapy. Pay attention to how the client moves, how they talk about the body, and how they respond whenever increased emotional material surfaces. The goal is to understand what the client is saying concerning how they make their bodies' expression. When you keep hearing a client consistently mentioning the hurting body parts, it could indicate something that requires more attention. Learning and carefully observing nonverbal language is quite vital and matters a lot.

Here are some of the guidelines to follow when working with the body.

When working with the client, the therapist should inform them when they intend to include the body-oriented interventions. Avoid surprising the client with new techniques but instead, explain the method you are having so that they are in the picture.

As a therapist, you should always ask for permission to explain the exercises and interventions you are doing. Consider providing the client with a range of options that they can choose from.

Safety is of great importance, and the therapist should find out what the client needs if they are to feel safe. For example, you can help the client identify the body's part where they feel solid and sound. Then have the client guided on how they can periodically connect with the specific place.

Resource for strength and wellness by identifying somatic places within the body, imagery, or therapy room where the client can associate with wellness and strength.

Track the client on how they are doing and distinguish if there is any disassociation or feeling overwhelmed. If you identify something, then take time and slow down, resource, or even stop. You should still continue with verbal contact, but if the client feels uncomfortable with the bodywork, you can stop then provide some alternatives. Never insist on providing interventions that the client is not interested in.

Track the client for signs of physical safety such as self-harm threads, suicidal ideation, and follow the professional, ethical guidelines as you provide therapy.

Consider being trustworthy. Ensure that you work within the ethical codes, honor the set boundaries, and avoid coming up with any surprise to the client.

Phrases that can help facilitate body trust:

How are you experiencing these feelings?

Where are you sensing?

How do you recognize these experiences right now?

Are you feeling....what do you sense?

How does the body experience of tension appear to you at this moment?

What is it that you need to stay with this feeling?

What are you curious now about?

One of the vital aspects of somatic psychotherapy is to prepare the mind and the body for the work that's ahead. The therapist should follow the techniques to understand the power of the methods and how they can be applied to the client. Evaluate yourself as a therapist by clarifying how you feel, the sensations in your body at the moment, and your balance. Knowing how you feel before you start working with your client will give you a measure and that you actually know what you need to do to stay balanced.

It is a crucial self-assessment that will help you understand what makes you experience burnout and that which rejuvenates you. Even as a therapist, you should consider making awareness as a practice to get to know how you feel in your body, mind, and heart as part of the practice to becoming a

486

somatically-oriented therapist. You should consider cultivating a body-questioning vocabulary as part of your somatic psychotherapy work.

Some of the tools and exercises to use for the therapeutic interventions are:

Taking a snapshot of the body

This exercise aims to help the therapist establish how they are feeling in the present moment. They should be able to take a quick inventory of how they are to establish that somatic baseline can help you compare how you are while working with clients.

A body snapshot should be a moment of awareness that is inwardly directed and focuses on the moment. Knowing what goes within is critical as it helps the therapist be aware of when they are off balance and how they can get their balance back. They will be more aware of getting overwhelmed, triggered, or when they are getting flooded emotionally with such knowledge.

Therapists can choose to take the inner snapshot in between therapy sessions to help them stay tuned into themselves.

Body awareness for therapy readiness

This is a technique that helps with grounding the therapist as they get ready for a therapy session. It allows the therapist to return to their inner balance when feeling thrown off balance after a session. The goal is to help the therapist attain that inner balance and alignment to access strength and balance. You can do that by taking some five or seven minutes in quietness. Engage in this exercise at the beginning of the day as you prepare to start the sessions.

You can sit on the floor as you assume an outer posture by sitting upright and having the shoulders aligned with the hips. Ensure that the head is also in alignment with the chin, not protruding. Ensure that you align your posture so that you feel upright.

You can then evoke an image that ignites that relaxed quality. Consider practicing this body awareness for therapy readiness after every session so that it becomes a healthy habit.

Grounding through the body

When you learn how to ground your body as a therapist, you can overcome any challenge that the client raises during therapy sessions. Grounding through the body is such a vital and primary tool and should be often used to become a habit. As a therapist, you can arrive in the body with your awareness regardless of how you feel, whether activated, disconnected, tired, or triggered. Learning how to have yourself grounded as a therapist is a health and wellness practice that will help you sustain your work.

Grounding through the body makes it possible for you to engage in that regular self-check that helps you understand how you are doing. The goal of grounding is so that you can reconnect with the joy that comes from engaging in your work, having a calm mind and heart despite the chaos that you might experience during the sessions. You can ground yourself through the body by sitting, standing, lying down, or modifying the body posture to feel suitable for you.

Shaking it off

Shaking is that natural body process that restores the body to that natural state after experiencing some shocking or frightening experience. This body response can be used consciously to help with restoring body awareness and equilibrium. Shaking helps with restoring the body to its inherent self-restoring capability. It is a tool that teaches one how to safely release tension or anxious feelings that exist within the body.

The exercise enables one to interrupt that mental chatter that might be going on to refocus the body. Through shaking, the body regains awareness and can be applied to a client, especially when they report feeling upset, ungrounded, or shaky.

If, as a client, you feel ungrounded after helping in facilitating a client's process, then you can consider the exercise. The exercise can take about 5 minutes, with the focus being relaxation and grounding.

Calling internal support team

This is an exercise that helps a therapist to get ready for work. It entails visualization that centers both the mind and body and also reminds the therapist of the resources that they already have available in their life. When one is connected to the internal resources, they become more present and available for the client. This exercise is ideal when you require some extra grounding for the sessions you anticipate to be challenging.

You can practice visualizing the exercise anytime you feel stuck and unaware of the following intervention to make. You can do the exercise by sitting comfortably in a quiet place then closing your eyes to establish that centering breath to the body. You can then allow yourself to calm down as you reflect. Visualize yourself as having supportive people around you that are more like a physical team sitting right around you. You can then notice what happens to your body posture as the team sends strength to you.

Self-Resourcing

As a therapist, you will have challenging sessions. There are times when you will feel exhausted and in need of quick rejuvenation before you commit to seeing more clients. The fastest way of self-resourcing is by connecting with the ground and the movement through your body. All you have to do is take about fifteen minutes, then slow down as you synchronize your movement with your breath. Begin by finding a comfortable spot on the floor, then take time to feel the floor that's beneath you as you let your weight drop on the floor.

Exhale as you let out any tension you might be feeling. You can then begin moving the body in a twist while leaving the lower body where it's located and only rotating the upper part of the body and your arms.

Repeat the motion several times and rest on the side once you are through with the exercise.

Somatic inventory on signs of burnout

Burnout or feelings of fatigue is a common occurrence when working closely with stress and trauma-related clients. This exercise will help you to evaluate your burnout level from the inside out. Burnout is usually a condition where you get both physically and emotionally drained as a therapist due to the therapy process you perform. You can identify the symptoms by paying attention to how your body responds.

You can undertake the exercise by tuning in to your level of somatic level and burnout distress. Some of the symptoms of burnout include:

Excessive blaming and feeling of being resentful;

Isolation from others;

The feeling of being easily overwhelmed;

Being stuck in emotions that you can't express;

Feelings of irritability and having a tendency of aggressive outbursts;

Misunderstandings and frequent troubles with others;

Compulsive behaviors;

Flashbacks of client's traumatic stories and nightmares.

Chapter 6: The Procedural Steps in Trauma Treatment

As a comprehensive approach, all somatic and EMDR therapy procedures and protocols should be geared towards contributing to the positive treatment effects through an interaction with the client to enhance containment and processing of information. Every treatment effect entails interaction with the client, the therapist,t and the method being used. Therapists should have a clear understanding of how to appropriately prepare the clients as they also stay attuned to their specific individual needs while still keeping the information processing system activated so that treatment and learning can occur.

Therapists should begin by taking a comprehensive history to identify the appropriate targets for developmental and processing deficits that might have to be addressed. Various studies have proven that the early traumatic experiences of all types have very similar long-lasting effects that are negative. For example, suppose the mind can scan back to childhood days and bring up some unfortunate incident. In that case, many people will realize that they still feel the flush of some negative emotion when such memories are brought up. You May realize that your body even flinches when such thoughts come up.

As per the adaptive information processing model used in guiding EMDR therapy practice, it would mean that the traumatic experience was insufficiently processed and that the automatically arising emotions could be coloring one's actions and perceptions inappropriately and in a way that's similar to the present circumstances. You may realize that such a person tends to react negatively to new learning, groups, authority, or whatever aspects in that memory.

Those are actually not conditioned responses but are responses that are inherent within the stored memory. When a traumatic event has been processed sufficiently, one can remember it. Still, they don't experience the old sensations or emotions in the present moment.

We should be informed by our memories and not be controlled by them. For therapists, a clear distinction between dysfunctionally stored events and the adaptively processed events is that the required learning has taken place in an adaptively processed event. It's already stored with the appropriate emotions that can help with guiding the individual in the future.

The dysfunctionally stored event still has some of the present thoughts and sensory perceptions when the event took place.

When the childhood perspective of traumatic memories is locked within the mind and body, it causes the person to perceive the present from a defective vantage point, making them feel without control or safety. Therapists should be able to observe such in their practices. As much as clients know that they shouldn't be feeling powerless, hopeless, and unlovable, they still do.

When speaking of their childhood experiences, they can slip into using the same intonation. Therefore, the therapist should identify the events that have been stored dysfunctionally by the client, those that are coloring and stunting the present perception of the client, and then assist them accordingly.

Somatic psychotherapy and EMDR therapy facilitate learning on multidimensional emotional, physiological, and cognitive levels. The processing of traumatic events that are dysfunctionally stored enables clients to become free from such feelings. For most clients, simply processing the childhood experiences releases appropriate emotional and cognitive connections. Adaptive behaviors can emerge spontaneously alongside positive self-concepts and insights. For clients who might have been poorly neglected or abused in their childhood, a therapist needs to take time in determining the developmental windows that might have closed before the development of essential infrastructures was in place.

The therapist should take time and find out about the following to ascertain the extent of neglect or abuse:

1.   *Did the child learn anything about object constancy, or will it have to be taught during therapy?*

2.   *What will the therapist need to model for the client?*

492

3. What experiences will have to be engendered for healthy relationship to emerge?

Once the therapist has established such positive interactions within the therapeutic relationship, they should be stored in memory. They can then be enhanced through the therapy process. Therapists should be careful and view clients as very complex people that function at all levels of thinking, feeling, sensing, acting, and believing.

Example 1

As a therapist, you can test your psychotherapy skills by working with those struggling with traumatic memories. As a therapist, you should consider the following when engaging with a traumatized client.

Ensure that you don't re-traumatize the clients. Therapists can do such when they keep prodding for too many details or when they come out as someone interrogating the client.

Consider that getting traumatic history in chronological order might be impractical or unsafe due to how the memories are stored. Taking time to determine the presenting issues and the related themes are of great importance.

Remember to as open-ended questions, questions that start with words such as "what" and "how" as they allow the client as much information as possible with very little detail.

Avoid being judgmental. It doesn't mean that you have to endorse any unhealthy behavior; however, it does mean that you should respect the client's dignity at all times.

Be genuine and work towards building rapport from the first encounter. When engaging in the therapy sessions, let the clients know that they can opt-out of answering the questions.

Have closure strategies in place. You can allow for about 10 minutes to close down, then consider teaching some brief coping skills towards the end of the session.

493

Remember that assessment should be an ongoing process and not just for getting the client's history.

Procedures and Checklists

History Taking

Begin by asking the client some general information about themselves. The session should take about 5 minutes and should allow for some rapport building. Here are some of the questions to ask:

What are some of your assets, strengths, and resources? You can also ask an alternative question such as "What are some of the things you have been going through both internally and externally?

What do you want to work on during these sessions? General themes and memories can be worked on.

What result do you expect to have out of this session? Get the expected goals and outcomes.

Target selection

It might not be possible for the client to give detailed chronological history. It can be a challenge if one has not processed the memories or may not feel ready to share the details. Instead, you can ask if there are themes that the client can identify with the issues that the client is presenting.

Theme: Negative Cognition

First float back memory

Worst float back memory

Most recent float back memory

As a therapist, you can then present a list of negative cognitions for the target selection then let the client select the negative beliefs that they still hold in the present.

CBT + DBT + ACT

If the client checks over three negative thoughts, you can ask them to go over the list again and rank the beliefs based on most charged or less charged ones.

Step 1:

Once they have identified the negative beliefs, ask them some three float back questions, for example;

Looking back at your life journey, when was the first time you thought, "I am not good enough. I can't.

.   Looking back over your life journey, when is the worst time you believed………………..

Step 2:

In this resourcing phase, you should list existing adaptive coping skills and the resources that the client can use to address both internal and external issues.

Review the resources/skills and how they can be used, then let the client try them if they can help.

For resourcing and stabilization, develop coping skills and exercises that the client can practice in every session. You can also come up with coping skills and exercises that will work after the session.

Step 3:

Target memory or Incident

Let the client identify the image or worst part by asking.

Looking back on the event now, what image represents the worst part? If in case there is no image available or that which exists doesn't carry much charge. You can guide the client to think about the target or use another sensory channel with more control, like sound.

1.   To identify negative cognition, you can ask the client this question. "When you bring the image or that worst part now, what is that negative belief about you that seems to go with it?

2.   For positive cognition, you can ask the client, "When you bring the image or the worst part of the event, what would you like to believe about yourself at the moment?

3.   For the validity of cognition, you can ask the client, "As you look back on the image or the worst part now, how accurate the positive belief is right now on a scale of 1 – 7 with 1 being false and 7 being true?"

4.   For subjective units of disturbance, ask the client, "What is your level of disturbance as you bring up the image or worst part of the event, the negative emotions and beliefs together on a scale of 0 – 10 with 0 being no disturbance and 10 being the worst you can imagine?"

5.   Location of body sensation, "What are you noticing within your body now as you bring up the image or worst part of the event with the negative emotions and negative belief together?"

Step 4:

Encourage the client to bring up the body sensations together with the negative belief of and the image or worst part of the event memory. Encourage the client to notice all that happens as the stimulation begins. You can check for tones, eye movements, and tactile stimulation. Try to stay out of the way as much as possible. After each set, you can invite the client to take a breath and also ask questions such as "What are you getting? What are you noticing at this moment? The question is quite broad, and that invites free association.

When the client reports what they are noticing, you can move on to the following stimulation. Encourage that by using statements such as "Just notice" that or "Go with that." If the client brings up an image, ask for a SUDs rating so that you can check on their progress as the responses become more adaptive. You can use statements such as "When you return to the event image or the worst part of where we began, what is the level of distress that you feel now with 0 being no disturbance and 10 being the worst you can imagine."

496

Step 5:

This is like the installation phase, where you get to check for positive cognition. "When you bring up the image, does that original positive belief of "I'm good enough" fit, or is there another positive belief that fits better now?"

Check VoC of the positive cognition that you have arrived upon, then ask, "What is your feeling of how true that positive belief is right at the moment as you look back at the image with 1 being completely false and 7 is completely true." You can then keep going on with that until VoC is 7 or as close as is reasonable. You can then ask the client to place that positive belief together with the original image.

Step 6:

Now that the client has installed the positive belief, you can ask, "What are you noticing as you scan your body? If there are some residual disturbances, let the client see them as you continue with the fast sets until the identified residue is neutralized. When the client's body becomes clear/adaptive, you can ask the client to "Hold that body scan together with the original target and the positive belief.

Step 7:

This is the closure phase, and in case you realize that the session is not complete, then it means that you might have jumped from step 4 or step 5 to step 7, and that's still permissible. During the closure, you can use the resources built and strengthened in step 2 to reduce any form of residual distress as you ensure a safe departure. You can also engage the client in general debriefing about the session and also be mindful of addressing any concerns that the client might have. Remember that processing may still continue after the session ends, so you should review with the client a plan for safety, stabilization, and even contact support if the need arises.

List of Negative and Positive Cognitions

Responsibility:

I should have known better

497

I should have done something

I did something wrong

I am to blame

I cannot be trusted

My best is not good enough

I did the best I could

I did the best I could with what I had

I do my best

I am blameless

I am not at fault

I can be trusted

Safety:

I cannot trust myself

I cannot trust anyone

I cannot show my emotions

I am in danger

I am not safe   Safety:

I can trust myself

I can choose who to trust

I can show my emotions

I am safe now

I can create my sense of safety

Choice:

I am not in control

I have to be perfect/please everyone

I am weak

I am trapped

I have no options   Choice:

I am in control

I have power now

I can't help myself

I have a way out

I have options

Power:

I cannot get what I need

I cannot stand it

I cannot succeed

I cannot let it out

I am powerless/helpless Power:

I can get what I want

I can handle it

I can succeed

I can stand up for myself

I am powerful

499

Value:

I am not good enough

I am worthless/inadequate

I am insignificant/I'm not important

I deserve only bad things

I am stupid

I do not belong

I am alone

I am good enough

I am a good person

I am whole

I am restored

I am special

I deserve to live

I am special

Conclusion

Traumatic experiences can be quite devastating and can have such a massive impact on one's overall health and wellbeing if not well processed. Somatic Psychotherapy and EMDR therapy is a book that has shared in detail valuable information that therapists can use for treating clients that are faced with traumatic experiences. The valuable information shared in this book helps promote trauma awareness and understanding and provides helpful tools and techniques that can be used to address diverse cases of trauma.

It enables therapists to view trauma in the context of the client's environment and other related factors. Once the recovery from trauma has been identified as the primary goal, therapists can provide the necessary support as they create collaborative relationships with the clients, minimizing the risk of re-traumatization. As shared earlier in this book, therapists should understand somatic psychotherapy and EMDR therapy to provide much-needed help to the clients.

If any part of this book is not well understood, then I would like to encourage you to take your time and reread the book for better understanding.

Thank you for purchasing the book and make the best use of the information learned from it.

SOMATIC

PSYCHOTHERAPY

Introduction

Many people accept that as you age, your body becomes stiffer, and you will be less able to do the tasks you currently take for granted. However, there is a study that suggests this is not the case. Somatics is the study of movement; it is believed that the modern, Western way of life contributes to many posture and stiffness issues. These can be improved by altering how you perceive your body and completing some essential exercises as you move around.

Somatics was touched upon as early as the beginning of the twentieth century by the philosophers John Dewey and Rudolf Steiner; they both advocated experiential learning advantages. However, it was the work and study of Moshe Feldenkrais in the 1970s which was to lead to a wider knowledge and understanding of this field of research. These studies came to the Chairman of Philosophy's attention at the University of Florida, Thomas Hanna. Moshe's research and theories fitted in with Hannah's work; his introduction to Moshe Feldenkrais shaped his life and reinforced his belief that that attitude towards your body can be changed to improve posture and movement no matter how old you are.

Thomas Hanna had a good understanding of biofeedback rules; he added this understanding to what he had already discovered and what he learned from Moshe. For several years in the early 1970s, Hanna studied Moshe's techniques and principles; by 1975, he had managed to get the first Feldenkrais training program established in America. At this stage, he was the Director of the Humanistic Psychology Institute; during the same year, he and Eleanor Hanna founded the Novato Institute for Somatic Research. It was thanks to his studies and teachings that people started to become aware of what somatics was.

He continued to study Moshe Feldenkrais's theories and added his own knowledge and research t them. It became increasingly apparent that many people developed the same postural difficulties, regardless of age or vocation. Groups of people had the same characteristics, although this was far more pronounced in Western civilization than elsewhere.

This naturally led to the development of various exercises that helped anyone improve their mobility and flexibility. As this theory evolved, these exercises would become known as Hanna Somatic Education.

Hanna has been described as a philosopher, a theologian, a professional writer and, even a revolutionary thinker. His studies led him to discover that there were far more people with movement issues and chronic pain in the Western world than in the less industrialized parts of the world.

It was this belief that drove Hanna to find a new way of approaching aging, to return mobility and flexibility to those who followed his teachings. He spent several years studying the neurophysiology of development and control before developing what is now known as Clinical Somatic Education.

Clinical Somatic Education is designed as a teaching method; it involves a student learning to move in slow, precise ways. The movements must be a product of your conscious, not your subconscious. With the instructor's aid, you will quickly discover a vastly improved range of mobility, flexibility, and movement. Most people can master the basic techniques within twelve sessions; providing you continue to practice what you have learned, you should enjoy a far greater range of movement than what you thought was possible. The principles behind this are so easy to realize that it is possible to learn and understand the movements without a professional teacher.

Sadly Thomas Hanna died in a car accident two-thirds of the way through his first somatics teaching course. Thanks to Eleanor Hanna's dedication, his students, and the skill in which he organized his work and teachings, clinical somatic education has become available to anyone who wishes to improve their mobility and flexibility.

The guiding principle behind somatics is based on the understanding that a person is a whole individual; you are not a separate mind, body, and soul. You are one entity capable of growing, learning, and evolving; as such, anything is possible, and healing is simply an extension of this; you can heal yourself.

Somatics is based on a sound understanding of the human body and the neurological pathways that operate inside you. Every function you perform is controlled by your brain.

504

Even sitting still, your body will constantly be sending messages to your brain via your nerves. This information is processed by the brain and returned to your muscles and tendons via the same nervous network.

Most movements you make are termed 'voluntary'; this is because you are thinking about them, even if you are barely aware. Making yourself a drink is a conscious, voluntary decision. However, suppose you repeat the same process too often. In that case, your brain will see a habit developing and stoop processing the information. It will accept that you sit in a certain way or walk a certain way. It can even recognize a leg's weakness in plaster and accept that you will always walk more gently on the leg. This process is known as habituation, and it is an essential part of your life.

It allows your brain to handle all the mundane tasks without using any real effort, saving your brainpower for the more important things in life. However, it is also this habitation that can become an issue. If you strain a muscle and continue to use it while healing, you are likely to develop a new way of moving; this will compensate for any weakness or loss of movement while the part is recovering.

However, once it has healed, your brain will not automatically return to its previous, subconscious way of moving; it will continue to operate in a new way. This will limit your movement unnecessarily. For example, if you break your leg and it is in plaster, you will be unable to bend it for several weeks. Your body will remember this and, even when the cast has been removed, it will continue to resist bending it. To gain active and full use of your leg again, you will need to tell it to start bending again. This is one of the techniques which can be taught by clinical somatic education.

In effect, habituation is the body's way of coping after trauma; however, this leads to tight muscles, tight because habituation has taken effect. It will quickly reach the point where your muscles are tight and will cause pain if you move a certain way. At first, you put up with this discomfort; ultimately, you stop moving that way to prevent the pain from occurring.

At that point, your movement, flexibility, and probably posture have all been compromised; your body will become stiffer and less mobile, just as you expected it to! It is a self-fulfilling prophecy!

Chapter 1: General Uses of Somatics

Understanding that your muscle is tight and causes pain because of an old injury is only part of the story. You then need to figure out a way of getting your muscle to relax. It is possible to use the services of a masseuse or a chiropractor; they are highly likely to give you some relief from the pain of your muscle tightness. However, they are also likely to last for a limited time only. The main reason for this is habituation; your brain will still tell your muscle to contract, and it will do so as soon as possible. Of course, you can repeat the massage or other treatment you undertook every three or four days. However, this is a time-consuming and expensive way to deal with the issue. It is also only successful as long as you keep up the treatment.

The inability to voluntarily contract or relax a muscle is known as Sensory Motor Amnesia (SMA): learning to regain voluntary control will stop your brain from sending a message to your muscles telling them to contract. This is the main use of somatics, preventing pain by relearning how to voluntarily control your muscles. The emphasis is on learning how to feel everything you sense; you can then change how you move and control your own body.

There are several key benefits from practicing somatics:

Flexibility

Learning somatic techniques is essential to improve the range of flexibility, movement, and posture. It can also help manage pain because it will deal with stiff muscles and body parts and help you control the nerves and the brain's response to various stimuli.

Flexibility is an essential but relative part of everyone's life. A professional athlete will probably need to be exceptionally flexible, especially if they are a gymnast or similar. Golfers may require an improved range of flexibility in their shoulders. At the same time, people practicing karate will need good flexibility in their hips and legs. Working in an office environment and living a relatively sedentary life will only need excellent general flexibility.

Of course, the more flexible you are, the better you will be able to adapt to any situation, and the less likely you will be to suffer from injuries or any stiffening as you age.

506

Being flexible is also the basic requirement if you are looking to correct your posture or improve your movement range. This is because if you are flexible, your muscles will be loose enough and relaxed enough to learn new ways of doing things.

If this is not the case, then you will be unable to effectively move individual body parts without the risk of injury. Stretching correctly is an essential part of keeping your body ready for anything.

Posture

Somatics is beneficial for posture in several ways. The most obvious benefit is that, by learning to control your own muscles, you can stop any strain being placed on your spine by tight muscles and tendons. Stresses and strains on your spine can lead to poor posture. In turn, this will increase the likelihood of vertebral degeneration, where the discs supporting the spine are no longer able to do so.

Problems with your spine can also cause constrictions to blood flow or even nerves, both of which can cause severe issues in other parts of your body.

Your spine is one of your body's most important parts; the central nervous system passes through and is protected by it. At the same time, it keeps your body upright and capable of a variety of tasks. Looking after it is essential to your long-term health and enjoyment of life.

Movement

Fluid movement, in any direction necessary, results from good posture and a good range of flexibility. Movement is essential to life; the more you move, the better the heart responds and the easier it will find it to pump blood around your body. A good range of movement will ensure a good blood flow to all vital organs and a plentiful supply of oxygen.

Suppose you have issues with your range of movements. In that case, you are likely to have reduced function and be less willing to push your body past any movement or pain issue. A reduction in movement will result in you doing less out of fear of making an injury or movement issue worse. Unfortunately, this is the exact behavior that worsens the movement issue and ultimately results in very little mobility.

To ensure your ability to move stays as good as possible, you should practice somatics for as little as five minutes per day. You will be amazed at the benefits which can be gained from such a short brain retraining period!

Pain Management

Pain is often the result of trauma; an accident can damage muscles and tendons in your body, no matter how big or small. After the accident has happened, you will likely discover pain in one of your muscles or tendons. The muscle is contracting to deal with the injury; it may have been damaged itself, or it may be reacting to protect another part of your body.

Many people will treat muscle injuries with hot and cold compresses, attempting to decrease the blood flow and minimize swelling while sending fresh, oxygenated blood to the muscles. The risk is that the muscle will continue to contract after treatment and cause pain. This is often treated by taking painkillers and not dealing with the actual issue; the result is that the injury is masked, your muscle remains contracted, and your brain learns to deal with the problem by operating differently. Unfortunately, this is avoidance instead of recovery. In the long term, the injury is likely to return to haunt you! Clinical somatic education can help you to learn how to control the muscle while ensuring it relaxes and stretches so that your body can return to a more mobile, active state.

By taking voluntary control of your muscles, you will also be able to alleviate any pain associated with your muscle's injury and repetitive use while contracted.

Although the primary uses of somatics are to improve flexibility, posture, movement and to assist with pain management, it is also an excellent technique to target a wide range of ailments with the human body:

Sciatica

The sciatic nerve can become trapped, pinched, or occasionally damaged. This will result in shooting pain down your leg, usually starting from your hip and extending as far as either your knee or even your toes. In extreme cases, this can cause a loss of feeling in your leg. The pain can cause a rapid reduction in movement or a dependency on painkillers.

Fortunately, somatics can help with these issues by teaching you to stand correctly and control your back muscle. It is usually this which is contracted and putting pressure on the sciatic nerve. By learning to take voluntary control of the muscle, you can ensure it is relaxed. The pressure is removed from your sciatic nerve. Movement and pain release can be provided very quickly!

Hips, Knees & Leg Muscles

This is a common area of concern for those who spend their day sitting at an office desk. It can also be a matter of concern for those who run or perform similar exercises regularly.

The issue will usually arrive through either injury or incorrect posture, leading to habituation of your muscles. These tightened muscles will imbalance your muscles as your joints tighten due to your muscles' pressure being placed on them. To correct this issue and relieve any pain and mobility issues, you can learn somatic techniques to relax your muscles and stand correctly. This will alleviate the pressure in your hips, knees, and even your leg muscles.

Plantar Fasciitis

This is the pain and inflammation which many people get in their feet. In fact, this is caused by the tightening of your muscles in your legs and your feet. These may be a result of trauma, bad posture, or just years of bad habits. Somatics will teach you how to stand and even to move, using conscious thought, which will, ultimately, replace your subconscious actions with a new set of actions. The new ones will be far more beneficial to your health, posture, and muscles.

TMJ Pain

TMJ pain occurs in the face and is usually linked with stress. Many people react to stress by grinding their teeth. Alternatively, you may simply clench them. It is merely a way of dealing with an issue and getting the job done within the confines of the timeframe available. Sadly, it is an increasing issue as the modern, technologically advanced world places more demands on everyone.

The cause of this pain is a tightening of the muscles in your face and jaw. To relieve this pain for the long term, you will need to learn how to relax your facial muscles and, preferably, stop clenching your jaw or grinding your teeth in the future!

In fact, it is possible that any muscle in your body could become contracted and remain that way. This is because every muscle in your body is used to some extent and has the potential to be either injured or misused for an extended period. Once it has learned to function incorrectly, it will continue to do so until you train it to do otherwise.

Training your muscle is not difficult; it simply requires you to perform a series of exercises daily, allowing to focus on your muscles and control them better. Every exercise must be performed slowly; this is the only way for your brain to learn a new method of doing something instead of continuing with the old way.

Somatics should also help you focus more on your own body, how it operates, and how you can improve the way it moves and deals with exercise and trauma.

As well as the issues listed above, somatics can help deal with the following conditions:

• *Carpal Tunnel Syndrome*

• *Tendonitis*

• *Bursitis*

• *Thoracic Outlet Syndrome*

• *Scoliosis*

• *Chronic headaches*

• *Myofascial Pain*

Treatment sessions are usually short, and an entire course of treatment is usually over within between ten and twelve sessions. However, unlike some alternatives, it is a highly effective, long-term strategy.

Chapter 2: Exercises

Somatics can be learned by anyone and can be used by anyone. Obviously, the exact exercises which will benefit you will depend upon the injuries and issues you have.

Before you start these activities, it is essential to understand the concept of pandiculation. It is this concept and way of exercising that is fundamental to somatics.

Instead of just stretching, you are doing three things in one exercise:

• The targeted muscle group is already contracted or tight. Your brain has become used to it being this way and accepts it. The first stage of this process is to tighten the muscle more; this will remind your brain that the muscle can have different levels of contraction.

• Next, you will need to lengthen the muscle or muscles as much as possible. The amount you can extend them will rapidly increase. The opposite side of this step is releasing the muscle. Again, this is a way of reminding the brain of every muscle's full range of movement.

• Finally, you need to relax completely; the brain will associate complete relaxation with the state that the muscle should be in and start to refocus its efforts on using the muscle correctly.

These three stages make a somatic exercise so effective; you will go through the complete range of physical movements and reset your brain to accept the possibilities. One of the most significant parts of starting somatic exercises is that you will feel a difference straight away. You'll develop a much better range of movement within a few weeks than you had thought possible.

There is an abundance of options available, but the following exercises can be beneficial to almost anyone; it is essential to remember that these exercises are designed to be completed slowly:

Body Awareness

This exercise should help you become more aware of your body, which points are tight and need to be worked on. Start by lying on your back and bend your knees so that your feet are flat on the floor.

Next, you need to spread your arms out as far as you can, keeping them on the mat. You should have your right hand with its palm downwards, and the left with its palm upwards.

Slowly roll your arms, moving both simultaneously, roll them in opposite directions three times. You can extend this movement by putting your knees towards the side, which currently has the palm facing down, and your head towards the other side. This exercise should be completed between five and ten times; keep the pace slow and focus on how your coordination changes.

Lower Back

Lower back pain affects the majority of people at some point in their lives. In fact, many people live with their back pain for many years as they believe it is simply the way things are. Fortunately, it does not need to be the case forever! The following exercise can loosen and relax your back muscles and provide relief from pain and improve your posture.

Lie flat on your back with your legs extended out in front of you. Then, with your eyes shut, twist your right leg outwards; your lower back should arch. Hold this for a few seconds before turning inwards; your lower back should flatten to the floor. You should then repeat this with the other leg. You will need to focus on how this exercise affects your lower back. Once you have done each leg several times, you will need to do both legs at the same time outwards and then inwards. Repeat the exercise five times, keeping your focus on what your lower back wants to do. Do not try and stop it from arching or flattening; simply pay attention to which it does.

Right and Left Back

This exercise is a natural extension to the lower back one you have just completed. Still laying on your back with your legs extended, bring them up slightly towards your body and bend them a little at the knees. Then, roll your legs together to the left, followed by a movement to the right.

You will feel the movement on the right and left sides of your back. You can obtain a more subtle feeling in your back by doing this exercise with your legs extended. You should repeat the exercise between five and ten backs, focusing on the way your back moves.

Spinal Freedom

Again, lie in your back with your knees bent and your feet flat on the floor. Start with your left leg and bend it to bring it towards your chest. Use your left hand to hold it in place. Next, put your right hand behind your head and lift your head towards your left knee. Exhale while lifting; you will feel your spine lengthening. To finish, inhale as you lower yourself back down, arching your back as you do so. Once you have repeated this exercise between three and five times, you will need to switch sides and move your right leg while your left hand holds your head.

Hamstrings

Start by sitting on the floor with your legs out in front of you. You will then need to bend your right leg so that your foot goes towards your crotch. Your thighs should extend to the side of your body, although they will probably not naturally touch the ground. Next, hold your left leg, which is still extended out in front of you. Then bring your head down towards your knee. Repeat this between three and five times before switching legs.It is also possible to stretch your hamstrings by sitting as above; instead of taking your head towards your knee, hold your extended leg and pull it towards you. Focus on keeping your back straight and your head up. This will provide a deeper stretch of the hamstrings and strengthen the lower back muscles.

Side Stretch

This exercise starts in a standing position. Your feet should be shoulder-width apart and your hands clasped behind your head so that your elbows stick out to each side. Take a breath in a while, lowering your body to one side. As the weight of your body pushes down, you will find it impossible to continue breathing in. After a few seconds, straighten and repeat between three and five times. You will then need to lower your body to the other side.

Alternatively, you can stretch your sides by standing with your legs shoulder-width apart and lift your right arm and shoulder straight up. To get them straight, your body will need to bend to the left. You should breathe in as you move your arm upwards and then breathe out as you start to bend. Your bodyweight should be lifted, and the pressure on your lungs will not be felt in the same way.

Stretching the Thighs

Start by standing up; again, your feet should be in line with your shoulders. Then lift one leg off the floor and bend it at the knee, placing your foot behind your buttocks. You will need to use your hands to hold and support your foot! Next, pull the top of your foot towards your buttocks. You will feel your thighs gently stretching.

Alternatively, you can Push your foot away from your buttocks while pushing your pelvis forward. This will increase your thigh's stretch potential and avoid any overarching, which can often happen when trying this exercise. Again, repeat between three and five times, slowly.

Neck and Shoulder

This exercise is started by lying down flat on your back, with your legs extending away from you. Lift both arms straight up towards the ceiling. Then, choose one arm and stretch it up further, as though reaching something approximately another foot higher. As you do this, your body will naturally roll slightly to one side as your shoulder, and upper body on the other side lift off the floor. Your waist should stay on the floor.

Hold the position for a few seconds before bringing your arms level again and repeating the move twice more. You will then need to switch sides and do the arm on the other side. Repeat the entire process two or three times, according to how you feel.

514

Many different exercises can be learned to assist with you your recovery from a life of pain. The above are a few ones that will get you started, but all the exercises are as simple and effective. Somatics is not designed to force movement or place any additional stress on your body. It is a method by which your body can relearn the balance and full range of movement which you were born with and are still capable of. Old age or accidents do not mean a lifetime of pain; these simple exercises will give you a new lease of life!

Chapter 3: What are somatic symptoms?

Pain

Pain is a sensation of extreme discomfort and abnormal hypersensitivity. It appears as a signal and a warning that something in our bodies is damaged. This could be caused by inflammation or trauma. Pain is the most common symptom. When pain indicates an injury or inflammation in the body and lasts until the damage is healed, it is helpful and purposeful. However, when the pain lasts even after the wound is healed and becomes chronic, lasts for weeks, months, years, it becomes troublesome and needs treatment.

Sometimes we can't find out where the damage is or with which mechanism the pain is induced, especially when there is no organ damage. There are different kinds of pain: somatic, visceral, and neuropathic.

Visceral pain comes from internal organs when they are stretched, damaged, or under inflamed. Nerves that surround these organs bring sensation to our brain. This pain is deeply aching, difficult to localize, and may increase in intensity and then abate before reappearing. It is difficult to find out where the pain is coming from. Abdominal organs can be the source of visceral pain.

Neuropathic pain appears when there is damage or inflammation of the nerve itself. It sends signals of pain associated with tenderness and numbness. There is no real damage to the surrounding tissue, just damage to the nerves. This can happen in facial neuropathy or in people with diabetes. It is difficult to treat.

Somatic pain is triggered when there is damage to the body surface, joints, tendons, blood vessels, or muscles. This is the most common type of pain. We can say that there are superficial and deep somatic pain. For example, if you cut your hand or finger, you would feel the pain on the hand's specific localization. Still, if you hit your hand on something firm, you experience deep somatic pain because your joints, muscles, and tendons hurt, and your whole hand hurts as well.

Pain in somatic symptom disorder can't be explained by any known medical condition, even though a doctor must first exclude somatic and visceral pain etiology. Pain can affect personal, professional, love, and family life.

The mechanism of pain appearance is in somatic disorder due to stress, which triggers the nervous system that stimulates adrenal glands and the sympathetic system, which induces bowel activity. It can be presented as pain or can cause muscular tension, which then hurts. Our perception of pain and how we notice and bring attention to pain may also play a role.

Suppose one has increased sensitivity to pain awareness. In that case, he/she may become intensely worried that pain can be, in fact, a sign of damage in the body. Worrying only increases the intensity of pain.

Pain in somatic symptom disorder is usually located symmetrically, and the most common places are the face and mouth. This pain may be time-related to some stressful situations in a person's life. It may prevent him/her from doing some activities. It can also affect work and personal life.

The most commonly reported pains that are medically unexplained are:

Generalized pain

Face pain

Leg pain

Back pain

Joint pain

Pain when urinating

If the pain appears in the last couple of weeks and up to three months, it is considered acute pain. Chronic pain lasts more than three months and can be present for years. It can be either constant, which is rare or amplified along with some stressful situations. Even though they are considered to come "from the mind," they are indeed real sensations. They can significantly affect a person's life. Other people may not understand it, and a person may experience stigmatized behavior from others.

A person may have some psychological issues that make him/her more sensitive to some sensations. According to other theories, there may be damage that happened before but didn't completely heal. The pain comes from it but is amplified. It is rarely possible for the pain to develop entirely from emotional factors.

Generalised pain and/or fatigue

Generalized pain is pain that spreads all over the body without a proper way to localize the source. Pain can be sharp or dull, depending on the location. It can include distant parts of the body with no connection to each other or in places close to each other. A person may complain about pain in the abdomen, one leg, and the head. This pain is usually chronic. If he/she has symptoms for months that induce trouble in their professional and personal life, stopping them from participating in various activities.

In general, all-over body pain can sign increased body temperature, chronic fatigue, or some illnesses that affect many joints and/or muscles. When these are excluded from the diagnosis, a doctor will consider fibromyalgia. Generalized pain is characteristic of fibromyalgia. It is an illness of unknown origin but includes pain all over in various parts of the body.

These locations experience pain with just the touch of a finger. It is known to have psychological disorders as a background. The pain they are experiencing is deep, sharp, or dull and can come and go. However, fibromyalgia doesn't satisfy the somatic disorder criteria because there is evidence that the nerves are abnormal in this illness. In somatic disorders, there are no anatomical damages at all. This is why when a person comes in with this complaint, they should be excluded from all of these illnesses and problems. If the diagnosis is still uncertain, the doctor will consider a different approach.

Generalized pain is most likely caused by stress and increased with anxious thoughts. It can present as pain in the legs, arms, and head simultaneously without any announcement or known pattern. It comes and goes, and it can last up to several months. A person may feel pain in various localisations: the chin, arm, leg, or lower abdomen.

These couldn't be otherwise explained by any known illnesses. A mechanism of how this happens would be known after the talk with the person.

It can be very common with young people, especially women, who find themselves in conflicts with themselves or other significant people. Also, that time may be a transient period when major goals are already achieved or on the way to be completed. Either way, a person can find himself/herself in a situation under great pressure from others and surrounded by rejection and feelings of being a failure. This can lead a person to have anxiety issues and problems with adjusting. These feelings may last for a long time and are expressing themselves through various ailments.

The pain may appear anywhere - in the head, arms, face, back, and may be associated with some bowel discomfort and pain in the pelvis (in women, this is especially in the uterus). A person has difficulty pointing out the exact location of the pain or the situation when it is magnified.

Generalized pain may be associated with known illnesses as aggravating factors. It may worsen the illness itself. It decreases a person's will and ability to participate in activities.

Generalized fatigue or weakness can appear with generalized pain. This fatigue is characteristic of persons who first complained about their symptoms when they were under 30 and have lasted for months or even years. There is confusion between chronic fatigue syndrome and fatigue caused by somatization. Chronic fatigue syndrome has clinical signs (on lymph nodes) that indicate the diagnosis, which can't be said for the latter. Somatization fatigue is present along with other somatization symptoms such as gynecological or abdominal discomfort. Fatigue itself isn't a symptom of somatization disorder. (14) Generalized or localized weakness may also be a part of conversion disorder in young people.

Face pain

Face pain appears very often in the population (12%). Face pain usually spreads in the upper, middle, or lower part of the face. There is a term that doctors refer to as atypical facial pain (persistent idiopathic facial pain). It is present in the exact prevalence in men as in women.

The pain often crosses the face's midline and is described as stabbing, throbbing, or burning. It lasts more than three months. Usually, a person would complain about numbness, pain, or tingling in one particular part of the face.

It gets worse in stressful, life-changing events. The first professional they turn to is usually a dentist. After diagnostic procedures and an exam, the right cause isn't found.

There is also a condition that is referred to as myofascial pain dysfunction syndrome. It is a pain around the teeth and in the jaws, pain in the jaw joint, and sensations in the mouth. It is very common for pain to be localized around the mouth area. Myofascial pain dysfunction syndrome is associated with pain in the jaw joints, pain while chewing and speaking, or moving chewing muscles in any way. This disorder is strongly related to depression and can appear along with other somatization symptoms. (15) A person may be very concerned about the pain because it seems so frequently during the day and almost every jaw movement.

A person may also experience trouble sleeping. The stressful component in causality is the muscle tension in people who are more sensitive to stressful events because of specific mild or severe psychological traumas previously experienced. Face and jaw pain are also related to stress and anxiety.

Back pain

Back pain is very common in our population. It can be caused by muscle injury or inflammation, spine malposition, illness of kidneys, pancreas, gallbladder, or nervous system problems. People who experience back pain have difficulties in everyday working life and find it as stressful and frustrating as the job itself (16). This is due to stress and its effect on the back and neck muscles that can't relax properly. These people often visit the doctor's office to search for a reason for back pain. They regularly have other somatic symptom disorder symptoms, like arm pain, headaches, chronic fatigue syndrome, etc. Usually, they have already been to physical medicine specialists. They have been given exercise samples to strengthen the muscles, even though that didn't help.

There are signs of depression and anxiety with some of them, but that isn't necessarily obligatory for sympathizers. Back pain in somatization is atypical. Between 10 and 20% of all people who suffer from somatization have back pain problems. Back pain is related to anxiety and depression. Neck and back stiffness are more reported in persons with post-traumatic stress syndrome and phobias of open spaces. There is a type of personality in which back pain is more common than others.

People who are well-organized, responsible, hard-working, and self-critical tend to be under great stress, even though they tend to push it to the subconscious. Some of them have some repressed memories or troubling issues from early development. The relation between them is inexplicable. Back pain is very resistant to treatment, and a lot of work needs to be put into the therapy. A person also needs to organize activity and rest since they are significant in treatment. Also, a healthcare provider will try to find out some emotional issues that might be bothering the person. They need to be resolved for treatment to work.

Back pain can vary from mild to severe. If touched or pressed, specific muscles are stiff and painful. A person may also feel numbness, tingling, or burning pain.

In somatic symptom disorders, back pain (previously referred to as tension myositis syndrome) is caused by tension and stressful situations. Tension myositis syndrome is a psychosomatic pain disorder.

The sympathetic autonomic system is activated with stressful events that induce emotional reaction and then stimulate blood vessels' muscles. As a response, it constricts, and blood supply begins to lower. This affects the back and their function's massive muscles since they don't get enough oxygen and nutrition. This leads to the accumulation of lactic acid, which is responsible for pain.

People usually complain about back or neck pain that moves from one spot to another. Pressing some areas on the back may be followed by intense pain all over the muscle. Because of the pain, people frequently change their sleep position. Thus, they become chronically tired. (17) This type of pain is similar to myofascial pain. The pain originates from the fascia (outer layer of the muscle) and muscles. Pressure on certain spots on the back triggers pain

521

in the whole area. Myofascial neck pain spreads pain to the face (temporal region) after putting pressure on the neck's back. There aren't any clinical studies that differentiate myofascial back pain from somatized back pain, and it might be that they have a mixed pathophysiology

Leg pain

Leg pain can be in one part of the leg or in the whole leg and in both legs. Also, it can appear while doing nothing, i.e., sitting or while standing or walking. Various illnesses of the internal organs can be followed by changes in the leg. Pain in the leg is mostly neurologic (diabetes, ischialgia), varicose veins, or joint pain. Pain in the leg can be in the form of cramps, deep pain, pain when walking that is sharp, dull pain, etc. In conditions that may be considered a somatic disorder, leg pain is sometimes caused by anxiety. This pain's mechanism may seem unbelievable, but negative and worrying thoughts can actually increase sensitivity in the legs. This condition isn't rare. The pain can be caused by anxiety attacks when muscles of blood vessels contract and deprive the legs of oxygen and tighten the leg muscles, which causes pain. In somatic symptom disorder, these symptoms last longer than the anxiety attack. It is hard distinguishing between the two. Pain in the leg may be disabling and last for months and years without a known cause.

Numbness, tingling, or even paralysis can appear as a symptom of conversion disorder in young people. In some cases, after an accident that's been avoided, they sometimes convert the stress and emotional shock into actual symptoms.

Joint pain

Joint pain may be associated with inflammation or injury. It may also be associated with muscle pain. When declared as a somatic symptom disorder, it is challenging to determine the main cause. It is often associated with other somatization symptoms. Knee joint pain is the most frequently reported somatic symptom that affects joints. Most of the studies actually proved that pain in the jaw joint can be affected by psychological disorders.

Unexplained menstrual symptoms

First, menstruation occurs when all the body factors are set to specific parameters, depending on the height, weight, production of hormones, percentage of fat in the body, and a regular, unimpeded psychological structure. This is all regulated by hormones in the pituitary gland, regulated by the hypothalamus in the center of the brain. As for later functioning and regular menstrual cycles, they are controlled by the pituitary gland and the hypothalamus, but they receive various stimuli, including environmental and stressful factors. It reacts when a person is under enormous stress, which impairs the production of hormones (estrogen and progestin), leading to irregular menstruation and even absence of it. Factors that can also affect menstrual disorders can be over-exercise, weight loss, and eating disorders, which all have some psychological background and induce exhaustion. Chronic stress and short-term worrying, and having anxious thoughts of one particular event/subject may have all the same effect on menstrual bleeding.

Other menstrual problems may be excessive pain during menstruation, such as dysmenorrhea and irregular bleeding between two menstruation cycles. Even pain during menstruation can be influenced by psychological issues and can be a form of expression. It develops similarly to other types of pain. Usually, a person may amplify the pain perception because of some subconscious anxious or depressive content, and menstruation becomes more painful. Painful menstruation-related to stress is linked to 75% of adolescent girls. Irregular bleedings may also be explained with somatization. This, however, happens with great pressure and stress on the person and occurs rarely. The bleeding isn't usually profuse.

Menstrual symptoms are often associated with other somatic symptoms like gastrointestinal symptoms and back and joint pain. Some sexual difficulties may be a part of the complaints. Menstrual symptoms may vary from mild to severe.

Unexplained sexual symptoms

It is more and more a subject of various discussions about how the psyche affects sex life. Usually, there could be some obvious life problems that put

523

pressure on both of the partners. There is a body complaint of any kind that brings discomfort to both of them. The key to a happy relationship is good communication between two partners, even if problems about different topics and not just within the relationship make a person more stressed and frustrated. He/she may not be aware of a large amount of stress he/she struggles with. Still, with more deep talk, he/she discovers that sexual problems have begun or are in some way linked to specific events or feelings.

Sometimes, a person is already having trouble but considers it to be just the way things are. The partner doesn't understand the situation. A lot of people bring their frustrations and insecurities into this delicate part of life. The negative background expresses itself through the inability to relax and through anhedonia, not just in sexual life but also in professional and family life. A person becomes unmotivated and unhappy, which turns the cycle around. The problems that are frequently reported are pain during intercourse and erectile dysfunction.

Pain during intercourse (dyspareunia)

Dyspareunia is pain associated with vaginal intercourse. It can appear in women as in men, but it is recently discovered that the problem exists in men. Women are frequently confronted with this problem, which then brings other problems as well. Pain during intercourse appears in between 10 and 20% of the female population. However, the reasons for this could be infections, sexual indifference, problems with lubrication, and vaginismus. Most of them, except infections, are caused by psychological factors: anxiety, worry about performance, fear of pain, etc. The severe type of dyspareunia and pain in the pelvis comprise a smaller part of those women. These women, not surprisingly, have sexual intercourse less frequently and have more interpersonal problems with their partners, which may lead to discord in marriage.

Vaginismus has already been proven to be directly linked to a woman's psyche. Vaginismus is the appearance of pain because of involuntary muscle spasms inside the vagina, which causes problems during intercourse. It appears when a woman is anxious about sex or inserting tampons or medical objects during a gynecological examination.

Pain can appear during entry or deep inside. It is unexplained or simply called dyspareunia when we exclude vaginismus as a possible diagnosis.

Most women actually don't report this problem to their gynecologists, which raises how often it actually appears in the population. Psychologists have found particular attachment and self-confidence problems with women who complained about pain during intercourse. Some inner frustrations and tension are expressing in the way of pain in the lower pelvis. (28) The reason may lie in internal or external conflicts as well as stress and tension of sexual intercourse. Somatization pain may be different from vaginismus, such as persistent Kegel's pelvic exercises. In vaginismus, women, particularly gynecologists, can feel the stiffness of the vaginal wall due to muscle spasms. Dyspareunia seems to be unfit for any other similar diagnosis and requires a psychological evaluation. Women usually say that the symptoms are present for more than 6 months.

Women are affected by this as well as their partners. They may have problems with self-image and motivation to conceive, and often they feel incapable or unfit. Continued and unsuccessful attempts and high expectations make it even worse. Sometimes, a man may, consequently, develop some sexual issues such as erectile dysfunction.

Pelvic pain is the lower abdomen's pain that is frequently noticed in women who had suffered sexual abuse. When they feel real pain, they may not necessarily consciously link it to what has happened in the past. Also, unresolved depression and anxiety problems cause the problem to stay persistent.

Unexplained headaches

Headaches are the most common severe symptom in adults. Half of the population has some kind of headache with mild to severe characteristics. Headaches are actually often left unexplained or developed from the influence of many factors combined. It is unsurprisingly the most bothering symptom. A person can't function properly at work and can't control his/her emotions. They'll have problems in general, day-to-day functions such as concentrating, driving, etc.

Headaches develop from cardiovascular, neurological, psychological, or other body problems such as dehydration or high fever. If all other organ functions are fine, we still have many possible causes. The exact mechanism of developing a migraine is unknown, even though cardiovascular factors and chemical imbalances are found to be responsible. A person may complain of headaches that happen for explainable reasons and in certain situations (after too much chocolate, cheese, caffeine, or alcohol). Others have headaches once or twice every month, with a tendency to chronicity.

Localization of pain may vary. Some complain of pain on one side, or back of the head, forehead, or in the whole head. Localization may suggest the type of headache. Psychological factors have proven to be responsible for pathogenesis.

It has been proven that when a person struggles with pain, he/she can't take their mind off the pain. When this happens, the effect of medication might not help them because of their expectations from the medications. From the early days of medical history, doctors have been practicing the placebo medication treatment with such patients, which proved to be valuable.

Nowadays, new studies suggest that we would expect the pain to go away at the exact moment as we ingest it, but thinking that way only makes the pain stronger since pain is a sensation created by the brain as an alarming sensation of damaged tissue.

Same but opposite, we may not think that the medicine will work, so we lower our expectations and stop thinking about its effect, which then leads to less pain relief. These mechanisms seem complex and not well-known for now. However, psychological and voluntary influences can modify pain or even create it.

The somatization of psychological issues is often the explanation for a headache. A particular type of personality is more likely to develop a somatization headache. These people are responsible, busy, and under great emotional stress.

Some personalities are subconsciously creating an image of something worse that would happen or fear pain itself, so they subconsciously create or enhance pain.

526

Scientists again can't accept the theory about emotional factors creating the pain, so more elements are included. For psychologists, a problem seems easier.

People struggling with headaches have no knowledge of when a headache might strike, and so they have big problems when it does. With a lack of concentration, patience, and attention to the environment, a person may have difficulties at work or at home and may injure himself/herself. Episodes of headaches usually have been present for more than 6 months.

Headaches with a psychological background are a pain in the entire head, with pressure or tension (this is why sometimes it may be called tension headache), light or sound nuisance.

Anything opposing to migraine criteria for diagnosis is better explained as somatization if associated with other symptoms. Otherwise, we can call it tension headache. Somatization disorder may help the back, arms, or legs. A stressful situation may be the onset of the headache. If the temporary situation becomes chronic stress, the headache becomes chronic too.

Somatoform headaches in children and adolescents appear in every tenth person. It usually follows the pattern of pain observed in their parents, which tells about parental influence in the pathogenesis.

Chapter 4: Be Aware

Mind what You Put into Your Body

Living mindfully means bringing yourself to a full sense of awareness about you and your body. And if you've been living the same busy lifestyle as so many others, chances are you haven't really given much thought to the types of fuel you've been living on.

This isn't going to be some sermon on how you should be living like a vegan or cutting out red meat or restricting your carbohydrate access. But the food you eat should be nourishing. Read the packaging carefully to see what vitamins and minerals each is providing you, care less about calories and more about chemicals and avoid as many as you can and put together a meal that can meet the energy demands of your lifestyle. There are several websites and smartphone apps that can help you determine what each food is providing you with. Use these to your advantage to create a diet that will nourish you, not just fill you up.

Of course, some junk foods, treats, desserts and even drinks may still find themselves lingering around your kitchen. And that's okay in moderation. This isn't about condemning particular food groups, or about judging you for not being the healthiest person on the block. Rather, this is to make you aware of the food you eat and aware of the way the food fuels your body.

Eat and Drink Slowly

If you're like most busy professionals, breakfast is something of a blur, lunch is probably nonexistent and supper is a blend of storytelling, last minute cleaning, and checking on tasks still left over from work. It's time to stop all of that. Eating mindfully means savoring each bite. Relishing every sip. Appreciating every breath you hold to swallow and the feeling of satisfaction as the food makes its journey down your esophagus. It means taking the time to really enjoy your meal and the nourishment that it is bringing to you. Additionally, listen to your body. Stop eating once your body is satisfied and nourished. No more worrying about whether or not you've cleaned your plate. No more eating so much food you feel sick and bloated.

Stay in the moment with each bite. Your body will feel better for it and so will you. Feel the textures bump against your tongue. Breathe in deep right before you take a bite and savor the aroma of each ingredient.

Having a burger? Close your eyes and concentrate on each and every topping: the way the pickles dance against the beef. The way the cheese sticks briefly to the roof of your mouth. The way the buttered roll crunches slightly when you bite down into it. The way the acid in the mustard teases at your senses and sets the nerves at the back of your tongue on fire. Savor every moment of your bite.

Take Your Day One Step at a Time

Multitasking is a wonderful and often desirable skill to have. However, without proper discipline, multitasking can quickly take over your life. When was the last time you sat down to eat and just ate? When was the last time you did anything without also either thinking about the past or planning out a bit of the future? Ever take a shower in the morning and not try to also map out your day? Ever take a bath at night and not think about everything you tried to do that day? To live mindfully means that while you are brewing yourself a cup of coffee, for that moment, that is all you are doing. No running to grab the paper real quick, no stepping over the cat to shove some bread into the toaster, and no sorting out the day's to-do list in your head as you stir in the creamer.

Just brew the coffee.

Have you ever seen a coffee commercial on television before? Are the people in the commercial ever enjoying their coffee while they run around, dodging each other's briefcases and tossing kisses at their children? No. In those moments of chaos and pandemonium, it's hard to even recognize what good can come from a cup of coffee.

But then the moment comes. The music slows down. The steam wafting up from the cup of coffee tickles the person's nostrils, and he or she smiles and closes his or her eyes. Then, the sip. They hold the coffee in their mouth for a moment, then swallow and lick their lips.

That is the epitome of mindful living.

Once you've finished brewing the coffee, move on to the next task, whatever that may be.

Move Slowly and Deliberately

Rushing through the task at hand is a sign of multitasking: you're trying to hurry so you can get to doing something else. For example, maybe you're speeding on the drive home so you can hurry up and get supper started. Rushing through one task in hopes of starting another task isn't staying in the moment. It's allowing the future to try to take over your thoughts again, and bring with it anxiety and stress.

Stick with one thing at a time, and give it your full attention. Make sure every second you spend on that activity is planned and deliberate. Doing this will help you to keep from rushing and possibly making mistakes.

During that drive home, try to monitor your breathing. Stuck at a red light? Rather than tapping your fingers anxiously awaiting the green signal to carry about your trip, try taking in a deep breath and thinking about how comfortable your seat is. Take a look around you and try wishing each person also stopped at the light a nice day. Concentrate on how the steering wheel feels gripped between your fingers. How the gum you're chewing feels as you gnash your teeth.

Take in each moment of the drive. Make each moment purposeful and meaningful, and you will find the drive to be more enjoyable.

Chapter 5: Meditation and Psychiatric Conditions

More and more studies are being done to see the link between the different types of meditation and psychiatric conditions. What is being found is very interesting indeed. The kind of meditation that has proven popular with people looking for peace of mind or may have been anxious or depressed is mindful meditation, transcendental meditation, and Buddhist meditation, and all be beneficial for different reasons.

However, the basic premise of these being beneficial is gleaned from the same reasons. One can slow down the mind, take control of the thoughts, and do this is more capable of coming to wiser conclusions. These meditation types have been used in substance abuse centers for years and help those with problems get their lives back on track. Since meditation is long term, the changes that are made during meditation really are essential to those who previously have been treated by psychiatric care:

- *One becomes more focused on life*

- *The cognitive skills are improved*

- *Panics are less likely to occur*

- *Fears can be overcome or controlled*

- *Life's crises can be put into perspective*

- *Practitioners of meditation are less likely to self-abuse*

You can see from this that people gain a better perspective of their lives and overcome many obstacles using this method, rather than traditional methods of psychiatric treatment. Thus, this helps them to gain better control of their lives. Since this is long-term, it also means that people become more aware of the body and mind's needs and can see things from a much healthier perspective. Thus, they are unlikely to make bad choices and are much more likely to live balanced lives, including the right foods, the right amount of exercise, and the right amount of rest and relaxation. One patient who was an addict explained his experience and felt that his meditation practice helped him respect his body and mind.

He felt that his teacher had taken his mind back to basics and had reconstructed it because the drug use had literally torn his life apart. Now, forty years later, the calmness that was learned through meditation is the only reminder of the folly of his youth. Still, it's a valuable reminder that has strengthened him through all kinds of indecision in the day-to-day running of his life.

One of the things highlighted in many illnesses of a psychiatric nature is that subjects find it difficult to sleep. Sleep is a vital factor when it comes to day-to-day health and wellbeing. Without that sleep, the psychiatric problems can be exaggerated and brought to the forefront because people become too tired to deal with their problems.

However, introduce meditation, and life becomes easier to manage. People also learn to breathe correctly, and that helps the levels of oxygen in the body to normalize. If you have ever seen someone in a panic breathing into a paper bag, it's done for a very good reason. When people panic, they tend to breathe in too much air, and oxygen levels in the body become too high. When you breathe into a bag, you rebreathe the same air and thus bring those levels down.

Breathing

The fact that meditation circles around breathing means that it's a natural thing. People who learn to breathe in the way that meditators do will get more control over themselves and their situations. People who have suffered from bereavement will be able to find a little peace away from depressive thoughts. Those who suffer from anxiety will also be able to find more control through the taught breathing methods.

Coupled with relaxation exercises, therefore, meditation really can be of help to those who are seeking to overcome obstacles placed in their lives by psychiatric conditions. However, that does not mean that this should replace any pills or medications prescribed to a patient.

In fact, it would be dangerous to stop treatments without proper supervision.

532

If this is your intention, you need to talk to professionals to work through the process with you to not make changes to your body that are drastic for your body to take. For example, some serotonin enhancers in the way of medications work long term, and cutting them instantly can return the patient to a very low feeling.

Thus, if you want to try meditation, then this should be included in your treatment at first, rather than replacing it. Today, many of the medications are for long-term, build-up use, so please do talk to your professional before making changes to prescription medications. All I can do is point out the benefits, but every individual will be different, and their needs will be different. I can say for sure that meditation will help people whose lives are troubled by anxiety, depression, or mood swings. Lack of sleep will also be tackled, as will over-eating and meditation can even help with eating disorders.

Chapter 6: Meditation for Stress Relief

Before we proceed with this guided meditation, I want you to find the most comfortable place in your house or office. Find a place where you can lie down entirely and feel at ease with your own body. My advice is to use a yoga mat or anything soft to spend the next several minutes in complete harmony with your body and with who you are. Stop thinking about pain, stress, what you have to do today at work, or what you left undone at work, what college your kids are going to, or even what to eat tomorrow.

Find a place where it's just you and your body, and then lie down. If you need more comfort, bring a pillow or a blanket to prop your legs up or support your head more. You should not feel distracted by anything, not even a sore inch of your body. The entire duration of this guided meditation is meant to make you feel fresh and anew. It is intended to give you a reboot, both mentally and physically.

Alright now. Are you lying down? Do you feel comfortable? And most importantly, do you think that you could stay there, like that, for the next fifteen minutes?

If you do, then let's go on.

Lie down and make sure you do not put any kind of stress on your body. This body is here to sustain your life on Earth, so treat it kindly every time you can. It is a sacred mechanism you have been given so that you can fulfill your goals. Your biggest dreams. Your most hidden, secret aspirations.

This body is all yours. Nobody has the right to do anything with it that you don't want them to. Not even yourself.

So lie down, stretch out your legs, and make sure your neck is not stiff. Let your whole body be loose. Let yourself go in the most meaningful way there is. Every muscle in your body deserves to be nothing less than 100% comfortable now. YOU deserve to be comfortable.

You have a whole world of stress and anxiety to deal with outside of this little bubble of comfort you have created for yourself here—but that world is outside.

You are here, perfectly in tune with your body, with who you are, with everything the world has given you, perfectly accommodated on this floor you have chosen to use while walking the path of meditation with me.

Nothing wrong can happen to you here, and the positive feelings you will gain throughout this meditation will overflow into your external life as well. You will smile more. You will be kinder to yourself and those around you. You will emanate nothing but light. Eventually, all stress will disappear as well, and for the first time in what is most likely a long time, you will finally be able to think clearly. You will finally be able to remove the dark clouds of stress and anxiety from your life and see it as it is: a gift, an opportunity, your own game in your own house.

How does your body feel right now? Do you feel the need to adjust a little? If so, do it slowly. You don't have to be anywhere right now, other than here, with your mind and body. You don't have to do anything else than treat yourself kindly and allow your body to fully relax.

There are hundreds of muscles in your body helping you move every day, helping you feed yourself, helping you talk, helping you smile, and helping you breathe. The muscles in your body are one of the main reasons you can function every day at your pace. Treat them kindly, for they are there to stay with you not for today or tomorrow only, but for the rest of your life.

Slowly start to relax as you continue lying down. Breathe in deeply. Breathe out. Inhale. Exhale. Deep and slow. You have all the time in the world right now. No rush, no deadlines, no places to be, no mad bosses to handle. You are everything, and you are sufficient. Right here, on your mat or on your bed, you are yourself in the fullest and most meaningful sense in the world.

There's nobody who can take you from this state of total and complete relaxation.

Because you are enough, and you are the only one who can control your life. Not your parents, not your boss, not your family, not your friends, not anyone on TV.

Just you.

You have a purpose here, and you are on your way to making your dreams come true because this wonderful body you have been gifted with, in its own shape, covered in a skin that is its own shade, is more than enough. Your muscles are now soft because you have finally given them time to take a break.

As you relax, you feel like you are sinking into the ground. You think that everything around you has been liquified, and you feel that every inch of your body becomes the surrounding space. There is no boundary between you and the bubble of relaxation and wellness surrounding you.

You are one.

One with yourself.

One with your past.

One with your present.

One with your future.

You are enough, and you have more than enough time on your hands to do everything you want.

What is it that you want to do?

What is your final purpose?

To build something? To raise your children beautifully? To achieve a life of equilibrium and wellbeing that emanates grace, just like the music you are listening to right now does?

Of course, you can do all that—and more! Because nature has engineered you to do it, you have a body that can help you and a brain that controls every single second of your life in a relaxed, beautiful way.

Your back is fully aligned with the surface you are lying on. There is no strain on it. There is no strain on your life anymore because you have taken control of every single inch and every single second of who you are from here on out.

Your fingers are completely unwound, and your palms are facing the world, ready to absorb all the positive energy in the universe. You are enough. Your body is enough as it is. Nothing can deter you from the path of pure success and happiness that lies ahead of you.

Deadlines do not exist. They are imaginary boundaries the world has placed on you. The only reason you adhere to them is because you feel that you have to.

But in reality, you don't have to do anything at all. Just be yourself. And yourself is enough.

Breathe in profoundly and absorb this state of wellbeing into your body and into your mind. This is your moment to recharge yourself before you go out again and efficiently handle everything. A way that leaves stress at the door, outside of your space of beauty and grace.

Your legs have sunk into the ground, and they have become one with it. From the tip of your thumbs to the top of your head, everything is fully at ease.

You don't have to run anywhere. You don't have to chase anything or anyone. You just have to be with yourself because you are the perfect mechanism—one that is fueled with clean air and positive energy only. One that is at ease.

No nerve in your body should feel any tension now.

You are one with everything, and everything is one with you. You are absorbing everything good in the universe and leaving behind everything that's bad. Yes, stressful situations happen, but you are handling them with a focused mind and a new, energized, recharged battery from this moment on.

Everything is mellow and soft around you, and you are sinking into this state of complete balance and love. Everything and everyone around you loves you, and you love them back. And from the infinite love in which you are sinking now, the face of the person you love appears.

They are smiling back at you and taking your hand, slowly leading you to the place where you went out on your first date or a place that means something to you. You still cherish that memory so much! With all that's been going on lately, though, you might feel that you have forgotten this memory and shoved it to the back of your mind where no beam of light ever reaches.

But your loved one is there to finally open the door to that place and let that wonderful feeling of excitement beam throughout all the darkness of the room it has been hiding in, exploding into pure energy. You see your loved one smiling, so happy that they have brought this memory back to your attention. You go back to that moment, and you can feel everything that is surrounding it: the perfume of the place; the beauty of your loved one; the light in the room or the sunset that was setting down on the two of you; the heat of the moment; the fact that, back then, it was just the two of you and all the dreams you shared with each other, and all the jokes, and all the minutes of bliss that brought you to love them deeply, uncontrollably, madly, and irremediably.

Your loved one is laughing with you, remembering a sweet moment of that first date or that time in space. They are taking your hand and bringing the palms of your hands together to absorb all the good energy of that moment and bring it to the center of your mind.

This is the well from which you will fuel yourself with grace and beauty from here on out. No matter what happens, you will always have this fantastic memory that makes you smile every single time. It is right there, at the very core of your mind, radiating happiness and relaxation and goodness all around you.

It is where you will go every time you feel the need to, now that you have finally pulled this memory out of the attic. You are ready to take on the world, knowing that you have an unbreakable shield of strength that can protect you from everything negative and stressful in your life.

Your loved one is slowly fading away now that they have made their purpose clear. They have created a moment of sheer joy you can always go back to, knowing that you can hydrate your mind with positivity and grace every time you feel like drowning.

Your loved one's image is fading out. Still, you hold on to the feeling of miraculous discovery, of sheer passion and calmness. The feeling, the emotion, will never fade completely, not when you are out in the world and not when you are here, with my voice, in this bubble of earnestness and beaming goodness.

Breathe in and out, slowly. Maintain a rhythm of breathing in full accord with your life and everything you have ever done. This is you here, nobody else, and you are not defined by anything other than the good things that have happened to you. Deadlines are nothing more than man-made limits. Speed is unnecessary in a world where everyone is heading in the same direction. Stress is futile because you are in complete control of your emotions, actions, thoughts, and how you achieve your own dreams.

In, out, in, out.

Right now, the core of your body feels warm and fuzzy, just like that memory you are holding on to. It feels that nothing can break this center of strength and beauty like nothing can derail you now from your path to happiness.

This core is the essence of everything you are excellent at. It might be that you make the best cookies in the world. It might be that you sing divinely. It might be that nobody can handle a spreadsheet as well as you do. Whatever it is, your core is made of positive thoughts, unforgettable memories, and the things you are absolutely best at.

Let this core of you expand slowly, reaching out past its imaginary boundaries and overflowing into your entire abdominal cavity and chest. Take your time; this will overflow in its own rhythm, just like the lava of a volcano reaches every crack of soil without rush, without a deadline.

The warmth in you is not destructive, though. It is only good, for your body this warm feeling reaches are blessed with energy, aptitude, loving grace, and miracle. Every inch of your body touched by this river of fuzziness that has sprung from your core is meant to be perfect just the way it is.

You are OK. You are MORE than OK. You are the kind of person that can really move mountains precisely because your core is made out of the things that truly define you: love, compassion, the power to change, and the power to be kind.

The feeling of warmth has now reached your lower abdominal cavity, and you can feel it flowing over the body itself into its extremities. Your shoulders and hips are the first ones to feel this incredible energy filling out your entire being. And from there on, your elbows and your knees will feel it too.

It's a slow process, but there's no need to rush anywhere. In this bubble you have created, the time has simply ceased to exist because time is nothing but a relative, man-made concept. This is the absolute zero of time—the moment from which the entire universe has sprung from. And you are there, one with the absence of time, one with the lack of any physical restriction.

By now, the fuzzy feeling has overflown into every inch of your body. Your toes, the tip of your nose, your eyes, your brain, and even your hair—they are all gracefully embraced by this feeling of utter well-being and relaxation. And from here, you start to overflow your state of calmness into your bubble and everything surrounding it.

Because you have the power to bring this not only upon you but on everyone that comes into contact with you. In fact, right now, the main source of your stress outside the bubble you have created with yourself is looking at you. And you feel nothing but kindness. You want to show them that you are enough and that your entire being can create pure positivity.

You reach out your hand and touch theirs with a firm but gentle touch. At first, they are skeptical about receiving anything from you, even if it's just a simple touch. But the more you reach out to them, the better it is. You are giving them some of your light and watching them being taken over by it.

They slowly start to become much less reticent to everything you are and everything you share with them. There is nothing more and nothing less than beauty between the two of you. This might be your boss, it might be a negative person in your family, or it might be an object in itself.

But right now, you can see nothing wrong and nothing dark in them, just the pure light you are sharing with them, watching them melt down their own walls and become one with this bubble of calmness.

The threat of their stress is basically null right now. It simply does not exist, the same way as nothing existed before the world and the universe were created. The negativity they had been bombarding you with is not there anymore. As you start to fill them with this positive feeling, they begin to melt down, and they reach out to you with their other hand.

You are now holding both of their hands, transferring goodness and calmness. Because, no matter who they are and what they do, people deserve to know you are this fantastic source of power, efficiency, and courage.

They start to smile back at you, flooded with the positive emotions you have been sharing with them. And the more they smile, the more they want to hug you, and you want to share this embrace.

You are slowly approaching each other, ready to embrace each other as you are. You are enough. They are enough. And this moment and this feeling of purity and love and commitment to goodness are enough.

Their image slowly starts to fade away, but you hold on to this emotion of grandeur and ultimate power as this happens. You have beaten your worst enemy, the thing that has been darkening your days and nights, the thing that was the primary source of negativity and stress in your life.From here on out, you not only manage each other. You are each other, and you are enough in the world, and you know that your goodness and calmness can contain anything negative that may come from them. You know that you can share this feeling of utter beauty, and you know that they will never affect you the way they have been doing until now.

Because whatever the reason behind your struggle may have been, it is now over. You have won over it, not by clenching your fists and baring your teeth, but by loving them as they are and by allowing them into your bubble of calm and relaxing vibrations.

As you realize you have the power to change not only yourself and your own mindset but also show it to the world that you are enough, you slowly start to come back to your room as well.

541

Your core is filled with nothing but greatness now because you are worthy of it and because you have created this within you, with that one good memory you had.

If one great event from the past can do so much for you, can you imagine how it would feel to open the door to every small joy and significant achievement you have ever had? Can you imagine a life where you don't have to roam the halls of your life? Hiding in fear of what might happen next because you KNOW for a fact that you are enough and that you can do anything, beyond time restrictions, beyond physical limits?

You are everything you have. The body on this floor is everything you need. The mind that controls it and who you are is all that you should ever turn to to make your dreams come true, to achieve a life of perfect balance and harmony.

You cannot change others. You cannot change the past, You cannot change all that is bad in the world. They will always continue to be there. But from here on out, you have a core of strength and light you can quickly turn to whenever times get rough. You have a life of happiness and excitement and love and compassion and kindness to share.

You can control how others make you feel because you know, deep inside, that you are who you are. They are who they are and embracing them.

Your body is slowly returning to its shape, maintaining the same amount of energy within it as you felt it at the peak of its light overflow. As you come back, you feel your legs are yours again, and the tips of your toes start to be there more than any time before. You can move them slowly, just a little, just to feel what a fantastic thing it is that you can control them, that your brain can send an order, and your toes can execute without fault.

The same happens with everything in your life. Your brain can send an order, and everything else will fall into place to make it come true. The materialization of your love is precisely that: the power your brain has to recharge itself and your body but also to show the world that you are powerful. Because you are a gift for the world, and the world is a gift for you.

CBT + DBT + ACT

Your fingers start to come to their senses too. As you breathe in and out, you slowly begin to acknowledge your physical space. You are on your mat or lying down on the bed, and you feel the warmth of your environment and the light, and you slowly start to become conscious of my voice again.

Breathe in and out. Take your time. No rush. It's just you and this voice and the energy you have been building inside of you all this time. You are here. Now. Breathing air because your body can do this. Holding on to the positivity and calmness you have gained because your mind can do this.

Take a very deep breath and, with your eyes closed, pull your body into a sitting position. Don't rush anywhere; there is no hurry. Inhale and exhale. Sit up in a lotus position or however else you feel comfortable in (maybe you want your legs stretched out or just slightly bent?). Breathe.

The air you breathe in fuels the wonderful feeling of calm, relaxation, and gratitude you have been working toward during this break.

Slowly breathe in and out, deeply. Open your eyes. Start to wiggle your toes and your fingers. Look ahead of you. There's a life of amazing grace waiting for you once you exit your room and start facing your tasks.

They might not always be easy. But what is essential is that you now know that you have the power and the energy to handle everything.

Chapter 7: Tools Needed to Meditate

Many people are under the impression that you need to invest money into meditation. Still, you don't need to, at all. The things that you are likely to need are simple. You may need a yoga mat for comfort that is not a costly item. It can be beneficial to have one because when you meditate outdoors, you can use this to protect yourself and cushion yourself from the ground. This is useful for other things than meditation, so it isn't a huge investment and can be used on the beach. It may also be a good idea to have a small cushion. This is used to sit on, as many people cannot achieve the lotus position easily since they may have limbs that are not flexible enough to get comfortable in that pose.

I don't want to add many illustrations to the book, but the lotus pose leg position isn't comfortable for people who are starting off with meditation. There's too much bend of the legs, and it's not easy for people to tuck their feet in. Thus, if you sit and bend your knees and cross your ankles, you will find it a whole lot more comfortable if you have a cushion to prop up your behind. You can use a meditation stool if you prefer, and some people find that this gives their back much better support.

It's a common misconception that you have to sit in any one given position to meditate. You don't. As long as you have a comfortable position, even a chair will be good enough. Those who do yoga and Buddhist meditation tend to choose this position because it's an excellent position to ground yourself. After achieving the lotus or beginner lotus, they tend to put their hands face upward onto their knees. This helps them to stay focused on what they are doing.

You will need loose clothing but don't necessarily have to spend money on fancy gear. That's your choice. Avoid clothing with a tight waistband or anything uncomfortable and likely to draw your mind away from the meditation you are about to do. Thus, even if you choose your most comfortable pajamas, these are very adequate for meditation.

Other things are really up to you. You may want to create a space within your home where you meditate and add things to it that you find to be inspirational.

Some people like to have a Buddha statue. Others like candles and scents. However, remember that the main purpose of meditation is concentrating inwardly, so these are not the most essential things in the world.

There is something that I found to be very helpful. I bought a set of beads for meditation for a specific purpose. When you are meditating, you are asked to concentrate on something – whether it's the environment around you, as in the case of mindfulness meditation – or your breathing in other types of meditation. Still, you may also be expected to count. By using meditation beads, I found that I could cut out the counting and simply move onto the next bead and that this acted as my counting method, thus taking away one more thing to think about. For people who have very active minds, like I had when I started, they can really help because you can concentrate on the breath rather than the counting.

There are some beautiful beads on Amazon.com for meditating, and once you have circled the whole set of beads, you will know that you have reached the number of 108. Instead of going back to one when you start to think of other things, you merely feel your way back to the beginning of the beads again, and this works a treat.

Although none of the extras are essential to your practice, I also found that having an Om singing bowl was useful. With one of these, which you can obtain on markets or on Amazon, you can set the mood for meditation because the sound that you make with the bowl is so mellow. The sound is produced when you move the mallet around the rim of the bowl. As well as being very aesthetically pleasing, I find that slowing down from the busy day is actually enhanced by starting a meditation session with a bit of Om from the bowl.

Of course, none of the items that I have suggested are obligatory. Still, they may just help enhance your meditation and allow you to enjoy your retreat into the world of meditation. Anything that positively enhances your experience or gives you the incentive to ensure that you practice daily is worth it.

These could also be little things that you ask friends for, for Christmas, or you can improvise and make things to fit into your meditation space that inspire you. These may be photographs. They may be flowers or plants or anything that makes you feel at peace within your chosen meditation area.

Chapter 8: Learning All About Relaxation

If you were to start meditating without knowing what relaxation is, then it's likely that you would fail. The reason is that you are going from a hectic life to a time when you are expected to sit and think of nothing. Not only are you making the task hard because of the contrast between your life and meditation, but you haven't yet learned to still your mind. Relaxation helps you do this, and this chapter is all about learning to still the mind and concentrating on the way you breathe.

Lie down on a bed or on a yoga mat, make sure that your head is comfortably propped without too many pillows. One is ideal because this puts your neck in the correct position to breathe the best you can. After all, your windpipe is freed up, and the air is allowed to pass through your body easily. You need to be dressed in clothing that is not restrictive and should ensure that your legs are straight out. When you eventually do the relaxation exercise, your hands will be down by your sides. Still, for the time being, we need to teach you to breathe correctly.

Place one hand on your upper abdomen. This hand is there for the express purpose of feeling the pivoting motion as you breathe. Many people breathe too lightly or do not allow sufficient air to enter their bodies. Some people breathe in too much and over-oxygenate. The way that you breathe is central to meditation.

Breathe in through the nose to the count of 3 and instead of thinking of what's going into your body as being air, think of it as energy. Hold that energy within you, and you should feel your upper abdomen rise to the count of three. Then, exhale through your mouth to the count of 5. The exhale is longer because you are trying to get rid of impurities that you may have built up within your breathing system.

Do this several times because you need to get accustomed to the rhythm of your breathing and the counting so that you do this without really thinking of the timing. It's worth spending a little time on the breathing exercise. Once it is automatic, you will be able to do the relaxation exercise that follows in a much more fluent way.

Relaxation exercise

This exercise can help you relax and help you sleep at night, but it's also a beneficial exercise to teach you to put thoughts out of your mind. When you start meditation, you will be expected to empty your mind of thoughts. Since this is something that you are not accustomed to doing, it's hard at first, which is why people concentrate on breathing. It gives the mind something to mull over.

As you continue to breathe in and out as we have shown you, we will turn our attention to each of the parts of the body. First of all, think of your toes. Tighten the muscles around your toes and feel them tensing up. Then relax them totally and feel them getting heavier. You need to do this with each area of the body, and it makes sense to start from the toes and work all the way up the body to the top of the head.

I have put down the things that you should be thinking of and should be concentrating on:

- *Sole of the foot*
- *The ankles*
- *The shins*
- *The knees*
- *The thighs*

Then move up to the items below:

The hips, the stomach, the waist, the chest or breast area, the wrists, the forearms, the upper arms, the shoulders, the neck, the back of the head, facial features if you want to include these (lips – nose – eyes – cheeks).

By the time you have worked over the whole body, you should be very relaxed indeed, but while you are doing these, concentrate on that part of the body that you are relaxing and do not think of other things. If you find that you are thinking about different things, you need to start back at the toes again.

Chapter 9: Treatment approaches

Somatization is a complex condition with combined causality of body and mind. Scientists have worked to find out the exact mechanism of development to find the correct and effective treatment. Usually, when a physician confronts symptoms that can't be explained, he/she becomes frustrated, and the patient becomes confused because they don't know whether the condition is severe. The doctor usually reassures him/her to be patient and does another analysis. As the person complains of symptoms more and more, a physician is forced to begin any treatment that may help in this situation. These treatments are often not helpful or only partly helpful. Still, the diagnosis stays unknown.

In general, these people searching for a diagnosis should improve their lifestyle, dedicate time to relaxation and doing what they like, and give up the bad habits and apply some new ones related to physical activity and healthy eating. This doesn't mean that the symptoms aren't being taken as seriously; it is a plan for the beginning of the effective treatment on a healthier body.

Treatment includes various methods - pharmacological, that is with medications, psychological, and life coaching. Some are more and some less effective. It is up to the healthcare provider to refer the patient to the right specialist to begin the appropriate treatment.

When you have unexplained symptoms that have been present for months or even years, you will seek a diagnosis. Not everyone around you will share your worries. They can't understand the severity of your symptoms. When the various diagnostic procedures don't clarify the cause, they are doubtful whether it is even real.

Many people experience a lack of support and trust. Some don't even share the issue with close people, knowing that they would be mocked or not trusted. The symptoms are usually characterized the wrong way because of their unusual characteristics. For example, there's pain present in one part of the body then moves to another part without any visible explanation. Therefore, a person may be given advice from family or friends to give up.

It will resolve by itself, that they are imagining or that it is only in their heads.

A person is usually confronted with non-acceptance and frustration, which may make the symptoms even worse. Creating a stable and supportive atmosphere is crucial for the treatment.

On the other hand, some patients experience rejection from various medical specialists, who tell them that their illness isn't their field of expertise. A person may find himself or herself trapped in their bodies, with no clear help in sight, and the symptoms can continue for a long time. However, with more scientific research, general medical practitioners can recognize that a person might have somatization disorder.

The leading cause is, in fact, psychological. Some unresolved frustrations, tension at work or in family, or unexpressed emotions and anxiety are transformed into physical symptoms without visible damage. Thus, the helpful treatment is also a psychological approach. These psychological methods require some time and motivation but are actually teaching you new ways to look at your life. A person might feel uncomfortable accepting that something is "mentally wrong" with them and can experience difficulty handling the stigma behind it, which is understandable.

A stable psychological structure is actually a part of our everyda

y functions, much like the digestive or respiratory system, and sometimes requires some help and treatment. The whole process needs time for adaptation. You should note that some treatments can't resolve the situation entirely, so you should be ready to try different approaches or combine them with others.

If other conditions have a known cause, your healthcare provider may first concentrate on them and treat that symptomatology. They may be responsible for your other symptoms. If that therapy is of little help, they will refer you to a cognitive-behavioral therapist since CBT has shown the best results in treating somatic symptom disorder.

Medical (pharmacological) treatment

Medical treatment is often used to cover the symptoms and make a person's life much easier. However, the condition may continue to exist even after treatment. Anxiety and depression may be associated with somatization. In these situations, the disorder is known, but the physical symptoms still exist with no explanation.

Medications that are commonly used are antidepressants.

Despite their name, they are used for depression and similar mood disorders and long-term neuropathic pain, eating disorders, phobias, anxiety, post-traumatic stress disorder, multiple sclerosis, etc. They are also helpful in the treatment of somatic symptom disorder.

Antidepressants may be divided into subcategories:

SSRIs Selective serotonin reuptake inhibitors

SNRIs Serotonin and noradrenaline reuptake inhibitors

TCAs Tricyclic antidepressants

Atypical antipsychotics

Antiepileptic medications

Herbal medication St. John's wort

1.) Selective serotonin reuptake inhibitors (SSRI) or SSRIs are the most commonly used antidepressant medications. They are efficient in treating depression, phobias, anxiety, eating disorders, obsessive-compulsive disorders, fibromyalgia, irritable bowel syndrome, and premenstrual syndrome. They are effective and have minimal side effects. They work by blocking serotonin absorption into the nerve cell, which prolongs its effects. Serotonin is a chemical in our body responsible for good mood, reduction of pain, social behavior, appetite and digestion (serotonin is also located in large amounts in the gastrointestinal system), sleep, memory, and sexual function. In depression and all of the above mentioned-disorders, serotonin levels are low, and the right way to increase it is with SSRI-s. SSRI-s are tablets that your healthcare provider may begin the treatment with, preferably in small doses. It takes 2-4 weeks for the treatment to take effect.

They are not recommended for pregnant women and those who breastfeed and for persons under the age of 18. Other medications should be considered if a person has some chronic illness like diabetes, kidney, heart, or liver disease.

People with glaucoma and epilepsy shouldn't use it either. Some caution is needed when drinking caffeinated drinks. Driving is not advised if a person experiences dizziness and nausea when using SSRIs. They can induce seizures in people with epilepsy.

Side effects are dry mouth, dizziness, nausea, nervousness, insomnia, blurred vision, headache, diarrhea, and erectile dysfunction. Serotonin syndrome appears when serotonin accumulates in the body, usually when SSRI is mixed with some other drugs that increase serotonin effects, which your healthcare provider will inform you. The symptoms are confusion, tremors, restlessness, irregular heartbeat rate, dilated pupils, high or low blood pressure, diarrhea, change in body temperature, nausea, and vomiting. These symptoms require treatment in a hospital.

Most commonly used are:

2.) Serotonin and noradrenaline reuptake inhibitors (SNRI)or SNRI are medications that work similarly to SSRI. Still, instead of only increasing the effect of serotonin, they also increase norepinephrine effects (noradrenaline). Norepinephrine is a sympathetic neurotransmitter, similar to adrenaline (epinephrine), and it is essential for energy and mood improvement. Serotonin and norepinephrine are low in people who suffer from depression, so these are indicated for this condition. Other indications for their use are anxiety disorders, chronic pain, fibromyalgia, back pain, osteoarthritis, and somatization.

They are not recommended for pregnant women and those who breastfeed, and people under 18. Other medications should be considered if a person has some chronic illness like diabetes, kidney, heart, or liver disease. They can induce seizures in people with epilepsy.

Side effects include dry mouth, dizziness, nausea, nervousness, insomnia, blurred vision, headache, erectile dysfunction, excessive sweating, change in appetite, cough, and weight loss. It is also possible for a person to develop serotonin syndrome.

Most commonly used are:3.) Tricyclic antidepressants (TCA) or TCAs are a group of antidepressants that could be helpful even in people with somatic symptoms based on the body-mind relationship. Their action mechanism is to block the serotonin and norepinephrine reuptake but in a different way than SNRI) and increase serotonin and norepinephrine effects. This may help improve mood, decreasing anxious and phobic thoughts, pain relief, eating disorders, managing premenstrual syndrome, and preventing migraines and headaches. TCAs can be used for children and adolescents. It takes 2 to 4 weeks for TCAs to take effect.

Persons who are taking this medication should note that they might induce sleepiness and drowsiness. Hence, they affect the ability to drive or operate machinery.

Possible side effects include dry mouth, dizziness, nausea, blurred vision, problems with urination, excessive sweating, weight gain or weight loss, tremors, erectile dysfunction, diarrhea, and abdominal pain. They can induce seizures in people with epilepsy.

Most commonly used are:

TCAs

Amitriptyline (Vanatrip, Elavil)

Amoxapine (Asendin)

Desipramine (Norpramin)

Doxepin (Silenor, Sinequan)

Imipramine (Tofranil)

Nortriptyline (Pamelor)

Protriptyline (Vivactil)

Trimipramine (Surmontil)

4.) Atypical antipsychotics can be used for pain relief and serotonin inhibition in cases where it is very high and induces the symptoms. Olanzapine (Zyprexa) and Clozapine may be helpful in repeated headaches and migraines. (43) Side effects may include low blood pressure, dizziness, drowsiness, blurred vision, confusion, dry mouth, abdominal pain, constipation, problems with urinating, heat intolerance, low white blood cell count, and irregular heart rhythm. There is particularly an increased risk if similar drugs are used. Vehicle driving and machinery operation are forbidden if a person is experiencing dizziness and drowsiness.

Paliperidone is a type of antipsychotic that is usually combined with SSRI (Citalopram) and may be used in somatic symptom disorder.

5.) Antiepileptics - Gabapentin and Pregabalin are not only used for epilepsy but for somatic symptoms disorder as well. They improve the general condition, provide relief from pain, and be used in fibromyalgia. They are also useful in treating conditions that are linked with anxiety and anxious thoughts. They are used in small doses. Side effects include dizziness, drowsiness, tremor, dry mouth, blurred vision, erectile dysfunction, swelling, and weight gain.

6.) Herbal medication - St. John's wort (Hypericum perforatum) many studies suggest this as a good remedy against many illnesses. St John's wort is a flowering plant widely known to help in depression, nervousness and anxious thoughts, difficulties sleeping, and even some infections. Active substances in this herb are hypericin and hyperforin, among others (rutin, quercetin, and kaempferol). Hypericin can help treat conditions linked with mild to moderate depression, and hyperforin is also helpful in infection treatment.

St John's wort grows on open space and has spread from Africa and Europe to Asia and America. Its effects are known from ancient history when Greeks used it to improve mood and to heal wounds. They can be used in tablets, capsules, teas, and tinctures (0.3% hypericin derivatives, 300-mg capsules Ze 117- 50% ethanolic extract, and some others). The recommended daily dosage is Ze 117.

554

Hypericin is found in plant flowers in the black dots. Hypericin and Hyperforin are used to treat somatic symptom disorders. The increase of serotonin, dopamine, and norepinephrine improves mood, relieves pain, prevents headaches and migraines, and treats gastrointestinal symptoms.

Side effects that might occur are gastrointestinal discomfort, allergic reactions, dizziness, confusion, nervousness, and dry mouth. It is possible to develop photodermatitis, which is an abnormal skin reaction to sunlight while using St. John's wort. A similar response could be noticed in the eyes. Normal precaution and protection are advised while spending time in the sunlight. All of the side effects are temporary and mild.

Precaution is also needed when using some medications (antihistamines, Digoxin, Amitriptyline, Verapamil, sedatives, oral contraceptives, warfarin, antifungal medications, SSRI-possibility for serotonin syndrome, and some other food supplements and herbs). It is advised to consult your healthcare provider before beginning to use St. John's wort because of possible adverse effects and to evaluate whether it is the appropriate medical agent for you. (44)

Pharmacological treatment is in many cases not advised for their adverse effects that may sometimes bring worse results than the symptoms themselves. That is why medications are not considered to be the main course of action for treating somatoform disorders. They are often used along with other treatment types (psychological) while carefully choosing the type of medications because of their possible side effects.

Another issue is the treatment of children and adolescents. Many of these medications, antidepressants mostly, are not suggested because of increased risk for adverse effects. Even though somatoform disorders are much more present in adults, adolescents and children have a higher chance of conversion disorder than adults. The best treatment for them is talk therapy, but it is sometimes not as helpful. However, in this situation, a specialist should evaluate the risks and benefits of using medication therapy. It is usually recommended that children and adolescents undergo psychosocial therapy, which includes therapy with the help of family members and close friends.

The psychosocial approach may be effective in the whole society to prevent psychological crises and prepare for managing emotions and stressful situations.

Psychological

A psychological approach has shown much more effects. A wide variety of methods can be deployed depending on the most comfortable and effective one. Scientists and psychologists developed various methods for relieving symptoms. Cognitive-behavioral therapy showed promising results and is usually the first type of psychological therapy. Others are combined with a CBT for better effect. Some of them are a part of cultural tradition to clear the mind.

Work with somatization begins not only when somatic symptoms appear but also with learning about properly confronting conflicts, frustrations, shocking situations, expressions of emotions, etc.

These are cognitive-behavioral therapy (CBT) with activity monitoring (increasing underactivity/reducing overactivity), overcoming unhelpful behavior, pacing activities, managing sleep problems, managing unhelpful thinking linked to anxiety and depression, assertive and social techniques, relaxation, psychoeducation, and some other non-specific approaches.

Cognitive Behavioral Therapy (CBT)

Cognitive Behavioral Therapy (CBT) is a crucial type of treatment on both psychological and physiological levels. CBT focuses on conversation with a psychologist or psychotherapist to create a healthy attitude for solutions of problems or importing attitudes into a person's behavior that would later become incorporated with his/her thoughts. These corrected behaviors and thoughts find use in confronting difficulties in life. Sessions usually don't take long, generally less than an hour of regular visits and talks once a week. The longevity depends on the needs of a person.

Example for cognitive behavioral therapy includes finding an approach for a person to participate in positive activities that would negate fear or stressful situations. In time, it would result in positive thoughts when negative situations come up. CBT's goal is to achieve specific results toward a subject of psychological imbalance.

CBT teaches a person how thoughts and attitudes reflect on behavior and the other way around. A therapist talks with persons about positive and negative thoughts and behavior. The key is to identify which and promote what is healthier and beneficial in managing all of the troubling events/situations. Somatoform disorders have an increased risk of occurring in people who are just prone to have a more negative perspective. This comes from automatically applied thoughts and beliefs established in childhood. In time, they triggered an adverse reaction in troubling situations. A therapist will help you detect those automatic thoughts and help you change them into useful ones.

You might be seeking reassurance from the doctor that your symptoms indicate a severe illness, even though the diagnostic tests have shown otherwise. You may try a different approach with CBT. A doctor will always have on his/her mind that he/she must take good care of you, and if there is any indication of a serious illness, he/she would determine it in time.

At the beginning of treatment, a therapist will ask directly about the current situation and troubles in your life (using the BATHE technique usually).

A person with unexplained symptoms likely to be somatization from psychological imbalance will probably have a subject to talk about. This subject doesn't have to be at first a clear cause for the frustration. Still, the conversation needs to be structured and following certain principles. During the process, a person will learn to cope with some problems, fears, or emotions and then change how they react to them.

A particular use of CBT in treating somatoform disorders is characterized by:

introducing relaxation techniques,correcting automatic thoughts and attitudes, and facing fears as well as gradually confronting them, creating new approaches to situations, and illness/symptoms, facilitation of emotional expression and giving value for certain emotions, elimination of preoccupational thoughts about symptoms,improving communication with other people regarding the illness or the problem, assertiveness, and social skills, introducing satisfactory and pacing activities and combining them with necessary and routine activities.

CBT also tends to include a spouse or a family member in the treatment, at least in the beginning. It is important to identify and single out specific thoughts that become blockages and try to restrict them, requiring support from a significant other.

A person's views on his/her illness should also be modified. No matter how strangely symptoms appear to a physician or a person, there is a background that explains it all without the need to announce the person as mentally ill or sick from an insidious disease. A person will need to change their approach to symptoms. They are present indeed and troublesome, but the illness's behavior has to change with giving less value and attention to it. With this, a lot of other techniques for positive thinking may be of help.

Some techniques can be attempted as a way of self-help. These include managing the frightening situations listed by hierarchy on a paper and working through them, from the least frightening to the most terrifying. Others may be mind experiments, such as thinking about previously experienced situations and thinking of other approaches to that situation, then finding resolutions and seeing them from negative and positive aspects.

Some people are given the advice to record their feelings or thoughts on something and then carefully and objectively think about them. The key is to learn to see things from another angle and change behavior accordingly. CBT is often used along with some relaxational methods such as visualization, breathing exercises, meditation (mindfulness methods), and yoga.

Cognitive-behavioral therapy isn't just about talk. Still, instead, it is about acquiring skills and learnings about thoughts and actions and their connection. Usually, the therapist gives a patient assignments that he/she has to achieve, and the effects are later discussed during the session. The treatment usually consists of planning and conceptualizing the problem and thoughts about it. Setting the goals isn't about not feeling the pain, nausea, or any other symptom, or not feeling anxious, but rather more specific, concrete, and actually achievable.

Goals are set using this formula:

Specific

Measurable

Achievable

Realistic

Time-bound

Solutions to the problem are discussed. A patient then gets an assignment for coping with the issue. CBT in severe somatization disorder can't be brief, but it should last for at least 10 months.

Very often, CBT is combined with antidepressants to treat the associated condition and to increase its effects. Sometimes the treatment can be done individually or in groups, both of which should be offered. CBT alone showed more results than relaxation methods. While having CBT treatment, patients are advised to also visit the general practitioner to evaluate physical symptoms once a month. (45) Activity monitoring-increasing underactivity/reducing overactivity/boom bust cycle.

Activity monitoring is one of the first steps of cognitive-behavioral therapy. Having somatic symptoms and confronting the fact that they are unknown and more likely psychological can be difficult to perceive and challenging to handle within interpersonal relationships. These people are often more likely to begin excluding themselves from society and becoming more and more inactive or start practicing some unbeneficial activities. A person may conclude that it is much safer or more comfortable to become passive and do nothing. A person will avoid certain activities with the fear of the pain becoming greater or that they would be embarrassed by the symptoms and what other people think about them.

Cognitive-behavioral therapy revolves around inclusion into activities. Activities are chosen by using the SMART formula. At first, a person needs to create a routine and activities that are repeated each day. These include everyday preparation of meals, buying groceries, reading, etc. Then, he/she needs to determine the necessary activities that occur daily.

These include going to work, paying the bills, taking the children to and from school, visiting parents, and cleaning. A person needs to create a list of everyday pleasurable activities and hobbies that involve different amounts of time. These activities could either be reading, relaxing, watching TV series, listening to music, painting, dancing, doing sports, etc.

It is preferred for a person to individually organize these activities to fit all three types of activities in a day. Activities should be sorted from the easiest to the hardest. A person should try doing all of them without exception but evenly organized. It is recommended that a person keep a diary of the activities, at least at the beginning.

Correcting activation and behavior may work the opposite way, especially to the persons who are overworking themselves to avoid unwanted thoughts. This can't be helpful because the underlying problem is only hidden and covered and not solved through healthy behavior. There is also another situation when a person forces him/herself to overwork.

This happens when symptoms appear from time to time, and a person tries to deal with the illness itself and its impact on the professional or personal life. This is called the Boom and Bust cycle. Boom and Bust cycle activity is a term that comes from business/economy. It refers to a person becoming more productive at work when the symptoms aren't present.

The boom and Bust cycle is more present in the professional area of activities. This situation pushes a person to achieve as much as possible until the symptoms are back again. This, too, arises from fear of the illness and requires a healthier attitude, which is difficult sometimes to manage.

A person feels that work needs to be done and feels incapable or guilty if it's not. It may be that when symptoms are gone, he/she will try to forget about them and ignore their existence, and working beyond the limits of physical possibilities. It can also lead a person to feel exhausted and less motivated and induce feelings of unhappiness. It brings more tension because of increased feelings of incapability or failure.

Professional activities are experienced as obligational. People become more unsatisfied with them and avoid doing them for fear of promoting the symptoms. With time, a person becomes less productive and less active and needs more time to recover and rest.

Setting time and effort limits to activity can prevent this cycle from happening. Also, activities should be equally organized throughout the day. The activity level should be the same on good days as bad days to avoid overactivity on good days and inactivity on bad days.

Some therapists recommend three Ps:

Prioritising

Planning

Pacing.

Pacing activities

Pacing is a skill that allows you to do activities, but in a reasonable amount and with the organization. Overactivation can make symptoms increase in intensity, and under activating or doing nothing makes you less motivated and depressed. That is why pacing is a good way to do activities. You may think that this way, your productivity becomes lower than if you had worked all day, or you may think of those activities as boring obligations.

However, pacing allows you to become constant with work without your symptoms increasing. With time, you shall see that this actually makes you happier and self-satisfied with the amount of work done and time spent for rest or relaxation.

Pacing is particularly suggested to people who are struggling with pain, headaches, and fatigue. They probably need more rest than other people. However, having more rest would solve problems only temporarily. Pacing is all about gradually taking control over your activities and how much you can handle. It may be challenging to cope with, but it would help you to feel better.

The time needs to be divided into activity time and rest time.

They should be equally distributed throughout the day. People who are becoming more and more tired and have increased their activity with pacing need to gradually increase the activity. They should set their own limits, and as they feel ready and full of energy, they may proceed and move the limits further.

Some activities need to be divided into those requiring more energy from those who require less energy. This way, the activities would be spread adequately throughout the day. Challenging activities can be divided into two parts with a pause. Planning in pacing is crucial. You should dedicate a certain amount of time to an activity that would require medium energy, which wouldn't induce symptoms in you. Planning should be taken seriously and with reasonable deadlines to perform productive activities and not as exhausting.

Some activities need to pass the priority test. Not all of the activities are necessary. It isn't a sign of weakness if you ask someone from your family or friends to help you with some exercises. You don't need to do things alone, or don't have to burden yourself because you feel that it is only your duty, because it isn't. You should also include activities that you enjoy and not just activities that you are obligated to do. Doing fun activities induces pleasure and makes us happier, taking our minds off the symptoms, pain, or fatigue.

So, with pacing, you will avoid overactivity during the days when you feel fine. Also, you will escape from pointlessness when you are experiencing symptoms. This requires a plan that you should be motivated to follow.

The time that you dedicate to a specific activity needs to be respected. Even though you are feeling fine, you are more productive, focused, and concentrated. You shouldn't forget about burn-out syndrome. It can be difficult to estimate how much time to dedicate to relaxation and how much to continue working when you don't feel tired or in pain at the moment. Good pacing is all about making sure you know when to quit. It's not when you're already experiencing symptoms because it will take you longer to rest and recover.

Pacing activities include doing one thing at a time. That way, energy is only used for one activity, and our focus is centered on one thing, which makes us more relaxed and less tense.

It may appear difficult as people are getting used to your pacing, or they will make their own appointments that would prevent you from following your schedule, or they will assign you tasks to do. However, you must have control over your energy and time, even if you disappoint others. Your schedule is as important as theirs, and you can't put everyone else first.

There are differences between cognitive behavioral therapy, adaptive pacing therapy, graded exercise therapy, and specialist medical care. They can benefit persons with somatization individually or combined. Even though they seem to overlap, some of them individually proved to be more useful than the others.

Adaptive pacing therapy revolves around letting the body fight with whatever the cause is while providing the best conditions for it to happen. A person organizes time and spreads activities so that he/she economically spends energy. This would prevent the boom and bust cycles and overuse energy for unnecessary purposes and then not be active.

Graded exercise therapy refers to approaching previously set activities step-by-step, increasing the effort and energy needed for the activity. Some people become less active due to symptoms and fear of symptoms intensifying.

Specialist medical care includes specific therapy for specific symptoms, even though they have no clear causality. Treatment usually includes medicines and advice on how a person can affect the symptoms through behavior.

Cognitive-behavioral therapy consists of changing the thoughts and behavior in ways that are more realistic and logical and, in the end, healthier and more helpful. Particular thought and/or behavior may be the key to treating some of the symptoms.

A study that compared those four approaches concluded that graded exercise therapy and CBT had more positive effects than adaptive pacing therapy and specialist medical care alone.

Overcoming avoidance behaviors and other unhelpful behavior. Overcoming fears.

With time, as symptoms seem to last too long and become chronic, a person becomes more distressed. Social, personal, and professional priorities come as second and third now that a person's health is unexplainably disrupted. Avoidance of social and professional activities may develop from fear of the symptoms increasing or from fear of rejection from other people due to symptoms. Many people don't show empathy in a way that is encouraging to people. This has to be changed since it creates a stigma against somatization disorder, which hinders coping with it.

Cognitive-behavioral therapy tends to focus on activities that are not beneficial for dealing with somatization symptoms. The not beneficial and unhealthy activities are:

Avoiding activities or overdoing things,

Constantly changing lifestyle and eating habits to try to improve symptoms,

Boom and bust cycle,

Fears of symptoms getting worse and from illness and behaving accordingly.

The natural response to any potentially harmful situation is to fight or flight (escape). These actions are both regulated by the sympathetic involuntary system, which starts a reaction for preparing to deal with potentially harmful situations: increased heartbeat rate, breathing, and others. In both, dealing with anxiety towards the symptoms is with creating the fear from the situation, and it prevents consequences from happening in the first place. Avoiding thoughts of a certain problem can make it all worse, but the same way a person may choose certain activities to prevent consequences from happening with excessive and extreme measures (for example, a person cleans the house thoroughly every day to avoid germs).

Avoidance and safety behavior are activities that a person performs due to fear or anxiety of something. Safety behavior includes taking extreme measures to prevent some events. They may not appear so evidently as avoidance. Hence, a person is usually not aware of all of the activities he/she does to escape from the symptoms.

564

Cognitive-behavioral therapy introduces the person to gradual exposure to real situations. It helps in overcoming difficulties or fear from difficulties with symptoms in everyday life. A person makes a list of fearful thoughts, specific ones regarding one situation/problem. The list is put in a hierarchy from the easiest to achieve and overcome to the hardest. The list is a person's ladder in overcoming unhelpful thoughts and behavior. During talks with a therapist, a person may discover those activities and focus on dealing with them gradually and switching to more helpful behavior. By gradually overcoming these situations stage by stage, a person becomes aware of different thinking benefits and how to deal with consequences or problems due to symptoms without negative thoughts.

You can actually break the fear itself into smaller pieces and try confronting them separately. Thinking of scenarios that could happen is sometimes healthy and sometimes not. However, there is no harm in trying. Sometimes, it is helpful to think of your greatest fear and writing a story about it. You shall notice that the more you think of it, the less you can change any unexpected negative outcome. Still, you can become aware of healthy ways to become involved in your health.

For example, suppose you are having very intense abdominal pain or headache. In that case, you may become fearful about a dangerous tumor that might be destructive to your body. However, there isn't much for you to do but watch from the positive and negative sides. After you finish the frightening story, you should read it repeatedly. At first, your emotions would interfere, and you would find it hard to continue reading. Still, as you read it many times, you will experience fewer emotions linked to the fear or event itself, which can lead you to the conclusion of the preciousness of life. You may feel more motivated to focus your attention, not overthinking the illness, and instead, try to live a fulfilling life.

Managing sleep problems

Disturbing thoughts during the day make the nights even harder. Sometimes when we're distracting ourselves from the core of the problem, we can't fall asleep. Now, this subconscious discomfort prevents the brain from shutting down and entering sleep mode.

You can improve sleep by making your room comfortable with fresh air and with proper ventilation. Loud sound and bright lights should be removed. You shouldn't watch TV or check your smartphone before sleep because it triggers your brain into delaying the process of falling asleep. Also, you should avoid drinking or eating before bedtime, especially caffeine. It also depends on how many hours you need to be asleep to recharge. Some people only need 6 hours, while others need 8 or 10.

The real reason behind not being able to fall asleep could be worrying thoughts that appear even in the most comfortable room for sleeping. Think of how many times you would think about your symptoms and how they interrupt and deconcentrate you during the day. Do they indicate an illness that you are afraid of? Lack of sleep will only make you feel worse. In any case, if you can't sleep, don't obsess over it. Relax and focus on finding different approaches to your worries.

Chapter 10: Treatments for Anxiety and Depression

Compared to people in a calmer state of mind, the thoughts and feelings of people with chronic anxiety and depression are heavily influenced by information coming in from the limbic system and brain stem. Hence, conscious, logical "top-down" approaches to calm the brain to be less effective than "bottom-up" approaches, which focus on the body, or hybrid "right-brain" approaches which combine talk therapy with body awareness.

The goal of somatic therapy is to guide the brain and body back towards homeostasis – a balanced state in which there is a moderate level of nervous arousal in most situations. The autonomic nervous system doesn't swing wildly between sympathetic over-arousal and parasympathetic under-arousal. This involves finding ways to release unnecessary muscle tension and desensitize yourself to stressful memories without triggering the brain's alarm center in the amygdala. This means it's crucial that you feel relatively safe and comfortable when trying to release chronic tension (the so-called "safe space" referred to in trauma therapy). Otherwise, you will subconsciously tense up (both physically and emotionally) to protect yourself from real or perceived threats.

When the inner critic in your mind is loud and persistent, as when you're anxious or depressed, it can be extremely difficult to calm yourself with rational thinking. Writing down your thoughts can be helpful, but this only tends to be of modest benefit and isn't a very practical solution when you're otherwise engaged in a hands-on task. However, shifting your attention from your negative thoughts and feelings to your physical sensations can be a powerful way of "grounding" yourself and feeling safer and more relaxed.

A key aspect of grounding is reducing unnecessary nervous arousal in the upper half of the body. When your nervous system is over-aroused, you can literally feel ungrounded because there is too much muscle tension (and blood flow) in the upper half of your body and too little in the lower half. So when you're in an over-aroused state, it often helps to focus on the lower, or peripheral, parts of the body such as the legs, feet, and hands.

In turn, this helps to slow down breathing, increase blood flow to hands and feet, and reduce unnecessary muscle tension throughout the body.

The Window of Tolerance

When the brain and body are in homeostasis, your ability to tolerate moderately stressful events is much higher than when your nervous system is dysregulated. *This is why somatic therapists focus on increasing their client's "window of tolerance" – how much mental and physical stress they can handle without becoming under or over-aroused. Hence, if a client's window of tolerance increases, they will find it easier to deal with stressful situations.

Limitations of Top-down Talk Therapy

If conventional talk therapy was as good as many of its practitioners claim, then rates of anxiety and depression would be a lot lower than they are.* However, there are several drawbacks to conventional talk therapy, limiting its usefulness in helping deal with these disorders. I've already mentioned that it's complicated for the logical, verbal neocortex to calm the instinct-driven brain stem and the emotion-driven limbic system. This makes it challenging for us to resolve symptoms of depression or anxiety by just talking about our personal problems.

Sometimes we may acquire helpful insights into why we are depressed or anxious (for example, we might find that one of the reasons we have social anxiety is because we were bullied as a child) but simply finding explanations for our emotional problems rarely helps us to feel much better. Think of a common psychological issue such as a phobia of spiders. Just talking about your fear of spiders with someone else isn't going to change your gut reaction when you next have a surprise encounter with a hairy arachnid. You're still going to experience the same feeling of dread that first triggered your phobia.

568

Another weakness of conventional talk therapy is that the emotional release from talking about or expressing powerful feelings rarely brings lasting relief or closure. Hence, you might gain some short-term benefit from punching a pillow or seeing a counselor and having a frank talk about your personal problems, but this "cathartic" emotional release rarely has long-term benefits.

When talking about emotionally-charged issues, clients can often feel threatened at a subconscious level, and flight, fight, or freeze responses can easily be triggered.

Once these instinctive survival responses are triggered, the brain's left-frontal part (which controls speech and self-talk) will shut down, and it can become very difficult for clients to express their thoughts and feelings in words.

Those who instinctively favor the fight response may become verbally aggressive. Those who prefer the flight response to threats may become fearful and defensive. In contrast, those who gravitate towards the freeze response may switch off emotionally and become mentally scattered.

Even just getting people to turn up for talk therapy can be a big challenge. Many (if not most) people are instinctively uncomfortable discussing personal problems with strangers, and regular one-on-one talk therapy with a qualified psychologist can be very expensive. People prone to freezing in stressful situations can also be quite shy individuals who don't like confrontation or draw attention. Hence they often have an instinctive aversion to therapy and can easily be scared off.

Since the 1980s, the most successful form of talk therapy has been cognitive behavioral therapy. According to some scientific studies, it has a 50 percent success rate in reducing anxiety and depression among those who follow through with it. CBT was developed in the 1960s and 70s and is based on the idea that our thoughts determine how we feel.

By recognizing your negative thoughts and replacing them with more positive or constructive opinions, you can eventually think yourself out of anxiety or depression. But despite being a relatively successful form of talk therapy, CBT requires a lot of commitment from the client, and relatively few people are willing to commit to an extended course of treatment.

In particular, clients with chronic depression find it very difficult to motivate themselves to stick with this therapy form. Those with major depression often have to take high doses of powerful antidepressants before they feel positive enough to try it.

Brain-body therapists say that while talk therapy techniques like CBT can be useful for some people with mental trauma and mood disorders, they need to be preceded with bodywork to calm the nervous system. Otherwise, the client will either abandon the treatment, emotionally disconnect themselves from the therapy, or become even more nervous by opening themselves up.

Challenging strongly-fixed beliefs can also lead to an ego-clash between therapist and client. Some clients can become angry, frightened, or resentful if the therapist tries to talk them out of beliefs that provide relief from problems they aren't able to deal with.

Limitations of Medication

While some people with anxiety and depression experience major benefits from using antidepressant medication, the majority who take them experience either modest improvements or no benefit at all. Furthermore, many people who do experience some benefit from medications find they are associated with unpleasant side-effects. For some users, these troublesome side-effects (such as nausea, dizziness, insomnia, weight gain, and sexual dysfunction in males) outweigh the modest benefits.

Another limitation of antidepressants is they aren't very effective at treating anxiety and depression moderate but long term. Hence, someone with low-grade, chronic depression, and generalized anxiety is less likely to find an antidepressant helpful than someone with major depression or an extreme case of obsessive-compulsive disorder. This suggests that antidepressants work best in people with chemical (or neurotransmitter) imbalances in their brains. Most people with mixed anxiety and depression of a moderate but chronic nature do not have neurotransmitter imbalances. Instead, they have dysregulated nervous systems and or maladaptive approaches with stress. Antidepressants can also make it harder to sense physical feelings while engaged in body-based therapies.

570

Many brain-body therapists recommend using low doses that allow patients to stay in touch with their physical sensations (such as half a Prozac tablet per day, instead of the standard adult dose of one to two tablets per day).

Limitations of Non-Specific Brain-Body Treatments

In addition to pills and talk therapy, many people with symptoms of anxiety and depression use non-specific forms of somatic therapy, such as yoga and aerobic exercise. While these approaches have some benefits, they are probably best regarded as somatic therapy-lite. By that, I mean they have some benefits. Still, they aren't focused strongly enough on calming the nervous system and discharging traumatic memories.

Arguably the most commonly used form of physical therapy for mood disorders is good old-fashioned physical exercise. Hundreds of scientific studies have shown that aerobic exercise and weight-lifting can positively affect mood and muscle tension. People who don't exercise are more at risk of developing mood disorders.

However, the short-term benefits of exercise only last a few hours.

According to somatic therapist David Berceli, physical exercise only gets

rid of surface muscle tension. So you can still experience a lot of deep muscle tension even if you engage in vigorous exercise regularly.

This physical exercise is a beneficial complementary therapy for managing nervous arousal daily. Still, it isn't powerful enough to have a significant, long-term effect on chronic anxiety and depression.

Another popular therapy for anxiety and depression is meditation. Various forms of meditation are all the rage these days. Still, as with physical exercise, meditation rarely goes deep enough to have long-term effects. Meditation is good for temporarily calming the mind and relaxing the body.

571

To get significant benefits, you need to meditate like a Buddhist monk and spend hours meditating every day - ten or fifteen minutes in your lunchtime will not cut it if you are trying to deal with a mood disorder. Sitting for long periods while meditating can also be very difficult for some people with high levels of nervous arousal, particularly those with the hyperactive/impulsive form of ADHD or "Type A" personalities. People who are prone to daydreaming and dissociation also tend to space out during meditation, and this makes it difficult for them to get any real benefit from it (if you're trying to use meditation to improve concentration, it's recommended you meditate for a very short periods, like a minute or so, and take a break whenever you lose focus)

Among the popular alternative therapies for mood disorders, yoga is arguably the most beneficial since it involves both the mind and body. Some of the poses can be very useful for achieving a relaxed yet focused state of mind. However, somatic therapy experts such as Peter Levine and Pat Ogden say that yoga is relatively non-specific and doesn't adequately address core physiological processes. As with meditation, some studies show that regular yoga practice can help reduce symptoms of anxiety and depression, but it usually takes many years of standard practice for significant change to occur.

Hence, while the stretching poses in yoga can help relax the body and mind when done regularly, they aren't particularly effective in releasing high levels of chronic stress and muscle tension that have built up over many years.

Similarly, suppose you do have a lot of chronic muscle tension. In that case, you are likely to have an insufficient level of physical flexibility. You may find it very frustrating and uncomfortable to do some of the yoga poses taught in a typical yoga session. For example, as a middle-aged male with chronically tight hamstrings, I found it impossible to do the famous "down dog" position, a core exercise in many yoga classes.

I eventually did get some benefit and enjoyment from incorporating some yoga poses into my exercise routine, but that was only after I had already made progress in loosening up my body through tension release exercises.

Admittedly, a yoga class that is specifically aimed at people with anxiety or depression is likely to be more effective than a more generic yoga class, but it's probably better to use yoga as a complementary therapy rather than a primary tool for tackling chronic symptoms of anxiety or depression.

Suppose you can't find a yoga instructor specializing in yoga for trauma or stress. In that case, you may get some valuable benefits from doing "intuitive" stretching exercises at home. Instead of doing a set routine of standard yoga poses, just close your eyes and do whatever form of stretching exercise you feel like doing at the moment. So rather than using your conscious mind to force yourself to do a specific set of poses (whether you want to or not), you are allowing your subconscious to decide what type of stretching you do (from particular yoga poses to dance moves, to very simple stretches). Sometimes this type of freestyle stretching can be a handy tool for reducing physical tension because you target particular areas of the body where your subconscious is sensing high-stress levels. For example, in a standard set of yoga poses, you will probably spend a few minutes on each of the main muscle groups in the body – which could include areas of the body where you aren't very tense. However, when you work intuitively, you might spend ten or fifteen minutes on just one area (such as the hips) where you subconsciously notice a lot of tension.

Music can be very helpful with this form of exercise. It helps you switch off your logical brain and get your body moving instinctively. When I first started doing this stretching routine, I was a bit afraid to injure myself, particularly when focusing intensely on one particular area of the body. However, not once in doing this form of exercise regularly have I sustained an injury. It seems that your subconscious has a pretty good idea of what your physical limits are and won't push you to do things that are likely to lead to pain or injury.

Chapter 11: Somatic or "Right-Brain" Psychotherapy

Most talk therapy forms focus on the left side of the brain that deals with talking and logical thought. For example, in cognitive therapy, you discuss your negative thoughts and feelings with your therapist and think of more positive or constructive ones. In "person-centered" counseling (the most common form of counseling), you discuss your personal issues with your counselor, and your counselor provides periodic feedback. In somatic therapy, the client shifts from discussing and analyzing their thoughts, behaviors, and personal history to focusing on their internal sensations. For example, the therapist might notice that the client looks uptight and distressed. She then asks where the client is experiencing physical tension.

The client mentions tension in their jaw and shoulders and a feeling of irritation and anger related to a relatively recent argument. Hence, there is a shift in mental activity from the logical, verbal, left neocortex to the right side of the brain, a more intuitive part of the brain that interacts more closely with the body, brain stem, and limbic system.

A significant advantage of this type of therapy is that it avoids many of the ego-clashes that often occur in traditional talk therapy. Instead of probing deeply into your personal history or situation, the main focus is on your physical sensations. This means that the therapist isn't challenging the client to radically change their attitude, thinking, or behavior. The client doesn't have to divulge lots of personal information if they don't want to.

The primary requirement is being willing to focus on your physical sensations. This process tends to peak most people's curiosity that can often be quite pleasant (particularly if you unlock an area of physical tension or discomfort). Another benefit of somatic therapy is that it tends to be less mentally demanding than cognitive therapy, which can require a lot of mental effort and discipline on the client's part.

Sometimes, the therapist may engage in small experiments with the client, such as asking them to exaggerate a tension pattern in the shoulders or see how they react if they increase or decrease eye contact.

As somatic psychotherapy progresses, the therapist works within the client's window of tolerance while slightly pushing their boundaries to widen their tolerance window.

For example, suppose the client is looking relaxed during therapy. In that case, the therapist can test their comfort zone by doing role-play exercises and seeing how their body language changes when they are forced to act in a way they aren't used to.

The client and therapist may also set specific goals, such as increasing social confidence or increasing their ability to tolerate feelings of restlessness and boredom without resorting to drugs or alcohol. Suppose the goal is to improve social confidence. In that case, the focus might be on sensing their posture and tolerating unpleasant sensations in the chest and belly. Suppose the goal is to explore feelings of sadness. In that case, body awareness might be directed towards facial expressions and the head's downward tilt.

The main drawback of somatic psychotherapy is a lack of trained therapists with the skills to take full advantage. It can take a lot of training and experience for the therapist to know what body language cues are meaningful indicators of underlying mental stress and which are not. Most psychologists and counselors receive very little training in somatic therapy or body awareness.

This is despite an increasing amount of research showing that somatic therapy can be useful for a number of stress-related disorders such as post-traumatic stress disorder. Some somatic therapists say the relative lack of interest in this form of therapy is cultural.* Over the last few hundred years, western culture has tended to see the mind and body as independent of one another. Some critics, such as medical historian Edward Shorter, say this tendency has been a problem in 20th-century psychiatry, with its over-emphasis on Freudian psychotherapy in the 50s and 60s.

However, the increasing popularity of eastern mind-body practices like yoga is sparking a greater interest in developing western mind-body practices that incorporate the latest scientific knowledge about the nervous system and its effects on the mind and body.

Where somatic psychotherapy is unavailable or unaffordable, body-based somatic therapy can be combined with self-administered cognitive therapy. In self-administered cognitive therapy, as outlined in popular self-help books like David Burns' Feeling Good: The New Mood Therapy, you keep a written record of persistent negative thoughts, then critique your thoughts and come up with constructive responses.

This basic DIY cognitive therapy approach can be combined with somatic, brain-body approaches, such as the following exercise suggested by Pat Ogden:

-Identify a persistent negative belief (e.g., I'm an angry person and can't do anything about it);

-Observe how your body reacts to the negative opinion (e.g., my jaw and shoulders tense up, and I can't think clearly);

-Think of a different physical movement you could make (e.g., I could clench my left hand or shake my shoulders);

-Make the alternative movement several times;

-Make a mental or written note of any improvement in your thoughts or feelings (e.g., I feel less tension in the upper body, and I don't feel quite so angry).

Self-administered cognitive therapy is quite effective for mood disorders, so there's every reason to expect positive benefits from combining self-administered cognitive therapy with body-based therapy.

Chapter 12: Genco Method Somatic Release

Preparation: Get ready for the Genco Method Somatic Release. Keep your eyes closed and your body still. If you would like to make any adjustments to your posture, please do so now. (Pause). Once you have adjusted yourself, invite the stillness and keep your body at rest until our practice is over (Pause).

Gradually become quiet within, as quiet as you choose to be at this moment. Take three deep, long breaths, and each time you breathe in, sense that your conscious breath is coming to you with the increased levels of peace and harmony. (Pause). And as you breathe out, know that you are releasing what is already expired by choice and needs to be removed from your mind-body. (Pause). Keep observing that you are inhaling peace and harmony with the flow of natural and conscious breath cycles and releasing toxicity and tension. A natural elimination process is taking place by your choice. (Pause). With each breath, you are reaching a state of enhanced peacefulness; your body is progressively feeling weightless while you are finding yourself sliding deeper and deeper into your consciousness. (Pause).

Now, imagine yourself in front of a door that opens into a quiet environment that will host only you and your higher consciousness. No external or internal chatter can exist in this Sacred Silent Space. See with your mind's eye that your name is on the door, and it is reserved only for you. Open the door, go inside, and before you close the door, but they "do not disturb" sign on the doorknob. This sign is an instruction to your subconscious mind not to interrupt the process. Your subconscious acknowledges this command.

During our practice, allow the sound of my voice to guide your journey into the depths of your consciousness. Use my voice as an informing white light that reveals what is on your path, just like a light on a helmet does in the darkness of a cave. Let the sound of my voice assist your journey in and out of the depths of your consciousness.

Resolution: Now is the time to intentionally state the resolution you wish to experience through this practice. Take a deep breath with conscious awareness and clear choice. State your resolution quietly in your heart space three times with full feeling and attentiveness.

Your resolution is your conscious choice that is given to your mind-body to undertake through our practice. Notice that your subconscious receives and acknowledges your instructions on what you choose to resolve.

Restoring the Wellbeing: Bring your attention to the organic, reverent, capable, quiet breath. Become aware of how the breath breathes you. Notice how the breath moves through in and out of the nostrils. (Pause) The organic breath flows through both nostrils, meets at the top of the nose to form a triangle. (Pause). The conscious breath enters through the nostril openings, moves upwards, and draws together to form a triangle with its apex in the eyebrow center. (Pause) Observe the breath passing through both nostrils like a gentle dance inside the nostrils... Notice the breath movements in each nostril separately (Pause) and simultaneously. (Pause) Observe individual movements of the breath in each nostril and their reunion at the eyebrow center. (Pause).

Continue your awareness of breathing. Imagine you are now breathing through alternate nostrils. In through one nostril, and out through the other; up and down the triangle's sides and back again. (Pause) Start practicing immersing your consciousness with the breath's consciousness and direct the breath in through one nostril and out through the other. Inhale through the left nostril and exhale through the right. Continue to practice directing the breath towards alternate nostril, breathing left in, right out, right in, left out. (Long Pause)

Now, enhance your capacity to interact with the breath. Deepen your connection with the awareness that brings the breath in and out of you. Locate the consciousness of the breath over the crown of your head. Continue engaging with the breath's consciousness by breathing through the crown of your head while inviting the conscious awareness into you, into your mind-body. (Pause). Once the breath starts to arrive at you with this directed awareness, you can guide the breath's consciousness to arrive at the places that feel uneasy or stuck to offer freedom from it.

Know that the conscious breath is arriving with the powerful vibration of the truth. Now see your awareness immersed with this consciousness, observing your body from the level of unattached and highest levels of perception.

From these heightened cognizance levels, start observing your body to identify where the information is stored inside your mind-body regarding the resolution you made. The cells that carry the emotional trauma or tension relevant to your resolve make themselves known to you by a dimmed grayish projection of light and denser texture compared to the healthier cells. See their grayish light and locate them inside of you. (Pause). Become fully aware of where they are in your body. (Pause) Take a moment to observe them just as if you observe a piece of art in a gallery, with full awareness, detachment, awe, curiosity, compassion, love, and care. (Pause)

Recall your resolve. Let the intention of your resolve charge your breath with the midnight blue light of consciousness. Allow this conscious breath to come in like a laser beam and touch the grayish cells that have made themselves known to you earlier. Grant permission to the midnight blue light to enable the change towards your resolve with its highly charged levels of truth, consciousness, mercy, peace, and harmony. Direct this breath to touch the cells that are ready to release the trauma.

Each time the beam of midnight blue light touches the illumined cell, you see gray matter leave that cell, and the cell starts to shine with the authentic midnight blue, the clear divine consciousness of that cell. Know that the original intention of that cell is restored. (Pause) Go through your mind-body cell by cell to clear all the outdated programming and ask the gray matter that has left your body to return to the source that it came from. Take 7 breaths in this level of freedom, release, peacefulness, truth, and heightened awareness. (Long Pause).

Confirm the completion of your practice by repeating your resolve quietly in your heart space three times with full feeling and attentiveness. Send your gratitude to your mind-body for its support and cooperation for the resolutions received.

You are now ready to return to the normal state of awareness. In a moment, I will play a chime for you. Once you hear that chime, you will return to normal consciousness levels, fully restored, rejuvenated, relaxed, and feeling much freer than before.

As you come out of this wonderful state of peacefulness, you will feel fully rested, energetic, healthy, and grounded. I will now ring the chime.

When you hear the chime, you will come out of the deep relaxation state, feeling an increased sense of peacefulness, freedom, and wellness, bringing with you all the benefits of this experience. (Chime). It is now time to return to normal levels of awareness.

Recall your resolve. Let the intention of your will charge your breath with the midnight blue light of consciousness. Allow this conscious breath to come in like a laser beam and touch the grayish cells that have made themselves known to you earlier. Grant permission to the midnight blue light to enable the change towards your resolve with its highly charged levels of truth, consciousness, mercy, peace, and harmony. Direct this breath to touch the cells that are ready to release the trauma.

Each time the beam of midnight blue light touches the illumined cell, you see gray matter leave that cell, and the cell starts to shine with the authentic midnight blue, the clear divine consciousness of that cell. Know that the original intention of that cell is restored. (Pause) Go through your mind-body cell by cell to clear all the outdated programming and ask the gray matter that has left your body to return to the source that it came from. Take seven breaths in this level of freedom, release, peacefulness, truth, and heightened awareness. (Long Pause).

Confirm the completion of your practice by repeating your resolve quietly in your heart space three times with full feeling and attentiveness. Send your gratitude to your mind-body for its support and cooperation for the resolutions received.

You are now ready to return to the normal state of awareness. In a moment, I will play a chime for you. Once you hear that chime, you will return to normal consciousness levels, fully restored, rejuvenated, relaxed, and feeling much freer than before.

As you come out of this beautiful state of peacefulness, you will feel fully rested, energetic, healthy, and grounded. I will now ring the chime. When you hear the chime, you will come out of the deep relaxation state, feeling an increased sense of peacefulness, freedom, and wellness, bringing with you all the benefits of this experience. (Chime). It is now time to return to normal levels of awareness.

Conclusion

Clinical Somatic Education is slowly becoming a mainstream option for treating mobility, flexibility, and posture issues. This is, in no small part, thanks to Eleanor Hanna's efforts, who has carried on the work of Thomas. Thomas Hanna was the first person to start using the phrase somatics when he developed the clinical somatic education treatment option. This resulted from his years of research, building upon the work of several other respected scholars. Unfortunately, Thomas died in a car accident just five days into his first training course. The course was never finished. Although thanks to his impressive organizational skills, the information had already been shared. The remainder of the course was intended to be reiteration and discussion. This made it possible for both his wife, Eleanor and two of his students to develop the program further and teach it to the rest of the world. Thomas Hanna and Eleanor Hanna established the Novato Institute for Somatic Research and Training. After Thomas died in 1980, Eleanor continued to run and build the institute to ensure that as many people could benefit from somatic exercises. As the name suggests, the facility continues to research new ways of applying somatics to help people lead a fuller, balanced life.

Somatic exercises are designed to reawaken the mind and help everyone discover their own ability to improve their movement and reduce pain which has been impossible to eliminate via more conventional or traditional means. They are founded on the belief that everyone has the power to control their own destiny, eliminate pain, improve mobility, flexibility and, ultimately, become more effective in any activity they choose to undertake. The institute is spreading the word and potential of this treatment method via regular newsletters, magazines, books, and training courses. It also offers a three-year study to become certified as a teacher of Somatics. The ultimate aim is to have a teacher in every town across the country, ensuring that everyone has the opportunity to benefit from this ability to awaken the mind.

Clinical somatic education allows you to release your body from the pain and suffering that you may have come to accept as part of life.

The exercises are designed to remind your brain that, despite the number of things demanded daily, it is possible and essential to control your own muscles and not become a victim of habituation.

It is only through regaining this level of control over your own body that you will be able to enjoy a pain-free life which will provide you with the opportunity to achieve anything.

It is essential to mention that although the book is focused on the ability for somatic exercise to relieve pain and aid in movement, many other conditions can be helped by using somatics.

Some of the more common ailments which have been shown to benefit are:

• *Arthritis*

• *Balance Problems*

• *Dizziness*

• *The need to urinate frequently*

• *Obesity*

• *Sciatica*

• *Tendinitis*

• *Uneven Leg Length*

• *Whiplash*

In fact, many other disorders can be aided by the intervention of somatic exercises. The list is likely to grow as research looks into how this technique can be applied to other issues. Somatic exercising may be a relatively recent addition to the list of alternative or complementary therapies. Still, it is proving to have a massive range of potential.

You will have probably started this book with a loose idea regarding what somatics is and how it may benefit you. The book has introduced you to a brief history of the practice and how it came into being. It has also disclosed the main uses for somatic exercises as originally envisioned by

Thomas Hanna, particularly how they can aid with movement, flexibility, and posture.

By now, you should also be aware that it can be of great benefit to a wide variety of other disorders or conditions. Learning to train your mind is surprisingly easy; the example exercises are simple yet effective.

They release the tight muscles and allow your mind to exercise complete control over all the parts of your body, eliminating pain and restoring full function to parts of you that you may have thought would be limited for the rest of your life.

There is also a range of tips and tricks for getting started practicing somatics, a list of the many advantages of this technique, and a few risks, which should be considered before you start practicing.

But perhaps the most important message that you should take away from this book is the power of the human mind. It is possible to heal your own body by applying your brain to the problem and not relying on human prescription medications. While there remains a place in anyone's life for traditional medical responses, it is an electrifying feeling to know that you have the power to heal yourself and live a better life. This feeling comes from an awareness of the power that resides within everyone and how it can be reached by focusing on the mind.

Somatic exercises are simply one key towards unlocking the full power of the human mind. This mind is currently only used to less than a tenth of its potential. This book should have opened your eyes to what is possible. Start by using small exercises to alleviate painful muscles and other injuries or illnesses. The logical end of this path is the ability to self-heal.

Clinical somatic education also has the potential to help people with mental health disorders and those with low self-esteem.

This is because learning to heal yourself will help you understand who you are and what you can. Somatics will open up your options; use this book as a guide to exploring the capabilities of your own mind.